Wissenschaftliche Untersuchungen
zum Neuen Testament · 2. Reihe

Herausgeber / Editor
Jörg Frey (Zürich)

Mitherausgeber / Associate Editors
Markus Bockmuehl (Oxford)
James A. Kelhoffer (Uppsala)
Hans-Josef Klauck (Chicago, IL)
Tobias Nicklas (Regensburg)

362

Laurie Brink

Soldiers in Luke-Acts

Engaging, Contradicting, and Transcending the Stereotypes

Mohr Siebeck

Laurie Brink, born 1961; currently Associate Professor of New Testament Studies at Catholic Theological Union in Chicago, IL, and associate editor for *The Bible Today*.

ISBN 978-3-16-153163-7
ISSN 0340-9570 (Wissenschaftliche Untersuchungen zum Neuen Testament, 2. Reihe)

The Deutsche Nationalbibliothek lists this publication in the Deutsche Nationalbibliographie; detailed bibliographic data are available on the Internet at *http://dnb.dnb.de*.

The book was printed by Laupp & Göbel in Nehren on non-aging paper and bound by Buchbinderei Nädele in Nehren.

Printed in Germany.

*For the late CPO Bradley A. Brink, Sr. and
TSgt Bradley A. Brink, Jr., Ret., and
all soldiers and veterans who strive to be
εὐσεβὴς καὶ φοβούμενος τὸν θεόν*

Preface

This book is a significantly revised and rewritten version of a dissertation accepted by the Faculty of the Divinity School at the University of Chicago in 2009 for the degree of Doctor of Philosophy.

Many colleagues, mentors, and friends have contributed to both the dissertation and this revision. Richard Saller, Dean of the School of Humanities and Science, Stanford University, provided valuable direction and feedback on issues of Roman history. Hans-Josef Klauck, Naomi Shenstone Donnelley Professor of New Testament and Early Christian Literature at the Divinity School of the University of Chicago, supplied helpful criticism and friendly advice throughout the dissertation process, and encouraged this revision's publication in the WUNT II series. I am grateful for the patient supervision and insightful comments provided by my dissertation advisor, Margaret M. Mitchell, Dean and Shailer Mathews Professor of New Testament and Early Christian Literature at the Divinity School of the University of Chicago.

My own ad hoc group of advisors supplemented the critique offered by my committee. Chief among them are Carolyn Osiek, R.S.C.J., Charles Fischer Catholic Professor of New Testament Emerita at Brite Divinity School of Texas Christian University; Dianne Bergant, C.S.A., Carroll Stuhlmueller, C.P., Distinguished Professor of Old Testament Studies at Catholic Theological Union; and Deborah Green, Greenberg Associate Professor of Hebrew Language and Literature at the University of Oregon. The faculty of Catholic Theological Union, most particularly its academic dean and vice president, Barbara E. Reid, O.P., and the members of the Department of Biblical Literature and Languages offered scholarly advice and personal encouragement. My colleagues, Robin Ryan, C.P., Carmen Nanko-Fernández, Roger Schroeder, S.V.D., and Harrietta Holloway were steadfast in their support. The late Barbara E. Bowe, R.S.C.J. modeled academic excellence for the sake of teaching. Her example continues to illuminate my professional path.

The editorial staff of Mohr Siebeck demonstrated exceeding patience and excellent professionalism. I am particularly grateful to Katharina Stichling, editorial assistant Theology and Jewish Studies, and Matthias Spitzner, production support. Despite their efforts, any errors remain my own.

From the beginning of my academic endeavors, the Dominican Sisters of Sinsinawa have inspired my efforts at scholarship, teaching, and learning. Judy Schaefer, O.P., encouraged my interest in doctoral studies. The late Candida Lund, O.P., directed me to the University of Chicago. Sisters Kaye Ashe, O.P.,

Patricia Dillon, O.P., Collette Mary White, O.P. and the Sisters of St. Clara Community and the Villa at Sinsinawa Mound provided enormous support throughout the lengthy doctoral process. Finally, I owe an immeasurable debt of gratitude to Patricia Mulcahey, O.P., and Betsy Pawlicki, O.P. for their patient endurance and long-suffering support of my academic efforts.

Ad Majorem Dei Gloriam

Chicago, Illinois   Laurie Brink, O.P.
November 4, 2013

Table of Contents

Chapter 1

Luke and the Military

1. Assessing the Situation

From the time of Homer[1] the topic of war has held pride of place in Greek and Roman literature. Herodotus' reports on the Persian invasions in the late 5th century B.C.E. mark the emergence of the Greek historic period. Greek and later Latin historiographers continued to chronicle the successive wars that gave rise to kingdoms and empires. So pervasive were military τόποι that they readily appear off the battle field. The rigors of military life became a metaphor for the austere lifestyle of the philosopher and the pursuit of virtue.[2] Long after the battle, the successful general embodied a model for rhetoricians in their creation of *encomia*. In the hands of playwrights and poets, the blood of battle became the source of inspiration for comic triumphs and dramatic tragedies.

So it is not surprising to find the use of military vocabulary and metaphor in the New Testament. Paul writes of breastplates, helmets (1 Thess 5:8), stipends (1 Cor 9:7), weapons (2 Cor 10:4), siege-works (2 Cor 10:5) and swords (Rom 8:35). The Apostle to the Gentiles calls Epaphroditus (Phil 2:25) and Archippus (Phlm 1–2) συστρατιώτης. The Gerasene demoniac in the

---

[1] As Lendon noted, "The Iliad is the baseline for understanding the military ethos of the Greeks and important for understanding the military methods of historical Greeks" (*Soldiers and Ghosts: A History of Battle in Classical Antiquity* [New Haven, CT: Yale University Press, 2005] 21–22). The debt to Homer is literary as well. "Homeric epic…bequeathed to historiography many of its most fundamental features: the predominantly third-person narrative of military deeds; the mimetic representation of deeds (*erga*) and words (*logoi*); the articulation of the causes of actions; the concern to immortalize great deeds and rescue them from oblivion; and the use of formal and elevated language" (John Marincola, *Greek Historians* [NY: Cambridge University Press, 2001], 10).

[2] "Antisthenes…adopted and elaborated the Spartan view of moral armament, thus initiating the development of a theme that would continue to occupy philosophers, Stoics and Cynics in particular" (Abraham J. Malherbe, "Antisthenes and Odysseus, and Paul at War," *HTR* 76, no. 2 [1983]: 143–73, here 150). A contemporary of Socrates, Antisthenes saw virtue as a weapon: ὅπλον ἡ ἀρετή (Diog. Laert. 6.12.). The philosopher so armed had no fear of the world, particularly if he possessed prudence (φρόνις), a most secure stronghold (τεῖχος ἀσφαλέστατον, Diog. Laert. 6.13).

Gospel of Mark names himself "Legion," a Latin loan word that the evangelist leaves undefined (Mark 5:9). All the Passion accounts speak of soldiers
(Mark 15:16; Matt 27:27; 28:12; Luke 23:36; John 19:2, 23, 24, 32, 34), and
the Synoptics place a centurion as the head of the crucifixion party (Mark
15:39; Matt 27:54; Luke 23:47). The use of military metaphors in the New
Testament texts demonstrates that the early Christian community was not only
familiar with martial language, but adapted it for its own evangelical purposes.[3] The author of Luke-Acts is no exception.

As the author of the Gospel of Luke expressly states, after investigating
everything accurately (ἀκριβῶς), he penned an orderly (καθεξῆς) narrative
(διήγησις) of the events that had been fulfilled among the community (περὶ
τῶν πεπληροφορημένων ἐν ἡμῖν πραγμάτων). To demonstrate his commitment
to accuracy and order, Luke uses imperial temporal markers, in order to establish the chronological setting of his narrative. Immediately following the prologue to the gospel, the story opens in the days of Herod (Luke 1:5). The birth
narrative of Jesus is set during the reign of Augustus (2:1) and the governor-
ship of Quirinius (Luke 2:2).[4] John the Baptist begins his preaching in the
fifteenth year of Tiberius' reign, when Pontius Pilate served as prefect in Judaea, Herod Antipas ruled in Galilee, and his brother Philip ruled in Ituraea
and Trachonitis (Luke 3:1). In Acts of the Apostle, Luke's second volume, the
author sets Saul and Barnabas in Cyprus during the proconsulship of Sergius
Paulus (Acts 13:7). While in Corinth, Paul is brought before Gallio, then pro-
consul of Achaia (Acts 18:12). Paul is sent to Felix, the Roman governor of
Judaea (Acts 23:26), who is later replaced by the next governor, Porcius Festus (Acts 24:27).

The use of imperial temporal markers draws attention to the larger Roman
world in which the narrative will take place. Luke populated this stage with
other quintessentially Roman elements, most notably soldiers. In his treatment
of the Imperial army throughout the two volumes, the author uses military

---

[3] Krentz demonstrated that Paul used extensive military metaphors in his letter to the
Philippians. In so doing Paul was not unlike the contemporary Greco-Roman writers of
his day ("Military Language and Metaphors in Philippians," in *Origins and Methods.
Towards a New Understanding of Judaism and Christianity*, [ed. Bradley McLean; Sheffield, England: Sheffield Academic Press, 1993], 105–27). Also see Laurie Brink, "A
General's Exhortation to His Troops: Paul's Military Rhetoric in 2 Cor 10:1–11," Part 1,
BZ 49 (2005): 191–201, and Part 2, *BZ* 50 (2006): 74–89. Harnack disagreed. Paraphras-
ing the beatitudes, he concluded, "We need say nothing more to confirm that the gospel
excluded all force and had nothing warlike about it, nor would it endure the same" (*Militia Christi: The Christian Religion and the Military in the First Three Centuries* [trans.
David McInnes Gracie; Philadelphia: Fortress Press, 1982], 26).

[4] Luke's dating of Quirinius is anachronistic, but that does not diminish the fact that
he thought it important to situate his διήγησις within imperial parameters. See Mark D.
Smith, "Of Jesus and Quirinius," *CBQ* 62 (2000): 278–93.

language and metaphor, omits from his sources negative aspects of the military, and, as will be demonstrated in this study, characterizes individual soldiers and centurions as possessing the qualities of disciples, thus cumulatively creating an apologetic portrait of Rome's military.

1.1 De re militari *in Luke-Acts*

By the end of the first century of the common era, the Roman legions and auxiliary cast a lengthy shadow over the empire.[5] With the imperial army's ubiquitous presence,[6] the use of military vocabulary and battle images added an air of verisimilitude to the Lucan narrative. Yet, the author demonstrates more than a causal interest in and knowledge of *res militaria*. Luke is acquainted with the rank and order of units, and he names several throughout the two volumes. Foot soldiers (Luke 3:14; 7:8; Acts 10:7; 28:16) are under the command of centurions (Luke 7:2; 23:47; Acts 10:1; 22:25; 27:1) who act under the orders of military tribunes (Acts 21:31). Auxiliary cohorts (Acts 10:1; 21:31; 27:1), Herodian soldiers (Luke 3:14; 23:11) and Roman legions (Luke 8:31) are each distinguished from each other. Luke presents his soldiers as a provincial police force (Luke 3:14) that maintains local relations (Luke 7:2–5), carries out executions (Luke 23:32–47), establishes order (Acts 21:31–33), interrogates suspects (Acts 22:25), and transports (Acts 27:1) and guards prisoners (Acts 28:16).

This familiarity with the military allowed the author to make ready use of martial metaphors and vocabulary. Luke creates an extended battle metaphor by inserting specific military vocabulary and references into his sources. Thus, at Luke's hand, a home invasion is embellished into a military siege

---

[5] The Empire reached is territorial zenith under Trajan. It included an area of nearly 5 million square kilometers and an estimated population of 55 million (Graham Paul Burton, "From Augustus to the Antonines [31 BC–AD 192]," in *The Oxford Classical Dictionary* [ed. Simon Hornblower and Anthony Spawforth; Oxford: Oxford University Press, 1996], 1329). For various other estimates and methods of estimation, see P.A. Brunt, *Italian Manpower* (Oxford: Oxford University Press, 1971); E. Lo Cascio, "The Size of the Roman Population," *JRS* 84 (1994): 23–40; and Keith Hopkins, "Rome, Taxes, Rents and Trade," in *The Ancient Economy* (ed. Walter Scheidel and Sitta Von Reden; NY: Routledge, 2002), 190–230.

[6] MacMullen estimated the size of the legionary forces at 142,560 ("How Big was the Roman Imperial Army?" *Klio* 62 [1980]: 454), with perhaps a nearly equal number of auxiliary troops (Tacitus, *Ann.* 4.4). A moderate military force was able to uphold the *pax Romana* in outlying provinces largely due to the reputation of the army for swift and thorough retaliation, and, in some cases, the memory of such havoc remained vivid in the minds of the conquered peoples (Josephus, *B.J.* 2.361–379). The extensive use of military insignia on imperial coinage served as a continual reminder of the power behind the Emperor. (See Louis C. West, "Imperial Publicity on Coins of the Roman Emperors," CJ 45 [1949]: 19–26; Christopher Howgego, "The Supply and Use of Money in the Roman World 200 B.C. to A.D. 300," JRS 82 [1992]: 1–31).

(Luke 11:21–22), a parable narrates the aspects of a formal surrender (Luke 14:31–32), and the coming destruction of the Temple becomes a city besieged (Luke 19:41–44). Luke embellishes Mark 3:27, so that the Lucan strong man wears full armor (καθωπλισμένος), guarding his αὐλήν, a more impressive abode with a courtyard than the mere οἰκία of Mark (Luke 11:21–22). His possessions (ὑπάρχοντα, as opposed to Mark and Matthew's σκεύη) are left in peace, unless a stronger attacker should be victorious. The stronger man would then remove the first one's trusted armor and divide the spoils (σκῦλα).

After the Lucan Jesus instructs the crowds on the conditions of discipleship, he illustrates the importance of appropriate preparation with a parable (Luke 14:31–32) that is absent in Mark and Matthew. Which person planning to construct a tower would not first figure the costs, so as to assure the successful completion of the project? What king going up against another king in battle (συμβαλεῖν εἰς πόλεμον, Luke 14:31) does not determine if he can match his ten thousand against the enemy's twenty thousand? If not, he will send an embassy to ask for peace (πρεσβείαν ἀποστείλας ἐρωτᾷ τὰ πρὸς εἰρήνην, Luke 14:32).

Elements of this parable are echoed in Luke 19:41–44, where τὰ πρὸς εἰρήνην are no longer negotiable by an embassy. A palisade of stakes (χάρακα) will be built around the city of Jerusalem, and the besiegers will destroy it to the ground (ἐδαφιοῦσιν). No stone will be left standing. In Chapter 21, Luke transforms Mark's reference to the temple's defilement (τὸ βδέλυγμα τῆς ἐρημώσεως, Mark 13:14) into the destruction of the city (ἡ ἐρήμωσις αὐτῆς, Luke 21:20). The source of the coming devastation is the surrounding legions (στρατοπέδα, Luke 21:20). Mark does not depict the θλῖψις, but Luke is graphic. The people will fall by the mouth of the sword and be led away at the end of a spear as captives (πεσοῦνται στόματι μαχαίρης καὶ αἰχμαλωτισθήσονται, Luke 21:24). Josephus describes at length and in vivid detail what Luke is proposing (*B.J.* 5.258),[7] suggesting that both Josephus and Luke or their sources possessed knowledge of Roman siege warfare.

At the Last Supper, the Lucan Jesus admonishes those who are unarmed among his disciples to sell their mantles in order to buy swords (καὶ ὁ μὴ ἔχων πωλησάτω τὸ ἱμάτιον αὐτοῦ καὶ ἀγορασάτω μάχαιραν, Luke 22:36). The disciples announce that they have two swords, and Jesus answers, ἱκανόν ἐστιν

---

[7] The question of Luke's reliance on Josephus or vice versa has been explored extensively. Mason (*Josephus and the New Testament* [2nd; Peabody, MA: Hendrickson, 2003]) concludes that Luke utilized Josephus, while Sterling recognizes a similarity in genre (Sterling, *Historiography and Self-Definition*). Pervo cites Luke's use of Josephus in determining an early Second Century date for the writing of Acts of the Apostles (*Dating Acts: Between the Evangelists and the Apologists* [Santa Rosa, CA: Polebridge Press, 2006], 149–200).

(Luke 22:38). Neither the Gospel of Mark nor the Gospel of Matthew includes the mandate to arm oneself.

In some instances, Luke has removed or omitted military references found in his sources. For example, Luke does not include the reference to walking an additional mile in his Sermon on the Plain, while the Gospel of Matthew,[8] the Didache[9] and Justin Martyr[10] include it. The statement found in Matt 5:41 is often thought to refer to the legal right of a Roman soldier to force a provincial to carry his pack for the length of one Roman mile.[11] Scholars presume that impressing local inhabitants into temporary service provided the traveling soldiers with directions through unfamiliar territory. The practice of ἀγγαρεία was so well-known that Epictetus (*Diatr.* 4.1.79) and Apuleius (9.39–42) make mocking mention of it. The frequency of such requisitions and the impressment of civilians into service necessitated imperial intervention.[12] Third Century Jewish sources indicate that the abuses perpetrated by the Roman army did not lessen in peace time.[13] If the recommendation to go the extra mile had been present in Luke's sources, his choice to delete it in the

---

[8] καὶ ὅστις σε ἀγγαρεύσει μίλιον ἕν, ὕπαγε μετ' αὐτοῦ δύο (Matt. 5:41).

[9] ἐὰν ἀγγαρεύσῃ σέ τις μίλιον ἕν ὕπαγε μετ' αὐτοῦ δύο (*Did.* 1.4).

[10] Παντὶ δὲ ἀγγαρεύοντί σε μίλιον ἀκολούθησον δύο (*Apol.* 1.16.2).

[11] See Michail I. Rostowzew, "Angariae," *Klio* 6 (1906): 250–51, 253–57; and Chrys Caragounis, "ΟΨΩΝΙΟΝ: A Reconsideration of its Meaning," *NovT* 16 (1974): 50–51. Owing to Matthew's use of the verb ἀγγαρεύω, the Roman practice known as *angareia* is exclusively cited as the backdrop against which to read Jesus' imperative to go the extra mile (Matt 5:41). However, a review of the inscriptional and literary evidence on ἀγγαρεία demonstrates that the official practice concerned the transportation of goods and not the wanton impressing of individuals into labor. Freed from a strictly imperial context, Matt 5:41 might more accurately be interpreted as an example of extortion – c compelling the services of another. See my article, "Going the Extra Mile: Reading Matt 5:41 Literally and Metaphorically" in *The History of Religions School Today: Essays in Honor of Hans Dieter Betz.* (ed. T. Blanton, R. Matthew Calhoun and C. K. Rothschild. WUNT; Tübingen: Mohr Siebeck, 2014).

[12] An inscription, dated to the reign of Tiberius and found in Pisidia, set the limits for requisitioned goods and impressed services according to the rank and status of the one making the request. A provincial was obliged to offer unpaid hospitality and housing to imperial officials, soldiers in the provinces, and freedmen, slaves, and animals of the imperial household (Stephen Mitchell, "Requisitioned Transport in the Roman Empire: a new Inscription from Pisidia," *JRS* 66 [1976]: 107). The primary use of such edicts was to ensure the appropriate access to transport and quartering for the military in the provinces, and to discourage the unlawful requisition and seizure of personnel and materials without payment to provincials. Frequent and widespread exploitation is evident in numerous imperial documents from the early imperial period to the fifth century (W. H. C. Frend, "A Third-Century Inscription Relating to Angareia in Phrygia," *JRS* 46 (1956): 49).

[13] Benjamin Isaac, "The Roman Army in Judaea: Police Duties and Taxation," in *Roman Frontier Studies* (ed. V.A. Maxfield and M. I. Dobson; Exeter: University of Exeter Press, 1991), 458–61.

Gospel adds to the argument of his specialized treatment of the Roman military.

In scenes where Luke could not wholly remove details involving soldiers, he tends to minimalize the negative aspects. The other evangelists attribute the abuse and mocking of Jesus to the Roman soldiers, but Luke avoids or delays linking soldiers with these actions. In Mark 15:16–20, soldiers take Jesus into the praetorium where they plait a crown of thorns and dress him in a robe of royal color. They then salute (Mark 15:18) and mock (Matt 27:29) Jesus, saying, "Hail, King of the Jews (Mark 15:18//Matt 27:29//John 19:3). Mark, Matthew and even John agree that the soldiers struck Jesus, and Mark and Matthew add that they spat on him as well. At the conclusion of this scene, the soldiers lead Jesus to his crucifixion. Unlike the story in Mark's Gospel, the Lucan soldiers do not physically abuse Jesus. Luke does recount an incident of the beating and mocking of Jesus, but he set it in the house of the High Priest (Luke 22:63–65), rather than in the praetorium.

The scene in which Roman soldiers do mock Jesus merits only a brief mention and is moved to the foot of the cross, where the soldiers do not initiate the taunting but do join the rulers in mocking Jesus by offering him a cup of sour wine (Luke 23:35–36). This propensity to minimize the Roman military's responsibility in the death of Jesus is further evidenced when Luke fails to designate who actually leads Jesus to his crucifixion. Mark states clearly: "The soldiers led him away" (Mark 15:16). But Luke simply writes, "they" (Luke 23:26). In editing his sources, Luke goes to great lengths to minimize the explicit reference to Roman soldiers in the abuse, mocking and death of Jesus.

Luke-Acts evidences the author's familiarity and dexterity with military images and metaphors. The insertion of extended military metaphors into his sources suggests a conscious choice to evoke a martial context. His editing of the Passion narrative placed the brutal beating and mocking at the hands of Herodian guards and limited the cruelty of the Roman soldiers. The omission of sayings that could vilify soldiers adds to the weight of evidence that Luke intended to construct an apologetic portrait of the Roman military. An exploration of his characterization of soldiers in the two volumes will further demonstrate that the author is purposely creating a portrait that counters stereotypes and upsets the expectations of his readers.

1.2 Scholarly Investigations of the Military in Luke-Acts

Despite Luke's demonstrated interest in aspects of the military, little scholarly attention has been focused on the topic. Indeed, the lacuna is not limited to Luke-Acts. As T. R. Hobbs has noted, "many studies of the Roman-Hellenistic social world of the New Testament offer a strange silence on things military, except as an unexplored background to 'politics.'"[14] In most major treatises, scholars investigate the military from a historical perspective, presuming that Luke-Acts provides a reliable witness to the events it depicts. More recently, Hobbs did address the literary aspects of the military, but only as found in the Gospels. Since no scholars have evaluated the characterization of soldiers across the two volumes of Luke-Acts, this monograph seeks to fill that void.

The topic of the Roman military in the New Testament is so understudied that recent commentaries continue to cite monographs originally published more than a hundred years ago.[15] One of the few monographs solely focused on the topic of the military in Early Christianity is Harnack's now dated *Militia Christi*.[16] Written as a response to the question of the appropriate Christian attitude toward war in light of World War I, *Militia Christi* is a more detailed commentary on the sources mentioned in Harnack's earlier work on Christian origins.[17] Though one of the earliest and most complete compilations of materials concerning the topic, *Militia Christi* is not the work of an exegete.[18] Har-

---

[14] T. R. Hobbs, "Soldiers in the Gospels: A Neglected Agent," in *Social-Scientific Models for Interpreting the Bible: Essays by the Context Group in Honor of Bruce J. Malina* (ed. John J. Pilch; Boston; Leiden: Brill, 2001), 334.

[15] Schürer is frequently cited in reference to Luke 7 and Acts 10. His *The History of the Jewish People in the Age of Jesus Christ* was first published in 1890, though most commentaries cite a later edition (*The History of the Jewish People in the Age of Jesus Christ* [ed. G. Vermes et al.; Edinburgh: T &T Clark, 1973, reprint 1993]). For example, see I. Howard Marshall, *Commentary on Luke* (NIGTC; Grand Rapids, MI: Eerdmans, 1978); Joseph Fitzmyer, *The Gospel According to Luke I–IX* (AB; New York: Doubleday, 1981); *The Gospel According to Luke X–XXIV* (AB; New York: Doubleday, 1985), and *The Acts of the Apostles* (AB; New York: Doubleday, 1998); H. Conzelmann, *Acts of the Apostles* (Hermeneia; Philadelphia: Fortress Press, 1987); John Polhill, *Acts* (The New American Commentary; Nashville, TN: Broadman Press, 1992); C. K. Barrett, *A Critical and Exegetical Commentary on the Acts of the Apostles* (Edinburgh: T & T Clark, 1994–98); Joel Green, *The Gospel of Luke* (Grand Rapids, MI: Eerdmans, 1997); Ben Witherington, *Acts of the Apostles* (Grand Rapids, MI: Eerdmans, 1998); and Beverly R. Gaventa, *Acts* (Abingdon New Testament Commentaries; Nashville, TN: Abingdon Press, 2003).

[16] Adolf Harnack, *Militia Christi: Die christliche Religion und der Soldatenstand in den ersten drei Jahrhunderten* (Tübingen: Mohr [Paul Siebeck], 1905). The English edition followed nearly eighty years later.

[17] Adolf Harnack, *The Mission and Expansion of Christianity in the First Three Centuries* (trans. James Moffatt; Theological Translation Library; New York: Putnam, 1904–5), most notably 204–17.

[18] In *Militia Christi*, Harnack set out to address three questions: "1) Has the Christian religion continuously or at any time in its history assumed a warlike character and preached the right and duty of the holy war? 2) Has the church, occasionally or continuously, adopted military organization (in a transferred sense) and disciplined its believers, or a part of them, as soldiers of Christ? 3) What position has the church taken with regard to the secular military profession and to war?" (Harnack, *Militia Christi*, 26).

nack wrote as a liberal theologian and historian, and his biblical citations serve as a proof text for his thesis. He limited the definition of "gospel" to the "sayings of Jesus," without comment on the evangelists or their editorial hand. Harnack neglected to evaluate the New Testament literature that included soldiers and only marginally investigated other scriptural texts that engaged military metaphors. Nonetheless, *Militia Christi* is one of the first works to recognize an implicit connection between the Roman military and the spread of Christianity.[19]

Those interested in a more focused interpretation of the Roman military usually begin with T. R. S. Broughton's "Note XXXIII. The Roman Army" in the fifth volume of *The Beginnings of Christianity*, edited by F. J. Foakes Jackson and Kirsopp Lake.[20] Broughton's work provides a map through the military maze in Acts of the Apostles. As he noted,

> Acts has several references to the Roman army, and in the background of the story there is always a dimly perceived and changing mass of tribunes, centurions, and soldiers who sometimes limit the freedom and sometimes preserve the lives of the Christians who are in the foreground.[21]

At the time of its publication, Broughton's "The Roman Army" contained the most comprehensive collection of inscriptions that related specifically to the army in Acts. The article's inclusion within the five-volume monumental work of Jackson and Lake guaranteed its wide readership. But, like Schürer and Harnack before him, Broughton's concern was the historicity of the military episodes in Acts of the Apostles and not their narrative function.

In subsequent years, various scholars have focused on aspects of the Roman military including its presence and impact in the province of Judea,[22] but

---

[19] "The special justification for developing this theme of the relationship of the Christian religion to the army in a monograph lies in the facts that the early Christians (especially in the West) perceived themselves as God's soldiers and that the historical shift from paganism to Christianity first took place publicly in the army" (Harnack, *Militia Christi*, 24).

[20] T. R. S. Broughton, "Note XXXIII. The Roman Army" in *The Beginnings of Christianity. The Acts of the Apostles* (ed. F. J. Foakes-Jackson and K. Lake; vol. 5; London: Macmillan, 1933; repr., Grand Rapids, MI: Baker Book House, 1979), 427–44.

[21] Broughton, "The Roman Army," 427.

[22] These include Benjamin Isaac, "Roman Colonies in Judaea: The Foundation of Aelia Capitolina," *Talanta* 12/13 (1980 January): 38–43; Denis B. Saddington, "The Administration and the Army in Judaea in the Early Roman Period (From Pompey to Vespasian, 63 BC–AD 79)," in *The Holy Land in History and Thought* (ed. Moshe Sharon; NY: Brill, 1988), 33–40; Shimon Applebaum, *Judaea in Hellenistic and Roman Times* (NY: Brill, 1989); Isaac, "The Roman Army in Judaea"; Michael P. Speidel, "The Roman Army in Judaea under the Procurators," in *Roman Army Studies 2* (ed. Michael P. Speidel; Stuttgart: Franz Steiner, 1992), 224–32; and Jonathan Roth, "The Army and the Economy

they have seldom investigated the portrayal of the army as presented in the New Testament texts and early Christianity.[23] In the mid-1970s, John Helgeland addressed the lacuna for the period following 170 C.E., but acknowledged that the lack of evidence from the earlier period made an investigation of Christians in the military difficult.[24]

The next scholar to focus on the question of soldiers in Luke-Acts was Denis Saddington in his 1996 work, "Roman Military and Administrative Personnel in the New Testament" in *Aufstieg und Niedergang der römischen Welt* II.26.3.[25] Saddington updated Broughton and occasionally disagreed

---

in Judaea and Palestine," in *The Roman Army and the Economy* (ed. Paul Erdkamp; Amsterdam: J. C. Gieben, 2002), 375–97.

[23] For example, see A. N. Sherwin-White, *Roman Society and Roman Law in the New Testament* (Oxford: Clarendon Press, 1963); G. R. Watson, *The Roman Soldier* (Ithaca, NY: Cornell University Press, 1969); J. B. Campbell, *The Emperor and the Roman Army: 31 BC–AD 235* (Oxford: Clarendon, 1984); Fergus Millar, *The Roman Near East: 31 BC–AD 337* (Cambridge, MA: Harvard University Press, 1993); Martin Goodman, *The Roman World: 44 BC–AD 180* (New York: Routledge, 1997); Lawrence Keppie, *The Making of the Roman Army: From Republic to Empire* (Norman, OK: University of Oklahoma, 1998); and J. E. Lendon, *Soldiers and Ghosts: A History of Battle in Classical Antiquity* (New Haven, CT: Yale University Press, 2005).

[24] John Helgeland, "Roman Army Religion," in *SBL Seminar Papers* (George MacRae; Missoula: Scholars Press, 1975), 199–205.

[25] Saddington's is one of only a few articles in *ANRW* that focus specifically on the intersection between the Roman army and the New Testament. Others that address the Roman military in general include D. J. Breeze, "The Career Structure below the Centurionate during the Principate," *ANRW* II.1 (1974): 435–51; R. W. Davis, "The Daily Life of the Roman Soldier under the Principate," *ANRW* II.1 (1974): 299–338; L. de Blois, "Volk und Soldaten bei Cassius Dio," *ANRW* II.34.3 (1997): 2650–76; H. Devijver, "The Roman Army in Egypt (with Special Reference to the Militiae Equestres)," *ANRW* II.1 (1974): 452–92; Brian Dobson, "The Significance of the Centurion and 'Primipilaris' in the Roman Army and Administration," *ANRW* II.1 (1974): 392–434; G. Forni, "Estrazione etnica e sociale dei soldati delle legioni nei primi tre secoli dell'impero," *ANRW* II.1 (1974): 339–91; J. Harmand, "Les origines de l'armée impériale: Un témoignage sur la réalité du pseudo-principat et sur l'évolution militaire de l'Occident," *ANRW* II.1 (1974): 263–98; J. H. Jung, "Das Eherecht der romischen Soldaten," *ANRW* II.14 (1982): 302–46; idem, "Die Rechtsstellung der römischen Soldaten: Ihre Entwicklung von den Anfängen Roms bis auf Diokletian," *ANRW* II.14 (1982): 882–1013; B. Lehmann, "Das Eigenvermögen der römischen Soldaten unter väterlicher Gewalt," *ANRW* II.14 (1982): 183–284; Denis B. Saddington, "The Development of the Roman Auxiliary Forces from Augustus to Trajan," *ANRW* II.3 (1975): 176–201; idem, "Tacitus and the Roman Army," *ANRW* II.33.5 (1991): 3484–3555; R. K. Sherk, "Roman Geographical Exploration and Military Maps," *ANRW* II.1 (1974): 534–62; Michael P. Speidel, "Legionaries from Asia Minor," *ANRW* II.7.2 (1980): 730–746; idem, "The Rise of Ethnic Units in the Roman Imperial Army," *ANRW* II.3 (1975): 202–31; idem, "The Roman Army in Arabia," *ANRW* II.8 (1977): 687–730; idem, "Nubia's Roman Garrison," *ANRW* II.10.1 (1988): 767–98; Michael P. Speidel and A. Dimitrova-Milceva, "The Cult of the Genii in the Roman Army and the New Military Deity," *ANRW* II.16.2

with some of his findings. Nonetheless, he trod the same historical path. Though providing a realistic backdrop upon which to set the military characters in the New Testament, Saddington's research does not allow for a more nuanced reading of the narrative. He inferred from Acts 22:28 that "Claudius Lysias is notorious for having purchased his Roman citizenship, granted to him by the emperor Claudius,"[26] but then overlooked the σύγκρισις[27] set up between Paul's citizenship and that of the tribune. Elements of the narrative are lost when scholars investigate solely for questions of historical accuracy.

A welcomed change of pace from the purely historical examinations is the more recent work by T. R. Hobbs, which focuses on the soldiers in the Gospels through the lens of social-science methodology. Where Schürer, Harnack, Broughton, and Saddington asked questions of history and reliability, Hobbs posits ones of social identity, power, and agency. He moves closer to recognizing the texts as stories and to considering how the reader might view the soldiers' actions. For his analysis, Hobbs employed a model that categorizes the military organization in relationship to its host society by "ideal types."[28] Such a pursuit attends little to the actual historical context.

(1978): 1542–55; and G. R. Watson, "Documentation in the Roman Army," *ANRW* II.1 (1974): 493–507. Articles pertaining to the Roman military and its religious practices include E. Birley, "The Religion of the Roman Army," *ANRW* II.16.2 (1978): 1506–41; J. Helgeland, "Christians and the Roman Army from Marcus Aurelius to Constantine," *ANRW* II.23.1 (1979): 724–834; idem, "Roman Army Religion," *ANRW* II.16.2 (1978): 1470–1505. And the Roman military and the New Testament are discussed in F. F. Bruce, "The Acts of the Apostles: Historical Record or Theological Reconstruction," *ANRW* II.25.3 (1985): 2569–2603; W. M. Swartley, "War and Peace in the New Testament," *ANRW* II.26.3 (1996): 2298–2408; S. M. Taylor, "St. Paul and the Roman Empire: Acts of the Apostles 13–14," *ANRW* II.26.2 (1995): 1189–1231, and "The Roman Empire in the Acts of the Apostles," *ANRW* II.26.3 (1996): 2436–2500. Taylor recognizes that the Acts of the Apostles paints a favorable picture of Roman soldiers as imperial agents, but does not investigate Luke's intent.

[26] Denis B. Saddington, "Roman Military and Administrative Personnel in the New Testament," 2416.

[27] For a detailed discussion of the function of σύγκρισις in the Greco-Roman world and the Pauline texts, see Christopher Forbes, "Paul and Rhetorical Comparison," in *Paul in the Greco-Roman World* (ed. J. Paul Sampley; Harrisburg, PA: Trinity Press International, 2003), 134–71.

[28] Hobbs develops his model after Feld's structural analysis (Maury D. Feld, *The Structures of Violence: Armed Forces and Social Systems* [Sage Series on Armed Forces and Society 10; Beverly Hills, CA: Sage Publications, 1977], 31–69).

It is a moot point whether that the writers of the Gospels themselves were fully aware of the details of the military situation, nor of the niceties of Roman military protocol. In true artistic fashion, the Gospels [sic] writers create their literary worlds through the narratives they construct, and the characters that occupy these worlds ... Nevertheless, there is a body of "background knowledge," presupposed by all the Gospel writers, which the mere mention of the word "soldier" evokes.[29]

According to Hobbs's analysis, the author of Luke-Acts may be creating a social organization, but he was doing so by means of a narrative.

By far, the majority of the scholarly work on soldiers in the New Testament has concerned the historical context out of which early Christianity emerged. Luke's own claim to be penning a narrative of actual events based on authoritative witnesses encouraged later interpreters to read the texts in search of reliable information. Social historians, both of the New Testament and of Roman history, have tended to evaluate the two-volumes in comparison with data from ancient historians, inscriptions, or archaeological findings. Research into the existence of certain cohorts in Palestine under a Judean king or the period of service for Pilate, Felix, and Festus have led to historical reconstructions of the Roman military in New Testament times. But such historical or, in the case of Hobbs, social-scientific endeavors often ignore the fact that the soldiers in the texts are narrative characters[30] and, as such, require an analytical approach that considers them within a literary context.

2. Methodology: A Strategic Approach

An investigation into the portrayal of soldiers in Luke-Acts begins with two related questions: How did Luke construct military characters within his two volumes? and Why did Luke present them as he does? The first question requires attention to the text of the Gospel and Acts in conversation with the works of other ancient authors. The second concerns Luke's intentional crafting of sources, in order to direct his authorial audience toward a particular view of the Roman soldier. If Luke has envisioned an authorial audience closely aligned with his real one, then the intended result should have an effect on his real audience as well.

Since, as Penner comments, "Methods bring with them particular ways of seeing and reading texts, and they can be, and often are, mutually exclu-

---

[29] Hobbs, "Soldiers in the Gospels: A Neglected Agent," 335.

[30] As Darr has observed, "historical methods were not designed to analyze characterization, and, in fact, have tended to obstruct our perception of this and other literary features of New Testament" (John Darr, *On Character Building: The Reader and the Rhetoric of Characterization in Luke-Acts* [Literary Currents in Biblical Interpretation; Louisville, KY: Westminster John Knox, 1992], 12).

sive,"[31] is it possible within the same academic enterprise to trace the development of literary characters within the narrative, and to ask questions about the author's intent? In other words, do literary analysis and redaction criticism make strange bedfellows? The distinction between these two methods is not to be found in the uniqueness of their tasks. The root difference lies in the answer to the question "What is a text and how does it function?"[32] Both methods may presume the canonical form of the text as the starting point. But literary criticism investigates the work as a complete whole with its own narrative integrity, plot, characters and themes, while redaction criticism looks at the seams in that text – the inconsistencies that hint at authorial intervention, the evident editing of sources. Literary analysis presumes the unity of a text as a governing principle. Redaction criticism is concerned less with integrity and more with diversity – in this case, the ways Luke differs from Mark.

2.1 Literary Criticism: Attending to the Narrative

The elements of plot, setting, and character are the locus of interest in literary investigations. Nonetheless, literary criticism of a New Testament text can also provide substantial insights into the author's theological concerns, formerly the purview of redaction criticism alone.[33] Scholars have used a literary method to explain seeming inconsistencies in a narrative. For example, Mikeal Parsons concludes that the differences in Luke's two ascension narratives result from creative choices made by the author and not from separate sources.[34]

Similarly, Daniel Marguerat demonstrates that the so-called "silent ending" in Acts was in keeping with ancient literary motifs and did not necessarily

---

[31] Todd Penner, "Madness in the Method? The Acts of the Apostles in Current Study," *CBR* 2 (2004): 225.

[32] Ibid., 250.

[33] For example, see David P. Moessner, *Lord of the Banquet: The Literary and Theological Signficance of the Lukan Travel Narrative* (Minneapolis, MN: Fortress Press, 1989; repr., Harrisburg, PA: Trinity Press International, 1998). Other examples of literary studies that have yielded theological results include J. H. Neyrey, "Acts 17, Epicureans and Theodicy: A Study in Stereotypes," in *Greeks, Romans and Christians: Essays in Honor of Abraham J. Malherbe* (ed. David L. Balch, et al.; Minneapolis: Fortress Press, 1990), 118–34; E. Reinmuth, *Pseudo-Philo und Lukas: Studien zum Liber Antiquitatum Biblicarum und seiner Bedeutung für die Interpretation des lukanischen Doppelwerkes* (WUNT 74; Tübingen: Mohr Siebeck, 1994); O. W. Allen, *The Death of Herod: The Narrative and Theological Function of Retribution in Luke-Acts* (SBLDS 158; Atlanta: Scholars Press, 1997); John Paul Heil, *The Meal Scenes in Luke-Acts : An Audience-Oriented Approach* (SBLMS 52; Atlanta: Society of Biblical Literature, 1999) and C. W. Stenschke, *Luke's Portrait of Gentiles Prior to their Coming to Faith* (WUNT 2.108; Tübingen: Mohr Siebeck, 1999).

[34] Mikeal C. Parsons, *The Departure of Jesus in Luke-Acts: The Ascension Narratives in Context* (JSNTSup. 21; Sheffield: JSOT, 1987).

indicate that the author had limited sources.[35] John Darr's literary approach to the question of the characterization of the Pharisees in Luke-Acts leads to a much more nuanced understanding of their role.[36] Both William Shepherd[37] and Richard Thompson[38] viewed the text through a literary lens, in order to understand how the Holy Spirit and the Church functioned within the narrative of Luke-Acts.

Literary studies of Luke-Acts have thus provided substantial interpretive payoff as a result of the overt methodological aim to analyze the narrative closely, looking at the function of language within a micro and macro literary context and in the process yielding notable insights into the unifying features of the Gospels and Acts.[39]

This type of literary analysis acknowledges that a narrative is written in a specific historical and social context but, at the same time, recognizes that its full meaning cannot be limited to that original setting. The primary interest of this investigation is the historical context of both the narrative and the author, and the author's intent in the construction of character. To that end, more modern literary approaches are best supplemented with attention to ancient literary theory.

Luke created characters according to the standards of first century literary expectations, which were based on earlier theory and contemporaneous literature. A comparison of the presentation of soldiers in Greco-Roman literature demonstrates the existence of several commonplaces that reappear across generic divides. Luke's construction of military characters demonstrates his familiarity with these stereotypes.

2.2 Redaction Criticism: Seeing the Seams

A literary analysis of the characterization of soldiers in Greco-Roman literature marshals a cohort of military characters, but it does not address how Luke changed or adapted his characters in light of these types. Redaction criticism, however, provides a vital foundation from which to launch a literary investigation of an ancient text precisely because it attends to the author's creative and editorial efforts within a particular historical context.[40] Such an analysis is

---

[35] Daniel Marguerat, "The Enigma of the Silent Closing of Acts (28:16–31)," in *Jesus and the Heritage of Israel: Luke's Narrative Claim upon Israel's Legacy* (ed. David P. Moessner; Harrisburg, PA.: Trinity Press International, 1999), 285–304.

[36] Darr, *On Character Building*, 85–126.

[37] William H. Shepherd, *The Narrative Function of the Holy Spirit as a Character in Luke-Acts* (SBLDS; Atlanta: Society of Biblical Literature, 1994).

[38] Richard P. Thompson, *Keeping the Church in Its Place* (New York: T & T Clark, 2006).

[39] Penner, "Madness in the Method? The Acts of the Apostles in Current Study," 248.

[40] "Each gospel, it now seems established, is crucially shaped by the socio-religious circumstances surrounding its composition, specific cultural attachments, the nature of

not without its opponents, who charge that redaction critics are overly concerned with questions of theology.[41] But investigating where the author chose to diverge from original sources or standard practices also hints at his creative artistry. Thus a redactional analysis of the Gospel of Luke also has a literary payoff. It shows not only how the author used his sources to serve his theology but also how he reworked them for the sake of his literary agenda.

The use of literary criticism and redaction criticism leads to the same conclusion: Roman soldiers are portrayed as possessing the qualities of good disciples. How does the implied author anticipate that his authorial audience will respond to this progressive portrait of the Roman military? Is the developing characterization meant to be literal, comical, ironic, or parabolic?

Whenever a writer of a work is unknown, his intent not recorded, or his relationship to sources and models only indirectly accessible, the philological question of how the text is "properly" to be understood, that is according to its intention and time, can best be answered if the text is considered in contrast to the background of the works which the author could expect his contemporary public to know either explicitly or implicitly.[42]

By comparing the literary portrayal of soldiers throughout Greco-Roman literature with those in Luke-Acts we are more fully able to understand how Luke's soldiers may function within the narrative and how the soldiers might

---

the audience, and perhaps most significantly by authorial will and ingenuity" (Werner Kelber, "Redaction Criticism: On the Nature and Exposition of the Gospels," *PRSt* 6 (1979): 11). But Spencer argues that such attention to the "backstage historical developments deflects the focus away from the final (canonical) presentation of the Lukan text" (F. Scott Spencer, "Acts and Modern Literary Approaches," in *The Book of Acts in Its Ancient Literary Setting* [ed. B. W. Winter and A. D. Clarke; Grand Rapids, MI: Eerdmans Publishing, 1993], 386). Against this critique, Stein earlier stated: "Redaction criticism is … concerned with investigating the final canonical product for its own sake, and not simply as a means of gaining historical information about the historical Jesus or the early Church" (Robert H. Stein, "Redaction Criticism [NT]," in *ABD* [David Noel Freedman et al.; New York: Doubleday, 1992], 649

[41] Redaction criticism came under fire both by those who accused it of undermining faith and by those who thought it overemphasized theology. Critics argued that stringent adherence to this method could cause one to over-read differences between a text and its sources. In their view Lucan deviations from Mark do not necessarily reflect theologically-motivated editorial changes. Defining the relationship among sources, redaction, and the narrative is complicated because, in its early stages, redaction criticism focused so minutely on individual pericopes that it tended to neglect the literary work as whole. In response, a modified redaction criticism, called "composition criticism," sought to investigate the theological intent of the author while respecting narrative integrity. See Stein, "What is Redaktionsgeschichte?" *JBL* 88 (1969): 50; and Stephen D. Moore, *Literary Criticism and the Gospels: The Theoretical Challenge* (New Haven, CT: Yale University Press, 1989), 4–7.

[42] H. R. Jauss, "Literary History as a Challenge to Literary Theory," *New Literary History* 2 (1970): 19.

be viewed by the authorial audience, and thus how they contributed to his wider theological and literary purpose.

Redaction criticism sees a text as a patchwork of seams where literary analysis admires the integrity of the narrative.[43] Taken together, these two differing lenses provide a keener insight into the text. Literary criticism investigates the narrative aspects of the text as a whole and has the potential to answer the first question: How has Luke constructed his portraits of soldiers? Redaction criticism concerns itself with the *Sitz im Leben* of the evangelists, and thus can aid in answering the second question: Why does Luke present soldiers as he does? Redaction criticism and a literary analysis of the narrative demonstrate that Luke utilized Greco-Roman stereotypes in his characterization of soldiers, in order to paint a particular portrait of the Roman military.

2.3 Assumptions about the Text, Author, and Audience

The variety of methodological lenses trained on the Gospel of Luke and Acts of the Apostles, particularly in the last fifteen years, belies specific, though often unarticulated and therefore unexamined, assumptions and ideologies.[44] Using two seemingly different methods requires a clear discussion of the underlying assumptions at the base of this investigation. They are assumptions about the text, about the author, and about the audience.

2.3.1 About the Text

As noted above, the question "what is a text?" has ramifications for methodological inquiry. What exactly is being studied: the seams or the whole? A second question is unique to the text(s) under study. Should Luke-Acts be read and analyzed as a continuous story with characters and actions in the first volume foreshadowing events in the second? Or is the reader meant to view them as separate entities – literary works that each have their own integrity? Since Henry Cadbury designated the third gospel and Acts of the Apostles by the hyphenated Luke-Acts,[45] the scholarly community has, by and large, consid-

---

[43] Against those who would advocate the use of only one method, Mitchell wrote, "I think we should resist in principle the assumption behind the dichotomy, i.e. that scholars only espouse or employ a single methodological perspective or commitment. Methodological flexibility seems to me to be most desirable, as curious readers ask questions which require different approaches" (Mitchell, "Patristic Counter-Evidence to the Claim that 'The Gospels Were Written for All Christians'," *NTS* 51 [2005]: 78, n. 116).

[44] "There is an increasing lack of reflection on and seeming awareness of the embedded values and assumptions – often of a conflicting nature – guiding the various methods frequently touted as complementary models of analysis," (Todd Penner, "Madness in the Method?" 225).

[45] Luke and Acts "are not merely two independent writings from the same pen; they are a single continuous work. Acts is neither an appendix nor an afterthought. It is proba-

ered the two works to be a production by the same author. Differences of opinion surround the question of how the two relate to each other.[46] Against the consensus view, Parsons and Pervo claim that differences in genre, narratives, and theology distinguish the two works as separate entities.[47]

The question of the unity of Luke's two volumes has implications for evaluating their narrative structure and the author's purpose. Michael Bird outlined several consequences for reading the two volumes as either one work or as separate books: the prologue of Luke's Gospel can be interpreted differently if it simply refers to the gospel; the genre of the two works is informed by their literary relationship; the narrative structure is impacted by the sense of relationship, so that any overarching theme, theology, or purpose is affected; addressing the question of unity forces other methodological evaluations; and finally, the unity or disunity of Luke and Acts influences one's approach to New Testament theology.[48] "Perhaps a solution to the unity of Luke-Acts will depend in part upon privileging a single methodology, be it literary criticism or reception history."[49]

My research locates the unity of the narrative at the level of audience interpretation, since readers stitch together earlier episodes with later ones, creating meaning as they proceed.[50] Luke could anticipate that his authorial audience would make the connections because "the assumption of narrative coherence is a convention that would have been shared by ancient readers and writers, including the writer of Luke-Acts and his audience."[51]

---

bly an integral part of the author's original plan and purpose" (Henry J. Cadbury, *The Making of Luke-Acts* [London: SPCK, 1927; reprint 1958], 8–9).

[46] I. Howard Marshall succinctly outlined the four models that address the possible relationship between the two works. In the first model, no connection exists, because the two works were written by different authors. In the second, the same author produced both, but they were autonomous works, perhaps later assimilated. In the third, an author designed and wrote one work in two parts: the Gospel and Acts. Finally, in the last model Luke-Acts originated as one work, which was later separated, requiring subsequent revisions. Marshall argues for the validity of the third model based on the presence of the two prologues ("Former Treatise," in *The Book of Acts in Its Ancient Literary Setting* [ed. Bruce W. Winter and Andrew D. Clarke; Grand Rapids, MI: Eerdmans Publishing, 1993], 165–72).

[47] Mikeal C. Parsons and Richard I. Pervo, *Rethinking the Unity of Luke and Acts* (Minneapolis, MN: Fortress Press, 1993), 18.

[48] Michael F. Bird, "The Unity of Luke-Acts in Recent Discussion," *JSNT* 29 (2007): 439–42.

[49] Ibid., 441.

[50] S. John Roth, *The Blind, the Lame, and the Poor: Character Types in Luke-Acts* (JSNTSup. 144; Sheffield: Sheffield Academic Press, 1997), 14.

[51] Ibid., 16.

2.3.2 About the Author

The second assumption underling this investigation is about the author. Whereas redaction criticism concerns itself with the actual author, literary criticism assumes that only the implied author is accessible because the object of study is the narrative, and the actual author is not explicitly present. This investigation focuses on the actual author's characterization of soldiers as evident in the narrative, but acknowledges that we only have access to the implied author. An analysis of Lucan characterization may hint at interests and predilections of the actual author but the historical person, whom tradition has named Luke, remains lost to us.

2.3.3 About the Audience

Writers write to be read. The rhetorical handbooks emphasize that the goal of rhetoric is response. A successful writer, like a successful orator, hopes to motivate the audience either by reason of logic, emotion or the speaker's credibility (Arist. *Rhet.* 1.2.1–2). After all, a loyal, attentive audience assures a writer's success. Such seems to be the case in Josephus' *Antiquitates judaicae*, when the author notes that those hunting glory are eager to write history and display their talent (1.1). In *De Historia Conscribenda*, Lucian recounts that some historians write falsehoods in order to entertain or flatter their audience (63).[52] Rhetoricians were not immune from the same tendency toward sycophancy. Encolpius, the narrator in Petronius' *Satyricon*, criticized his teacher, Agamemnon, and others of his profession, for providing honey-balls of words, sprinkled with poppy and sesame seeds, so as to please their audience. One need not rely on the witness of contemporaneous writers to establish that writers are attentive to their readers. The narrator of Luke-Acts has addressed his audience in the two prologues (Luke 1:1–4; Acts 1:1). But exactly what audience did the author have in mind and how might we breach the divide of historical distance to discover the answer?

To this point, the terms "reader" and "auditor" have been used interchangeably. Contemporary literary theorists deal with texts that are most often engaged visually and not aurally, so that "reader" is an appropriate term. However, the Gospel of Luke and Acts of the Apostles, as ancient productions, were, in all likelihood, heard by an audience and read by only a few.[53]

---

[52] Also see A. Georgiadou, "Lucian and Historiography: 'De Historia Conscribenda' and 'Verae Historiae,'" *ANRW* II.34.2 (1994): 1448–509.

[53] "It is more accurate to speak of the audiences of the Gospels and Acts as *listeners* rather than readers because of the low literacy levels in antiquity and because reading was conducted as a presentation before an audience" (Patrick E. Spencer, *Rhetorical Texture and Narrative: Trajectories of the Lukan Galilean Ministry Speeches* [Library of New Testament Studies 341; New York: T & T Clark, 2007], 5 n. 9). I prefer the term "auditor" to listener since it parallels the authorial audience.

To think of Luke's audience as listeners affects the critical analysis of the text.[54] If the original audience is listening to the narrative, it does not have the benefit of rereading a passage or skipping over sections. It engages the text solely as a consecutive narrative, so that what is presented earlier in the story must be brought to mind as the plot progresses. To emphasize the aurality of the ancient audience's encounter with Luke-Acts, the term "auditor" will be preferred over "reader," though certainly there were those who "read" the text in the traditional sense.

2.3.3.1 Which Audience(s)?

In more recent studies of Luke-Acts, scholars who engage reader-response or audience-oriented theory are more specific in describing the reader or auditor to whom they refer. After a lifetime of studying the texts through a literary lens, Talbert has articulated "a concern for a synchronic reading of the final form of the text with a focus on the milieu within which Luke and Acts were written."[55] He credits the work of Rabinowitz and Jauss with distinguishing types of audiences and recognizing the historical expectations of the authorial audience. John Paul Heil acknowledges that the authorial audience for Luke-Acts is situated both in and beyond the text. For Heil, the audience has a historical location and a literary context.[56] Parsons is, likewise, noteworthy. He establishes a specific audience and articulates how that audience guided his analysis.

I am also interested in the way the "authorial audience" hears the rhetoric of Luke and Acts. By "authorial audience," I mean the audience Luke had in mind when he wrote Luke and Acts, that is a general Christian audience, living in the Roman Empire near the end of the first century.[57]

---

[54] Moore saw a conflict for those biblical scholars who would too readily apply "reading strategies" to texts that, in their original context, were received aurally. "Where the guild *has* missed out, however, in the view of the orality-literacy specialists, is in failing to realize that the *aural* appropriation of a text (in a public reading, say) fosters a markedly different way of conceptualizing it than the predominantly *visual* appropriation of a private, silent reading....Clearly, in attempting to play out the roles of the audiences envisioned by the evangelists, historical exegetes have failed to give due weight to the fact that these audiences were *listeners* first and foremost" (Stephen D. Moore, "Doing Gospel Criticism as/with a 'Reader,'" *BTB* 19 [1989]: 86).

[55] Charles H. Talbert, *Reading Luke-Acts in Its Mediterranean Milieu* (NovTSup 107; Leiden: Brill, 2003), 15.

[56] Heil, *The Meal Scenes in Luke-Acts: An Audience-Oriented Approach*, 3. Though he appeared to be drawing on the conclusions of Jauss and Rabinowitz, he cited neither.

[57] Mikeal C. Parsons, *Luke: Storyteller, Interpreter, Evangelist* (Peabody, MA: Hendrickson, 2007), 19.

Spencer uses the terms implied readers and authorial audience in his investigation of Lucan narrative rhetoric.[58] For aspects of his analysis trained on the narrative itself, he invokes the implied reader. To investigate ideological influence of the narrative, he employs the authorial audience. By making these distinctions, he recognizes that the hermeneutical effects of a text can best be determined from outside the narrative itself, which is the privileged perspective of the authorial auditor.

Much of reader-response criticism in biblical studies has tended to invoke Iser[59] and Fish,[60] fostering, albeit unknowingly, an approach that focuses on the reader's encounter with the text,[61] which leaves the determination of meaning to each individual. A more nuanced use of terms, situated within an audience-oriented theory, yields a richer analysis. Rabinowitz recognized the existence of multiple levels of audience within and outside a narrative.[62] He delineated the simultaneous roles any reader plays when encountering a text: actual audience, authorial audience, narrative audience, and ideal narrative audience. The actual audience includes the flesh and blood readers or auditors situated in time and space, possessing a specific historical, cultural, social, and religious perspective. The actual audience is the only audience over which the author exercises no authority.[63] These real readers are always just beyond the grasp of the author,[64] though "all responsible readers try very hard to respond in accord with what they take to be the intention or vision of the author and the work. They try as best they can both to understand and feel the point of view, attitudes, tone, mood, biases, and so forth which inform what they read."[65] In selecting specific literary and linguistic conventions, the au-

---

[58] Patrick E. Spencer, *Rhetorical Texture and Narrative*.

[59] Wolfgang Iser, *The Implied Reader* (Baltimore: Johns Hopkins University Press, 1974) and "The Reading Process: A Phenomenological Approach." *New Literary History* 3, no. 2 (Winter 1972): 279–99.

[60] Stanley Fish, *Is There a Text in This Class? The Authority of Interpretative Communities* (Cambridge, MA: Harvard University Press, 1980).

[61] George Aichele, *The Postmodern Bible: The Bible and Culture Collective* (New Haven, CT: Yale University Press, 1995), 27.

[62] Peter J. Rabinowitz, "Truth or Fiction: A Reexamination of Audiences," *Critical Inquiry* 4 (1977): 121–41.

[63] Ibid., 126.

[64] The reader "cannot become merely a carbon copy of an authorial point of view, because not enough of the copy is written. He cannot passively undergo the author's experience of the work because the most the author can provide are guides and stimuli to the experience" (Walter J. Slatoff, *With Respect to Readers: Dimensions of Literary Response* [Ithaca, NY: Cornell University Press, 1970], 65).

[65] Ibid., 59.

thor anticipates that the readers bring a literary competence to the act of reading.[66]

Rabinowitz defined the authorial audience as the intended reader or the hypothetical audience presupposed by the text and created by the author from assumptions about the actual historical audience he or she has in mind. The author creates the authorial audience so that it stands in close proximity with the actual audience. "But even if an author makes a serious attempt to write for the 'real people out there', the gap between the actual and the authorial audience will always exist."[67] This authorial audience "is a heuristic literary construct," the author's ideal reader who would understand the author's intent and read the narrative as it was designed to be read.[68] The artistic and stylistic choices made by the author are related to his assumptions about the actual audience's beliefs, values, and literary expectations.[69] These assumptions about his real audience form the foundation for his authorial audience. What is learned or experienced at the narrative level affects the authorial audience, "and, unless the authorial audience is very distant from the actual audience, [affects] the actual audience as well."[70] Actual readers must take on the role of these intended readers if they are to understand the intended meaning of the text.[71]

Investigating the authorial audience aids in determining the author's rhetorical goal for his real audience.[72] This distance between actual audience and the author's intended audience may be cultural, temporal or geographic. In the case of Luke-Acts, the gap may be between Luke's perception of where his audience stands with respect to what they have been taught and where he thinks they should be. "We are often forced to call upon the 'best part' of ourselves when we join the authorial audience. But most novelists, even if they do call on our better selves, will only call upon those moral qualities which they believe the actual audience has in reserve, just as they try not to rely on information which we will not in fact possess."[73]

The third type of audience proposed by Rabinowitz exists only within the text. Like the authorial audience, the narrative audience must possess specific

---

[66] Steven Mailloux, *Interpretive Conventions: The Reader in the Study of American Fiction* (Ithaca, NY; London: Cornell University Press, 1982), 91.

[67] Rabinowitz, "Truth or Fiction: A Reexamination of Audiences," 127.

[68] Mary Ann Tolbert, *Sowing the Gospel: Mark's World in Literary-Historical Perspective* (Minneapolis, MN: Fortress Press, 1989), 53.

[69] Rabinowitz, "Truth or Fiction: A Reexamination of Audiences," 126.

[70] Ibid., 133.

[71] Talbert, *Reading Luke-Acts in Its Mediterranean Milieu*, 19.

[72] "Starting with the question, 'How would the authorial audience have heard this text,' leads to a conclusion about what the author of the text probably intended" (Talbert, *Reading Luke-Acts in Its Mediterranean Milieu*, 19).

[73] Rabinowitz, "Truth or Fiction: A Reexamination of Audiences," 126.

knowledge in order to participate in the story.[74] The narrative audience is not expected to believe "facts" that would be either unfamiliar or unbelievable to the authorial audience. Like the authorial audience, the narrative audience does not exist. The authorial audience and the narrative audience are fictions, though in very different ways. The authorial audience attempts to reflect the original audience, while the narrative audience is limited to the confines of the narrative world. James Phelan further modifies Rabinowitz's narrative audience by defining it as "the actual audience's projection of itself into the observer role within the fiction. In taking on that role, we will always become believers in the reality of the fictional world."[75]

The final audience level refers to the audience that the narrator addresses within the story. Unlike the narrative audience, which may or may not accept the narrator's statements, the ideal narrative audience believes him or her even if the narrator is unreliable.[76] The ideal narrative audience is "the audience for which the narrator wishes he were writing."[77] In later writings, Rabinowitz collapsed the ideal narrative audience with the narrative audience.[78]

2.3.3.2 The Lucan Authorial Audience

The Gospel of Luke and Acts of the Apostles have various narrative audiences that require the actual auditor to play several roles simultaneously. The prologues of both volumes appear to address the authorial audience directly (in the person of the one named recipient), while the remainder of the story involves the narrative audience(s). But the authorial audience is never completely out of the picture. For instance, the author intends for his authorial audience to ask, along with Peter, κύριε, πρὸς ἡμᾶς τὴν παραβολὴν ταύτην λέγεις ἢ καὶ πρὸς πάντας (Luke 12:41). Throughout the two-volume work, the auditors are asked to "see, hear, and do" (Luke 6:47), situating themselves among the various fictive listeners (οἱ ὄχλοι, ὁ λαός, οἱ μαθηταί, οἱ γραμματεῖς καὶ Φαρισαῖοι, οἱ τελῶναι καὶ ἁμαρτωλοί), in order that they might know with greater certainty the things that they have been taught. Luke expects his authorial audience to recognize the various allusions to the Septuagint (for example the references to Num 6:3 and 1 Sam 1:11 in Luke 1:17, and the echo

---

[74] Ibid., 127.

[75] James Phelan, "'Self-Help' for Narratee and Narrative Audience: How 'I' — and 'You'? — read 'How.' Lorrie Moore's Short Story 'How' from the Collection 'Self-Help' — Second-Person Narrative," *Style* 28 (1994): 357.

[76] Rabinowitz, "Truth or Fiction: A Reexamination of Audiences," 134.

[77] Ibid., 134.

[78] Peter J. Rabinowitz, *Before Reading: Narrative Conventions and the Politics of Interpretation* (Columbus: Ohio State University Press, 1998). "Most rhetorical theorists have felt Rabinowitz's first three audiences have been sufficient to account for most author-narrator-reader relationships" (Phelan, "'Self-Help' for Narratee and Narrative Audience," 354).

of the words of the Prophet Isaiah in Mary's encounter with the angel in Luke 1:26–38). When Zechariah exits the temple, ὁ λαός presume that his muteness results from his having seen a vision (Luke 1:22). The narrative audience knows for certain that he has seen a vision but also possesses additional information: Zechariah has been struck dumb not simply because he saw a vision but because of his disbelief. When Mary experiences a similar encounter, the narrative audience knows what happened to Zechariah and anticipates how Mary may respond.[79]

> As a result we are not only regaled with a history, but drawn into a drama, and our own experience as audience – measured against or coinciding with the experiences of audiences *within* the text – becomes the narrative's way of making the history meaningful, 'true' and instructive to Theophilus and to us.[80]

The construction of an authorial audience is mostly (though not entirely) a literary endeavor. To uncover the authorial audience, we must first investigate the text for signs within the narrative that indicate a particular interest or view that might belong to a specific group. Additionally, we take note of those events or terms that the author defines and those that he or she does not. These explanations indicate the information the authorial audience would not know. We can assume that the authorial audience would understand the references hinted at through allusions in the text. The portrait that emerges is sparse. We can determine more of what the authorial audience does not know that what it does.[81]

An analysis of the author's literary efforts, use of imagery, vocabulary, and rhetoric further adds to the portrait of the audience, whom the author presumes understands his literary genius. The horizon of expectations – the authorial audience's knowledge of other literature, history, culture, etc. – permits the author to leave unspoken what he could readily expect his authorial auditors to know. This cultural knowledge and the gleanings from the narrative lead to the following portrait of the authorial audience.

The Lucan authorial auditor is a culturally literate member of the late-first- or early-second-century Mediterranean world who knows basic facts about the Roman Empire, including its history, politics, and geography, and the way it functioned politically and militarily. Luke uses the reigns of emperors to situ-

---

[79] "A comparison, therefore, of the two angelic annunciations gives us *both* a complete understanding of the identity of Jesus (a knowledge which will itself often privilege us, the gospel audience, over audiences within the text), and of His coming triumph, *and* a model for the selfless acceptance of God's words and God's ways" (Cornelia Cook, "The Sense of Audience in Luke: A Literary Examination," *New Blackfriars* 72 [1991]: 21).

[80] Cook, "The Sense of Audience in Luke: A Literary Examination," 20.

[81] Culpepper, *Anatomy of the Fourth Gospel: A Study in Literary Design: A Study in Literary Design* (Philadelphia: Fotress, 1983), 212.

ate his narrative in a specific historical period (Luke 2:1; 3:1). In Acts 11:28, the famine predicted by Agabus is placed during the reign Claudius. Aquila and Priscilla are in Corinth because the Edict of Claudius has forced them to leave Rome (Acts 18:2). Though not always chronologically accurate, Luke identifies known Roman political figures such as Quinius (Luke 2:2), Gallio (Acts 18:12), Felix and Festus (Acts 24:27).

Luke presumes his authorial audience possesses a knowledge of major cities and ethnic groups. The litany of the nations from whence the Jews have gathered for Pentecost includes visitors from parts of the Roman empire (Judea, Cappadocia, Pontus, Phrygia, Pamphylia, Egypt, Libya, Rome, Acts 2:9–10) and those areas never under Roman jurisdiction such as Parthia (Acts 2:9).[82] Luke places Paul's travels along main Roman thoroughfares including the Via Sebaste (Antioch Pisidia, Acts 13:14; Iconium, Acts 13:51; Lystra and Derbe, Acts 14:6; and back again, Acts 14:21)[83] and the Via Egnatia (Philippi, Acts 16:12; and Thessalonica, Acts 17:1).[84]

The authorial audience is also familiar with popular Greco-Roman literature[85] and some of its literary features including prison breaks (Acts 12:4–10; 16:23–29)[86] and shipwrecks (Acts 27:13–44).[87] The unusual feature of this contextualized auditor is his or her knowledge of the Greek Bible, which Luke engages through his use of Septuagintalisms,[88] and biblical allusions.[89] As a Greek-speaker, he or she understands rhetorical conventions.[90] Members of this audience belonged to the wide social network of Theophilus, which in-

---

[82] Gary Gilbert, "The List of Nations in Acts 2: Roman Propaganda and the Lukan Response," *JBL* 121 (2002): 497–529.

[83] Taylor, "St. Paul and the Roman Empire: Acts of the Apostles 13–14," 1189–1231.

[84] Taylor, "The Roman Empire in the Acts of the Apostles," 2490.

[85] D. R. MacDonald, *Does the New Testament Imitate Homer? Four Cases from the Acts of the Apostles* (New Haven: Yale University Press, 2003).

[86] Richard Pervo, *Profit with Delight: The Literary Genre of the Acts of the Apostles* (Philadelphia: Fortress Press, 1987), 21; and John B. Weaver, *Plots of Epiphany: Prison-Escape in Acts of the Apostles* (BZNW 131; New York: DeGruyter, 2004).

[87] D. R. MacDonald, "The Shipwrecks of Odysseus and Paul," *NTS* 45 (1999): 88–107.

[88] For example, πρός + the accusative after a verb of speaking is rare in the Synoptics, but Luke uses it frequently. See Luke 1:13; 4:36; 5:22; 7:24; 15:3, 22; 22:15, 70; 23:4; 24:18, 44; Acts 2: 37, 38; 5:8; 7:3; 9: 10, 11, 15, etc. (Fitzmyer, *The Gospel According to Luke I–IX*, 114–16).

[89] William Kurz, *Reading Luke-Acts: Dynamics of Biblical Narrative* (Louisville: Westminster John Knox, 1993), 13; and Robert L. Brawley, *Text to Text Pours Forth Speech: Voices of Scripture in Luke-Acts* (Bloomington, IN: Indiana University Press, 1995).

[90] "Since Luke's authorial audience presumably knew how to respond appropriately (if unconsciously) to persuasive rhetoric, we should determine then how the same authorial audience would have understood his rhetorical strategies and literary conventions." (Parsons, *Luke: Storyteller, Interpreter, Evangelist*, 19).

cludes men and women, slave and free, patrons and clients, Jew[91] and Gentile, Roman citizens and noncitizens.[92] The authorial auditor resides within a Hellenistic urban setting and may be an artisan or small-business owner (Acts 16:14; Acts 18:2; 19:24, 38). The audience is likely composed of both Christians[93] and God-fearers[94] and is aware of Greco-Roman religious beliefs and practices (Acts 14:11–13; 19:27; 28:4–6).

This study contributes to the composite portrait of the authorial audience by suggesting that its members are familiar with the Roman military and recognize the differences among various military ranks (tribune, centurion and soldier, Acts 21:31–32) and those units typically located in the provinces (Acts 10:1, 27:1). Additionally, the authorial auditor knows a variety of literary stereotypes of soldiers, which the author often engages, contradicts or transcends. Attending to an approach that considers the authorial audience in light of its "horizon of expectations" provides a way to understand how Luke's particular characterization of soldiers might have functioned. As Rabinowitz has stated, an author attempts to write for an authorial audience that closely mirrors his actual audience.[95] The more thorough our composite of the Lucan authorial audience, the closer we may come to seeing the elusive Lucan community.[96]

---

[91] Tyson disagrees that the Jews were part of the authorial audience, because the auditor "is not well informed about certain significant aspects of Jewish religious life" ("Jews and Judaism in Luke-Acts: Reading as a Godfearer," *NTS* 41 [1995]: 25).

[92] Patrick E. Spencer, *Rhetorical Texture and Narrative*, 34.

[93] Luke-Acts was composed for a Christian authorial audience, according to Kurz (Kurz, *Reading Luke-Acts: Dynamics of Biblical Narrative*, 14), while Tyson proposes an audience with "a limited knowledge of Christianity" (Tyson, "Jews and Judaism in Luke-Acts: Reading as a Godfearer," 26).

[94] For Tyson, the implied reader is "a pious Gentile who has deep affinities with Judaism but has not yet made a total commitment" (Tyson, "Jews and Judaism in Luke-Acts: Reading as a Godfearer," 26). Spencer also places God-fearers among the auditors (Patrick E. Spencer, *Rhetorical Texture and Narrative*, 34).

[95] Rabinowitz, "Truth or Fiction: A Reexamination of Audiences," 126.

[96] Johnson recognizes that a link could be forged between the literary aspects of the text and its actual original audience. "The task of discovering the literary function of the diverse elements in Luke-Acts does not by itself preclude the possibility of ultimately finding out something about Luke's readers (Johnson, "On Finding the Lukan Community: A Cautious Cautionary Essay," *SBLSP* 1 [1979]: 94). Talbert, however, does not believe that an authorial audience indicates a specific Lucan community. "By authorial audience one is not necessarily referring to a particular localized community from which and for which a text is alleged to have originated. Rather, the authorial audience refers to the larger cultural milieu within which a document was read/heard" (Talbert, *Reading Luke-Acts in Its Mediterranean Milieu*, 17). Contrary to Talbert, I hold that Luke shapes that image of his authorial audience based on his interpretation of an actual historical and localized community.

3. Plan of Action

Previous investigations of the soldiers in Luke-Acts have focused primarily on questions of historicity. Was the centurion of Capernaum a member of the Roman army or the Herodian militia? Were legions quartered in Judea under a Jewish king? Was the Italian cohort composed solely of Roman citizens? Yet, these questions do not address the literary aspect of the portrayals of soldiers – that they are characters within a narrative and not necessarily meant to be historical figures. Such a literary analysis has received little scholarly attention.

This investigation provides an examination of the soldiers in Luke-Acts that considers them primarily as literary characters, subject to the audience's ideas of verisimilitude. Additionally, this project takes seriously the *realia* of the Roman military and attempts to integrate the findings of archaeology and epigraphy, in as much as they provide insight into what a first-century audience would reasonably know and expect. If readers or auditors build characters as they encounter them in the text, then what tools must they bring to the table? By what categories might an ancient reader or auditor assess a narrative persona? Jauss recognized that an audience held a "horizon of expectations" – literary and cultural – as they approached the text. In the reading process, an audience measures a text according to these expectations.

A corresponding process of the continuous establishing and altering of horizons also determines the relationship of the individual text to the succession of texts that forms the genre. The new text evokes for the reader (listener) the horizon of expectations and rules familiar from earlier texts, which are then varied, corrected, altered, or even just reproduced."[97]

Jauss's work on reception history attends to the socio-historical context of the actual audience. As the horizon of expectations changes over time, other audiences in later historical periods will understand the text differently.[98] Taking the role of the audience seriously requires attention to ancient literary theory and the expectations of character development, since characters are designed to motivate the audience toward a particular moral judgment.[99] Chapter 2 discusses the construction and function of characters within ancient literature, with particular attention to generic expectations.

Due to the prevalence of the topic of war in ancient literature, military personae are ubiquitous. Chapter 3 focuses on the characterization of soldiers in Greek and Latin narrative texts, in order to discover the variety of stereotypes that Luke may have had available for his characterization of soldiers. In the

---

[97] Hans-Robert Jauss, *Toward an Aesthetic of Reception* (trans. Timothy Bahti; Minneapolis: University of Minnesota Press, 1982), 23.

[98] Rabinowitz, "Whirl without End," 91.

[99] James T. Laney, "Characterization and Moral Judgments," *JR* 55 (1975): 408.

vast majority of cases, soldiers are presented as merely elements and not developed fully enough to be categorized as characters.[100] If the soldier is more
than simply a prop, his character is depicted through traits directly or indirectly inferred within the text.[101] Evaluating the actions of the military character
requires attention to the narrative setting. For the warrior who kills on the
battlefield is a hero, but if he kills on the home front, he is a murderer.

This broad review of soldiers in Greco-Roman literature results in a collection of military stereotypes, which are variously employed in the process of
characterization. The collection of military stereotypes only demonstrates that
commonplaces were prevalent and that Luke's inclusion of soldiers is not
unusual. A more focused analysis is required in order to evaluate if Luke's
engagement with those stereotypes is unique. Chapters 4 and 5 analyze those
soldiers, centurions, and tribune found within the Gospel of Luke and Acts of
the Apostles. Essentially, Luke's portrayals fall into three categories. He uses
stereotypes as a basis of description, building on the expectations of the
Greco-Roman reader. He also contradicts the stereotypes, upsetting the reader's expectations. Finally, Luke transcends these stereotypes, demonstrating
that the military character is capable of change.

The characterization of soldiers in Luke-Acts could be designed to serve
the narrative structure, to foster Luke's agenda, and, if the authorial community closely mirrors the actual one, to encourage a particular response on the
part of the Lucan community. The stereotypical portrayals seem most limited
in their broader impact. Luke does not develop them beyond their immediate
task in the narrative. Examples of stereotypical soldiers are found in Luke 23
and Acts 12 and 27. The contradictory descriptions include the soldiers coming to John for baptism (Luke 3:14), the centurion at the cross (Luke 23:47),
the Tribune Claudius Lysias (Acts 21–23:32), and the soldier attending to
Paul in Rome (Acts 28:16). The portrayals of the Roman military that transcend the stereotype are limited but significant. Not only do the centurion of
Capernaum (Luke 7:1–10) and the centurion of Caesarea (Acts 10) impact the
narrative and promote Luke's theological agenda, but they – and perhaps the
contradictory portraits as well – serve as parabolic exempla, demonstrating to
the authorial audience the appropriate response of a disciple. Chapter 6 evalu-

---

[100] The distinction between character and element is made by Chatman (*Story and
Discourse: Narrative Structure in Fiction and Film* [Ithaca, NY: Cornell University
Press, 1978], 96–145), and explored more fully in the next chapter.

[101] According to Garvey, "A full and systematic account of characterization must
provide each character with a set of structural attributes, and set of non-structural attribu-
tions, as well as an identification and a temporal orientation which indicates any change
in attributes" (James Garvey, "Characterization in Narrative," *Poetics* 7 [1978]: 63).
Because several of the texts in the research pool are brief or the portrayal of the military
figure is limited, the temporal aspect of Garvey's definition could not be considered.

ates Luke's portrayal of soldiers and proposes that the cumulative characterization serves both a narrative and a rhetorical function.

Chapter 2

Characterization in Ancient Literature

1. Introduction

In the preface to the Gospel, the author of Luke-Acts acknowledges that other narratives have been written about all that Jesus did and taught (Luke 1:1), and he does not claim any unique literary invention on his part. The contribution his gospel makes is one of organization and accuracy (Luke 1:3). His intent is to instill confidence in Theophilus, so that he can trust what he has been taught (Luke 1:4). The author will follow standard literary conventions if he hopes to meet his goal, since novelty would not enhance the work's credibility. Evidence abounds to demonstrate Luke's knowledge of Greek literature. He has Paul quote the Greek poet Aratus (Acts 17:28).[1] Acts 5:39 and Acts 26:14 may have their origin in Euripides' *Bacchae*,[2] leading Weinreich to propose Luke's literary dependence on the work.[3] The miraculous prison breaks in Acts (5:18–20; 12:6–11; 16:23–34) are a literary motif found in other ancient narratives (Ovid, *Metam.* 3.690–700; Lucian, *Tox.* 28–33).[4] Low literacy levels notwithstanding, the Lucan authorial audience would know the texts of Greco-Roman *paideia*, especially the works of Homer.[5] Likewise, readers and auditors came to expect

---

[1] M. J. Edwards, "Quoting Aratus: Acts 17,28" *Zeitschrift für die Neutestamentliche Wissenschaft und die Kunde der älteren Kirche* 83 (January 1, 1992): 266–269.

[2] Abraham Malhberbe, *Social Aspects of Early Christianity* (Eugene, OR: Wipf & Stock, 2003), 42–44.

[3] Otto Weinreich, *Gebet und Wunder: zwei Abhandlungen zur Religions- und Literaturgeschichte* (Tübinger Beiträge zur Altertumswissenschaft 5; Stuttgart: Kohlhammer, 1929), 179. Weinreich's thesis has been critiqued by Vögel ("Lukas und Euripides," *TZ* 9 [1953]: 421–25, 428ff); John Hackett ("Echoes of Euripides in the Acts of the Apostles?" *Irish Theological Quarterly* 23 [1956]: 218–27; 350–66); and more recently by Weaver (*Plots of Epiphany,* esp. 12–14).

[4] For a compilation of ancient narratives in which prison breaks occur, see Richard Pervo, *Profit with Delight,* 147, fn. 15.

[5] MacDonald is most notable among New Testament scholars who advocate Luke's use of Homeric legends (*Does the New Testament imitate Homer?*). MacDonald's methods have received various critiques, but his recognition of the prominent role of Homer in the literary imagination of the evangelist Luke is well-taken. In her review of MacDonald's *The Homeric Epics and the Gospel of Mark* (New Haven, CT: Yale University Press, 2000), Mitchell argued for a more nuanced interpretation and "less wholesale literary mappings." But she also noted the likelihood that early Christians would have been familiar with the

that novels would include sea voyages and shipwrecks (Acts 27:1–28:16).[6] "The first readers would have approached the Gospel guided by the same hermeneutical principles that he used when he read the tragedians or the historians."[7]

Since Luke demonstrates familiarity with Greek literature and literary motifs, we would expect his mode of characterization to follow the standards of other Greco-Roman writers. The characters in ancient literature, and no less in Luke-Acts, were portrayed as heroes and villains modeling human virtues and vices,[8] with whom the audience could identify or shun. We begin our investigation of ancient characterization with Aristotle who, unlike his teacher Plato, viewed poetry and prose not as mere imitation but as creative action.[9] A review of the principles of Aristotle's literary theory provides a basis on which to assess characterization in ancient literature, and, more specifically, in Luke–Acts. The *Poetics,* though not a complete synthesis of Aristotle's literary theory, influenced ancient critics and grammarians alike.[10] Greek plots were recycled into new Roman contexts, and the revival of classicism and Atticism led Hellenistic writers "to follow Aristotle and his rules for characterization."[11] Aristotle's analysis of logic, rhetoric and poetics accedes to the "intentions of the speaker, the susceptibilities of the audience addressed, and the nature of the

---

writings of Homer. Concerning the possible allusions in Acts 14:8–18, she added, "It is not at all unthinkable that Luke would have deliberately intended such an explicit Homeric allusion, but, even if not, there is very little to prevent an early Christian reader from bringing the Homeric narrative portraits and conceits about disguises – human and divine – to a reading of this passage, especially since Zeus and Hermes are directly invoked in a parodistic fashion that depends for its sting on general cultural knowledge of Homeric lore" ("Review: Homer in the New Testament," *JR* 83 [2003]:258).

[6] Susan Marie Praeder, "Acts 27:1–28:16: Sea Voyages in Ancient Literature and the Theology of Luke–Acts," *CBQ* 46 (1984): 683–706.

[7] Theodore J. Weeden, *Mark: Traditions in Conflict* (Philadelphia: Fortress Press, 1971), 17.

[8] Elizabeth Struthers Malbon, "The Jewish Leaders in the Gospel of Mark: A Literary Study of Marcan Characterization," *JBL* 108 (1989): 260.

[9] As Richter pointed out, "For Plato, that artists were not always faithful to the truth counted against them; for Aristotle, artists must disregard incidental facts to search for deeper *universal* truths" (David H. Richter, *The Critical Tradition. Classic Texts and Contemporary Trends* [New York: St. Martin's Press, 1989], 40).

[10] G. M. A. Grube, *The Greek and Roman Critics* (London: Methuen, 1965), 70, 103.

[11] Fred W. Burnett, "Characterization and Reader Construction of Characters in the Gospels," in *Characterization in Biblical Literature* (ed. Elizabeth Struthers Malbon and Adele Berlin; Semeia 63; Atlanta: Scholars Press, 1993), 8. Also Thomas Hägg, *The Novel in Antiquity* (Berkeley: University of California Press, 1983), xii.

communications for which it serves as medium."[12] Since attending to the author, his audience and the narrative's function are the concerns of this investigation, Aristotle's reflections on literary theory are particularly pertinent.

Despite Gorgias' claim to the contrary,[13] Aristotle proposed that prose and poetry differed significantly from each other. The lexis of prose should not include the use of poetic devices or elevated language (*Rhet.* 3.2–12). Prose (generally just λόγος in Aristotle)[14] is marked by the iambic meter and a vocabulary that most closely resembles ordinary conversation (*Rhet.* 3.1.9). It is the purview of the historian (*Poet.* 9.2). Poetry concerns itself with probable actions while history deals with actual occurrences (*Poet.* 9.4–5). As a poetic genre, tragedy is composed of a beginning, middle and end (*Poet.* 23.1), but history covers a duration of time (*Poet.* 23.21–23) and the course of events and people during that time, regardless of their causal relationships.

Elements of plot, characterization, spectacle, diction, melody and thought were presented differently according to the goal of the genre. For example, distinctions between poetry and prose led to differences in the process of characterization.[15] Aristotle lent much more weight to the characters in tragedies and epics, admitting that those in comedy had not always been treated seriously (*Poet.* 5.31–33). Characterization in tragedy depicts people as better than they are, while characterization in comedy presents them as worse.

If one is to represent morally inferior people, one must (logically) represent them doing and saying morally inferior things. By Aristotle's own poetical criteria, therefore, the contents of comedy must deviate from the ethical norms of polite social intercourse.[16]

Comedies and tragedies did share in common the use of masks, which produced characters that were immediately recognizable.[17] Pollux reported that there

---

[12] Richard McKeon, "Aristotle's Conception of Language and the Arts of Language," in *Critics and Criticism: Ancient and Modern* (ed. R. S. Crane; Chicago: University of Chicago Press, 1952), 176.

[13] Gorgias held that prose emerged from poetic imitation and that poetry itself was "simply 'logos with meter' (Helen, 9)" (Richard Graff, "Prose verses Poetry in Early Greek Theories of Style," *Rhetorica* 23 [2005]: 307).

[14] English translations read λόγοι as "speeches" when Aristotle discusses the three species of rhetoric (*Rhet.* 1.3.1) but as "prose," when it is found in the singular and is being contrasted to ποίησις (*Rhet.* 3.1.9). See Aristotle, *Art of Rhetoric* (trans. J. H. Freese; LCL; Cambridge, MA: Harvard University Press, 2000) and Aristotle, *Rhetoric and Poetics* (trans. W. Rhys Roberts and Ingram Bywater; New York: Modern Library, 1954).

[15] "In comedy, tragedy, and epic at least the fixed type characters of rhetorical theory were subjected to modifications in accord with the genre in which they chanced to appear," (William Charles Korfmacher, "Three Phases of Classical Type Characterization," *Classical Weekly* 27 [1934]: 86).

[16] Malcolm Heath, "Aristotelian Comedy," *The Classical Quarterly* 39 (1989): 345.

[17] For example, Menander does not introduce the name of his characters, "since they wore readily recognizable masks.... It is probable that certain names were associated with certain masks, and that unique names were established in dialogue" (W. Thomas MacCary,

were three categories of masks: tragic, satirical and comic (*Onom.* 133–154). "Although [Roman] comedy has a wider choice than the twenty-eight masks of tragedy and comprises forty-four in all, they are distributed, with variations of age, of traits and of sex into three main urban classes – prosperous citizens, household slaves, and courtesans."[18] Epics, because of their longer length, often included a fuller development of the character's attributes.

Another generic distinction in characterization is the use of proper names for individuals.[19] The characters in comedies have fictitious names, while tragic, epic, and historical characters most often have real names (*Poet.* 9.15). Comedies deal with probable but not certain incidents (*Poet.* 9.12–14), so a sense of reality engendered by an actual name is not necessary. Rather, the names of comic characters are meant to describe their personality. Plautus's Pyrgopolynices is a combination of πύργος, πόλις, and νίκη, making him "Conqueror of Tower and City." Terence's Thraso may be derived from θράσος, and therefore would be something like "Mr. Emboldened."[20] The soldiers of Roman comedy do not reflect real-life military men; they are parodies. However, the military figures found in the Hellenistic and Roman novels are meant to be believable and thus have realistic names. For example, in the work of Xenophon of Ephesus, "for most of the unimportant characters, he seems to have chosen the names quite at random among those in use in daily life, utilizing them for individualization but not for characterization."[21] Since histories concern actual events (*Poet.* 9.3–5), writers were obliged to use the actual names of soldiers and generals or risk their own credibility.

A quick perusal of character names in Luke-Acts demonstrates that the author did not adhere to generic boundaries. As would be expected in historical accounts, political figures are identified accurately (emperors: Augustus, Luke

"Menander's Soldiers: Their Names, Roles and Masks," *The American Journal of Philology* 93 [1972]: 283, fn 14).

[18] Alan McN. G. Little, "Plautus and Popular Drama," *Harvard Studies in Classical Philology* 49 (1938): 205.

[19] "What is important is that drama is much more intensely concentrated and meaningfully shaped, 'purer' than ordinary unscripted experience, so that everything the stage figures do and say, and everything said about them, has to be taken as significant, even their names," (Stephen Halliwell, "Traditional Greek Conceptions of Character," in *Characterization and Individuality in Greek Literature* [ed. Christopher Pelling; Oxford: Clarendon Press, 1990], 89).

[20] Blume suggests that Thraso derived from a different stem, one shared with Homer's Thersites. In this reading, Thraso means "'Tollkühn', vom gleichen Wortstamm abgeleitet wie der Name Thersites" (Horst-Dieter Blume, "Komische Soldaten: Entwicklung und Wandel einer typischen Bühenfigur in der Antike," in *Rezeption des antiken Drama auf der Bühne und in der Literatur* [ed. Bernhard Zimmermann; Stuttgart: Metzler, 2001], 187).

[21] Thomas Hägg, "The Naming of the Characters in the Romance of Xenophon of Ephesus," *Eranos* 69 (1971): 59.

2:1; Tiberius, Luke 3:1; Herodian rulers: Herod, King of Judea, Luke 1:5; Herod the Tetrarch and Philip the Tetrarch, Luke 3:1; Herod Agrippa I; Acts 12:1; Agrippa II, Acts 26:1; Roman magistrates: Quirinius, Luke 2:2; Pontius Pilate, Luke 3:1; Felix, Acts 23:24; Porcius Festus, Acts 24:27; Sergius Paulus, Acts 13:7; Gallio, Acts 18:12). But Luke also includes comic characters with names that serve as descriptions: Elymas, which the author translates for his audience as μάγος (Acts 13:8),[22] and Eutychus is fortunate that Paul possesses healing powers (Acts 20:9–10). The vast majority of Lucan characters have the typical monikers with which his authorial audience would be familiar. In the Palestinian context of the Gospel of Luke, the characters' names reflect the Jewish setting (Zechariah, Elizabeth, Mary, John, Judas, etc.).[23] As the narrative moves beyond the borders of Judea, characters in Acts of the Apostles bear Hellenistic names: [Paul] "was accompanied by Sopater son of Pyrrhus from Beroea, by Aristarchus and Secundus from Thessalonica, by Gaius from Derbe, and by Timothy, as well as by Tychicus and Trophimus from Asia" (Act 20:3). Roman soldiers have common Latin names (Cornelius, Claudius, Julius). Whether there actually was a Cornelius or Julius serving in Caesarea, their names enhance the sense of realism, reflecting the historical presence of the Roman military in the provinces. The Gospels and Acts have been called mixed genres,[24] so it's not surprising that the Aristotelian distinctions among genres are little followed. Nonetheless, Luke does attempt to name characters as befits their narrative setting.

The following section focuses on the development and formulation of characters in ancient literature before turning to a discussion of the how those characters function within the narrative. The final section focuses on the characterization of soldiers and generals. In the historiographies, the author's own military experience as well as changes in military practices affected how soldiers were portrayed. In addition to personal experience, the narrative setting set parameters for probable behavior. The majority of military characters are found on the battle field. Some are depicted on assignment in the provinces, and a few

---

[22] The narrator of Acts "uses the translation of a name as a way of further identifying a character, and presumably providing information unavailable to the narratee, ostensibly because in the cases of Barnabas, and Elymas, the narratee does not know Aramaic" (Parsons and Pervo, *Rethinking the Unity of Luke-Acts*, 70.)

[23] H. J. Cadbury, "Some Semitic Personal Names in Luke–Acts," in *Amicitiae Corolla: a Volume of Essays Presented to James Rendel Harris, D. Litt. On the Occasion of His Eightieth Birthday* (ed. H. G. Wood; London: University of London Press, 1933), 45–56.

[24] Kermode labels the gospels *genus mixtum* (*The Genesis of Secrecy: On the Interpretation of Narrative* [Cambridge, MA: Harvard University Press, 1979], n. 20, 162–163); and Karris gives the same designation to Acts of the Apostles ("Windows and Mirrors: Literary Criticism and Luke's Sitz im Leben," *SBL Seminar Papers* [1979]: 53).

are portrayed on the home front. A brief survey of the characterization of soldiers in Greco-Roman historiographies, tragedies, comedies, novels and satires will conclude the chapter.

2. The Process of Characterization and the Function of Narrative Personae

2.1 Creating Characters

Aristotle held that the chief element of both poetry and prose is the plot, around which character, thought, diction, music and spectacle are merely structural supports (*Poet.* 6.8–10). Nonetheless, the poet should attempt to integrate all, since they enhance the plot and improve the quality of the work. Our primary concern is character, which Aristotle defined as an agent of moral action possessing certain qualities, which, when acted upon, lead to happiness or its opposite (*Poet.* 6. 19–20). As an agent, a character performs actions that are essential to the drama, but the character's description is not necessary and is included only for the sake of the actions (*Poet.* 6. 20–21). Emphasizing character's supporting role, Aristotle concluded that tragedies do not need to have characters, but they cannot exist without a plot (*Poet.* 6.21).

For a character to function appropriately within a work, four aims must be achieved (*Poet.*15.). First, the character is to be morally good (χρηστός), which is revealed through his or her speech and action (ὁ λόγος ἢ ἡ πρᾶξις). Second, the character must be suitable (ἁρμόττον). Third, the character is to manifest likeness (τὸ ὅμοιον), possessing basic, shared human qualities. Finally, the portrayal of a character is to be consistent (τὸ ὁμαλόν). The character introduced early in the narrative should resemble this same character encountered later. Any changes that occur should be reasonable, so that the character behaves in probable ways.

2.1.1. The Importance of Ἔνδοξα in Characterization

Aristotle asserted that across the genres vividness and verisimilitude are the tests of viable characters who behave in probable and likely ways.

With character, precisely as in the structure of events, one should always seek necessity or probability – so that for such a person to say or do such things is necessary or probable, and the sequence of events is also necessary or probable (15.1454a [Halliwell, LCL]).

The determination of what is probable is a communal act or, as Aristotle termed it in *Topica*, an endoxic act:

Generally accepted opinions, on the other hand, are those which commend themselves to all or to the majority or to the wise – that is, to all of the wise or to the majority or to the most famous and distinguished of them" (Top. 1.100b18.22–24 [Tredennick and Forster, LCL]).

The prominent decide what is expectable and therefore probable. "Thus endoxa would be both what is recognized as reasonable and respectable by anyone and what is endowed with power because it is believed and circulated by the legitimate representative of power."[25] The idea of ἔνδοξα undergirds our concept of verisimilitude, which leads the audience to expect characters to behave appropriately to their type within their narrative setting. Though verisimilitude most often guides the development of characters across all genres, exaggeration is to be expected in comedies. The exaggeration is, nonetheless, an amplification of the behavior that the audience would consider probable. In the end, the audience will "sharpen his or her sensibility and social competence in this direct experiencing of human behavior, and in concrete actions, he or she will create more precise typifications, that is, *topoi* and *endoxa*, which make the actions of others easier to anticipate."[26] The endoxic tendency of characterization leads to the creation of stereotypes. When an author engages a stereotype, he or she is calling to the mind of the reader or auditor all previous characters who have exhibited the same behaviors. Thus:

the presence of a literary ancestor for a fictional character is of course in some measure critically significant: in so far as the author and audience can also be presumed to be aware of the ancestry, it is a contributing factor to the understanding of the character in his own environment.[27]

2.1.2 Modern Literary Theory and the Creation of Character

Aristotle's discussion of characterization in the *Poetics* focused on its role within the genre of tragedy. As genres developed, the Aristotelian categories no longer fit neatly. To understand the complexity of characterization as it would develop in emerging genres, modern literary theory holds the most promise. Aristotle emphasized the importance of a character's actions, but modern literary theory focuses of the emergence of a character's qualities

Literary theorists hold that characterization is a collection of attributes or traits[28] that an author gives to an identified character within a narrative text

---

[25] Ruth Amossy, "Introduction to the Study of Doxa," *Poetics Today* 23 (2002): 371.

[26] Ekkehard Eggs, "Doxa in Poetry: A Study in Aristotle's Poetics," *Poetics Today* 23 (2002): 413.

[27] John Arthur Hanson, "The Glorious Military," in *Roman Drama* (ed. T. A. Dorey and D. R. Dudley; London: Routledge & Kegan Paul, 1965), 51.

[28] Chatman defines a trait as "a narrative adjective out of the vernacular labeling of a personal quality of a character, as it persists over part or whole of the story" (*Story and Discourse*, 125). Rimmon-Kenan used "character trait" (*Narrative Fiction* [London:

through a process of repetition, similarity, contrast and implication.[29] Repetitive behavior leads the audience to infer character traits. If a character is continually biting his nails, for instance, the audience may identify him in that scene as nervous. The similarity of behaviors also affects character identification through generalization. A soldier who boasts of his war successes may also boast of his love conquests. Contrasting behavior can affirm a generalization. The soldier in Apuleius's *Metamorphoses* bullies a gardener and in the end steals his donkey. The same bully hides from the authorities so he will not be punished for losing his sword. This contrasting behavior leads the audience to conclude that the soldier is selfish. Implication follows behavior. In Acts 10, Cornelius prays daily. The implication is that he is pious. Attributes or character traits such as being "nervous," "selfish" or "pious" emerge from the text. For example, Plautus's Pyrgopolynices appears crooning about the luster of his shield in the opening scene of the *Miles Gloriosus*. His sycophant responds that Pyrgopolynices is, indeed, a successful hero and greater than the god Mars. In Act Two, the soldier's servant, Palaestrio, speaks directly to the audience, calling his master *gloriosus, impudens, stercoreus, plenus periuri* (90). The behavior of the soldier, the dialogue of his sycophant, and the direct address by his servant confirm that Pyrgopolynices is a self-centered braggart, and we anticipate that his behaviors will lead to his undoing, which, indeed, they do.

Authors present a character's attributes either directly (through the statements of the narrator or other reliable characters) or indirectly (by means of settings, clothing, names and actions).[30] The latter requires more attention on the part of the author and anticipates the reader has an "inferential capacity," which allows for the inferring of more details about an individual than are explicitly stated.[31] The use of direct or indirect characterization makes differing demands of the reader, who must evaluate the details presented.

The lower end of this scale – character revealed through actions or appearance – leaves us substantially in the realm of inference. The middle categories, involving direct speech either by a character himself or by others about him, lead us from inference to the weighing of claims. With the report of inward speech, we enter the realm of relative certainty about character: there is certainty, in any case, about the character's conscious intentions, though we may still feel free to question the motive behind the intention. Finally at the top of the ascending scale, we have the reliable narrator's explicit statement of what the characters feel, intend, desire; here we are accorded certainty.[32]

Routledge, 1983], 59), while Garvey preferred "attribute" in his definition ("Characterization in Narrative," *Poetics* 7 [1978]: 74–75).

[29] Rimmon-Kenan, *Narrative Fiction*, 39–40.

[30] Garvey, "Characterization in Narrative," 68.

[31] Chatman, *Story and Discourse*, 29.

[32] Robert Alter, *The Art of Biblical Narrative* (New York: Basic Books, 1981), 117.

The process of character creation – regardless of whether traits are revealed directly or indirectly – can be minimal or extensive, depending on the character's role within the narrative. If a figure has no cumulative development and appears in only one episode, he or she can be considered a minor or less-developed persona. In contrast, round or major characters affect the plot as a whole and develop through the course of the story.[33] Round characters have a variety of traits, some of which may even contradict each other.[34] These more developed narrative personae instill in the auditor a stronger sense of intimacy,[35] since the audience comes to know these major characters throughout the narrative. The same cannot be said of the minor characters, who appear only within specific scenes, and have only minimal impact on the plot. A third category includes "elements" – those characters who are best described as part of the setting,[36] since they appear as props, adding realism or dimension to the scene, but do not influence the plot.

2.1.3 Filling in the Gaps: The Role of the Audience

The author's characterization requires active participation on the part of the readers or audience, in order to bring the narrative figure to life. Characterization thus depends upon a relationship between the author who penned the work and the audience who will enflesh the narrative persona from the author's skeleton. To achieve successful characterization, the author anticipates that his authorial audience possesses an "inferential capacity"[37] and will draw on a horizon of cultural knowledge, so as to fill in the gaps. The author expects his actual audience to behave as does his authorial one.

We must reconstruct – to the fullest extent possible – the extratextual repertoire, literary skills and basic orientation of the original audience. In doing so, our ultimate purpose is hermeneutical, not historical: we are less concerned with discovering the identities of intended addresses than with ascertaining the type and degree of "cultural literacy" the author seems to have assumed for his audience.[38]

---

[33] Darr and others have debated whether ancient characters could be described as "developing." "Narrative characters – even those in historical works – were largely illustrative, symbolic, and typed, rather than representational, mimetic, and heterodox as they tend to be in modern novels" (*On Character Building*, 48). In the section on the function of characters, I will discuss Gill's treatment of ancient character and the question of a fixed nature (Gill, "The Question of Character-Development: Plutarch and Tacitus"), which addresses Darr's concerns.

[34] E. M. Forster, *Aspects of the Novel* (New York: Harmondsworth, 1962), 75.

[35] Chatman, *Story and Discourse*, 132.

[36] See Chatman for a lengthy discussion of the difference between characters and elements as "existents" in a story (Ibid., 96–145).

[37] Ibid., 29.

[38] John Darr, *On Character Building*, 26.

This horizon of cultural knowledge or, as Darr defines it, "extratextual reper-toire," (extratext) includes the skills and knowledge necessary to "fill in the gaps" of the text.[39] Darr listed the criteria of 1) language; 2) social norms and cultural scripts; 3) classical or canonical literature; 4) literary conventions and reading rules; and 5) commonly-known historical and geographical facts.[40] The author assumes his authorial audience has this repertoire of skills and knowledge to "construct" the text and to build the characters by filling in what is unstated in the text itself. For example, Luke introduces a centurion stationed in Capernaum, without an explanation as to who a centurion is or what he might be doing in a small Jewish fishing village (Luke 7:1 2), likely presuming his authorial audience would fill in the blanks. The methodological implications of the "extra text" are well appreciated by Fred Burnett. "Theories of characteri-zation that are drawn from modern narrative poetics can be applied to biblical texts only when the horizon of expectations for what constitutes a character in a particular biblical text has been clarified."[41] Though speaking of biblical nar-ratives, Burnett's statement is no less accurate in terms of other ancient texts.

Aristotle would agree that the construction of character occurs both in and beyond the text. "What is striking is that (Aristotle) seems to conceive the pro-cess of dramaturgy essentially in terms of the relationship between poet and audience, rather than in terms of the imaginative creation of characters and their emotions."[42] The audience or reader encounters the actual textual indicators, such as proper names, direct description by a reliable narrator, and depicted action, and subsequently engages in a process of character-building, in order to "bring to life" the author's text. This encounter is cumulative: the audience brings to bear what it has learned about a character throughout the narrative.[43] As Thompson recognizes for Acts of the Apostles, "Since the actions that the Acts narrative depicts infer possible 'character' traits or motives of the charac-

---

[39] As Darr notes, the reader's cultural background would impact how he or she engages in this process of evaluating the text, so that the skill set would differ depending on the reader (Ibid., 22–23).

[40] Ibid., 22.

[41] Burnett, "Characterization and Reader Construction of Characters in the Gospels," 6.

[42] Christopher Gill, "The Ēthos/Pathos Distinction in Rhetorical and Literary Criti-cism," *CQ* 34 (1984): 152.

[43] "Character is not given to us like a gift in the hand, or like a picture on the wall, but …it does in fact accumulate. This must make perfect sense since the story, unlike the pic-ture on the wall, moves across time – we must turn the page in order to find out what else there is to know about the character…" (Mary Doyle Springer, *A Rhetoric of Literary Character: Some Women of Henry James* [Chicago: University of Chicago Press, 1978], 179). Darr came to a similar conclusion. "Because character is cumulative, it is essential that we be cognizant at all times of the degree to which a character or a character group has been constructed at each point along the text continuum" (Darr, *On Character Building*, 42).

ters, these portrayals function within the narrative much like the specific episodes: each incidental depiction of a character contributes cumulatively to the
narrative plot and to the character's portrayal in the narrative."[44]

The cumulative nature of characterization requires that a narrative be read
in sequence because the author builds on earlier appearances of a particular
figure. And, as Thompson acknowledges, the reader must continually reform
the developing portrait.

> The characterization of a given narrative refers *both* to the cumulative images of characters *and*
> to that part of the reading process in which the reader constructs and reevaluates the characters
> in light of new information, scenes, and images.[45]

By investigating the portrayal of Jews across Luke–Acts, Tannehill has successfully demonstrated that the role of Israel in the Gospel of Luke is much
more nuanced and complicated than previously thought.[46] Likewise, Darr
demonstrates Luke's facility in creating multi-dimensional characters such as
Herod the Fox[47] and the Pharisees[48] by noting that characters develop over the
course of the narrative. This project demonstrates that the same cumulative construction of character is active in Luke's presentation of Roman soldiers.

2.2 The Narrative and Rhetorical Functions of Characters

Our analysis is stalled from the start if we fail to answer a primary question:
What purpose does a text serve? More specifically, for our ancient author,
whom we call Luke, what might he have envisioned as the response to his two-
volumes from his authorial audience? Fortunately, Luke has left us a preface in
which he speaks directly to this authorial audience, describing his intent. But
exactly how does one create an assurance of things that have been taught (Luke
1:4)? This interplay between the author and his audience is precisely what Aristotle described as a cathartic encounter. As noted above, the primary function
of characters is to enhance the events of the drama; thus, characters take a back
seat to plot. Yet, the audience's ability to identify with the characters is a key
factor in achieving Aristotle's goal for tragedy: κάθαρσις (*Poet.* 6. 28). Under-

---

[44] Richard P. Thompson, *Keeping the Church in Its Place* (New York: T & T Clark,
2006), 26.

[45] Richard P. Thompson, "Believers and Religious Leaders in Jerusalem: Contrasting
Portraits of Jews in Acts 1–7," in *Literary Studies in Luke-Acts: Essays in Honor of Joseph
B. Tyson* (ed. Richard P. Thompson and Thomas E. Phillips; Macon, GA: Mercer Univer-
sity Press, 1998), 330.

[46] Robert Tannehill, "Israel in Luke–Acts: A Tragic Story." *JBL* 104 (1985): 69–85.

[47] John Darr, *Herod the Fox: Audience Criticism and Lukan Characterization*. JSNTSS.
Sheffield: Sheffield Academic Press, 1998.

[48] Darr, *On Character Building*, 85–126.

standing the function of Luke's characterization of soldiers requires a prelimi-
nary discussion on the function of characters and the role characters plays in
the creation of catharsis.

According to Plato, the gods granted the gift of music and poetry as a means
of restoring balance during periods of emotional instability that plague all human beings. Rising out of the natural rhythmic movements and cries of an in-
fant, music and poetry were thus part of human nature (*Rep.* 653d). As such,
they could be judged for moral content and moral effect (654e), for the pleasure
music and poetry created (655c–e), and for their quality of imitation (668c). In
Platonic thought, music serves a recreational purpose; its rhythm and harmony
becomes a pleasurable path to self-control. Aristotle develops this idea of emotional release in a slightly different direction. Like Plato, Aristotle argues that
excess emotions could be stirred, purged and returned to a balanced state by
means of music (*Pol.* 8.7), tragedy (*Poet.* 6.28), and, indeed, all artistic acts of
mimesis. "The rousing of pity and fear in their audience was, as we have seen,
the recognized goal of the art of words, of orator, rhapsode and poet."[49] Aristotle describes how this emotional reordering works.

For any experience that occurs violently in some souls is found in all, though with different
degrees of intensity – for example pity and fear, and also religious excitement; for some persons
are very liable to this form of emotion, and under the influence of sacred music we see these
people, when they use tunes that violently arouse the soul, being thrown into a state as if they
had received medicinal treatment and taken a purge (καθάρσεως); the same experience then
must come also to the compassionate and the timid and the other emotional people generally in
such degree as befalls each individual of these classes, and all must undergo a purgation
(κάθαρσιν) and pleasant feeling of relief; and similarly also the purgative (καθαρτικά) melodies
afford harmless delight to people (Arist *Pol.* 8.5–16 [Rackham, LCL]).

In the *Politics*, Aristotle envisions a less refined audience (8.7.20), one likely
to have less control of its emotions. He places no such limitations on the term
in his discussion in the *Poetics*. Aristotle may have recognized that the need for
catharsis was more broadly shared. Citizen and non-citizen alike were able to
identify with a character and "experience" a vicarious cleansing of their own.
But the character must be one whom the audience recognizes and with whom
it feels a sense of affinity or aversion. For most, an extremely virtuous person
or an abject villain does not inspire a kinship.

This leaves, then, the person in-between these cases. Such a person is someone not preeminent
in virtue and justice, and one who falls into adversity not through evil and depravity, but
through some kind of error; and one belonging to the class of those who enjoy great renown
and prosperity, such as Oedipus, Thyestes, and eminent men from such lineages (*Poet.* 13.5–
10 [Halliwell, LCL]).

---

[49] Grube, *The Greek and Roman Critics*, 75.

For characters to lead the audience to a cathartic experience, they must be morally good if they are found in tragedy, and morally inferior if found in comedies. The questions of morality are at the heart of the character's role within the plot.

The chorus or audience (for our purposes, those who are to make moral judgments) are drawn into the action by means of dramatic empathy. We have tended, following the elements of tragedy, to identify this emotional response primarily in terms of catharsis. But, it may well be that pathos is a more common mode of interpretative response, a pathos (not pity) called forth by privation (steresis) or loss that becomes evident.[50]

The catharsis, or purging, which Aristotle envisions[51] is contingent on the presence of empathy. The audience must feel with the characters to the point of possession (ἐνθουσιασμός, *Pol.*8.5.11), in order to experience a purging of its own emotions. This dramatic empathy allows the audience to enter into the world of the character and to understand better his or her actions so as to make moral judgments.[52] L. A. Post distinguished the cathartic goal of tragedy, which is centered on an experience of πάθος, from the moral concerns of the other genres.[53] Comedy, for example, seeks to elicit a response from its audience by softening the hearer, making him pliable and allowing moral precepts and examples to do their work of persuasion.[54]

The actual audience naturally identifies with the characters, either feeling affinity with the characters or discontinuity. This affinity or lack of it is experienced in the auditors as either an attraction to or repulsion from a character.[55] Though the author has no control over his actual audience, he does anticipate how his authorial audience may respond and designs characters with that in mind. When an auditor identifies with a character, he or she may vicariously take on the qualities of the character, if only during the reading of the story.

---

[50] Laney, "Characterization and Moral Judgments," 408.

[51] Grubbe discussed the possible translation of catharsis as "purification," making the term an Orphic metaphor. But he suggested that "purging" was more consistent with its usage in elsewhere. "Even if we did not have the Politics, the purification of pity and fear is a strange idea for Aristotle, the son of a doctor and the most un-Orphic and unmystic of men" (*The Greek and Roman Critics*, 75).

[52] O'Donoghue proposed that a vicarious emotional bond was set up between character and reader (*Pathos and Significance* [Philosophical Studies, National University of Ireland 19; Dublin: National University of Ireland, 1970], 122–23). "In any case, the moral power of portrayal consisted in evoking those feelings which in turn render judgment both more meaningful and more realistic. By means of such portrayal, we are enabled to enter into the world of the subject (character), participate in the emotional atmosphere, and appreciate the range and force of moral agency and agony. Yet, at the same time we remain and never quite lose our awareness that we remain set apart, both spectator and judge" (Laney, "Characterization and Moral Judgments," 407).

[53] L. A. Post, "Aristotle and Menander," *TAPA* 69 (1938): 12.

[54] Ibid., 20.

[55] Robert C. Tannehill, "The Disciples in Mark: The Function of a Narrative Role," *JR* 57 (1977): 392.

Such modeling may lead to changes in behavior or to self-understanding. But what happens when one encounters a repulsive character? Tannehill suggested that the negative aspects of a character could spur the auditor into recognizing his or her own limitations and also lead to change.[56] Iser's description of the function of negation in modern novels may indicate how ancient authors also anticipated such contrary characterizations to work.

The challenge implicit in the negation is, of course, offered first and foremost to those whose familiar world is made up of the norms that have been negated. These, the readers of the novel are then forced to take an active part in the composition of the novel's meaning, which revolves round a basic divergence from the familiar.[57]

According to some modern scholars, this cathartic effect and the reader or auditor's ability to develop empathy with a character are limited, since Greco-Roman literature presents individuals as static or immutable.[58] One way to address this critique is to distinguish between character-viewpoint and personality-viewpoint.[59] In the former, the person is an agent determining his or her course of action. Those actions can then be evaluated as virtuous or not. In the latter, the person possesses personality traits, which are not evaluated morally. Both ancient historiography and ancient philosophy tended toward character-viewpoint, while modern biography in an age of individualism focuses on personality-viewpoint.[60] "It is the adult character [the ancient writers] are normally concerned with, the character of the developed moral agent, to whom virtues and vices can properly be ascribed."[61] Thus, the character-viewpoint presents not a complete interpretation of the figure but rather an evaluation of his ἀρετή.

These writers, Greek and Roman alike, talk as if their job was to pass judgments on the qualities of the great men of history, and to see how they measure up to certain preconceived norms of excellence, as statesmen and as men. They do not suggest that their job is to understand these people as interesting individuals or personalities, to give a sympathetic or "empathetic" picture of them, to "get inside their skin," psychologically, as a modern biographer might.[62]

---

[56] Ibid.

[57] Iser, *The Implied Reader*, 34.

[58] "The psychology of the Romans was based on the assumption that a man's character is something fixed, something given to him at birth. Nothing could ever alter that character or the action which flowed from it" (R. M. Ogilvie, *The Romans and Their Gods in the Age of Augustus* [New York: Norton, 1970], 18). Likewise, Syme comments, "It was the way of thought of the ancients to conceive a man's inner nature as something definable and immutable" (Ronald Syme, *Tacitus* [Oxford: Clarendon Press, 1958], 421).

[59] Christopher Gill, "The Question of Character-Development: Plutarch and Tacitus," *CQ* 33 (1983): 470–71.

[60] Ibid., 471.

[61] Ibid., 477.

[62] Ibid., 473.

Gill cited authors, such as Plutarch, who understood the role that φύσις, λόγος, and ἦθος play in the construction of a character (*Mor.* 2a–b). In Plutarch's portrayal of Brutus, for instance, the young Brutus leans toward the good, but when he becomes an adult, his nature has hardened so that his ἦθος has become harsh (*Brut.* 1). Sallust depicts Jugurtha similarly – a young man who has good qualities negatively influenced by ambition (*Bell. Jug.* 8). Tacitus's detailed presentation of Tiberius demonstrates that the emperor's choices reflect his true character (4.31.1). The personality of the individual matters little. Rather, characters function as moral agents whom the authors expect their audiences to evaluate. Such an assessment is part of a process of characterization in which both author and auditor participate.

Regardless of the expectations of the genre, the ancient audience identified with the characters, often being called upon to judge the actions of the characters as either morally superior and justified, or inferior and without merit. The goal of the author was to evoke an emotional response from the auditor that would lead to virtuous action or at least suggest the direction for such action.

In summary, within the process of characterization, ἔνδοξα sets the limits of verisimilitude by which a character is judged as probable or realistic. The character is brought to life as the audience, engaging its "extra text," interprets the various attributes and actions presented by the author. On the level of the story, characters function to forward the plot. At the level of the narrative rhetoric, characters provide a cathartic encounter for the audience, who either identify with or are repulsed by the character.

3. The Characterization of Soldiers in Greco-Roman Literature

Within the limitations set by genre, the literary figure created in the process of characterization must be "recognizable," behaving in probable and expected ways, suitable to his or her role in the narrative setting. So the successful literary portrayal of generals and soldiers in ancient literature must meet, to some degree, the ancient audience's expectation. Whether resembling an actual person, such as Thucydides' Cleon, or an imagined one, like Plautus' Pyrgopolynices, the military character need possess verisimilitude. The audience of Menander's *Perikeironmene* and the citizen reader of Xenophon's *Anabasis* measured the military characterizations against their own experience as hoplites. The portrayals needed to be realistic if the audience's expectations were to be met. Since the works of Aristophanes received repeated awards in the dramatic festivals and Thucydides himself became the subject of another historian's work,[63]

---

[63] For Dionysius of Halicarnassus, Thucydides was the greatest of historians (*Thuc.* 2).

we can assume that the ancient authors, among other things, were successful at creating realistic characters.

Not surprisingly, the greatest number of literary soldiers investigated in this study are found in the Greek and Roman historiographies, in which war is the central theme. But the soldier is also a frequently occurring stock character in comedies. The emergence of the genre of the novel provided yet another front on which to marshal soldiers, though they appear mostly in minor roles. The following section describes how various authors present military characters within specific genres.

3.1 Soldiers in the Historiographies

The writers of ancient histories understood their work to be the production of accurate records of the events they detailed. However, two factors – the author's own military experience and changes in military practice – affected how those events were recounted and how commanders and foot soldiers were presented.

3.1.1 The Experience in and of Battle

[Homer] had no thought of explaining, formally, a military system. He had no need to do so; war was a part of the daily life of his audience, and the military system was a part of the civil organization in which that life was lived.[64]

As citizens, Greek and Republican Roman writers served in their respective armies, giving their military accounts a greater veracity. According to Polybius, only those with such experience should endeavor to write history.

It is neither possible for a man with no experience of warlike operations to write well about what happens in war, nor for one unversed in the practice and circumstances of politics to write well on that subject. (12.25.g [Paton, LCL]).

Of the historiographers surveyed, Thucydides, Xenophon, Polybius, and Josephus explicitly refer to their military experience in their writings, though none had celebrated careers. Polybius (6.19–42) and Josephus (*B.J.* 3.70–109)[65] also include lengthy descriptions of military camp life and the training of troops.[66]

---

[64] Oliver Lyman Spaulding, *Pen and Sword in Greece and Rome* (Princeton: Princeton University Press, 1937), 7.

[65] In all likelihood, Josephus gained an intimate knowledge of camp life after his surrender to Vespasian, when he became first a chained prisoner (*B.J.* 4.623–9) and later a Flavian client. Perhaps some of Josephus' appreciation for the Roman military and its practices was acquired during his first trip to Rome. The term he used for describing his organization of his Galilean forces was ῥωμαϊκώτερον (*B.J.* 2.577), which Goodman aptly translated as "more along Roman lines" ("Josephus as Roman Citizen," in *Josephus and the History of the Greco-Roman World* [ed. Fausto Parente and Joseph Sievers; Leiden: Brill, 1994], 337.)

[66] For a comparison of Josephus and Polybius, see Shaye J. D. Cohen, "Josephus, Jeremiah, and Polybius," *History and Theory* 21 (October 1982): 366–81.

The fifth century B.C.E. historian Thucydides lived through the entirety of the Peloponnesian War and had been an unsuccessful general in the first battle at Amphipolis. His subsequent banishment at the instigation of Cleon led to a twenty-year exile, during which he became familiar with Athens's enemies (Thuc. 5.26.5). A contemporary of Thucydides, the philosopher Xenophon, served as a cavalry leader for his native Athens before political disagreements led him to enroll as a mercenary in Cyrus' army (*Anab.* 3.1.4–10). Subsequently, he served in the Spartan army. Like Thucydides and Xenophon, Polybius had first-hand knowledge in the ways of war. His experience, in both the diplomatic and military arenas, provided him with the political connections to weather the vicissitudes of Rome's rise to Mediterranean dominance. The Jewish historian Josephus by his own admission was an unwilling commander impressed into service in Galilee at the outbreak of the First Jewish War. After being taken captive at the battle of Jotapata in 67 C.E., Josephus came to the attention of Vespasian and Titus, eventually becoming a Flavian client (*Vita*, 75).

Personal experience in battle allowed writers like Thucydides to vividly portray the military figures who would populate historiographies. But verisimilitude required that not only the characters but the setting be accurately described. Though remarkably stable, military organization and strategy did evolve over time, moving the markers for appropriate and probably behavior.

As the Greek city-states of the fifth century gradually gave way to Hellenistic monarchies of the fourth, so the citizen soldier – the cornerstone of the Greek phalanx – declined in prominence. The Peloponnesian War had changed the face of battle. "By its long duration, and by the distance and complexity of its campaigns, it rendered the old type of citizen soldier gradually more obsolete."[67] No longer were citizens willing to endure the hardships of battle with little possibility of reward. In addition, the tactics of war required a better-trained and better-prepared army. The close of the Peloponnesian War saw the emergence of the paid soldier not simply as μισθόρος but as a professional soldier. This development, fueled by Cyrus and promoted by Alexander, would culminate under Augustus.

Rome's fight for Mediterranean dominance, its' war against Jugurtha and the Civil Wars forced sweeping reforms of military practices, equipment and recruitment. Though Marius received much of the credit, the reforms were the culmination of tactical changes made by Scipio, minor reforms issued by Gracchus, and Marius' coup de grâce: opening military service to the proletariat (Sallust. *Bell. Jug.* 86). This move earned Marius the title of father of Rome's professional army, now organized into individual legions each with its own identity, signaled by its sacred *aquila*. Though a brilliant general who com-

---

[67] Spaulding, *Pen and Sword*, 20.

manded the esteem and devotion of his soldiers, Julius Caesar did little to improve on Marius' army. It was the adopted son of Caesar, Octavius, who would prove an apt military reformer. One of his first significant changes was the establishment of a standing army of citizens. In addition, Augustus set limits for the length of service at sixteen years for those in the ranks. Veterans served four additional years and were organized into a separate unit with its own standard and reduced workload (Tacitus, *Ann.* 1.78). The creation of the *aerarium militare* in 6 C.E. provided retirement pay for the army. Augustus bank-rolled the new war chest with 170 million sesterces from his own funds and promised a yearly annuity (Dio 55.25).

As the legions were becoming professionalized, the auxiliary underwent a similar development. Auxiliaries were levied troops supplied by client kings or subject provinces. Originally, the *cohortes* and *alae* were ethnically distinct, wearing their own military garb and utilizing indigenous modes of warfare. Even their commanders were local men. However, these ethnic and often specialized contingents soon became professional forces under Augustus, though their hierarchy of appointments and benefits at discharge were yet to evolve.

The soldier portrayed in Imperial literature is the product of a different military milieu than his literary ancestors. The hoplite tactics of an earlier age had given way to new formations, new equipment and a new career – that of a professional soldier. With these changes came different expectations on the part of the audiences for Rome's imperial period literature. No longer could it be assumed that military service was a shared experience. Though, as Saddington notes of Tacitus, "most of his readers would have been familiar with the features of military life."[68]

3.1.2. Historiographers' Characterization of Soldiers

The Greek historians focused almost exclusively on the deeds of generals and commanders. In the Greek phalanx, the hoplite's name or distinguishing characteristics mattered little. In the imperial period, the individuality and moral agency of the character came to the fore. Where Thucydides would applaud excellent actions in battle, Livy would simply extol individual excellence of character. The following highlights the presentation of generals and soldiers in Greek and Roman historiographies.

---

[68] Denis Saddington, "Tacitus and the Roman Army," 3485.

Thucydides organized his history like a general creating a battle strategy set within seasonal limits.[69] Only commanders of note are singularly described and then only by narration of their actions and through their speeches.[70]

To only a few preferred individuals does the historian give such distinctive features and these sparingly touched, as to lift them from the mass. The private life and personal character of historical personages come into consideration only as these influence the course of public events.[71]

Thucydides aligned his characters according to their military and diplomatic abilities and not their moral goodness.[72] The absence of portrayals of the rank and file indicate that at this juncture in the writing of ancient histories, the individual soldier had yet to be distinguished from the mass of other hoplites. Thucydides becomes important for our analysis because his histories recognize the theater of war as a backdrop of human drama on which future historians would stage ever more complex scenes.

Like Thucydides, Xenophon recounted no individual rank and file soldier of note. However, his descriptions of generals implicitly describe the men under their command. For example, Xenophon reports that soldiers found Clearchus' harshness and punishment to be an inspiration and an encouragement (*Anab.* 2.6.12). A certain love of austerity was a sign of a good soldier. One wonders if the character of Clearchus, so detailed by Xenophon, has a touch of autobiography.

Polybius, like his predecessors, characterized the commanders and only occasionally portrayed individual soldiers. However, his description of the selection of centurions (6.24.9) and the narration of the centurion who raped his captive (21.38) indicate that the enlisted officers were becoming more visible within the Roman military structure. Amid the battles among and against Rome's enemies, Polybius situated a description of the republican army in which he detailed the enlistment and division of recruits among the four existing legions (6.24–25).

---

[69] "Battles in the Archaic period were fought during the summer because for Greece's farmer soldiers, fighting at other times of the year was impractical if not impossible" (P. Krentz, "Fighting by the Rules: The Invention of the Hoplite Agôn," *Hesperia* 71 [2002]: 27). Also see W. R. Connor, "Early Greek Land Warfare as Symbolic Expression," *Past and Present* 119 (1988): 3.

[70] "If one wishes to discover what (Thucydides) feels about the ability or character of any individual – or indeed how far he is prepared, or is conscious of any obligation, to commit himself even by implication – it is necessary to examine thoroughly all the relevant narrative and speeches" (H. D. Westlake, *Individuals in Thucydides* [Cambridge: Cambridge University Press, 1968], 5–6). Also see Charles Forster Smith, "Character-Drawing in Thucydides," *The American Journal of Philology* 24 (1903): 370.

[71] Charles Forster Smith, "Character-Drawing in Thucydides," 369.

[72] Westlake, *Individuals in Thucydides*, 7.

In general, the soldiers in Dionysius' history of Rome are citizens who protect their *patria* and benefit from its victories and its security. But the Roman army of Dionysius' day was a professional one. They were no longer citizen soldiers levied for temporary duty. One reads in Dionysius' history a wistful look back when the glory of Rome resulted from the bravery of its citizens cum soldiers, and not its paid armies.

History, for Livy, had a decidedly moral function, which affected his characterization of soldiers. "The aims of characterization determined the selection of material and the structure of the narrative, even at the expense of historical truth."[73] Livy's concern for the moral state of Rome and her citizens may explain the apparent contradiction between his artistry and his perceived incompetence.[74] Using speeches, dialogues and actions, Livy portrayed numerous soldiers, centurions, tribunes and prefects during the course of his 142 books on the history of Rome. Yet it was not their military skill but their moral aptitude that interested Livy.

Josephus characterized the soldiers in his histories through their actions on the battlefield. A few received adjectival epitaphs. Rank and file soldiers were not distinguished, but centurions are often named, though given little further description. On the whole, however, Josephus reserved his praises for groups of auxiliary soldiers, like the Sebastenian cohort (*B.J.* 2.51, 58, 63, 74, 236). After the death of Herod, most of the royal troops defected to the rebels, except a cohort of auxiliaries from Sebaste (Samaria) under the command of Rufus and Gratus, both noted for their strength and intellect (*B.J.* 2.52). This cohort from Sebaste came to the aid of a Roman century when it was ambushed while conveying supplies to the legion. This legion's centurion, Arius, and forty of his most noble soldiers were killed in the assault (*B.J.* 2.63).

When centurions are characterized by Josephus, they are singularly brave and intelligent, in many cases losing their lives in the heat of battle. Rank and file soldiers are likewise portrayed, but normally as part of their unit and not as individuals. Whether Josephus' respect of the Roman military was genuine or the result of a client writing for his patron, he demonstrated a clear and direct relationship between the general who would be Caesar and the forces that would carry him to the purple. Both Titus and Vespasian are lauded, Vespasian for his innate virtue (*B.J.* 4.33), and Titus for his clemency and mercy (*B.J.*

---

[73] Edwin M. Carawan, "The Tragic History of Marcellus and Livy's Characterization," *CJ* 80 (1984): 141.

[74] For a critique of Livy's use of sources and factual accuracy, see Heinrich Nissen, *Kritische Untersuchungen über die Quellen der vierten und fünften Dekade des Livius* (Berlin: Weidmann, 1863); and Hermann Tränkle, *Livius und Polybios* (Stuttgart: Basel, 1977), 193–228. For a more sympathetic analysis, see Walsh, *Livy: His Historical Methods and Aims*; T. J. Luce, *Livy: The Composition of his History* (Princeton: Princeton University Press, 1977); and Gary Forsythe, *Livy and Early Rome: A Study in Historical Method and Judgement* (Stuttgart: Franz Steiner, 1999).

1.10). Given the valor and virtue of its commanders, is it any wonder that Rome's soldiers were likewise portrayed?

While Josephus tended to praise the deeds of the auxiliary, Tacitus saw the legions as the true center of Roman's military might. "Even where other branches of the armed forces were involved in operations, they are frequently ignored or at best accorded brief mention."[75] It is no wonder, then, that members of the legions are more often characterized. According to Saddington, nearly 50 senior officers and 61 soldiers and centurions, but only 33 auxiliaries, are mentioned by name in the *Annales* and *Historiae* of Tacitus.[76] As with all ancient historiographers, Tacitus gave greater attention to the characterization of significant generals, but even centurions and foot soldiers are portrayed, if indirectly, through their actions. Heroes receive two names (Atilius Verus, Gaius Volusius, Arrius Varus, Julius Agrestis, Julius Mansuetus), whereas mutineers have only one name (Percennius, Vibulenus). Through his details and characterization, "Tacitus makes us aware how versatile and all too human an institution the Roman army was."[77]

Mommsen labeled Tacitus *dieser unmilitärischste Schriftsteller*, owing to the lack of specific military detail in his writings.[78] Saddington counters, "it should be clear at the outset that Tacitus retails only the newsworthy and the morally significant."[79] For our purposes, Tacitus' lack of attention to tactical information is less important than his interest in creating vivid characters. Though Mommsen may have disparaged Tacitus' military completeness, others see him as "the individual who introduced man's personality into history."[80] His style was influenced by Sallust and his own experience in oratory, but the literary atmosphere of Rome in the late first and early second century is credited with producing in authors like Tacitus an interest in the *narrative persona.*[81]

3.2 Soldiers in the Comedies, Novels, and Satires

When the generals of Thucydides' and Xenophon' histories returned home, they became the target of comedians. The military characters found in Old Attic Comedy are often parodies of historical figures whom the playwrights derided as part of their social critique. Like their contemporaries, the writers of history,

---

[75] Saddington, "Tacitus and the Roman Army," 3494.

[76] Ibid., 3506–48.

[77] Ibid., 3504.

[78] Theodore Mommsen, *Römische Geschichte V* (Berlin: Weidmann, 1885), 165.

[79] Saddington, "Tacitus and the Roman Army," 3504.

[80] Stephen G. Daitz, "Tacitus' Technique of Character Portrayal," *The American Journal of Philology* 81 (1960): 30.

[81] "Persius, Martial, Petronius, and Juvenal all may be considered representatives of this spirit which tended to focus the attention of the writers upon personalities, and, more especially, upon their faults" (Daitz, "Tacitus' Technique of Character Portrayal," 30).

these poets were familiar with the hoplite army of fifth century B.C.E. Greece. However, they and the comedians to follow did not place the soldier on the stage of battle. Military characters in comedies are found on the domestic front where they are heralded as either retired soldiers cum successful citizens or braggart warriors who continue to live out their past glories. And though Aristophanes' political satire would evolve into Menander's domestic comedy and finally emerge as the farcical works of Plautus and Terence, the character of the soldier remained limited.

Where historiographers wrote about the actions of the state, particularly at war, Aristophanes understood himself in some ways as the guardian of the polis, "the enemy of the demagogues, the sycophants, the innovators, the hypocrites who were the curse of the Attic state and of Athenian society."[82] As such, the literary portrayals of military men in Aristophanes' comedies are parodies of real soldiers for purposes of political critique. Aristophanes' would-be general Lamachus is touted for his strength early in the play, *Acharnenses*, only to become a whining weakling after his injury. As would be expected in stage productions, characterization is developed indirectly through action and speech, either that of the speech of the soldier, or other characters speaking about the soldier. Aristophanes paved the way for the emergence of the comic soldier who would be variously redressed by comedians to follow.

By the period of New Comedy, the stock characters of the courtesan, the cook and the soldier had been established.[83] Engaging but also moving beyond the stereotype, Menander's portrayal of soldiers is more complex than that of Aristophanes. The soldier is no longer a political lampoon against a real military leader as in the works of Aristophanes. He is violent, but capable of change. Several of Menander's plays present soldiers who succeed at acquiring the girl of their dreams.[84] The violent Polemon is redeemed by the love of Glykera in *Perikeiromene*. The soldiers Thrasonides in *Misoumenos*, Stratophanes in *Sikyonios* and Kelostratos in *Aspis* all win the girl in the end.

---

[82] H. Lloyd Stow, "Aristophanes' Influence upon Public Opinion," *CJ* 38 (1942): 83. Aristophanes' "favored weapons are parody, satire, and exaggeration to the point of fantasy, and his favourite targets are men prominent in politics, contemporary poets, musicians, scientists and philosophers, and – as is virtually inevitable in a comedian writing for a wide public – manifestations of cultural change" (Kenneth James Dover, "Aristophanes," in *OCD* [ed. Simon Hornblower and Anthony Spawforth; Oxford: Oxford University Press, 1996], 164).

[83] MacCary, "Menander's Soldiers," 279.

[84] *Perikeiromene, Misoumenos, Sikyonios, Aspis* and *Karchedonios* have sympathetic military characters (MacCary, "Menander's Soldiers," 297). They are not portrayed as wholly violent, vain or braggadocious. The fact of their military affiliation has little to do with the play's action. "Unless the play is set in a military environment, which would be utterly incompatible with a domestic setting, the soldier cannot pursue his occupation except outside the home and beyond his local community" (Wilfred Major, "Menander in a Macedonian World," *Greek, Roman and Byzantine Studies* 38 [1997]: 66).

In Menander's *Kolax*, Bias provided the template for the *miles gloriosus* who would appear frequently in Latin comedy. Though little remains of Menander's original, it can be deduced from the extant fragments that Bias is a wealthy rival for a woman's affections. Both Pheidias and Bias are suitors for the same ἑταίρα, but Bias' finances place him in a more suitable position. The wealthy, braggart soldier vying for the woman's favor only to be out done by another suitor becomes a standard plot line for the comedies to follow.

When the Roman writers adapted the works of Menander, the stock characters were presented more rigidly, less apt to behave contrary to the audience's expectations. Of the extant works of Plautus, seven plays include soldiers portrayed as caricatures rather than fully developed characters.[85] They are "of the 'stock variety', and cannot stand up to serious criticism: nor is it intended that they should."[86] By far the most frequent behavior of Plautus' soldiers is bragging, and his *Miles Gloriosus* epitomizes the stereotype. All of Plautus' soldiers who appear on stage brag about their accomplishments. Characterization is developed indirectly through the speech of the characters and their actions. Only twice is the description of a character explicit, and this is in the *argumentum* of the play.

A couple of decades after the death of Plautus, the *miles gloriosus* had become a standard character. In the prologue of *Eunuchus*, Terence defended himself against those who would accuse him of "copying" other Latin playwrights. In his list of such "copied" characters, he included the *miles gloriosus*, arguing that he had borrowed this character from Menander's *Kolax* and not from a fellow Roman playwright, whom we can suppose may have been Plautus. Except for the author's statement in the prologue, the textual indicators for characterization are indirect through the speech of the characters and their actions. Terence's soldier, Thraso, is allegedly skillful and braggadocious, but also insecure and gullible, making him the perfect wealthy host for a parasite. Thraso resembles Plautus' soldiers indicating not so much wholesale borrowing from the previous playwright, as the emergence of a stereotyped *miles gloriosus* in Roman comedy.

With the advent of the romance novels, the use of stereotypes continues, though the characters are now located in exotic settings. "The domestic focus, situational comedy, stock characters and melodrama of New Comedy all find happy homes in the Greek novels."[87] Only a couple of references are made to any type of military presence in Xenophon's *Ephesiaca*: Araxus, the retired soldier who is killed by his wife (3.12) and the police prefect Polyidus (5.3.1–5.5.7).

---

[85] George E. Duckworth, *The Nature of Roman Comedy* (Princeton, Norman, OK: Princeton University Press, University of Oklahoma Press, 1952), 264.

[86] Morris Marples, "Plautus," *Greece and Rome* 8 (October 1938): 4.

[87] Kathryn Chew, "Achilles Tatius and Pardoy," *CJ* 96 (2000): 58.

In the mid-second century, Achilles Tatius portrayed soldiers as skillful, efficient and ready fighters in his novel, *Leucippe and Clitophon* (3.13.4).[88] Their commander, Charmides, displays hospitality in his attention to Clitophon and skill in the face of battle. His weakness is love of Leucippe, but this does not interfere with his military duties. He leaves her immediately when called to battle (4.11.1). The bandits are portrayed as villainous and lawless, while the military characters are presented as brave and civilized. They guard and protect the Nile delta, rescuing those held hostage and fighting to their death.

"A creative synthesis of Greek fiction with Roman satire and mimic motifs,"[89] Petronius' *Satyricon* is only partially extant, so the plot is difficult to reconstruct. The main characters include a homosexual pair, Encolpius (the narrator) and Giton, and Ascyltus, a fellow adventurer. Much of Book 15 (26.6–78.8) encompasses a comic banquet given by the freedman Trimalchio wherein the food is grossly abundant and the tales told by guests equally as vulgar. Other tales are interspersed throughout the various misadventures of the three. Of particularly note are the story of the soldier-werewolf (62) and the tale of the Widow of Ephesus (111–112). Within these two tales, Petronius offers differing portraits of the Roman soldier. In the first, the soldier has the potential of becoming a ravaging beast, terrorizing the countryside. As a beast, he is portrayed as both brutish and violent. In the second, the soldier is fully human. He is portrayed as a virtuous man, but easily led by his lust. He is protective of the Widow and her maid, hopeful of repayment and duty-bound to rectify his error.

Where Aristophanes used comedy as a mode of social critique, Juvenal relied on satire. In *Satire* 3, Juvenal gave expression to the conditions in Rome through his portrayal of Umbricius, a poor man who must leave the city in order to survive. Even the great Roman general, Corbulo, known for his physical strength, would struggle under the weight born by the slaves who carry huge vessels through the streets (3.251). Umbricius' tirade recognized that even the mighty soldiers and great generals were no match for the chaos that Rome had become.

Nobilitas sola est atque unica virtus, advised Juvenal to Ponticus, a young man living a life of wanton luxury (8.20). Juvenal encourages him to be first a strong soldier, good guardian and a just judge (8.79–80). The appropriate task when one had outgrown boyhood was to do one's military service rather than to cavort about town driving one's own chariot (8.169). Juvenal gave the example of Marius, whom he depicted as a low-born citizen who had to hire himself out in order to farm. Working his way up in the ranks, he distinguished himself in the army and celebrated a triumph after the defeat of the Cimbri and

---

[88] Jean Boorsch, "About Some Greek Romances," *Yale French Studies* 38 (1967): 74.

[89] P. G. Walsh, *The Roman Novel* (Cambridge, London: Cambridge University Press, Bristol Classical Press, 1970, reprint 1995), 7.

Teutones (8.245–253). Juvenal closed with an admonishment. It would be better to have Thersites as a father but to fight like Achilles, then to have lineage with Achilles and be like Thersites (8.270–271). For Juvenal, the soldier of old embodied the *virtus* out of which true nobility sprung. Juvenal's most extensive discussion on the Roman army is found in the Sixteenth Satire, of which only 60 lines remain. He opens with a question: who can number the benefits given to the soldier (16.1)? Juvenal then outlines the various privileges afforded a soldier, most often at the expense of the citizenry.[90]

Apuleius' description of the centurion who encounters the gardener is no less disparaging than Juvenal's assessment of the Roman military. With respect to the provincial folk, the soldier is characterized directly by the narrator as superior and arrogant (9.39), filled with insolence and violence (9.40), lacking self-restraint (10.1), terrorizing to travelers and greedy (10.13). With respect to his military obligations, his actions demonstrate that he is a good soldier. He is appropriately worried about losing his sword (9.41). He reports immediately to his superior (10.1) and he is dutifully obedient in fulfilling his mission (10.13). His *commiles* live up to the camaraderie indicated in their appellation. They hunt down the gardener, in order to retrieve the soldier's sword and to seek revenge (9.41). From the narrator's perspective the centurion is a terrorizing brute and, at the same time, a dutiful soldier. The actions of his comrades indicate the same probably could be said of them.

Whether set within a historiography or strutting across the stage, military characters are generally little developed. Generals of note receive greater descriptions in histories, and braggarts are the comic foil in comedies. But the rank and file soldier is seldom depicted despite his ubiquitous presence.

4. Conclusion

Characterization is a process by which an author presents a character's attributes through direct and indirect means, and a reader or auditor uses his or her "extratextual repertoire" to enflesh the author's sketch. The genre establishes the boundaries for the creation of characters. For example, tragic characters have less opportunity for prolonged development than do those in epics since the plot of a tragedy is limited by the action on the stage (*Poet.* 24.6). In a historical account, the goal is an accurate portrayal of events as they occurred, so the words and deeds are to be recorded truthfully and evaluated as to their effectiveness (Polb 12.25g). Thus a person's speech and actions in a historical account serve chiefly as a vehicle of information, and only secondarily as a mode of personalization.

---

[90] Stanley Allen Iverson, "The Military Theme in Juvenal's Satires" (Ph.D. diss., Vanderbilt University, 1975).

Though the setting and stage directed the mode of characterization available to the writer, differences in genre did not impact the types or function of characters. Both major and minor characters are found throughout the historiographies, comedies, and novels. Authors would engage either direct or indirect means to the lay the foundation for characters, often invoking stereotypes of stock characters. In ancient literature, characters were agents of action, forwarding the narrative's plot. They were also endowed with certain qualities, portrayed from what Gill called the "character viewpoint." This viewpoint tended to show a figure as exhibiting particular virtues or vices. The ancient audience participated in building character by filtering the cues in the text through their own extratextual lenses. This process invited the auditor or reader to make a moral judgment about the character's qualities. The goal was catharsis, πάθος or moral action. The audience was to identify either positively or negatively with the character, and thus be motivated to a change in behavior.

As the brief survey of the characterization of ancient soldiers demonstrates, historians, playwrights, novelists and satirists followed the standard modes of characterization. Leaders are presented more frequently and better developed. An author's experience in the military and the current standards and practices of the army factored into the characterization of military figures. The next chapter will focus on the military stereotypes often used as the foundation of an author's characterization. The use of such stock figures presumed that the authorial audience would recognize the stereotypes, and respond as the author anticipated.

Chapter 3

Literary Stereotypes of Greco-Roman Soldiers

1. Introduction

The creation of characters is only partially in the hands by the author, who lays a foundation by means of the narrator's statement or indirectly through the depiction of a character's actions, dress, or dialogue. In the process of reading or listening to the text, the author's skeletal portrait is enfleshed by the reader from his or her own cultural repertoire. To aid in this process, the author engages stereotypes, which allow one to evaluate the character's behavior based on his or her understanding of the particular τόποι. Thus, character-building is a cumulative activity shared between the author and the audience.

1.1 Restricting Expectations: The Creation of Stereotypes

Of particular importance in this study of the characterization of soldiers is the role of verisimilitude and setting. Aristotle's concept of ἔνδοξα discussed pre-viously is the basis of verisimilitude. Characters are to behave in probable ways, which mirror how a real person could be expected to act. But those expectations of behavior change over time. For example, since the Greek phalanx system discouraged hoplites from personal acts of bravery, the portrayal of an individual hoplite who breaks ranks in an act of daring would be an improbable character. As military practices developed, so did reasonable expectations of behavior. In the Roman Imperial army, competition among individuals was encouraged, with awards being distributed to the first to scale an opponent's fortifications or capture the standards of the enemy.

The parameters of probable behavior also depend on location. What is ac-ceptable, and even expected, in the heat of battle would be intolerable at home. The rape of the captive noblewoman, Chiomara, by the unnamed centurion (Polyb. 21.38) is a case in point. It is not his behavior toward the woman that provokes the historian's ire, but his greed and incapacity for discipline (21.38.3).[1] Plutarch includes Chiomara among his women of virtue, and describes her rape as the fortune of a soldier (τῇ τύχῃ στρατιωτικῶς, *Mulier. virt.* 258E). Had the centurion raped the noblewoman at home, he would have

---

[1] Livy altered the version, noting that the lust and greed of the soldier led him to violate her body (38.24.2-3).

been subject to fines (Plutarch, *Sol.* 23). Plutarch recounts the story of the women of Amphissa who stood guard over the sleeping female revelers of Bacchus, fearing that the mercenaries quartered in their city would defile the women (*Mulier. virt.* 249E–F). Here, the word for rape does not pertain to the prerogative of a soldier but to the act of treating one unfairly (ἀγνωμονέω). Plutarch himself seems to recognize that the setting has implications for the moral judgment of the behavior. What serves the soldier well in the field would brand him a brute back home.

For the most part, the military characters in the histories are set on the battlefront, where they are depicted as skillful, virtuous, and violent as would be expected of actual soldiers in battle. The soldiers in the satires and novels of imperial writers are most often individuals who are on assignment away from their legion or cohort. Like actual soldiers, this military character is often depicted as the imperial representative, policing the province on behalf of the Roman governor. The setting for comedies is the domestic scene, with its concomitant expectations of civic behavior. When a soldier on this stage fails to hang up his helmet and don the robe of civic responsibility, he becomes the subject of the playwright's comic pen. If he were a foreigner and flashed his wealth and self-made status, he suffered doubly.

The τόποι of characters have their origin in the ancient listing of virtues and vices. Aristotle defines virtue as the mean of positive behavior as determined by a reasonable person. In Theophrastus' *Characters*, the individual τόποι fall on either side of Aristotle's virtuous mean.[2] They are either excessive, like the man who possesses κολακεία or the one who is filled with ἀλαζονεία, or they are deficient, like the person who embodies μικρολογία and the one who is filled with δειλία. Theophrastus may have had in mind the characters of Athenian comedy, for Aristotle acknowledged that the φαυλότεροι belong to comedy (*Poet.* 5.1). Tragedy, on the other hand, required characters who are, first and foremost, χρηστός. But goodness must correspond to a character's class (ἔστιν δὲ ἐν ἑκάστῳ γένει, *Poet.* 15.19). In Aristotle's male-world view, even the characters of a woman and a slave can be portrayed as good according to their state in life (καὶ γὰρ γυνή ἐστιν χρηστὴ καὶ δοῦλος, *Poet.* 15.20).

When various virtues and vices are repeatedly exemplified, particular characters have the potential to develop into stereotypes. The good man is the character whose chief trait is ἀγαθός. Once a stereotype is fixed, a writer can upset the expectations of the audience by having the character behave in a contradictory or unusual manner. The author anticipates that the manipulation

---

[2] Theophrastus, *Characters* (LCL; Jeffrey Rusten and I. C. Cunningham; Cambridge, MA: Harvard University Press, 1993). Aristotle's discussion on virtues and vices is likely the inspiration for Theophrastus' work, which was originally meant to be a guide for the young.

of expectations will direct the authorial audience toward a particular conclusion. Thus, not only does an auditor build character, he or she also responds to the character being constructed.

Since the narrative rhetoric of a text is meant to evoke a response in the audience, authors utilize stereotypes because they are emotionally provocative, and the audience recognizes how they are to react to the stock character presented. The τόπος or stereotype has potency because it presents normally unambiguous characters with whom the audience can quickly identify and evaluate. But the stock character need not be all good or all bad. As will be seen, the soldier-turned-werewolf of Petronius is generous in accompanying the slave on his sojourn, but he is also violent. A good man in battle can become a braggart at home. The evaluation of the character is often related to the situation in the narrative. Aristotle recognizes that virtues and vices are setting specific, since at certain times we praise an ambitious person as courageous and desirous of what is noble, and other times we praise the unambitious as measured and temperate (*Eth. nic.* 4.4.4).

Investigating Luke's use of military stereotypes requires a diachronic analysis of the literature in which soldiers are portrayed. This chapter uncovers the origins of the stereotypes and charts how they may have been reborn over time or reshaped due to generic constraints. Most military characters are portrayed as part of a larger force and little individuated. Noteworthy exceptions are military leaders of renown to whom historiographers paid homage. Upon their lips, Thucydides, Polybius and others placed *adlocutiones* that contained, if not the actual words of the general, at least his intent. The success of the campaign was often credited to the leaders' motivational call to arms. Playwrights, like Aristophanes and Menander, were less interested in recounting historical events, preferring to portray only slightly veiled parodies of actual στρατηγοί whose heroic antics on the battlefield had little value at home. The development of the centuriate under the Romans created a class of petty officers whose names and significant actions later writers immortalized.

The narrative characters that form the basis of this survey on military stereotypes are culled from the historiographies of Thucydides, Xenophon, Polybius, Julius Caesar, the epitomist of 2 Maccabees, Dionysius of Halicarnassus, Livy, Josephus and Tacitus; the comedies of Aristophanes, Menander, Plautus and Terence; the romance novels of Chariton, Achilles Tatius, Xenophon of Ephesus and Petronius; and the writings of Plutarch and Juvenal. This is by no means an exhaustive list of Greco-Roman military characters, and more extensive research will likely uncover a greater variety of stereotypes. However, after analyzing more than a hundred characters, the following distinct stereotypical categories emerge: the good soldier, the undisciplined soldier, the rescuer, the brute, the good citizen and the braggart.

The following list of military stereotypes was determined by a reading process that distinguished repetitive character traits within a particular setting, and then measured them against an endoxic yardstick. The τόποι are situated according to the three locales in which the military characters are found: the battlefield, on assignment, and on the home front. Because reliance on and reference to the auditor's own cultural memory limits the endoxic lens, and, therefore, the recognition of stereotypes to a specific cultural and historical milieu, the realia and expectations of each locale are described. For example, the land allotments and retirement given to a veteran upon his release from military service allowed a former soldier to gain prominence on the home front. The soldier who took advantage of his new status and integrated into the community becomes typified as the "good citizen," while the one who preferred to dwell on his military accomplishments was labeled the "braggart."

Before reviewing the τόποι, due homage must be paid to the father of the military stereotype. In the works of Homer we are first introduced to the good soldier and his foil, the braggart, who will set the trajectory for the future development of the literary stereotypes of soldiers.

1.2 The Homeric Origins of Divergent Military Stereotypes

Some of the earliest narrative portrayals of soldiers are found in the *Iliad*, a foundational narrative that inspired the battle plans of generals and kings, and the narrative endeavors of dramatists and historiographers alike. "In all periods Greek authors quote, echo, and allude to Homer in a manner that assumes a warmy familiarity in the readers."[3]

Advocating a pan-hellenic war against the Persians, Isocrates suggests that Homer's significance in the musical contests and even the Greek παιδεία[4] resulted from the poet's recognition of the long-standing enmity between the Greeks and the barbarians.

Moreover, I think that even the poetry of Homer has won a greater renown because he has nobly glorified the men who fought against the barbarians, and that on this account our ancestors determined to give his art a place of honour in our musical contests and in the education of our youth, in order that we, hearing his verses over and over again, may learn by heart the enmity which stands from of old between us and them, and that we, admiring the valour of those who were in the war against Troy, may conceive a passion for like deeds (Isocrates, *Paneg.* 159 [Freese, LCL]).[5]

---

[3] J. E. Lendon, *Soldiers and Ghosts*, 37.

[4] "Homer was 'the teacher of Greece,' memorized and recited and in later times read and reread with a concentration that no modern system of education devotes to a single set of texts....And at least by Hellenistic and Roman times (when the papyri of Egypt reveal such things) the *Iliad* had established dominance over the *Odyssey* as a teaching text" (Lendon, 36–37).

[5] A similar sentiment is echoed in Plato, *Res.* 606e.

The fact that Isocrates invokes an epic as an encouragement to fight reflects the significant place the *Iliad* had in the Greek mind-set, particularly in relation to war. Philip II is said to have devised the very successful Macedonian phalanx based on his reading of Homer (Diodorus Siculus, 16.3.2). The deeds of Patroclus and Teucros are to be matched by the manly citizens when the call to arms sounded (Aristophanes, *Ran.* 1034). Because of his knowledge of Homer, Ion claims to be the best general in Greece (Plato, *Ion* 541B), for apparently if one sang the epics repeatedly, one would gain military insight. "The heroes of epic always sat invisible upon the shoulders of the Greeks, whispering their counsel."[6]

The origins of the soldier as a stereotyped literary character are thus found in the ancient Greek epics of Homer, who portrays two general types among the troops in the *Iliad* – the hero and the braggart. One garners the trust and support of his fellow soldiers; the other is a laughingstock. Such an intentionally drawn comparison between two characters can highlight their similarities and their differences. The use of σύγκρισις in characterization allows the author to play characters off each other, imply qualities not directly stated, and insinuate a character's importance by comparing him with illustrious persons. As Aristotle notes, a σύγκρισις with illustrious persons enhances the character being described, particularly if he had few noteworthy accomplishments. Even a comparison with ordinary people can amplify one's virtues (*Rhet.* 1.9.39). Menander Rhetor recognized that such comparisons could be minor (μερική, Sp. III, 377, 5), or much more extensive (τελειοτάτην σύγκρισιν, Sp. III 376, 31). The σύγκρισις of Odysseus and Thersites sets up the divergent paths that the noble warrior and the *miles gloriosus* will take in future literary works.

We are first introduced to Odysseus in Book 2. When Agamemnon, heeding a dream from Zeus, attempts to rally his troops for an assault on Troy, his ploy backfires and the soldiers ready their ships to return home. Athena speedily departs Olympus to avert a tragedy. She finds Odysseus as equal to Zeus in counsel (2.169). She urges him to speak kindly (2.180) and restrain the soldiers, so that they might not abandon the fight. Odysseus' ability to encourage with gentle speech is noted in line 189. He chides those who would leap to their boats as being unwarlike and weak (2.201).

Later in Book 3, Odysseus' physique is described. Priam notes that Odysseus is shorter but more broad in the chest than Agamemnon (3.194). As Priam watches, Odysseus casts his battle gear on the ground, and like a thick-fleeced ram (3.197–8), he passes through his troops, readying them for battle. Helen identifies this κτίλος (3.196) as Odysseus, son of Laertes, from the land of Ithaca. He is known for his cunning and shrewd schemes (3.203). Antenor agrees with Helen's assessment, recounting a previous encounter with Odysseus when he was part of an embassy. Though he appeared harsh and angry,

---

[6] Lendon, *Soldiers and Ghosts*, 37.

and seemingly without sense, his voice echoed from his chest and the words fell like snowflakes in winter (3.222). The one who resembles an unrefined brute on first appearance turns out to be godlike (θείοιο); his willing heart and courageous spirit exceed others in effort (10.243). Odysseus is also modest: "Do not speak so much praise about me" (10.249).

A far different portrait emerges of Thersites, who plays the foil to Odysseus.[7] He is not identified by his father's name, but, rather, by the epithet "unmeasured in words" (2.212). Thersites, with his careless words and condemnation of kings, would do anything for a laugh (2.215). The description of Thersites alone is enough to evoke laughter from his fellow soldiers (2.217–219). The bandy-legged, lame-in-one-foot, stoop-shouldered and pointy-headed warrior is comic not only in words but in appearance.

When the mouthy Thersites meets the gently speaking Odysseus, Odysseus tells him to desist from his treasonous talk. Odysseus strikes him on his stooped shoulders with the golden staff, causing Thersites to cower and wipe away a tear (2.266–8). The Achaeans announce that although Odysseus has accomplished many great deeds, none are so excellent as silencing this annoying babbler (2.274–5).

The battle continues and Odysseus goes on to greater endeavors, but the comic Thersites disappears from the scene. The character types defined by Odysseus and Thersites appear in later literature. The rugged soldier endowed with strength and courage who is a darling of the gods contrasts with the braggart warrior whose unattractive features are compounded by his boasting, vanity, and dupability, and to whom the fates have turned a deaf ear.[8]

2. The Heirs of Odysseus and Thersites

The heirs of Odysseus and Thersites are legion. Appearing on stage or the pages of histories, the good soldier demonstrated the virtue appropriate for the setting while the braggart demonstrated vice. As Aristotle notes, the good person (ὁ ἀγαθός) will choose rightly that action which is either noble, expedient, or

---

[7] Rose and others suggest that the true foil to Thersites is Achilles (Peter W. Rose, "Thersites and the Plural Voices of Homer," *Arethusa* 21 [1988]: 19). Certainly Achilles is the central hero of the *Iliad*, and can be compared with the comic Thersites. However, the stereotypes of soldiers that will emerge are a measurement of how much a warrior exceeds human expectations or fails to meet them. Odysseus and Thersites, both born of human parents without the benefit of divine intervention, are more readily juxtaposed.

[8] Blume recognizes in Thersites the seeds for the stereotyped braggart soldier who will blossom in later comedies. "Diese Einzelheit weist schon auf die Komödie voraus, und erst recht die Anmaßung des Thersites, der keifende Ton seiner Rede und sein Buhlen um Gelächter, was ihn zum niedrigen Possenreißer (βωμολόχος) machtö (Blume, "Komische Soldaten," 176).

pleasant and avoid the shameful, harmful, or painful. The bad one (ὁ κακός) will choose wrongly (*Eth. nic.* 2.3.7). In the following sections, the illustrations of various military stereotypes are categorized according to their narrative setting and their dominant virtue or vice.

2.1 Soldiers on the Battlefield

With the exception of Lamachus's brief battle charge and his subsequent fall into the ditch (Aristophanes, *Ach.* 1173f), the soldiers in the comedies under study do not muster on the field. Rather, the battlefield is the purview of the historiographers and their military characters. Wartime deeds of bravery (Thuc. 4.81.1; Polybius 1.69.4; 1.78) and vicious acts (Thuc. 3.37–40; 3.84.1; Polyb. 1.85.1) receive equal attention in the historiographies.

However, the battlefield is not the only setting in which Greco-Roman historians placed their military characters. Thucydides reports the speeches held in assemblies when various στρατηγοί advocated for or against war (3.36.6– 50.1; 4.16; 4.27.3–29.1; 4.114.3). Xenophon writes that when the exiled Alcibiades returns to Athens and meets with the assembly to clear his name (*Hell.* 1.4.20), the floor of the assembly becomes a pseudo-battleground, where not military but rhetorical strategy wins the day. Though the commander as orator is not without his skill, his λέξις leaves something to be desired. Dionysius comments that Iphicrates' speech is filled with vulgar army talk (φορτικὸν καὶ στρατιωτικὸν, *Lys.* 12.43). Individual orations in the assembly, which are acceptable in the polis, are a sign of treason in the field. Spendius, the runaway slave turned mercenary, uses both speech and action (λέγειν καὶ πράττειν) to incite his fellow mercenaries to revolt (Polyb. 1.69.5). Polybius reports that the soldiers were incited by his arguments and turned to mutiny (1.69.8).

Only officials could speak at an assembly and only a general could legitimately address soldiers on the battlefield.[9] The *adlocutio* of a commander before battle is found throughout the Greco-Roman historiographies, indicating that it was a commonplace technique for rallying the troops and a useful literary form for historiographies. Because of its deliberative nature, it sets a choice before the soldiers. Either they fight bravely and honorably, or they behave as cowards and quit the field. These ἔνδοξαι define the boundaries for the literary stereotypes of the soldier on the battlefield. The good soldier demonstrates bravery and piety, while the bad soldier is typed as cowardly, greedy, and treasonous.

---

[9] Mogens Herman Hansen, "The Battle Exhortation in Ancient Historiography: Fact or Fiction?" *Historia* 42 (1993): 161–80.

2.1.1 Ἀνὴρ Ἀγαθός

The most frequently reoccurring stereotype in the historiographies is that of the noble warrior. He is portrayed as possessing bravery and zeal, and his actions demonstrate his skill. He embodies both moral goodness and military superiority. From the general's exhortation speeches found in the historiographies, we have the expectation of what qualities indicate moral goodness on the battlefield. A good soldier is first a good man[10] (ἀνὴρ ἀγαθός, Thuc. 4.95.1; 4.126.2; 5.9.9). He is eager for battle (ἡ προθυμία τῆς ἐπὶ τὸν ἀγῶνα ὁρμῆς, Ant. rom. 9.9.2) and superior in daring (τόλμῃ προύχετε, Thuc. 2.87.4; audeatis, audaciam, Livy 25.38.11). The ideal soldier possesses three virtues: zeal, respect, and obedience to his commanders (Thuc. 5.9.9). The successful demonstration of these virtues merits him awards and honor (οἱ δὲ ἀγαθοὶ τιμήσονται τοῖς προσήκουσιν ἄθλοις τῆς ἀρετῆς, Thuc. 2.87.9). He exemplifies ἀνδρεία.

Another element of the corporate portrait of the ἀνὴρ ἀγαθός on the battlefield is the soldier who manifests *pietas* or εὐσέβεια, which is defined as "a combination of devotion to the deity with the proper respect for one's superiors and responsibility toward one's dependents, especially as a familial duty."[11] Judas Maccabeus (2 Macc), the Horatii (*Ant. rom.* 3.17.2) and the son of Julius Mansuetus (Tacitus, *Hist.* 3.25) visibly demonstrate their supreme reverence for their superiors, for their *patria*, and for their gods on the battlefield.

2.1.1.1 The Brave Soldier

Thucydides' writings depict the embodiment of the noble warrior par excellence: the commander of the Spartans. Brasidas is characterized as worthy of esteem, virtuous, intelligent, and courageous. The Spartan commander is introduced in Book 2, where he comes to the aid of the besieged city of Methone in Laconia. With only a hundred hoplites, he successfully leads a daring campaign to rescue the city (2.25.2). In a battle at Pylos, Brasidas displays leadership and courage, distinguishing himself from all the naval commanders (4.11.3). When the Spartans meet the Athenians at the city of Megara, his strategy wins the city without need of a single blow (4.73). He is similarly successful in winning the city of Torone (4.110–16). He effectively uses exhortations to rally his troops and to impart strategy (4.126; 5.9.2–8). Brasidas is energetic (δραστήριος, 4.81.1), worthy of esteem (ἄξιος, 4.81.1), and just and

---

[10] "The adjective ἀγαθός was the prime epithet of worth for a man" (Walter Donlan, "The Origin of Καλὸς Κἀγαθός," *American Journal of Philology* 94 [1973]: 367).

[11] Mary R. D'Angelo, "Εὐσέβεια: Roman Imperial Family Values and the Sexual Politics of 4 Maccabees and the Pastorals," *Biblical Interpretation* 11 (2003): 158. D'Angelo holds that the Pastorals and 4 Maccabees participated in the Imperial propaganda of "family values," seeing εὐσέβεια as being constructed along the lines of Roman *pietas*.

moderate (δίκαιος καὶ μέτριος, 4.81.2). His virtue (ἀρετή, 4.81.2) and intelligence (ξύνεσις, 4.81.2) inspire Athenian allies to feel favorably toward the Spartans because he has gained the reputation of being a good man (ἀγαθός, 4.81.3). When he is killed in battle, the local town accords him a hero's funeral.

Using rhetorical comparison or σύγκρισις, Thucydides portrays Brasidas as the personification of soldierly goodness, in opposition to Cleon's violent actions and empty speech. Brasidas is a man of skill and virtue (4.70, 79; 4.81.2), while Cleon is characterized as exceedingly violent and eventually weak as he flees his final battle (5.10.9). Cleon, the Athenian commander whom Aristophanes so railed against, receives equal ire from Thucydides[12] who describes him as the most violent of Athenians (3.36.6). According to Thucydides, Cleon orders the slaughter of all the men of military age in Mitylena (3.37–40), and two years later, he proposes a similar action be taken against the citizens of Scione. When Sparta sends envoys to negotiate a peace, Cleon is the one who speaks harshly against it (4.22.2). Thucydides describes Cleon's talk as laughable (4.28.5). At the second battle of Amphipolis, Cleon is surprised by Brasidas's shrewd attack and flees, only to be killed in the process (5.6–11).

In *Anabasis*, Xenophon depicts Clearchus, the Spartan officer turned Persian mercenary, as a φιλοπόλεμος (*Anab.* 2.6.6).

Now such conduct as this, in my opinion, reveals a man fond of war. When he may enjoy peace without dishonour or harm, he chooses war; when he may live in idleness, he prefers toil, provided it be the toil of war; when he may keep his money without risk, he elects to diminish it by carrying on war. As for Clearchus, just as one spends upon a loved one or upon any other pleasure, so he wanted to spend upon war– such a lover he was of war. On the other hand, he seemed to be fitted for war in that he was fond of danger, ready by day or night to lead his troops against the enemy, and self-possessed amid terrors, as all who were with him on all occasions agreed (Xenophon, *Anab.* 2.6.6–7 [Brownson, LCL]).

Further, Xenophon describes Clearchus as an excellent and demanding leader who successfully supplied his army, kept severe discipline, and punished heavy-handedly (*Anab.* 2.6.8–11). Yet his soldiers respected him like schoolboys respect their teacher (2.6.12). Xenophon concludes his lengthy description of the mercenary leader by noting that he was indifferent to both friendship and kindness, making soldiers of whomever he was sent (*Anab.* 2.6.13–14). Although Clearchus commands the absolute obedience of his troops, he does not like being commanded by others (*Anab.* 2.6.15).

Clearchus is also a shrewd strategist on and off the battlefield. While in exile, he is recruited by Cyrus to raise a mercenary army (*Anab.* 1.1.9). When these

---

[12] As Smith noted: "In the case of Cleon, the greatest historian and the greatest satirist of the world, who knew all the facts, have both branded him as the arch-demagogue; and their verdict will stand. Cleon is pilloried forever" (Charles Forster Smith, "Character-Drawing in Thucydides," *The American Journal of Philology* 24, no. 4 [1903]: 379).

troops sense that Cyrus is leading them against his brother, the Persian king, they refuse to advance, throwing stones at their commander whenever he tries to urge them forward. Clearchus addresses them, saying he has two choices: either to obey his paymaster or to acquiesce to his troops (*Anab.* 1.3.6). The soldiers fall into step. Though Clearchus did not have a lengthy career (*Anab.* 2.6.15b), his leadership represents the type of warmongering commander that would fuel Aristophanes' satires.[13] By direct characterization and through the character's actions and speech, Xenophon describes Clearchus as violent towards his men when necessary, skillful at leadership, and courageous in battle.

In Xenophon's *Hellenica*, Alcibiades is another exiled commander. However, rather than serving as a mercenary, as Clearchus had, Alcibiades is recalled from his ignominy to serve Athens once again (*Hell.* 1.4.10). Xenophon reports Alcibiades' actions and the response of the Athenian assembly, which paint a portrait of a capable leader, successful at acquiring spoils and pressing his allies for money (*Hell.* 1.3.3–4). The Athenian assembly declares him ἀπάντων ἡγεμῶν αὐτοκράτωρ (*Hell.* 1.4.20). The tides turn when Alcibiades loses the naval battle of Notium. The assembly replaces him, fearing he lost the ships through neglect and a lack of self-discipline (*Hell.* 1.5.16).

Polybius describes Naravas, a young Numidian commander fighting with the Carthaginians, as honorable and filled with military zeal (1.78.1). Polybius demonstrates through Naravas' actions that the youth is both virtuous and skillful (1.78.8–9). The ἀνὴρ ἀγαθός is equally found among the literary portrayals of Roman soldiers. Julius Caesar describes Titus Balventius, the former chief centurion, as a brave man possessing great authority (*Bell. gall.* 5.35) who is pierced in both thighs by a javelin. Caesar also applauds Quintus Lucanius, who is killed after fighting most valiantly, while assisting his son (*Bell. gall.* 5.35).

Dionysius introduces Marcus Flavoleius, the chief centurion (*primus pilus*), who was formerly a plebeian and small farmer. Flavoleius spurs the disheartened troops to battle. Having just been exhorted and chastised by his commander, Fabius (9.9.1–9), Flavoleius holds up his sword and swears the traditional oath that he would be victorious (9.10.4). The act of the loyal centurion inspires others to do likewise until the whole army is filled with good humor (9.10.4), despite its earlier threats of mutiny.

Livy notes how obstinate courage (*pertinax virtus*, 25.14.1) could turn the tide of battle. For example, Vibius Accaus, a leader of the Paelignian cohort, excites his men to battle by throwing the auxiliary's banner over the enemy's trench. He utters a curse on himself and his cohort if the enemy should retrieve

---

[13] Aristophanes' critique of Athenian political leaders is evident in his characterization of Lamachus and Cleon. See T. A. Dorey, "Aristophanes and Cleon," *Greece & Rome* 3 (1956): 132–39; and W. G. Forrest, "Acharnians," *Phoenix* 17 (1963): 1–12.

their *signum* before they do, and then he leaps over the trench into battle
(25.14.4–5). The centurion Titus Pedanius, the *primus pilus* of the first cohort,
responds in a similar vein. After being reproached for the soldiers' cowardice
by Valerius Flaccus (the Roman tribune of the third legion), Pedanius seizes
the legion's standard from its bearer and announces:

This standard and this centurion will in a moment be inside the enemy's wall. Let those follow
who are to prevent the standard from being captured by the enemy (Livy, 25.14.7 [Foster,
LCL]).

He is followed first by the soldiers of his own cohort and then by the whole
legion. This act of bravery alters the planned retreat, and the Romans successfully capture the Carthaginian camp, killing more than six thousand and taking
seven thousand captives (25.14.11).

   A set of military characters is introduced in tandem in Livy's Book 26. After
the successful siege of New Carthage, Scipio announces that he will reward the
man who had scaled the city wall first. He calls the claimant forward. Two come
forth – a centurion of the fourth legion named Quintus Trebellius and a marine,
Sextus Digitius. Livy notes that the two are not so much in competition with
each other as they are representatives of their respective military branches
(26.48.6). A heated partisan argument ensues, forcing Scipio to set up a tribunal
to determine the winner. The tribunal is little more restrained than the men in
the field, so Scipio awards the crown to both men (26.48.13). The military
characters are shown as equally skillful, having successfully scaled the city wall
in the heat of battle. Though they step forward to receive their crown, Livy does
not indicate that this action is an indication of vanity. Trebellius is seen as one
of the legionaries, while Digitius is grouped with his fellow marines. They
represent a class distinction present within the republican and later imperial
Roman military. Only citizens could be legionaries, but non-citizens could join
the auxiliaries or the navy.[14]

   A nameless Roman soldier distinguishes himself not for his physical
prowess, but by his cunning. He discovers that his sister's new paramour is a
member of the enemy guarding Tarentum for Hannibal (27.15). This enemy
prefect is duped by the sister into giving away security information, which leads
to the capture of the city (27.15.11). The soldier skillfully sets up the deception
in conjunction with his general, Fabius (27.15.9–11). Livy notes that the
Tarentines were no match for the Romans who excelled in spirit, arms, the art
of war, vigor of body, and vitality (27.16.1). Given the successful trickery by

----

[14] For more on the distinctions between the land and sea forces of the Roman military,
see Graham Webster, *The Roman Imperial Army of the First and Second Centuries A.D.*
(3rd ed.; Norman, OK: University of Oklahoma, 1998); and Chester G. Starr, *The Roman
Imperial Navy 31 B.C.--A.D. 324* (3rd ed.; Chicago: Ares Publishing, 1993).

the nameless soldier, Livy could have added deception to this list of soldierly attributes.

In Livy's estimation, the Roman military man par excellence is Publius Scipio. Livy's brief encomium to Scipio is recorded as the thoughts of the Numidian Masinissa, who had conjured up an image of the ideal man after he heard of Scipio's many achievements (28.35.5). He anticipates that Scipio must be tall and magnificent. Masinissa imagines Scipio's physical features solely in light of his military accomplishments. Scipio's presence exceeds the Numidian's expectations. He is described as truly manly and soldierly (28.35.6).

Josephus credits Julianus, the centurion of the Bithynian cohort, with teaching him about Roman military science, presumably after the author's capture (*B.J.* 6.81). When Titus and his troops are besieged, Julianus inspires the commander and his men by leaping into the crowd of attackers. Julianus fights with such ferocity that his assailants fear that his strength and daring are superhuman (*B.J.* 6.82). His hobnail boots cause him to slip on the stone pavement, and his enemies attack him when he falls. Nonetheless, he continues to fight to his death. Titus himself is moved by Julianus's might (*B.J.* 6.89). Julianus receives the greatest reputation (*B.J.* 6.90) among both the Romans and his enemies. Josephus also recognizes Aebutius, a decurion who participates in the battle against Josephus' stronghold at Jotapata. Aebutius is noted for his remarkable ability and intelligence (*B.J.* 3.144) and is called a noble gentleman (*B.J.* 4.36).

Tacitus portrays the noble soldier as one who loses his life in a heroic act. The *primus pilus* of the Seventh Legion, Atilius Verus, rescues the eagle after the standards of his legion are captured. He is able to slay many of his enemies before he himself is killed (*Hist.* 3.22). In a similar feat of daring, the soldier Gaius Volusius of the Third Legion is the first to mount the Vitellian rampart, where he proclaims he has captured the camp (*Hist.* 3.29). The *primus pilus* Arrius Varus is a more complex character. He is a vigorous fighter (*Hist.* 3.6), whose fame increases after his exploits with Corbulo. But Tacitus records that Varus had ingratiated himself to Nero by presenting secret charges against his general's character. This action provides him with a promotion to chief centurion, but Tacitus calls it an award of shame (*infami gratia*). Varus is portrayed as rash when he leads his cavalry against the troops of Vitellius and inflicts only a small loss (*Hist.* 3.16). Despite his impetuousness, he is later promoted to praetorian rank (*Hist.* 4.4). Varus is popular with his troops and the people because he has drawn his sword only in battle (*Hist.* 4.39).

A less dubious character is Julius Agrestis, whom the author characterizes directly by explicit description and indirectly by the portrayal of his actions. Tacitus reports that Agrestis is a centurion who has demonstrated conspicuous resolve (*Hist.* 3.54). Agrestis volunteers to investigate what had occurred at Cremona. When he meets the opposition's general, Antonius, he does not try to deceive him, but speaks frankly and directly about his purpose. When he reports back to Vitellius, the emperor refuses to accept the truth and accuses the centurion of taking a bribe. Agrestis offers proof of his statements by committing suicide. Tacitus remarks that all agreed to Agrestis's fidelity and resolve.

In the romance novel *Callirhoe*, Chaereas desires to join the Egyptian revolt against the king of Babylon, who held Chaereas's wife in his entourage. He announces to the Egyptian pharaoh that his bravery is motivated by a desire for revenge (7.2.4). The Egyptian pharaoh provides him with armor and a tent (7.2.5) and eventually invites him to become his mess mate (7.2.5). The pharaoh favors Chaereas because he has shown intelligence, courage, and trustworthiness (7.2.5). In addition, he has both a noble character and a good education (7.2.5), which evidently are the Pharaoh's expectations of a good soldier. Considering that the novel begins with Chaereas striking Callirhoe and allegedly killing her, the reader might question the Pharaoh's judgment. In a page out of Xenophon's histories, Chaereas selects the Corinthian and Spartan mercenaries among the Egyptian troops, praising them as the best soldiers. He addresses his hand-picked troops, admitting that he is not seeking personal glory but communal success (7.3.10) and saying that they are free to choose any among them as their general. They chose Chaereas, and under his command, they successfully capture Tyre.

The depictions of military characters demonstrating ἀνδρεία in the historiographies and novels show larger than life heroics. The generals and centurions are competent and successful or they are quickly replaced. Even enemy leaders are portrayed as brave and worthy of praise. But the heroic warrior seems to possess in nearly equal parts both excellence in bravery and astounding acts of violence. Like Clearchus, he is merciless in his discipline and quick to punish disobedience. The Latin *virtus*, equivalent to the Greek ἀνδρεία, is the only spoil of war for which the wife at home awaits in Plautus' *Amphitruo*:

I want my man to be cried as a victor in war: that's enough for me.
Virtus is the greatest prize,
virtus comes before everything, that's for sure:
liberty safety, life, property and parents, homeland and
children it guards and keeps safe.
Virtus has everything in it: who has virtus has everything good.[15]

2.1.1.2 The Holy Warrior

Though the brave soldier is depicted more frequently, the pious soldier is also presented as an ἀνὴρ ἀγαθός. It is not his bravery that is virtuous but his respect for the gods. Isocrates defined εὐσέβεια as reverence toward the gods and justice

---

[15] Plautus, *Amph.* 648-53. Translated in J. E. Lendon, *Soldiers and Ghosts*, 176.

toward human beings (*Paneg.* 12.24). Likewise, Menander Rhetor lists piety as a component of justice along with fair dealing and reverence (*Treatise* 1.17–20). Josephus understands piety as a particular stance towards God (*Vita* 14). Such a view may have arisen from his background as a Hellenistic Jew but is found equally among Greek philosophers.[16] Pseudo-Aristotle recognizes a relationship between righteousness and piety, which includes duties to the gods, the spirits, as well as to one's country, parents and ancestors (*Virt. vit.* 5.2). Thus piety is the practice of virtue and a right understanding of the divine.

The Roman concept of *pietas* combined duty towards one's family and commitment to the *patria* (Cicero, *De Inv.* 2.22.66; 53.161), and developed from the Greek concept of εὐσέβεια[17] into a legitimization for Roman expansion.[18] Livy's history becomes a testament to Rome's greatness and conquest, which resulted from its practice of *pietas*.[19] Fraternal *pietas* bonded fellow soldiers as brothers, sworn to protect their homeland.[20] Though few literary portraits demonstrate the impact of pietas in the creation of troop cohesion and identity, tombstone inscriptions testify to the camaraderie experienced among the rank and file soldiers.[21] For the military characters who demonstrate εὐσέβεια, it appears to be the motivation for their courage.

As an example of Jewish national history, 2 Maccabees is much like other Hellenistic historiographies in its portrayal of significant figures. The hero, Judas Maccabeus, is characterized mostly through his actions and by way of comparison with his archenemy, Antiochus Epiphanes. But Judas is also reflective of the biblical character of David, Israel's ideal religious warrior. In the narrative, Judas is portrayed as a guerrilla fighter, secretly entering villages to enlist soldiers (8:1), and then at night setting fire to towns and villages (8:6). His military success is attributed to God (8:5), and his valor is well known (8:7). Like a military general, he exhorts his troops (8:17), reminding them of the outrage done to them by the Gentile Syrians (8:17) and assuring them that God has aided them in the past and will continue to do so (8:19–20). His words meet with success (8:21). He then divides his troops and sets commanders over each

---

[16] L. V. Semenchencko, "The Conception of Piety in the Jewish Antiquities of Flavius Josephus," *Vestnik drevnej istorii* 3 (2003): 36–45.

[17] "The idea of *pietas*, taken from Greece but brought to flower in Rome…is inseparable from the names of Posidonius and Cicero" (Hendrik Wagenvoort, *Pietas: Selected Studies in Roman Religion* [Leiden: Brill, 1980], 20).

[18] "The age of Augustus chooses as its catchword the *pietas* which formed the theme, as it were, of Virgil's epic and provided the standpoint from which Livy wrote his works of history" (Ibid., 3).

[19] Ibid., 17.

[20] Cynthia J. Bannon, *The Brothers of Romulus: Fraternal Pietas in Roman Law, Literature, and Society* (Princeton: Princeton University Press, 1997), 137–73.

[21] Richard Saller and Brent D. Shaw, "Tombstones and Roman Family Relations in the Principate: Civilians, Soldiers and Slaves," *JRS* 74 (1984): 134.

division (8:21–22). His exhortation and strategy prove successful: the Maccabean troops rout Nicanor's army. Only the coming Sabbath prevents the Jewish troops from pursuing their enemies in retreat (8:25).

On another occasion when members of his army are bribed to release their enemies, Judas kills them for their treasonous offense (10:22). When Lysias besieges Beth-zur on his march to Jerusalem, Judas is the first to take up arms (11:7). The narrator describes Judas as noble (12:42), virtuous and brave (14:18). His religious zeal is evident when he advocates prayer as a military strategy (13:10) and arms his men with inspiration (15:11). After the death of Nicanor, Judas severs his head and arm and displays them in Jerusalem. He hangs his enemy's head on the citadel as a sign of God's providence (15:35). By means of his actions, Judas Maccabeus is characterized as a skillful, virtuous, and pious leader,[22] who nonetheless engages in violent, guerrilla-like warfare.

As Judas Maccabeus is blessed, so Antiochus Epiphanes, who profaned the Jewish Temple (5:15ff), is cursed. He is responsible for a torrent of evil that flooded Jerusalem (6:3). The narrator describes him as a murderer and blasphemer (9:28), filled with arrogance (9:7). As he rushes to attack Jerusalem, he is struck down by the God of Israel, who deals him an incurable wound (9:5). The stench of his rotting flesh is so repugnant that even his soldiers are repulsed (9:9). His agonizing death counters his superhuman arrogance (9:8). For the author of 2 Maccabees, Antiochus is the embodiment of impiety, and Judas Maccabeus is the mighty hand of God.

Dionysius personifies the good soldier in his paradigmatic story of the *virtus et pietas* of the Horatii and the Curiatii. When a stalemate results between the Albans and Romans, the two tribes agree that representatives of each army will fight to the death (3.12–13) in order to determine the winner. As a point of honor, soldiers and officers argue among themselves about who will represent their side. However, the criteria for selection precluded most, for one had to have descended from a notable family, be excellent at arms, handsome in appearance, and have experienced a remarkable birth. As chance would have it, these encomiastic qualities are found in two sets of triplets. Sicinius, an Alban, married his twin daughters to a Roman, Horatius, and an Alban, Curiatius. Both women gave birth to triplet boys on the same day. The two sets of triplet brothers now serve in the Roman and the Alban armies (3.13.4). While the Alban brothers agree immediately to the fight to determine the victor of the battle, the Roman sons ask if they might first consult their father (3.17.1). Such piety is recognized by their general (3.17.2) and by their father who commends them (3.17.6). The two sets of brothers are evenly matched and fight bravely

---

[22] For further discussion on Jewish piety in the Second Temple Period, see Adolf Büchler, *Types of Jewish-Palestinian Piety from 70 B.C.E. to 70 C.E.* (London: Oxford University Press, 1922).

(3.18), until only the youngest Roman remains alive. After the battle, he returns to his father to announce the death of his brothers. Along the way he encounters his sister who had been engaged to one of his now-dead cousins. Because she is grieving for her lost love and not her lost brothers, the remaining son decries that she is a false virgin, a hater of her brothers, and a betrayer of his ancestors (3.21.6) and then kills her on the spot (3.21.7).[23] Dionysius's portrait of the good soldier is one who zealously guards family honor on and off the battlefield.

Tacitus paints a vivid picture of the horrors of war, particularly during the civil battles between Galba's death and Vespasian's ascension. The story of Julius Mansuetus of Vitellius's Rapax legion and his unnamed son is an example of the tragedy of battle (*Hist.* 3.25). Mansuetus has been enrolled in Spain, leaving behind a young son. When the son grows up, he is conscripted into Galba's Seventh Legion. The son meets his father on the battlefield, recognizing him only after he has mortally wounded him. The now-weeping son embraces his dying father, praying that his father's spirit will forgive him. He then buries his father, performing his official duties as a son. The rest of the soldiers curse the most horrible war. The demonstration of *pietas* by the son of Julius Mansuetus (*Hist.* 3.25) stands starkly against the story of the unnamed cavalry soldier seeking an award for killing his own brother (*Hist.* 3.51). He approached the generals for a commendation for his act, which they could neither reward, because of its brutality against blood, nor punish due to the necessity of war.

Appropriate piety assured the army on the verge of battle that the gods were fighting on their side. But, despite the importance of incense and auguries, few military characters are distinguished for their religious zeal. When a soldier is depicted as εὐσεβής it is often described as the motivation for his bravery. The manifestation of ἀνδρεία continued to be the most excellent example of the ἀνὴρ ἀγαθός, since the good man endures even to death for the sake of what is noble – the end to which virtue aims (*Eth. nic.* 3.7.2).

2.1.2 The Undisciplined Soldier

Generals and lower officers attended heavy-handedly to unruly troops whose lack of discipline often led to disobedience and, on occasion, to mutiny. "Roman *disciplina* was understood to be more a curb than a spur, and it formed an opposed pair with Roman *virtus*."[24]

---

[23] Due to her lack of modesty and her affront to the family, her father refuses to bury her in the family tomb (3.21.8). Dionysius comments on the sternness of the old Roman traditions, which upheld the victory of the state and reverence (i.e., εὐσέβεια) for the family at such dire costs (3.21.7).

[24] Lendon, *Soldiers and Ghosts*, 178.

Tacitus records that during the chaos that followed Galba's death, Vitellius made his way to Rome, accompanied by his cumbersome army of 60,000 soldiers slack in discipline (*Hist.* 2.87). Even the slaves of the soldiers were most insolent. It is no wonder that the soldiers and their *lixae* are undisciplined for, as Tacitus recounts, their commanding officers were equally incapable of obedience. Seven miles outside Rome, the horde set up camp, where Vitellius distributes cooked meals to the soldiers. Civilians infiltrated the camp and begin to harass the soldiers who are not accustomed to such mockery (2.88). They attacked the unarmed but provocative civilians, even killing the father of one of the soldiers.

Meanwhile in Rome, other soldiers, who had left the ranks in order to be first in the forum to view Galba's body, terrorized the citizens by their frightening appearance:

> They themselves presented a sight that was equally savage, dressed as they were in shaggy skins of wild beasts and armed with enormous spears; while, in their ignorance, they failed to avoid the crowds, or, when they got a fall from the slippery streets or ran into a civilian, broke out in curses and soon went on to use their fists and swords. Even tribunes and prefects hurried up and down the streets spreading terror with their armed bands (Tacitus, *Hist.* 2.88 [Moore, LCL]).

Tacitus does not seem to fault the army or its immediate commanders for the utter lack of discipline and order. Vitellius is to blame (*Hist.* 2.89). The *sacramentum*, which obliged the soldier to obey his emperor, became void when several contenders vied for the imperial purple.

If the good man is distinguished by his bravery and his noble motivation, the base one errs in his rashness or in his cowardliness, both actions motivated by fear. The stereotype of the undisciplined soldier has several subcategories that include the coward, the greedy soldier, and the mutinous orator. The coward is less often depicted in detail by the historiographers, who would not want to call attention to such behavior. The mutinous soldier, on the other hand, receives extensive description, since more than the actual enemy, this soldier has the potential of destroying the ranks from within. It is often greed, not power, that fuels the mutiny, so that the characterization of an undisciplined soldier may show him to be both greedy and seditious. The sole motivation for the coward is fear, so he is not likely to seek extra spoils or incite trouble.

2.1.2.1 The Coward

The motif of the punishment of the coward or malcontent found in the general's exhortation speeches introduces another stereotype. Such a soldier is slow and hesitant to fight (*Ant. rom.* 9.9.2). He lacks courage, and his inexperience leads to bad behavior (Thuc. 2.87.3). He is easily struck by panic and flees (Thuc. 4.125.1). But fleeing will most assuredly lead to loss of life (*Ant. rom.* 9.9.9;

Cyr. 3.3.45). Should the deserter survive the battle, he will live in shame (Plb. 15.10.3) or be punished severely (Thuc. 2.87.9).

Theophrastus paints a vivid portrait of the military coward or δειλός. When the coward is serving in the military, he makes excuses to avoid the front lines. He hides his sword under his pillow and claims to look for it (*Char.* 25.4). He will care for a fallen comrade rather than fight, and when the others return from battle, he recounts his "brave" deeds covered in another man's blood (*Char.* 25.5). Aristophanes' Lamachus enfleshes the δειλός. He returns from his brief battle nursing his war "injury," which resulted from his having stepped on a stake in his retreat (*Ach.* 1175–1195).

2.1.2.2 The Greedy Soldier

The spoils of war were the right of soldiers and often supplemented their pay, so that the stereotype of a greedy soldier must demonstrate more than simply a desire for gain. The military φιλοκερδής seeks a financial windfall at the expense of his military duty and beyond the bounds of the soldierly prerogative. The definition of such a soldier is often subjectively tied to the perspective of the author. The brave and pious Judas Maccabeus kills his own soldiers when he discovers that they have taken a bribe and released their enemies (2 Macc 10:20-22). The cavalry soldier who demands a financial reward for killing his own brother (*Hist.* 3.51) is greedy in Tacitus' estimation, since he has violated the higher Roman value of εὐσέβεια. Livy's account of Spendius shows that the runaway slave turned mercenary begins his mutinous path out of desire for more pay (1.69–86).

Polybius describes just such a fellow in Book 21 of his *Histories*. Chiomara,[25] the wife of a Galatian ruler, Ortiagon, is among the women and children captured when the Romans defeat the Gauls. She is taken as the spoils of battle by a nameless centurion. The centurion then rapes her, which Polybius describes as "acting in a soldierly way" (στρατιωτικῶς, 21.38.2), and thus dishonors her (21.38.2). Polybius describes the centurion as uneducated and incapable of disciplining himself (21.38.3). He is enslaved by both pleasure and money (21.38.3), but his love of money gets the best of him, and he accepts a ransom for the woman. As he is handing her over to her rescuers, she signals to them and they chop off his head. Later she deposits the centurion's head at her husband's feet, and announces: ἕνα μόνον ζῆν ἐμοὶ συγγεγενημένον (21.38.6). This unnamed centurion is portrayed as brutish, violent, greedy, and in the end, stupid. Thus our earliest portrayal of a Roman centurion by an ancient historian is none too flattering.

---

[25] Plutarch includes Chiomara among his virtuous women (*Mulier. virt.* 249.E–F). Livy also includes the story (38.24).

2.1.2.3 The Mutineer

A general feared dissension among his troops as much as he feared the enemy. The mutinous rabble-rouser in the guise of the orator strikes at the heart of military order. When the rank and file soldier gives an *adlocutio* this elevated portrayal is, indeed, a surprise because only generals addressed the troops.

An example of one such soldier is the mutinous Spendius, a runaway Roman slave who became a mercenary in the war against Rome (1.69–86). After Carthage surrenders to Rome in the First Punic War, the mercenary soldiers on the defeated city's payroll demand substantial reimbursement and eventually incite a revolt led by Spendius and a Libyan freeman, Mathos. The three-year war between Carthage and the mercenaries produces horrific acts, mostly under the direction of Spendius and Mathos. Polybius explains that Spendius desired to provoke war with Carthage so as to prevent capture by his slave owner, who would then torture and kill him (1.69.5). Polybius contrasts the runaway slave's fear of punishment with the violence and acts of torture he spawns in order to avoid his own suffering. The narrator characterizes Spendius as skillful and at one point even virtuous. Spendius is both physically strong and daring in battle (1.69.4), but he is also extremely violent, and even brutal. He is one of those whom Polybius characterizes as possessing an ulcerous soul (1.81.5–7). Spendius, who directs the crucifixion and mutilation of the Carthaginian soldiers and allows his own men to be stoned if they disagreed with his dictates, in the end faces a death more violent than the feared punishment from his owner. He is crucified and hung on the walls of Tunis.

The army at peace is equally susceptible to mutiny. Livy recounts that as Scipio's army had achieved a level of peace, the soldiers could no longer freely plunder the territory (28.24.6). Adding to their frustration, rumors of Publius Scipio's untimely death arose among the ranks. Two soldiers, Gaius Albius of Cales and Gaius Atrius of Umbria, hatch a plan to incite the troops to mutiny (28.24–29.12). The soldiers are dissatisfied that their pay has been delayed by Scipio's "demise" (28.25.6). In addition, they feel that notoriety has been denied them after a recent victory (28.25.7). The calculating Albius and Atrius recognize the volatile nature of the ranks and push the mutiny forward (28.25.13). When it is made known that Scipio was alive and well and ready to quell the mutiny, the two instigators rationalize that since they have not drawn blood, the general will be merciful (28.25.14). After demonstrating vanity and greed, they end their lives as portraits of stupidity, for mercy is not Scipio's response. Scipio charges that these soldiers have violated the *sacramentum* (28.26.4). The culprits are scourged, bound at the stake, and beheaded.

Tacitus' Percennius is a private who has an insolent tongue (*Ann.* 1.16) and formerly worked in the theater. He incites the troops who were already worried about the death of Augustus and its effect on their military service. Percennius asks why they should continue to obey a few centurions and fewer tribunes as if they, themselves, were slaves (*Ann.* 1.17). The incendiary speech is effective, and the troops begin to talk of joining three legions into one. Eventually, the centurions stave off mutiny and execute Percennius (*Ann.* 1.29).

On the heels of Percennius' near mutiny, Tacitus introduces a rank-and-file soldier by the name of Vibulenus, who is hoisted onto the shoulders of other soldiers so that he can address Blaesus's tribunal. He begins by complimenting Blaesus's attempts to restore hope to the soldiers, but then Vibulenus claims that his brother was put to death by gladiators in the general's entourage. He pleads with Blaesus for his brother's body so that he might bury him properly and, after that, die himself. Then he and his brother would have died not because of a crime they had done but because they had served the legion. After this rousing speech, Vibulenus cries, beats his breast, and leaps down from the soldiers' shoulders into the crowd (*Ann.* 1.23). He creates such frenzy that the gladiators are placed in irons while others go in search of his brother's body. But the body is nowhere to be found and, after torture, the slaves confess there had been no murder. When the soldiers whom Vibulenus had roused into a frenzy are about to attack the general, they discover that Vibulenus never even had a brother!

2.1.3 Conclusion: Responding to the Call to Arms

The stereotype of the ἀνὴρ ἀγαθός, with its roots in Homer's Odysseus, meets various incarnations of the mutinous Thersites on the battlefields of Greco-Roman historiography. The good man is above all brave, willingly facing death. He may also be noted for his piety toward his family and his country. The base military man is one who avoids the fight or breaks rank, endangering his fellow soldiers. Or he may exceed in greed, so that his motivation in battle is only for the spoils and what greater gain he may acquire. But the greatest vice that an undisciplined soldier could manifest is that of treason. The soldier who encourages his fellows to mutiny violates his oath of obedience and assumes a role reserved solely for the general: that of addressing the troops.

The stereotypes of the soldier on the battlefield, like those we will see in the narrative settings of the province and the home front, are not one-dimensional. The good soldier may be exceedingly brave but he can be equally violent. Or the undisciplined soldier may be mutinous, but his skill and leadership are what enable him to summon a hearing and garner support. The designation of a stereotype is made based on the most dominant trait evidenced in the portrait and the motivation for the character's actions. No doubt Spendius acquitted himself well as a Carthaginian mercenary and on this basis could have been deemed a good soldier. But his desire to avoid punishment as a runaway slave and his hunger for profit drove him to mutiny. His crucifixion on the walls of Tunis signal Polybius's final estimation of his character.

2.2 Policemen in the Provinces

When military campaigns began in the spring and ended before winter, soldiers were culled from citizen land-owners whose responsibility it was to perform military service or provide a substitute in their place. But as campaigns became more lengthy and enemies more varied in their military tactics, a standing professional army was established. While the legion was stationed on the frontiers of the provinces, the need would arise for a quick assault elsewhere. For such assignments a vexillation of soldiers, numbering between 1,000 and 2,000 men, would be dispatched to quell the crisis, sometimes remaining on assignment away from their legion for several years.[26]

Though only a percentage of the legion's strength, the vexillation served as a synecdoche for the full-force of Rome's military might. Likewise the individual soldier, through his oath of allegiance, was bound to his cohort, his superiors and finally to the emperor himself. As such, he represented the emperor and could expect certain privileges. This is made clear when a veteran soldier requested that Augustus himself appear in court on the soldier's behalf. When Augustus sent a friend instead, the soldier replied, "But I, as often as you had need of my aid, did not send another to you instead of myself, but I myself bore the brunt of battle for you."[27]

During periods of relative peace, these professional soldiers were given various tasks to occupy their time and their hands. By the imperial period, if a Roman soldier on active duty is not on the battlefield or guarding the frontiers, then he is stationed in the provinces. The actual soldier at battle is chiefly concerned with fighting, while the soldier on vexillation serves multiple functions. As epigraphic and literary evidence shows, this soldier is responsible for tax protection and collection, police work, and mediation between the governor and the provincials.

Egyptian papyri testify to the use of soldiers for protection during the collection of taxes or, in some cases, for actual collection of the taxes themselves.[28] In addition to protecting the collection and delivery of taxes and customs, soldiers were used to gather vital information. Documents from the Babatha archive found in the Judean desert "show that in A.D. 127 what was clearly a province-wide census was carried out in which the commanders of the auxiliary units stationed in the province served as local or regional *censitores*."[29] The

---

[26] Lawrence Keppie, *The Making of the Roman Army. From Republic to Empire* (Norman, OK: University of Oklahoma, 1998), 197.

[27] Dio 55.4.2. The incident may also be referred to in Suetonius, *Aug.* 56.4.

[28] A second-century papyrus lists soldiers from three cohorts – I *Flavia Cilicia*, II *Ituraeorum* and I *Lusitanorum* – and one *ala* as the collectors of a salt tax (*ChLA* 4. 264).

[29] Werner Eck, "Provincial Administration and Finance," in *The Cambridge Ancient History XI The High Empire A.D. 70–192* (ed. Alan K. Bowman et al.; Cambridge: Cambridge University Press, 2000), 288.

prefect of the auxiliary cavalry unit, Priscus, received and signed Babatha's census registration.[30]

Vexillations of soldiers frequently engaged in policing the provinces, particularly in those provinces on the border of the empire.[31] "There is increasing evidence for governors stationing special soldiers, the so-called *beneficiarii consulares*, outside towns, at major road junctions and on the frontiers of the empire. These should not, however, be seen as administrative outposts: their purpose was to fulfill the governor's duty to provide for the public safety in his province."[32] Legionaries culled from frontier forces maintained police posts on major routes throughout the provinces.[33] Ostraca found near watch towers on the eastern desert confirm the presence of both local Egyptians and Roman soldiers guarding the desert road.[34] The papyri from the trash heaps of Egypt provide abundant evidence that centurions in the rural areas not only provided security for the residents but also acted as *de facto* judges in civil matters. In August 198 C.E., Gemellus wrote to the epistrategos Calpurnius Concessus and included a copy of an earlier petition to and the response from the prefect.[35] The final subscription indicates that Concessus referred the matter to the centurion of the nome as Gemellus had requested. Evidently Gemellus believed that the centurion would be able to adjudicate his claim. If Gemellus's trust was not in vain, then perhaps, "far from being a remote and specialist military, the Roman army would have a real influence on village life, not merely as a vague threat of overwhelming violence which could destroy any challenge to the established order, but as a real and active presence in the local administrative and power structures."[36] Alston investigated numerous papyri addressed to centurions stationed in Egypt, in which locals solicited their assistance in legal matters or asked for protection.[37] More than half of the petitioners in the papyri

---

[30] Naphtali Lewis et al., *The Documents from the Bar Kokhba Period in the Cave of Letters. Greek Papyri* (Jerusalem: Israel Exploration Society, 1989), 65–70.

[31] For a recent and detailed analysis of the Roman army used as a policing agent, see Christopher J. Fuhrmann, *Policing the Roman Empire: Soldiers, Administration, and Public Order* (Oxford; New York: Oxford University Press, 2012).

[32] Eck, "Provincial Administration and Finance," 282.

[33] J. J. Wilkes, "The Danube Provinces," in *The Cambridge Ancient History XI The High Empire A.D. 70–192* (ed. Alan K. Bowman, et al.; Cambridge: Cambridge University Press, 2000), 586.

[34] Ibid.

[35] *P. Mich.* 425, inv. 2979 probably originated in Karanis in the Arsinoite nome of Egypt and is one of several papyri in the Gemellus family archive. See H. C. Youtie and O. M. Pearl, *Michigan Papyri VI. Papyri and Ostraca from Karanis* (Ann Arbor: University of Michigan, 1944), 118.

[36] Richard Alston, *Soldier and Society in Roman Egypt: A Social History* (London: Routledge, 1995), 87.

[37] Alston separates the papyri into assault cases (representing nearly half), military or administrative wrong-doings, and violence against property (*Soldier and Society*, 88–89).

that Alston studied claimed special status as a way of bolstering their claim, but only "a few people appealed to the chivalrous instincts of the centurions by suggesting that they had no one else to safeguard their interests."[38]

Despite the "chivalrous centurions" these petitions hoped to solicit, most papyri suggest that the military police force may have acted less as the just extensions of the Roman administration and more as terrorists with free reign. A centurion stationed in Ein Gedi acted as the local loan shark, according to a loan agreement found in the Babatha archive. Magonius Valens of Cohors I Milliaria Thracum[39] originally loaned Judah, son of Elazar Khthousion, 40 denarii, but the number was scratched out and 60 was written above it.[40] A passage from the second-century *Tosephta* indicates the fear with which Judean provincials lived. Discussing the prohibition against preparing foods on festivals for dogs and Gentiles, the passage recounts why Simeon Hatemani did not attend the synagogue on the eve of a festival:

A patrol of Gentiles came into town and they (the townspeople) were afraid that they (the soldiers) might harm them and therefore we prepared them a calf and we fed them and gave them drink and rubbed them with oil so that they would not harm the townspeople (*tos. Betzah* ii 6).[41]

On the basis of such evidence, Isaac concludes that Roman rule in Judea as reflected in the rabbinic sources demonstrates "a reality of intensive army interference which takes brutality as a matter of course."[42] In the Egyptian papyri, the verb διασείω, which means literally "to shake violently," came to refer to the extortion of the peasantry by soldiers. The noun διασείσμος is found in a mid-second-century financial account indicating the payment of extortion money to police agents and a soldier.[43] An earlier papyrus, dated around 37 C.E., records the testimony of a village scribe who denies knowing about a particular soldier's extortion scheme. This behavior occurred despite the fact that, among his various other duties, the governor was responsible for overseeing the soldiers in his administration. He was supposed to ensure that soldiers did not take advantage of the provincials under the guise of "requisitioning" needs for the army (*Dig.* 1.18.6.6–7). As is evident in the above examples, such oversight was lacking.

---

[38] Ibid., 91.

[39] This cohort was stationed at Hebron and had outposts at Ein Gedi. See Michael P. Speidel, "A Tile Stamp of Cohors I Thracum Milliaria from Hebron/Palestine," *Zeitschrift für Papyrologie und Epigraphik* 35 (1979): 170–72 .

[40] Lewis, *The Documents from the Bar Kokhba Period,* 11.

[41] Cited by Benjamin Isaac, "The Roman Army in Judaea: Police Duties and Taxation," in *Roman Frontier Studies* (ed. V.A. Maxfield and M. I. Dobson; Exeter: University of Exeter Press, 1991), 459.

[42] Isaac, "The Roman Army in Judaea," 459.

[43] L. Robert, "Sur un papyrus de Bruxelles," *Revue de Philogie* 3rd series 17 (1943): 111.

If the papyri soliciting the help of the local centurion are any indication, not all provincials lived in fear of the soldiers operating as agents of imperial administration. As Tacitus recounts, "the provincials (of Syria) were accustomed to live with soldiers, and enjoyed association with them" (*Hist.* 2.80 [Moore, LCL]). However, one wonders if the positive portrayals resulted from petitioners, such as Gemellus, who were former soldiers or family members of veterans themselves. The evidence of abusive soldiers acting as agents of imperial administration appears throughout the Roman provinces, from improper requisitioning of transport in Pisidian Antioch to extortion in Judea and Egypt. The papyri indicate that the experience of many provincials confirms the portrait of the brutish soldier found in several literary texts, and little historical evidence points to the probability of more positive portrayals. Only in the ancient novels do we find brief portrayals of the good soldier who appears as the "White Knight" rescuing damsels in distress – a decidedly romantic if not frequent characterization.

2.2.1 The Rescuer

As petitions to adjudicating centurions indicate, actual soldiers could be perceived as potentially helpful. Some of these military officials appear as literary characters in the Greek Romances.[44] Xenophon of Ephesus and Achilles Tatius depict prefects who rescue captives, hunt down bandits and befriend wayward strangers. In Xenophon's *Ephesiaca*, the governor sends Polyidus, the commander of an Egyptian contingent, to quell the raids instigated by Hippothous (5.3.1–5.57). Under Polyidus's leadership, his soldiers are successful. However, the bandit escapes, forcing Polyidus to pursue him. During the search of the countryside, Polyidus finds and rescues the captured Anthia (5.4.1–7), with whom he falls in love, despite the fact that he is already married (5.4.5). Though Polyidus rescues Anthia from the den of the bandits, she is still not safe and must implore Isis to save her yet again from Polyidus' amorous intentions (5.4.6).

Tatius's Charmides mirrors Polyidus. He, too, is a commander of an Egyptian cohort, who rescues Clitophon and then generously outfits him as a member of the cavalry. Impressed with Clitophon's abilities, Charmides offers him a place at table (3.14.2). After hearing Clitophon's tale of woe, the general is moved with pity (3.14.3) and makes plans to attack the brigands who had captured Clitophon's love. Unfortunately, very much like Polyidus, Charmides

---

[44] Xenophon's plot and the hero and heroine's adventures may appear fantastic, but "the novel's depiction of actual officials of the Roman provinces...contributes to an atmosphere of historical verisimilitude....Moreover, local and provincial security officers appeared not infrequently as *personae* in the genre" (J. L. Rife, "Officials of the Roman Provinces in Xenophon's Ephesiaca," *ZPE* 138 [2002]: 107).

also falls in love with the woman he rescues but, in the end, he responds to the call of duty (4.11.1).

Petronius also introduces a soldier captivated by a woman (111–112). In Ephesus, a *matrona* of great virtue is mourning the death of her husband so deeply that she remains in his tomb day and night, refusing to eat or drink. All praise her as a woman of singular character as she spends her fifth day without food or water. She is hailed as the one true example of chastity and love. Meanwhile, the governor gives orders that some robbers are to be crucified near the tomb of the widow's husband. A soldier is set to guard the bodies of the crucified robbers, lest they be removed and buried properly. Seeing the light coming from the tomb and hearing the mourning, he succumbs to human weakness and is curious to know the source of the lamentations. He encounters the beautiful widow weeping over her husband's corpse. He then brings his supper down to the tomb and urges her to end her mourning. While she pays no attention to his urgings, her maid succumbs and takes the food from the soldier. Refreshed from the nourishment, the maid urges her mistress to break her fast. Finally, the good widow of Ephesus agrees and eats heartily.

After the soldier successfully persuades the widow to eat, he hopes to impose upon her virtue for, as the narrator says "You know which temptation generally assails a man on a full stomach" (*Satyr.* 112. [Heseltine and Rouse, LCL]). While the soldier is in the tomb, the family of one of the crucified thieves notices that the guard has gone and takes the opportunity to remove their loved one in order to bury him properly.[45] Where Charmides responds immediately to the call to duty, this soldier is derelict. Fearing a greater punishment from his superiors, he intends to take his own life. The woman suggests that her husband's corpse be substituted for the body of the missing thief. The soldier follows the woman's advice, and those who saw the dead man wondered how he had ascended to the cross! The response to the tale within the larger narrative of the *Satyricon* offers a lens through which to interpret the story. One of the listeners responds, "If the governor of the province had been a just man, he should have put the dead husband back in the tomb, and hung the woman on the cross" (*Satyr.* 112 [Heseltine and Rouse, LCL]).

The Widow of Ephesus is not raped nor are her belongings looted. In fact, in this tale, the soldier brings the widow all the fine things he can. He encourages her to eat and she finally does so greedily. She consents to his desires, and the first night together is called their wedding night. When the soldier threatens suicide for his dereliction of duty, it is the once virtuous widow who suggests her husband's corpse as a substitute for the missing thief. The character of the soldier is a foil to the women's alleged chastity.

---

[45] Part of the ignominy of crucifixion was the denial of burial for the one crucified. However, Philo indicates that during some festivals, the authorities relented and allowed the family members to bury their dead (*Flacc.* 10.84).

2.2.2 The Bully

The most prevalent stereotype of a soldier on assignment away from his legion is that of the terrorizing brute. This stereotype occurs solely in the imperial literature. "As is generally recognized now, nothing could be further from the truth than Rostovtzeff's idea that the army of the Imperial period somehow represented an oppressed peasantry. On the contrary, the soldiers were a privileged official class whose presence was feared by ordinary people."[46] Satirists and novelists alike characterize soldiers as bullying, violent, and greedy.

Petronius's story of the soldier-turned-werewolf is the most striking example of the soldier literally as a terrorizing beast. During the banquet hosted by the extravagant Trimalchio, a guest by the name of Niceros is encouraged to tell a story (61–62). He recounts that when he was still a slave, he had fallen in love with an inn-keeper's wife, Melissa of Tarentum. When the inn-keeper died, Niceros took the opportunity to visit Melissa. He invited a guest who had been staying at his master's house to accompany him as far as the fifth milestone. This "guest" was a soldier and as brave as Orcus. Leaving at night under a full moon, they passed the tombs lining the side of the roadway. The soldier went over to the tombs while Niceros sat down and began to count the graves. When Niceros looked again for his traveling companion, the soldier had stripped off his clothes and placed them on the roadside. The soldier then made a circle around his clothes and promptly turned into a wolf! He began to howl and then ran into the woods. When poor Niceros went to pick up the soldier's clothes they had turned to stone. Drawing his sword, Niceros inched his way to Melissa's house, only to hear that a wolf had gotten into the house and attacked the sheep. One of the servants had pierced the wolf's neck with a spear. When Niceros returned in the safety of daylight, he passed the place where the clothes had turned to stone. Only a pool of blood remained. Reaching his master's house, he discovered the soldier in bed, with a doctor tending his neck wound. Realizing the soldier was actually a werewolf, Niceros knew he could never eat with him again.

In the *Metamorphoses*, we have a detailed portrayal of the military brute. Apuleius depicts not a soldier who turns into an animal but his protagonist. In Book 9, Lucius the ass, is now in the hands of the gardener. Having just witnessed a horrendous slaughter in the house of a man whom he had earlier offered hospitality, the gardener is returning home when he encounters a tall man whose dress and manner reveal him to be a soldier from the legion (9.39). The soldier gruffly asks in Latin where the gardener is taking the donkey. Not

---

[46] Millar cited Rostovtzeff, *The Social and Economic History of the Roman Empire* (1957), Chapter 11, no. 24 (Fergus Millar, "The World of the Golden Ass," *JRS* 71 [1981]: 68).

knowing the language, the gardener continues past the soldier. Unable to contain himself, the soldier strikes the gardener with his staff.[47] The gardener then answers that he does not know Latin. The soldier now responds in Greek. When the soldier discovers that the donkey is being taken to the next city, he attempts to confiscate it in order to transport the commander's baggage. Calling the centurion, "fellow soldier" (*commilito*), the gardener tries to dissuade the requisition of his animal. The soldier turns his staff intending to strike the gardener again. In self-defense, the gardener attacks the soldier first, pummeling him with his fists, elbows, teeth and even a rock from the road (9.40). The soldier, unable to move, continues to threaten that when he does get up, he will cut the gardener to pieces. Quickly, the gardener removes his sword from his reach. The centurion's only recourse is to play dead.

The gardener then takes the soldier's sword and rides his ass into town, seeking a hiding place from a friend. Eventually the much beaten soldier stumbles back, barely able to walk (9.41). He informs his fellow soldiers of the mishap – both the beating and the loss of his sword. Like the gardener, the centurion also goes into hiding, fearing that the gods of his military oath will extract revenge since he has lost his sword (9.41). His fellow soldiers hunt for the culprit and his ass. The soldiers concoct a story about a missing silver cup that the gardener allegedly stole, so that the magistrates will allow them to search the town. When they discover the friend who has hidden the gardener and his animal, the soldiers swear by the genus of the Emperor (9.41) that the gardener is hiding inside. The friend calls on his gods as witnesses that he is not hiding the culprit in his home. Finally the donkey sticks his head out of the second story window, giving away their hiding place.

Afterwards, the soldier takes possession of the donkey and piles him high with his baggage. The narrator explains that the soldier did this not because of army regulation but to terrify passing travelers (10.1). The soldier arrives at a town on his journey where he is then quartered with a member of the town council. He goes immediately to report to his commanding officer, who we are told oversaw a thousand troops. Eventually, the soldier sells the animal for eleven denarii and, in obedience to an order, carries a letter to the emperor (10.2).

With respect to the provincial folk, the soldier is characterized directly by the narrator as superior and arrogant (9.39), filled with insolence, violent (9.40), lacking self-restraint (10.1), terrorizing to travelers and greedy (10.13). With respect to his military obligations, his actions demonstrate that he is appropriately worried about losing his sword (9.41), that he reports immediately to his superior (10.1) and that he is dutifully obedient in fulfilling his mission (10.13). His *commiles* live up to the camaraderie indicated in their appellation.

---

[47] While the narrator did not identify the rank of the soldier, centurions carried a twisted vine stick as an indication of their rank (Webster, *The Roman Imperial Army*, 130).

They hunt down the gardener in order to retrieve the soldier's sword and seek revenge (9.41). From the narrator's perspective the centurion is a terrorizing brute and, at the same time, a dutiful soldier. The actions of his comrades indicate the same probably could be said of them.

The soldiers in Juvenal's Satire 16 are not only violent but legally privileged. Juvenal opens with a question: who can number the benefits afforded the soldier (16.1)? If the author could be promised a career under a favorable star, he would consider joining the ranks (16.2–3). No citizen would dare attack a soldier, and if the citizen himself were attacked by a soldier it was better to remain silent. The beatings by a soldier left one without teeth, with the likely loss of an eye and with black and blue swelling of one's face (16.11). Apuleius' gardener could certainly attest to this. But if the victim sought redress, likely the judge would be a centurion and the whole cohort would become one's enemies (16.20). Besides the camp was a great distance from the city (16.25). It was easier to find a false witness to testify against the wronged civilian than to entice one's friends to bear witness against the soldier (16.32–34).

Juvenal continues, noting that soldiers enjoy legal benefits not afforded to the average citizen. Soldiers did not have to wait for their cases to be heard at trial and they could write wills and keep their military earnings even if their fathers were still alive (16.51–54). Hence Coranus, a soldier, became the patron of his own father who sought the aid of his son (16.54–56). Hard work was rewarded and the most brave of the soldiers were the most fortunate (16.59). The piece ends abruptly with the mention of awards earned by soldiers. This satire does not mean that Juvenal was necessarily "anti-military, but that he saw what he considered undue advantage given to this sphere of the ancient Roman institution of the military at the expense of the civilian."[48]

Stories of the brutish soldier depicted in these novels and satires reveal an unflattering portrait. As the papyri demonstrate, general and widespread experience confirmed this stereotype.

2.2.3 Conclusion: Good Cop, Bad Cop

Auditors and readers expect military characters on the battlefield to engage in violent and savage acts. The battlefield stereotypes depict soldiers as motivated toward noble intentions or acting out of fear or over-confidence. When the setting changes to that of the province, the soldier is more often depicted as an individual, separate from his cohort and serving as a provincial policeman. Some officers and soldiers are characterized as rescuers who save citizens in distress from bandits, only to become victims of love. The opposite stereotype is that of the brute who bullies the very provincials he is meant to protect. By

---

[48] Iverson, "The Military Theme in Juvenal's Satires," 101.

Juvenal's account, a soldier need not fear civil authorities. However, the military powers-that-be was another matter. How else does one explain the sheepish behavior of Apuleius's beaten centurion when he loses his sword or Petronius's derelict soldier who contemplates suicide after he quits his post? In the novels, the soldier stationed in the province frequently is characterized as a brute who abuses civilians. He is also obedient to his commanders. But his ready obedience appears to result from his fear of punishment rather than from a sense of honor and responsibility.

2.3 Veterans on the Home Front

The stage of battle most clearly marks the expectations for good and bad behavior for a military character. When the character is placed in the province, the zeal that would have earned honors on the battlefield can manifest as daring rescues of captive maidens or bullying attacks on civilians. The military character located at home, like his real life counterpart, has even less opportunity to demonstrate the virtues that the historians praised: bravery, zeal, and obedience. Because the actual soldiers and commanders of ancient Greece and Republican Rome were most often citizens of their πόλις, their military status held sway on the home front only if they were the currently elected στρατηγός, or general. When the hoplite hung up his armor, he returned to the civic and economic duties at hand. In battle, he demonstrated his great deeds by force, but at home, he should accomplish his work by virtue of his will rather than his strength (Xenophon, *Oec.* 21.8). Conflict arises within the comedies when returned soldiers, flaunting their military successes, fail to return to their civic identities. The braggart mercenary soldier neglects to respect the greater status of the citizens among whom he lives. Instead, he exalts himself because of his wealth and military success.

Concomitant with the development of a standing Roman army, the soldier in literary works begins to appear as a professional with specific job requirements and prescribed length of service. He is the "new recruit," as Juvenal depicts, who chooses to do military service rather than cavort about town driving one's own chariot when one has outgrown boyhood (8.169). He is a long-serving centurion (Tacitus, *Hist.* 3.54) or a police prefect (Xenophon, *Ephesiaca* 5.3.1–5.5.7). And in the novels, if he is not serving in the provinces, he is on the home front, now retired (*Ephesiaca* 3.12). In reality, a soldier retired either to his native homeland,[49] his current location, or a land allotment[50]

---

[49] Michael P. Speidel, "Legionaries from Asia Minor," 744.

[50] Julius Caesar recognized that the creation of veteran colonies was a way to quickly disperse potentially mutinous soldiers. Because North Africa remained a relatively undeveloped part of the empire, he gave his older soldiers land grants along the coast. Augustus continued his policy (*Res Gestae* 27), and legionary soldiers could anticipate resettlement in a veteran colony until the reign of Hadrian. Such colonies were located

provided to him. With a sizable pension, he had the potential of becoming a significant member of his community, as epigraphic evidence has shown. These veterans never forgot the source of their wealth or their military exploits, as depicted on numerous funerary monuments. For example, a burial stele in Aquileia records the life of L. Pellartius Celer who, after 43 years of service, received a monetary award from Domitian and boasted a golden crown from Titus that was awarded for his bravery during the First Jewish War.[51] He was an *evocatus* in the Praetorian Guard, which meant he had voluntarily re-enlisted after his initial 16 years and served under Domitian. His unit was the 15th Legion Apollinaris. He died at 73 and was commemorated by his son.

When the home front is a narrative setting for literary soldiers, they often possess wealth and status in imitation of actual veterans. In Plautus's *Epidicus*, Stratippocles is a returned soldier (46) who brings back a beautiful woman as part of his modest spoils of war. His father, Periphanes, had been a mercenary soldier, and he amassed great wealth (449–51). That his son followed in his military footsteps – not as a mercenary but as a citizen doing his military service – is a literary example that reflects the epigraphic material. Two general military stereotypes, the good citizen and the braggart, are found in the narrative setting of the home front. The measurement of a person's virtue is not his or her actions, but the appropriateness of those actions (*Eth. nic.* 4.4.4). When the soldier returns home, the courageous deeds on the battlefield are to be replaced by the appropriate duties of a citizen. The braggart refuses to relinquish his glory days, preferring a nostalgic past to an appropriate and productive present.

2.3.1 The Good Citizen

The soldiers on the home front are expected to hang up their armor and reenter the domestic world as citizens "who discharge adequately all the responsibilities the community places on them – maintaining a stable family situation and keeping their household secure despite any disruptions from external forces."[52] In this narrative setting, the ἀνὴρ ἀγαθός is the sincere man who is truthful in speech and behavior (*Eth. nic.* 4.7.7) and the one who is temperate in all his actions according to the law (*Eth. nic.* 5.1.14).

---

either in depopulated areas of Italy (*Ann.* 14.27) or in newly acquired Roman territories, where they were often a "civilizing" influence and a ready paramilitary force should barbarians cross the borders. For a discussion of the creation of veteran colonies for border defenses, see A. N. Sherwin-White, *The Roman Citizenship* (Oxford: Oxford University Press, 1973), 243–4. Unlike the legionary recruits, the auxiliary forces of the Roman army were non-citizens from various provinces throughout the Roman Empire. In all likelihood, the veterans of these auxiliary *cohortes* and *alae* did not receive land grants upon retirement, so they would have returned to their province of origin.

[51] Giovanni Lettich, *Itinerari Epigrafici Aquileiesi* (Trieste: Editreg SRL, 2003), no. 92.

[52] Major, "Menander in a Macedonian World," 69.

Polemon in Menander's *Perikeiromene* is a literary example of a soldier who integrated back into his home community, albeit awkwardly. Though scenes are missing, including the opening, other lines indicate the setting. A Corinthian street is the stage, and Polemon is a recently returned (250)[53] Corinthian soldier (9) of low rank (91). He purchases property in Corinth (25) and, at the play's conclusion, marries a fellow Corinthian (434–437), which are both indications that he had returned to his civic responsibilities.

Pitting an unnamed soldier against the aged Periphanes in *Epidicus*, Plautus develops both characters in opposition to each other. The boastful unnamed soldier meets his match when he encounters the old man who was a former soldier of distinction. Periphanes admonishes the soldier for his hubris, on the grounds that Periphanes' own acts of bravery far exceeded that of the soldier's (451–2). Periphanes has left his brash youth, and now behaves like an Athenian citizen, making financial arrangements with the soldier, restoring his lost daughter to her rightful place in the household, and manumitting his cunning, if not trustworthy, slave.

Livy introduces the epitome of the noble Roman soldier as a good citizen on the home front. Marcus Curtius distinguishes himself not on the foreign battlefield but in the middle of the Roman forum. The situation that catapults Curtius into glory results from an odd act of nature. A gaping chasm occurs in the center of the forum, and nothing has been able to fill the breech. After consulting the gods, the seers determine that Rome must sacrifice the source of its strength (7.6.2) if the Republic is to endure (7.6.3). Marcus Curtius, an excellent young soldier, chastises the seers for not recognizing that Rome's blessing is to be found in her arms and valor (7.6.3). After turning to the temples above the forum and the Capitol, he extends his hands first to heaven and then towards the chasm. Then he mounts a finely decorated horse and plunges into the gulf as the crowds throw offerings in after him. Livy portrays Curtius as an exemplary citizen who, after due reverence to the gods, sacrifices himself in order to save Rome.

In Xenophon of Ephesus's romance novel, the hero, Harbrocomes, is purchased by Araxus, a retired and elderly soldier (3.12.2), who has the misfortune of having an exceedingly ill-tempered wife (3.12.3). Xenophon portrays Araxus only briefly but shows him to be a kindly owner, who loves Harbrocomes as a son (3.12.4). The good citizen attends to his slaves as members of his family. Unfortunately for this veteran, his home front becomes a battlefield. The good citizen, Araxus, is killed by his not so noble wife, Cyno, who also loves the handsome Harbrocomes.

---

[53] Line designations for *Perikeiromene* are taken from Menander, *Menandri quae supersunt* (ed. and trans. Alfredus Koerte; Leipzig: Teubner, 1945).

2.3.2 The Braggart

Motive determines whether a soldier boasting in the army camp is termed a braggart or not. As Xenophon writes, the soldiers who exaggerate for the betterment of a story are not to be called ἀλαζόνες, unless their motive is not entertainment, but gain (*Cyr.* 2.2.12). When the narrative setting becomes the home front, the braggart exaggerates deeds of valor or claims abilities that he does not actually possess solely for his own aggrandizement. "If war appears on the comic stage, it appears perforce as *alazonia*, and the great soldier cannot be drawn otherwise than as the great boaster, the *miles gloriosus*."[54] Military characters in the comedies who fail to promote domestic harmony are viewed either as tragic, as in the case of Cleostratus in Menander's *Aspis*, who dies on the battlefield, leaving his family financially bereft, or as comic, as in the case of Bias in Menander's *Kolax*. For the non-citizen mercenary, the problem is similar. The foreign mercenary fails to behave appropriately as a ξένος, or stranger, exalting himself because of his wealth and military success. The historians rarely place a soldier on the home front, but when they do, like the comedians, they note the character's participation in civic and domestic life.

One of the earliest examples of the braggart soldier is found in the character of Lamachus who enters the stage as a military man, flaunting his plumed helmet and weapons. Lamachus is the stereotypical warmonger whom the peace-seeking Dicaeopolis deplores. As his slave reports, Lamachus is a terror, brandishing a gorgonian-headed shield (964–5). As "the Great Battler," as his name indicates, prepares to march, Dicaeopolis prepares for the festival. Aristophanes uses σύγκρισις to his comic benefit. The dialogue between the two evidences the author's political point: festivals are better than battles (1094–1142). The dramatic action further substantiates the point when Lamachus is injured. He steps on a stake, an ignominious injury that he then wears like a badge of honor. The true hero is Dicaeopolis, whose private treaty of peace provides him with wealth, women, and wine, while the injured warmonger is carried off to the healer.

Plautus set the Roman standard for the braggart warrior when he created Pyrgopolynices in *Miles Gloriosus*. Pyrgopolynices is a soldier of undistinguished rank, who carries off a young woman, Philocomasium, from Athens to his home in Ephesus. Pyrgopolynices vacillates between self-aggrandizement and the solicitation of fawning sycophants. He suffers woefully under the affliction of his own beauty: "It really is such an affliction to be so handsome" and "That I may be no handsomer than I am! Ah yes, my beauty is an endless source of trouble to me" (*Mil. glor.* 68, 1086–7 [Nixon, LCL]). He relishes the retelling of his mighty deeds and the counting (however inflated) of the seven thousand he has slain. He fulfills his current military duty by paying for recruits

---

[54] Hanson, "The Glorious Military," 68.

for King Seleucus instead of going himself. His parasitic side-kick acknowledges the colossal nature of the soldier's self-promotion (21-3). Pyrgopolynices cannot help his marvelous nature. He is the grandson of Venus (1265) and favored by the gods – Mars, the god of war, as well as Venus, the goddess of love (1382). Milphidippa, the servant of a woman feigning interest in the soldier, lauds his god-like beauty and bravery in encomiastic terms:

Mercy me, sir, it's no wonder you do set store by yourself – a man so handsome and so famous for his bravery and beauty and daring deeds! Was ever any man more worthy to be a god? (1041–4 [Nixon, LCL])

The conniving servant, Palaestrio, makes the most accurate assessment of the soldier's intellect: *Nullumst hoc stolidius saxum* (1024). The soldier is dumb as a post. Indeed, the assessment of others falls woefully short of the soldier's self-perception: others view him as a bragging nuisance and a perfumed fornicator (923–4). In short, his character is vain, absorbed with his own accomplishments, and easily misled, but he thinks himself the offspring of the gods and, therefore, the best example of both beauty and bravery. The one who would capture and kill thousands on the battlefield is himself captured by the snares of his own ignorance. His sword and shield afford little protection, for the rules of engagement on the domestic front favor cunning over brawn and sleight of hand over frontal assault. The returned soldier becomes the *miles gloriosus* when he fails to recognize that a different war on the home front calls for a different set of weapons. The character of Pyrgopolynices is the most fully developed of Plautus's soldiers, while the others dutifully line up in his shadow.

Another of Plautus's soldiers, Stratophanes, whose name means "parader of armies," is a Babylonian soldier, again of no distinguished rank. In *Truculentus*, he returns home to his lover who, after ten months' absence, presents him with his alleged son. The entrance of Stratophanes on stage counters that of Pyrgopolynices. Stratophanes claims that his hands and not his mouth should announce his successes (483). He does not seek the eloquent praise of the citizens but rather believes his valor speaks fluently for itself (494). But his modesty is false, and as soon as he learns about the birth of his son, his braggadocious nature becomes apparent (505ff). Like Pyrgopolynices, Stratophanes lets his self-aggrandizement overshadow his good sense, and he fails to recognize the ploy of his deceptive lover.

"Renowned of battle," Cleomachus of *Bacchides* is less showy than Pyrgopolynices and Stratophanes, but, nonetheless, he is threatening and greedy, willingly selling Bacchis, a young woman whom he had purchased in Ephesus. A similar tale is told in *Curculio*, where a soldier intends to buy a young woman who turns out to be his sister. Although Therapontigonus[55] is less of a braggart

---

[55] Webster argues that the name, "Therapontigonus" is a Plautine fabrication (*Studies in Later Greek Comedy* [Manchester: Manchester University Press, 1970], 197).

than Plautus's other military characters, he threatens greater violence. Enraged when he discovers that his money has been swindled, he announces that he who had forced kings to obey him has now become a laughing stock (556–7). His successes in battle and the number he had slain are proof that he will resort to violence unless the young woman is returned to him (566–7). When Therapontigonus finally confronts the man from whom he planned to purchase the woman, he promises to turn him into a javelin and send him off a catapult if the man does not repay him (689–90). In *Poenulus*, the soldier Anthemonides, slays 60,000 flying men in one day, a feat his hearers disbelieve (470–3). He casts a string of obscenities at the father of his lover, whom he mistakes as a rival (1306ff), and in the end, unlike Plautus's other soldiers, Anthemonides receives the woman he loves. The *miles gloriosus* of Plautus's plays is situated in a domestic setting-turned battlefield. The enemies in his midst are his own cunning servants, who quickly unmask his bravado. Though he feigns the blessings of Venus and the strength of Mars, he is easily duped. His failure to see his own limitations blinds him to the deceit of others.

In Terence's *Eunuchus*, Thraso, like some of Plautus's soldiers, makes an appearance late in the play, not arriving on stage until the third act. And similar to some of Plautus's soldiers, he has purchased a girl while on his journeys. He plans to present her as a gift to his lover, Thais, if only she would abnegate her other suitor, Phaedria. Thraso is vain, notes his parasite, Gnatho (248). He demonstrates his vanity when he enters the stage and claims that he possesses a gift that graces everything he does (391ff). He brags not so much about his military endeavors as about his clever repartee at the dinner parties of significant men (421). In addition to his vanity and braggadocious nature, Thraso is also gullible, a trait readily apparent in Plautus's braggarts. A parody of the general's attaché, his parasite repeatedly appeals to his vanity while laughing behind his back (425ff). The soldier does appear a bit skillful when he plans an assault on Thais' house (772), and gathers an army from among his servants (784). Thraso is also wealthy and able to provide not only superior gifts but also excellent dinners (1080). Despite these points, Thraso is essentially weak. He is a foreigner who has no political clout (758ff) and who lacks courage (618). Rather than enhancing his status on the home front, the braggart veteran becomes the target of ridicule and deception.

2.3.3 Conclusion: Honorable and Dishonorable Discharge

The ἀνὴρ ἀγαθός on the homefront is the veteran soldier who no longer seeks glory in battle, but desires honor in civic settings. His speech and manner of life are truthful and his behavior temperate. Where he once offered obedience to authority, he now expects it from his family and servants. He has made the transition from warrior to citizen. His counterpart is the ἀλαζών.

The stereotype of the *miles gloriosus* sets up an expectation that the returned soldier will not integrate back into the domestic field without a fight. The battlefield is now the home front, but the sword and shield about which the *miles gloriosus* so boasts are of little use. The rules of engagement have changed. In the comedies, the braggart warrior is bested by cunning slaves and taken captive by love. He is outmaneuvered by cleverness and led into an ambush by his own ignorance. Though he may have been a hero on the battle-field, he is incapacitated by the domestic scene and unable to transition from one setting and its expectations of success to another.

3. Evaluation of Literary Military Stereotypes

For the most part, portrayals of military characters in ancient literature are one-dimensional, and develop little over the course of the story. As discussed in the previous chapter, this seemingly static presentation, in part, results from an ancient understanding that one's moral character was fixed at birth and be-comes evident in adulthood. Characterization is thus concerned with the individual's demonstration of ἀρετή, rather than a presentation of personality. So it is not surprising that literary portrayals appear as personifications of virtues and vices.[56]

The previous examples of military stereotypes were drawn from the author's presentation of the soldier's dominant attribute manifested in a particular narrative setting. The comedians and satirists tend to portray military characters as personifications of vices. The historiographers are more balanced. When they do characterize a "bad" soldier, they often mention some talent in addition to his vice. The purpose of stereotypical depictions is to direct the audience's assessment of the character.

3.1 Virtuous Military Stereotypes

Aristotle defines virtue with respect to the point between deficiency and excess. "Concerning then fears and boldness, the mean is courage" (*Eth. nic.* 2.7.2 [Rackham, LCL]). The good soldier in the field exemplifies courage, being neither fearful nor overly bold. In the Roman Army, he is an example of *virtus*, fortified by *disciplina*.[57] The stereotype is not limited to the higher officers. Foot soldiers, decurions, centurions, tribunes and generals can all be portrayed as brave warriors.

---

[56] The characterization of virtue and vice has a long literary history. For a discussion on the formation of character and its importance in Greek literature and thought, see Stephen Halliwell, "Traditional Greek Conceptions of Character," in *Characterization and Individuality in Greek Literature* (ed. Christopher Pelling; Oxford: Clarendon Press, 1990).

[57] Lendon, *Soldiers and Ghosts*, 221.

The ἀνὴρ ἀγαθός may also display εὐσέβεια. Reverence towards one's gods, εὐσέβεια, finds its Latin equivalent in *pietas*. Cicero defines this virtue as "that which urges us to carry out responsibility to country or parents or others related by blood."[58] Elsewhere Cicero adds that *pietas* is justice towards the gods (*Nat. d.* 1.116). Augustus assumes *pietas* as a central value, creating legislation designed to restore the Roman family[59] and promoting appropriate reverence for the gods.[60] The soldier demonstrating εὐσέβεια or *pietas* is much less frequent in literature than the stereotype of the brave warrior, since piety is demonstrated towards one's family and homeland, and the soldier is most often far from both.

The good soldier in the province is cast as a rescuer, who saves those in distress, similar to our more modern stereotype of the "knight in shining armor." Additionally, these military characters extend friendship to the one rescued, inviting him to dine at their tables and providing for his needs. Nothing, it would seem, is able to stop this virtuous soldier, particularly when he is protecting the province from brigands. Nothing, that is, until he happens to save a damsel in distress. Not even the war god Mars can shield the rescuing soldier from the arrows of Eros, for every rescuer portrayed is struck down by love. Polyidus, Charmides, the Egyptian soldier who accidentally poisons the object of his affections, and the unnamed soldier in Petronius's Widow of Ephesus are all soldiers on assignment who become captives of love.

The noble soldier on the home front is the good citizen concerned with the affairs of his home and city, promoting honor and avoiding dishonor. A military character exemplifies the good citizen when he finds that the source of honor now resides in his domestic sphere. Livy portrays the noble actions of the soldier cum citizen when Marcus Curtius sacrifices his life to save the city of Rome. In the comedies, the good citizen is concerned with his sons' success and his daughters' safety, while protecting his fortunes from his wily servants.

3.2 Ignoble Military Stereotypes

The heirs of Thersites fall far below the virtuous mean of bravery. They are portrayed variously as a coward, a greedy man and a mutineer. Few cowards are personified in the literary texts, but the definition of a coward is clearly stated by the historiographers. The coward avoids the fight, but willingly takes credit for any successes.

Particularly for the hoplite of the Greek phalanx, the spoils of war were the wages of soldiers. Roman legionaries were paid a base salary, but, nonetheless, all soldiers looked forward to the abundant booty to be pillaged from a sacked

---

[58] Cicero, *De Invention. De Optino Genere Oratorum. Topica* (LCL; H. M. Hubbell; Cambridge, MA: Harvard University Press, 1969), 2.65.

[59] D'Angelo, "Εὐσέβεια."

[60] According to the *Res Gestae*, Augustus restored eighty-two temples in Rome (20).

city. To be labeled as such, the greedy soldier must be excessive in his desire for gain. He tries to make a profit anywhere he can (*Eth. eud.* 2.3.7). As Polybius recounts, after raping the captive noblewoman, the centurion loses his head when he ignores personal risk to ransom her for a profit.

The mutinous orator presumes the right of the commander to address the troops. Like their literary ancestor, Thersites, mutineers use speech to incite the ranks to disobedience. Percennius, having been an actor, is well trained for the part of inciting a crowd (Tacitus, *Ann.* 1.16). Vibulenus climbs upon the shoulders of fellow soldiers, mirroring a general's stance on the βῆμα before his *adlocutio*. However, if a soldier's speech is a call to arms for his compatriots (Titus Pedanius, Livy 25.14.7, Gaius Volusius, Tacitus, *Hist.* 3.29), it evidences not the vice of boldness but the mark of bravery often leading to a noble death. The soldier on assignment in the province is most often depicted as a violent and gruff man, easily provoked to anger. A product of imperial writers, these soldiers no longer represent the noble imperial army expanding the frontiers of Rome or assuring the *pax Romana*. They are individuals who abuse provincials and fear their officers.

The final stereotype, the braggart warrior, is synonymous with ἀλαζονεία. Where ἀλήθεια is the central virtue of the good citizen, the braggart embodies the opposite. An element of truth may have once been the kernel of his tale, but his boasts have grown so outrageous as to be laughable (Pyrgopolinices' sex appeal) and ridiculous (Anthemonides' slaying of 60,000 flying men!) to everyone, it would seem, but the *miles gloriosus* himself.

The military stereotypes are positive when the characters' most prominent trait is virtuous. The examples of the good soldier, the rescuer, and the good citizen compare to qualities that Aristotle lists as belonging to his virtuous mean.[61] The undisciplined man, the brute, and the braggart warrior fall on either side of Aristotle's mean. Literary soldiers are occasionally depicted as possessing other attributes in addition to their dominant characteristic. A good soldier may also possess vices, though to a lesser degree. He could be excessive in violence or overly-zealous. Likewise, a negatively stereotyped character may still demonstrate some virtuous qualities. Spendius may be a mutineer but he is also touted for his valor.

---

[61] The virtue of εὐσέβεια or *pietas* and the activities of the rescuer are not part of either Aristotle's or Theophrastus's lists of virtues or vices, but both gain importance in Republican and Imperial Rome. See Andrew Wallace-Hadrill, "The Emperor and His Virtues," *Historia* 30 (1981): 298–323; J. R. Fears, "The Cult of Virtues and Roman Imperial Ideology," *ANRW* II, no. 17.2 (1981); and Paul Zanker, *The Power of Images in the Age of Augustus* (Alan Shapiro; Ann Arbor: University of Michigan Press, 1988).

My task in the next chapter is to determine where the military characters in Luke-Acts line up in comparison to these literary τόποι. Luke's use and manipulation of military stereotypes are indicative of the function of soldiers and officers within the larger narrative.

Chapter 4

Stereotypical or Against the Grain?
The Portrayals of Military Characters in Luke-Acts

1. Introduction

In his characterization of soldiers, Luke demonstrates that he is familiar with the various stereotypes found in Greco-Roman literature. He depicts soldiers who are known for their brutality and greed, soldiers who are obedient, and soldiers who rescue those in need. He also, on occasion, paints a portrait of a soldier that is contrary to the stereotype. Paradoxically, some Lucan military characters appear to seek repentance for their abusive behavior (Luke 3:14). While the soldiers at the cross join in the mocking (Luke 23:36–37), the centurion declares Jesus δίκαιος (Luke 23:47). Julius of the Augustan cohort may ignore Paul's suggestions, yet he exhibits φιλανθρωπία towards his prisoner (Acts 27:3). This chapter examines the depictions of soldiers and centurions in Luke-Acts and demonstrates that Luke knows and builds on the stereotypes found in Greco-Roman literature. Further investigation evaluates whether Luke perpetuates the literary stereotypes or contradicts them. Luke creates a more complex portrayal of the centurion in Luke 7 and the centurion of Caesarea in Acts 10, where he not only employs the stereotypes but transforms them. Both of these characters will be studied in the next chapter.

The author of Luke-Acts stands apart from the other gospel writers in both the number of military characters he mentions and the details he includes in their characterization. Luke recognizes distinctions among military units: auxiliary cohorts (Acts 10:1; 21:31; 27:1), Herodian soldiers (Luke 3:14; 23:11) and Roman legions (Luke 8:30). His military characters are of various ranks: foot soldier (Luke 3:14; 7:8; Acts 10:7; 28:16), centurions (Luke 7:2; 23:47; Acts 10:1; 22:25; 27:1), and tribunes commanding a thousand men (Acts 21:31; 25:23). As seen in other ancient literature, the officers are the most developed military characters in Luke-Acts. The centurion of Capernaum (Luke 7), Cornelius the centurion of Caesarea (Acts 10), the Tribune Claudius Lysias (Acts 21:31ff), and Julius the centurion of the Augustan cohort (Acts 27) are described directly by the narrator and indirectly by their actions and the dialogue with others. In comparison, the characterizations of the common soldiers are one-dimensional, relying almost exclusively on the authorial audience's knowledge of military stereotypes.

Luke expressly states that others have attempted to pen a διήγησις and that his will be an accurate (ἀκριβῶς) and ordered (καθεξῆς) account that confirms the certainty (τὴν ἀσφάλειαν) of what Theophilus has been taught (Luke 1:1–4). Both the Gospel and Acts reference Roman emperors, administrators, and client kings in order to situate the narrative within a specific historical setting (Luke 1:5; 3:1–2; Acts 18:12). Such attention to actual political chronology suggests that Luke is demonstrating his claim of accuracy. Perhaps the distinctions Luke makes among the military characters are another attempt to create a realistic setting so that his reader or auditor may know the steadfastness of his words. Certainly Luke appears to present an accurate portrait of the military in the region of Judea, in which the majority of his military characters appear. Since ἔνδοξα allows an audience to reasonably expect that literary soldiers behave similarly to actual soldiers, a brief introduction to the role and function of the military in the provinces will provide a measuring stick against which to assess Luke's portrayal.

1.1 The Province of Judea

With the exception of Paul's travels to Rome under military guard, soldiers appear in Luke-Acts only in the narrative setting of the province of Judea. Historically, Judea came under direct Roman administration after the deposition of Archelaus in 6 C.E. Except for a brief period under Herod Agrippa I (41–44 C.E.),[1] military prefects and then civilian procurators managed the province, though they remained subject to the legate of the larger province of Syria.[2] As Strabo recounted, Augustus kept those provinces most in need of military oversight under his direct control (17.3.25). The remaining provinces, pacified after the Civil Wars, were under senatorial administration.[3] Until the breakout of the First Jewish War, Judea was a backwater province of little importance. Thus its Roman appointees were notably of lower rank and status. Hall proposes that this lack of leadership ability on the part of the prefects adversely affected the administration of the province.[4]

---

[1] After the death of Herod Agrippa, Claudius reinstated Judea as a Roman province (*B.J.* 2.20).

[2] John F. Hall, "The Roman Province of Judea: A Historical Overview," *BYU Studies Quarterly* 36:3 (1996-1997): 329. On provincial administration also see Millar, *Roman Near East: 31 BC – AD 337* (Cambridge, MA: Harvard University Press, 1993), 31-36.

[3] Cities within the provinces often operated separately from the province, some having their own city constitutions. See Fergus Millar, "Empire and City, Augustus to Julian: Obligations, Excuses and Status," *JRS* 73 (1983): 76–96. For information on imperial administration during the Flavian period, see G. P. Burton, "Proconsuls, Assizes and the Administration of Justice," *JRS* 65 (1975): 92–106. The province of Egypt had a unique administration. See Alan K. Bowman and Dominic Rathbone, "Cities and Administration in Roman Egypt," *JRS* 82 (1992): 107–27.

[4] Hall, "The Roman Province of Judea," 329.

To enforce Rome's edicts, the prefect of Judea had cohorts of regular and auxiliary troops at his disposal, but the closest legions were stationed in Syria and under the jurisdiction of the Syrian legate.[5] However, a moderate military force was able to uphold the *pax Romana* in outlying provinces largely due to the reputation of the army for swift and thorough retaliation, and, in some cases, the memory of such havoc remained vivid in the minds of the conquered peoples.

Reporting the speech of Agrippa II, Josephus demonstrates how one client king may have kept his people in check under the shadow of Rome. The might of Rome's army should deter acts of war, proffered Agrippa II, in an attempt to prevent a revolt in Jerusalem (*B.J.* 2.345–402). The conflict began when the procurator Florus had ignored the violent altercation in Caesarea between the city's Jewish and Gentile residents (*B.J.* 2.284–292), and then had set his sights on the treasury in the Temple at Jerusalem. Agrippa's own sister, Bernice, had been nearly killed by the soldiers as they pillaged the city (*B.J.* 2.312). Hoping to quell the revolutionaries and calm the elders, Agrippa gave a speech to the residents of Jerusalem.

Agrippa outlined the various ἔθνη that Rome had subdued. The people of the Bosphorus and those around Pontus were now subject to 3,000 soldiers and 40 battleships (*B.J.* 2.367). Likewise the Thracians, whose land took five days to march through, were subdued by 2,000 Romans (*B.J.* 2.368). Even the Dalmatians, who had often fought for freedom, were pacified under a single legion (*B.J.* 2.370). Similarly, the Gauls allowed themselves to be a source of revenue for the Romans with only 1,200 soldiers stationed over them. This occurred, Agrippa announced, not because the Gauls were ignoble, but because they were overwhelmed by the power and good fortune of the Romans (*B.J.* 2.373). For those Jews undeterred, Agrippa ended with the example of Britain, where, like Jerusalem, the inhabitants thought a wall was an extensive defense against Rome's attack. After the British revolt, the entire island was subjected to four legions (*B.J.* 2.379). As Agrippa recognized, Rome's reputation maximized the benefit of its military.

Only during Herod Archelaus's ascension to the throne, and in response to the First Jewish Revolt, were legions quartered in Judea (*B.J.* 2.3.1; 18.9).[6] In Luke-Acts, the only mention of a Roman legion occurs in Luke 8:30, where the Gerasene demoniac names himself λεγιών, but this is borrowed from Mark 5:9. Most of the military officers and soldiers in the two volumes seem to be auxiliaries,[7] which is in keeping with the textual and inscriptional evidence for the first half of the first century in Palestine, the setting for Luke's narrative.

---

[5] Josephus reports that under Augustus, three legions were stationed in Syria (*A.J.* 17.286). Under Tiberius, the number increased to four (Tact. *Ann.* 4.5).

[6] T. R. S. Broughton, "The Roman Army," 439.

[7] Saddington, "The Administration and the Army in Judaea," 33–40.

1.2 Roman Auxiliary Cohorts

The auxiliary forces of the Roman army were a significant source of manpower, perhaps nearly equal to the number of legionary troops.[8] Like the growth of the professional legionary army, the auxiliary developed over the first two centuries of the common era. Even the term, *auxilia* was in flux. According to Tacitus, it could refer to a detachment of professional troops (*delectis auxiliis, Ann.* 6.41.1) or those supplied by a client king (*auxilia regum, Ann.* 13.4). Soldiers recruited from provinces were also considered *auxilia*.[9] A former soldier under Augustus, Velleius Paterculus used the terms *cohors* and *ala* to refer exclusively to the auxiliary.[10] This language is used on auxiliary diplomas as well. Greek authors referred to the auxiliary as σπεῖρα (Strabo, 17.1.12; Matt 27:24; Mark 15:16; John 18:3, 12; Acts 10:1) or σπεῖρα πεζῶν (*B.J.* 2.500) or by the name of their place of origin (τὴν τῶν Σεβαστηνῶν ἴλην καὶ πεζῶν τέσσαρα).[11] Auxiliary cohorts were also called by their weaponry or armor; for example: archers (*sagittarii, Ann.* 2.17.6) and light armed-troops (*leuis armature, Ann.* 2.8.4). Provincial units often retained the name of the region from which the cohort had been originally recruited. For example, Tacitus records the presence of the *Raetorum Vindelicorumque et Gallicae cohortes* (*Ann.* 2.17). But by the mid-first century, the cohort's ranks were replenished with new recruits from its present location and not necessarily from its place of origin.[12] The Nabatean Proculus joined the *Cohors II Italica* when it was stationed in Syria.[13]

Members of the provincial auxiliary, for the most part, did not possess Roman citizenship.[14] Claudius granted citizenship upon retirement after 25 years of service, and also gave the right of *connubium* or legal Roman marriage to auxiliary veterans (Dio 76.15.2). The granting of citizenship gave rise to the creation of *diplomatae* or discharge papers, actually carved on two bronze

---

[8] According to Tacitus, the auxiliary cohorts may not have been much smaller in size or strength than the legions but their numbers were not readily known because their location and size often changed, or the entire cohort would be dissolved. (*Ann.* 4.4)

[9] Denis B. Saddington, *The Development of the Roman Auxiliary Forces from Caesar to Vespasian (49 B.C. – A.D. 79)* (Harare, Zimbabwe: University of Zimbabwe, 1982), 36.

[10] Velleius Paterculus, *The Caesarian and Augustan Narrative (2.41–93)* (trans. A.J. Woodman; New York: Cambridge University Press, 1983).

[11] Josephus, *A.J.* 20.122. The author of Acts of the Apostles may be referring to the same cohort (σπείρης Σεβαστῆς) in Acts 27:1.

[12] Anthony Birley, *Garrison Life at Vindolanda* (Charleston, SC: Tempus Publishing, 2002), 41–42.

[13] *Inscriptiones Latinae Selectae* no. 9168.

[14] However, some citizen cohorts did exist. The title *civium Romanorum* in the cohort's title may indicate a band of Roman citizens who formed an auxiliary cohort rather than join an existing legion. After the Flavian period, the title *civium Romanorum* could also indicate a grant of citizenship given to the whole cohort for outstanding service rendered. See Michael P. Speidel, "Citizen Cohorts in the Roman Imperial Army. New Data on the Cohorts Apula, Campana, and III Camestris," *TAPA* 106 (1976): 339–40.

plates.[15] The possibility of citizenship may have motivated voluntary enlistment. However, unlike their legionary brothers, auxiliary veterans may not have received the *praemia militiae* or retirement pensions, nor an allotment of land upon discharge.[16]

From the time of Augustus until that of Trajan, auxiliary cohorts were not stationed permanently outside their home province,[17] which bore the cost and burden for maintaining its auxiliary. In addition to assessing taxes, the census of the population set the number of cohort units and yearly intake of auxiliary recruits.[18] Certain tribes seem to have been exempt from taxes, in turn for which they were expected to supply greater numbers of soldiers during times of battle (Tacitus, *Germ.* 29). Although some cohorts may have always retained indigenous leadership, most auxiliary troops were under the command of Roman officers, who were to encourage and enforce military discipline (Tacitus, *Agr.* 28). Though, as their name suggests, one would expect the *auxilia* to supplement the work of the legions, the auxiliary were often used as "cannon fodder."[19] In fact, Tacitus once boasted that Rome achieved victories without the loss of Roman blood, because the non-Roman auxiliary troops formed the first line of battle (*Agr.* 35.2)!

Due to fragmentary and sometimes contradictory evidence, the number of auxiliary cohorts and their respective sizes are debated. Generally, auxiliary forces were divided into mounted (*ala*) and infantry (*cohors*) troops. The *cohortes equitatae* were partially mounted. The cohort likely consisted of six centuries of 80 men, though its official name, *cohors quingenaria* indicates a number of 500 (Hyg. *De met. castr.* 28).

Auxiliary cohorts were commanded by a centurion who was either drawn from the ranks of the auxiliary and of provincial status, or who had been transferred from the legion and was thus a Roman citizen. Though Sherwin-White asserts, "There can be no certainty that any of the centurions in the stories of

---

[15] The plates were engraved with the discharge formula, the recipient's name, commanding officer, date and witnesses. The veteran could purchase copies of the bronze tablets, but the originals were placed in the Temple of the Deified Augustus and Minerva in Rome (Webster, *The Roman Imperial Army of the First and Second Centuries A.D.* [3rd ed.; Norman, OK: University of Oklahoma, 1998], 143).

[16] Brunt argues that it is unlikely that auxiliary soldiers serving side by side with legionaries would not have complained if they had received fewer benefits than the legionaries. However, the only evidence of an auxiliary taking part in the establishment of a colony is an inscription found in the Neronian colony of Antium (*ILS*. 2574). See P. A. Brunt, "Pay and Superannuation in the Roman Army," *Papers of the British School at Rome* 18 (1950): 66.

[17] The emergence of established frontiers "resulted in more and more units being assigned to the virtually permanent occupation of a particular fort unless transferred" (Denis B. Saddington, "The Development of the Roman Auxiliary Forces," 198).

[18] Graham Webster, *The Roman Imperial Army*, 142.

[19] Saddington, *The Development of the Roman Auxiliary*, 180.

Acts or Gospels was a Roman,"[20] Saddington, proposes that the centurions of auxiliary cohorts, particularly in the early imperial period, would be Roman citizens.[21] They may have served their twenty-five years as an auxiliary soldier and received a citizenship diploma before being promoted to the centurionate. This scenario could explain the age of several centurions who were promoted after a lengthy military career.[22] The statement made by the centurion of Luke 23:47 has greater authority coming from a Roman citizen than a local auxiliary provincial. The discourse between Claudius Lysias and Paul on the topic of citizenship suggests that Luke would have considered it significant that his officers possessed this Roman privilege, particularly because he regards them as imperial representatives.

The region of Judea was unusual in that its leaders were responsible for the recruitment and maintenance of its auxiliary troops from among the non-Jewish residents. Josephus recounts that Jews were exempt from military duty and were not obliged to quarter soldiers (*A.J.* 14.204–205).[23] The auxiliary army of Judea was, for the most part, made up of local Gentiles and was "only 'Roman' in the sense that it was organized and commanded by Rome."[24] The auxiliary cohort, composed of Gentile residents from Caesarea and its sister city, Sebaste, was stationed in Caesarea, where it responded inappropriately to the death of Agrippa, nearly costing itself removal to Pontus.[25] Sometime later, this same cohort joined forces with the Gentile residents of Caesarea and attacked the Jewish residents. What began as a controversy over equal civic rights erupted into a violent brawl (*A.J.* 20.176). The procurator Felix allowed the soldiers to pillage the houses of the Jews (*A.J.* 20.177). Some of the Jews appealed to Felix and persuaded him to call off the soldiers (*A.J.* 20.178). When Festus replaced Felix, an embassy of Caesarean Jews petitioned Nero that Felix be held accountable. Unfortunately, not only did Felix go unpunished, but Gentile resi-

---

[20] A. N. Sherwin-White, *Roman Society and Roman Law in the New Testament* (Oxford: Clarendon Press, 1963), 156.

[21] Saddington, "Roman Military and Administrative Personnel in the New Testament," 2414.

[22] Paul A. Holder, *Studies in the Auxilia of the Roman Army from Augustus to Trajan* (Oxford: BAR, 1980), 86.

[23] Though Jews could claim an exemption from military service, some Jews did join the imperial ranks. "That these Jewish soldiers actually thought of themselves as Jews is clear from the fact that they are mentioned as such in their inscriptions, were active as officials and members of synagogues, and were buried in Jewish cemeteries with religious symbols on their tombstones and sarcophagi" (Andrew J. Schoenfeld, "Sons of Israel in Caesar's Service: Jewish Soldiers in the Roman Military," *Shofar: An Interdisciplinary Journal of Jewish Studies* 24 [2006]: 126).

[24] Saddington, "The Administration and the Army in Judaea," 36.

[25] Josephus *A.J.* 19.354-365. The local troops were able to stay their immediate removal from Judea, but Vespasian transferred them later.

dents of Caesarea persuaded Nero to nullify the rights that the Jews had previously enjoyed. According to Josephus, the abuse of the Jews by the soldiers under Felix's command and the subsequent rescindment of rights led to the outbreak of the First Jewish Revolt (*A.J.* 20. 182).[26] These particular accounts of the auxiliary in Judea corroborate literary portrayals of soldiers in the provinces.

2. The Characterization of Soldiers and Officers in the Gospel of Luke

In most of Luke-Acts, the soldiers and officers depicted are on assignment in the province of Judea, stationed either in Jerusalem or in Caesarea. The temporal setting of Luke-Acts is prior to the outbreak of the First Jewish Revolt, and the narrator gives no indication of tension between Gentile auxiliary and Jewish provincials. But Luke recognizes that the actual audience and his authorial audience would have been aware of the revolt and its harsh suppression (Luke 19:43–44; 21:20, 24), so that they likely held expectations of violent and brutish behavior from the soldiers – expectations that Luke invokes and occasionally overturns in his literary portrayal of soldiers and officers.

2.1 The Soldiers Questioning John the Baptist: Luke 3:14

After situating the opening scene of Chapter 3 within the political and religious framework of Rome and Judea, Luke introduces the first soldiers encountered in the two-volume work. They appear among the crowd that has gathered at the Jordan River where John is preaching a baptism of repentance for the forgiveness of sins. The Lucan version differs from Mark most notably in the characters who come to John the Baptist. Mark limits them by geography (πᾶσα ἡ Ἰουδαία χώρα καὶ οἱ Ἱεροσολυμῖται πάντες, Mark 1:5). Matthew categorizes them, rather, by their religious affiliation (πολλοὺς τῶν Φαρισαίων καὶ Σαδδουκαίων, Matt 3:7). But Luke distinguishes those in the crowd by their economic status:[27] those wealthy enough to have more than what they need (ὁ

---

[26] Josephus can portray soldiers more positively, but these positive portrayals are often of legionaries, and the narrative setting is no longer "on assignment in the provinces" but active duty on the battlefield. For example, Arius *(B.J.* 2.63, *A.J.* 17.282), Liberalius (*B.J.* 6.262), and Furius and Fabius (*A.J.* 14.69-70).

[27] Luke-Acts contains numerous exhortations about the appropriate use of money: the disciples left everything, Luke 5:11, 28; the admonition not to invite the rich but the poor to dinner, Luke 14:12–14; the widow's mite, Luke 21:1–4; Judas's betrayal for money, Acts 1:18; Ananias and Sapphira, Acts 5:1–11; the anger of the Philippian slave-owners (Acts 16:16–19); and Ephesian silversmiths when their livelihoods are threatened (Acts 19:25) .

ἔχων δύο χιτῶνας, Luke 3:11), tax collectors (τελῶναι, Luke 3:12), and those doing military service (στρατευόμενοι, Luke 3:14). Luke apparently follows Q in vv. 7–9 and 15–18, but he redacts vv. 10–14 from another source or independently creates the three part τί ποιήσωμεν and its inquirers out of whole cloth.[28]

Luke 3:10–14 is programmatic for the Gospel, introducing both a Lucan theme about appropriate use of possessions,[29] and indicating the demands of discipleship. The crowds are consistently the sympathetic listeners of Jesus (Luke 4:42; 5:15; 7:24; 8:42–45), whom Jesus welcomes (οἱ δὲ ὄχλοι γνόντες ἠκολούθησαν αὐτῷ· καὶ ἀποδεξάμενος αὐτοὺς ἐλάλει αὐτοῖς περὶ τῆς βασιλείας τοῦ θεοῦ, καὶ τοὺς χρείαν ἔχοντας θεραπείας ἰᾶτο, 9:11) and teaches (Luke 5:3; 12:54; 14:25). The ὄχλοι respond with amazement at the casting out of a demon (Luke 11:14), and Jesus is interested in their understanding of his identity (Luke 9:18).

Those possessing more than one garment foreshadow what Jesus will command of his disciples, who, if their coat is taken, are to give up their χιτών as well (Luke 6:29). Jesus sends the twelve out with strict orders not to have two χιτῶνες (Luke 9:3). In Luke 9:12–17, those listening to Jesus have no food, and he tells his disciples to feed them (δότε αὐτοῖς ὑμεῖς φαγεῖν, v. 13). Appropriate use of clothing and food not only distinguish those coming to John for baptism but it is also the expectation for the disciples of Jesus. The summary in Acts 2 may indicate that a community of believers continued to uphold the expectations after the resurrection (Acts 2:45). Sharing of possessions in the Gospel is

---

[28] Most scholars accept that Luke 3:10–14 is not from Q (see W. Grundmann, *Das Evangelium nach Lukas* [THKNT 3; Berlin: Evangelische Verlagsanstalt, 1966], 103; Joseph Fitzmyer, *The Gospel According to Luke I–IX* [AB; New York: Doubleday, 1981], 464; James M. Robinson, et al., *The Critical Edition of Q* [Hermeneia; Minneapolis: Fortress Press, 2000]; and François Bovon, *Luke 1* [Minneapolis, MN: Fortress Press, 2002], 118). However, Marshall argues that the vocabulary does not reflect unique Lucan material, nor does his special source contain traditions about John, hence it must derive from the Q source (*Commentary on Luke*, 142). Likewise, Plummer (*The Gospel According to Saint Luke* [5th; ICC; Edinburgh: T & T Clark, 1901], 90) and Schürmann (*Das Lukasevangelium* [HTKNT; Freiburg: Herder, 1969], 169) claim verses 10–14 originated with Q. According to these scholars, Matthew chose to omit the verses so as to leave all ethical instructions to Jesus. As will be shown, Luke's penchant for reworking the military characters found in his sources suggests that these verses with their repentant soldiers came from the hand of the author.

[29] See Johnson for a thorough analysis of the Lucan concern for possessions (Luke Timothy Johnson, *The Literary Function of Possessions in Luke-Acts* [SBL Dissertation Series; Missoula, Mt: Scholars Press, 1977]). Also Philip Francis Esler, *Community and Gospel in Luke-Acts* (Cambridge: Cambridge University Press, 1987); and Halvor Moxnes, *The Economy of the Kingdom. Social Conflict and Economic Relations in Luke's Gospel* (Philadelphia: Fortress Press, 1988), particularly 109-126 and 139-153.

the response to conversion. Sharing of possessions in Acts of the Apostles becomes an example of a community of the converted, created by the Spirit.[30]

Like the crowd, tax collectors in the Gospel are portrayed as responding positively to Jesus. Levi, the τελώνης, becomes a disciple in Luke 5:27, precisely because, as Luke states, Jesus did not come to call the righteous but to call tax collectors and sinners (Luke 5:32). Luke casts the parable of the Pharisee and the tax collector (Luke 18:9–14) as a narrative retelling of that same statement. Tax collectors joins the crowds, who draw near to Jesus in order to hear him (Luke 15:1). Like the tax collectors seeking the baptism of John, tax collectors encountering Jesus also make some form of reparation. Zacchaeus gives half of his wealth to the poor and makes four-fold restitution if he has defrauded anyone (Luke 19:8).

Luke introduces the last group that comes to John, calling them στρατευόμενοι (a term he uses to describe the soldiers who rescue Paul, Acts 23:27). He may mean Jewish soldiers serving under Herod Antipas (*A.J.* 18.113).[31] Verse 8 (πατέρα ἔχομεν τὸν Ἀβραάμ) seems to indicate that those in attendance (οἱ ὄχλοι) were Jewish and may include the tax collectors and soldiers as well.

In the historical imagination of Luke, these soldiers could be mercenaries of Herod Antipas .... But it is not out of the question that the evangelist, in view of the future pagan Christian congregations, is thinking of Roman soldiers.[32]

This episode is recounted by Jesus in Luke 7:24–28 following a visit from the disciples of John the Baptist. Three times τί ποιήσωμεν had been asked of John by the three groups. It is now Jesus who repeats a question three times: what did you go out to the wilderness to see? (Luke 7:24, 25, 26).In response to Jesus' praise of John (Luke 7:28), the λαός[33] and τελῶναι justify God since they had been baptized by John. But the soldiers are absent. Instead Pharisees and Sadducees are mentioned as those who rejected the will of God since they had not been baptized by John (Luke 7:29). Those baptized by John are mentioned again in Luke 7:29, but only the people and tax collectors are listed. Those doing military service are absent. The following story in Chapter 7, in which Jesus commends the centurion of Capernaum for his πίστις (7:1–10), may serve as a narrative substitution. If Bovon is correct, and we are right to think of the

---

[30] Johnson, *The Literary Function of Possessions in Luke–Acts*, 184.

[31] Fitzmyer, *The Gospel According to Luke I–IX*, 470.

[32] Bovon, *Luke 1*, 124, Fn 44.

[33] The ὄχλοι (Luke 3:10) are replaced by λαός (Luke 7:29), here not necessarily to be understood in the "people of God" (e.g., ὁ θεὸς τὸν λαὸν αὐτοῦ, Luke 7:16). "In Luke *laos* ("people") takes a wider role. *Laos* with the article retains its specific LXX connotation of Israel as the covenant people (1:10, 17, 21, 68, 77; 2:32; 7:16; 20:1; 23:2, 13; 24:19), but can also be used more generally of crowds (9:12-13)" (D. F. Watson, "People, Crowd," *DJG*: 605-609).

soldiers in 3:14 as potentially Roman, Luke may be purposely postponing the mention of "baptized" soldiers because the baptism of such soldiers will not occur until Chapter 10 in the Acts of the Apostles.

2.1.1 Bullies Shaking Down the Provincials

Luke does not narrate how the soldiers came upon John in the wilderness. Perhaps the reader is meant to see these soldiers as on patrol, like those under the command of Polyidus in Xenophon's *Ephesiaca*. Soldiers policing the provincial hinterlands in search of bandits is a recurrent scene in the romance novels. For instance, in Achilles Tatius's novel *Leucippe and Clitophon*, the hero is freed when a patrolling vexillation of armed troops (3.13.1) attacks the bandits who have held him captive.

Those doing military service come upon the Baptist and the associated crowds and pose their own question: τί ποιήσωμεν καὶ ἡμεῖς? John tells the στρατευόμενοι to stop "shaking down" people for their property (μηδένα διασείσητε, Luke 3:14). Egyptian papyri confirm that actual soldiers were associated with such "shake downs" and were accused of extorting money from provincials. In a papyrus in the Oxyrhynchus cache dated to 37 C.E., a scribe swears that he knows of no villager extorted by a soldier (P. Oxy II.240). A few years later, the Prefect L. Aemilius Rectus announces that soldiers, police, or those working in his administration who extort or use force for gain will be punished (P. London 1171, verso).[34]

If the soldiers are Jewish, then their extortion of their own people for profit resembles the tax collector Zacchaeus – who likewise makes money off his fellow Jews. The verb συκοφαντέω, which means to secure something through extortion by false accusation,[35] is found in both pericopes. Zacchaeus promises, ἰδοὺ τὰ ἡμίσιά μου τῶν ὑπαρχόντων, κύριε, τοῖς πτωχοῖς δίδωμι, καὶ εἴ τινός τι ἐσυκοφάντησα ἀποδίδωμι τετραπλοῦν (Luke 19:8). The pair of words (συκοφαντέω and διασείω) also appears in papyri.[36] John the Baptist commands the soldiers to stop making false accusations that may provide financial gain (συκοφαντήσητε), and Zacchaeus uses the word in his pledge to repay anyone he may have cheated out of money (Luke 19:8). The prohibitive subjunctive in Luke 3:14 indicates that the soldiers are to stop extorting once and for all, suggesting that they had previously been engaged in that behavior, marking them as stereotypical bullies on assignment in the province.

---

[34] The papyrus is dated to 42 C.E. (see F. G. Kenyon, et al., *Greek Papyri in the British Museum III* [London: Oxford University Press, 1907], 105–7; and S. R. Llewelyn, *New Documents Illustrating Early Christianity. Volume 7* [North Ryde, N.S.W. Australia: Macquarie University, 1994], 66–67).

[35] DBAD, 955.

[36] BGU 1756, 11; PTebt I.43; P. Tor I. 1.

2.1.2 Soldiers Capable of Repentance

The startling aspect of Luke's portrayal of these soldiers is not their abusive behavior, which John enjoins them to change. Rather, it is that they would pose the question: τί ποιήσωμεν καὶ ἡμεῖς in the first place. Could these soldiers, known for their harassment, actually be interested in repentance? Luke seems to indicate that they could. The inclusion of the emphatic pronoun ἡμεῖς may indicate that the soldiers do not wish to be left out.[37]

If the soldiers truly seek repentance, John exhorts them to forsake their economic greed. They are to stop acquiring financial gain through violence and false accusation, and are to be content with their ὀψώνιον. Soldiers worried about their recompense is a commonplace cited by Paul (Τίς στρατεύεται ἰδίοις ὀψωνίοις ποτέ, 1 Cor 9:7).[38] The continuity of Luke-Acts[39] suggests that the author intended to foreshadow the admission of soldiers into the Christian community by placing the repentant, baptism-seeking στρατευόμενοι alongside οἱ ὄχλοι and τελῶναι, who had been baptized by John (Καὶ πᾶς ὁ λαὸς ἀκούσας καὶ οἱ τελῶναι ἐδικαίωσαν τὸν θεὸν βαπτισθέντες τὸ βάπτισμα Ἰωάννου, 7:29). The people and the tax collectors praise God's righteousness, while the Pharisees and lawyers reject the will of God, having not been baptized by John (οἱ δὲ Φαρισαῖοι καὶ οἱ νομικοὶ τὴν βουλὴν τοῦ θεοῦ ἠθέτησαν εἰς ἑαυτοὺς μὴ βαπτισθέντες ὑπ᾽ αὐτοῦ, Luke 7:30).

Luke does not narrate whether these repentant soldiers are actually baptized. Luke 3:21 vaguely announces that Ἐγένετο δὲ ἐν τῷ βαπτισθῆναι ἅπαντα τὸν λαόν, but it is unclear whether ἅπαντα τὸν λαὸν are the same cohort of questioners found in 3:10–14, and if so, whether the soldiers are included. The next military character Luke introduces, the centurion of Capernaum, seems to indicate that some soldiers not only abide by John's requirements but actually exceed them (Luke 7:5). The actual baptism of a soldier does not occur until Acts 10. The authorial auditor of Luke 3:14 is simply meant to ponder whether the soldier, so often stereotyped as the brute, might actually be capable of conversion.

---

[37] Marshall, *Commentary on Luke,* 143.

[38] In 2 Cor 11:8, the term has a more negative connotation. It is the result of robbing another church, though undoubtedly Paul is being metaphorical here: ἄλλας ἐκκλησίας ἐσύλησα λαβὼν ὀψώνιον πρὸς τὴν ὑμῶν διακονίαν. Paul continues his metaphorical use of ὀψώνιον in Rom 6:23 (τὰ γὰρ ὀψώνια τῆς ἁμαρτίας θάνατος, τὸ δὲ χάρισμα τοῦ θεοῦ ζωὴ αἰώνιος ἐν Χριστῷ Ἰησοῦ τῷ κυρίῳ ἡμῶν).

[39] "Luke has grasped the story about Jesus and the story of the early Church in a single vision, and has communicated that vision so effectively that at every point Jesus' story anticipates that of the Church, and the story of the Apostles and first Christians is inexplicable apart from what Luke has said about Jesus" (Johnson, *The Literary Function of Possessions in Luke–Acts,* 14).

2.2 The Soldiers at the Detainment and Crucifixion of Jesus: Luke 23

In the Passion narratives, all of the gospel writers recognize a distinction between the guards under the direction of the chief priests (οἱ ὑπηρέται, Mark 14:65; Matt 26:58; οἱ στρατηγοὶ τοῦ ἱεροῦ, Luke 22:52 [D text reads τοῦ λαοῦ], οἱ ἄνδρες, Luke 22:63; ἡ σπεῖρα, John 18:3, 12) and the Roman soldiers of Pilate (οἱ στρατιῶται, Mark 15:16; Matt 27:27; 28:12; Luke 23:36; John 19:2, 23, 24, 32). In Luke, despite the significant role they must have played in the actual death of Jesus, the soldiers present at the death of Jesus are only expressly mentioned in 23:36. Like the other gospel writers, Luke does attribute to a centurion at the cross an announcement at Jesus' death; however, the utterance of his centurion is significantly different from that of centurion in the Gospel of Mark.

Though the Gospel of Mark provides the main source for Luke's passion narrative, Luke has substantially changed the ordering for his own narrative purposes.[40] In the Gospel of Mark, Jesus is mocked twice – after the Sanhedrin passes sentence (14:64–65), and after Pilate hands him over to be scourged and crucified (15:15). When Jesus is condemned to death by the members of the Sanhedrin, "some" (τίνες) spit on him, cover his face and hit him (14:65a–b). The assistants (οἱ ὑπηρέται) also slap his face (14:65c). Luke places this scene prior to Jesus' questioning by the Sanhedrin, and explicitly identifies Mark's τίνες as οἱ ἄνδρες οἱ συνέχοντες αὐτὸν (Luke 22:63).

While Jesus' tormentors in Mark 14:65 are unidentified, those in 15:16 are obviously Roman soldiers: Οἱ δὲ στρατιῶται ἀπήγαγον αὐτὸν ἔσω τῆς αὐλῆς, ὅ ἐστιν πραιτώριον, καὶ συγκαλοῦσιν ὅλην τὴν σπεῖραν. Either Mark is unaware that a cohort (σπεῖρα) would include nearly 500 men or he is purposely exaggerating the military presence. Schmidt proposes that verses 16–20 parody an Imperial triumph where Jesus is the royal ruler who in the end becomes the captive leader.[41] The soldiers dress Jesus in a purple robe and place a crown of thorns on his head (15:17). They then salute Jesus as the King of the Jews while striking his head with a reed and spitting upon him (15:18–19). When the soldiers in Mark conclude their mock military triumph, they strip Jesus of the purple cloak, redress him in his own clothes, and lead him to be crucified (15:20). Jesus is now like the captive leader who is ceremonially executed at the conclusion of the Imperial Triumph (*B.J.* 7.154). "The crucifixion of criminals on

---

[40] I. Howard Marshall, *The Acts of the Apostles: An Introduction and Commentary* (TNTC; Grand Rapids, MI: Eerdmans, 1980), 827. Fitzmyer argues for a Marcan source but notes that Luke transposed various scenes of the Passion in order to collect the material about Peter and present only one appearance of Jesus before the Sanhedrin (*The Gospel According to Luke I–IX*, 66–71). Bovon proposes that Luke had extensively adapted Mark's passion narrative or that he had a different account (*Luke 1*, 7).

[41] Schmidt posited this correlation. "Mark designs this 'anti-triumph' to suggest that the seeming scandal of the cross is actually an exaltation of Christ" ("Mark 15:16–32: The Crucifixion Narrative and the Roman Triumphal Procession," *NTS* 41 [1995]: 1).

either side of Jesus is a conscious expression of the mockery of his kingship on the part of the soldiers."[42]

Luke's editorial hand is most evident in how he uses and adapts Mark's Passion narrative so that the presence and actions of Roman soldiers in the arrest, trial, and crucifixion of Jesus are minimized. Luke rewrites Mark's mock Roman triumph, so that Jesus is an innocent victim of mob violence. The Roman procurator of Judea, Pilate, declares him guiltless on three occasions (23:4, 14, 22). In Mark 15:15 Pilate wishes to please the crowd (Ὁ δὲ Πιλᾶτος βουλόμενος τῷ ὄχλῳ τὸ ἱκανὸν ποιῆσαι), but in Luke 23:25, it is the will of the people that Jesus be crucified (τὸν δὲ Ἰησοῦν παρέδωκεν τῷ θελήματι αὐτῶν), against Pilate's desire. It is not the Roman soldiers, but those of Herod who dress Jesus in royal robes (23:11). Such alterations evidence the attentive hand of the editor and not necessarily a separate source. The appearance of Roman soldiers in Luke 23, despite their role in the crucifixion, is so brief as to suggest the author means to purposely downplay their role in Jesus' death.

2.2.1 Herodian Soldiers as Bullies

Luke transposes the Marcan order so that the Herodian soldiers – not the Roman ones – humiliate Jesus. With the exception of Acts 12:4, 6, and 18, where the guards of Herod Agrippa I are called στρατιῶται, Luke intends that Roman legionary or auxiliary soldiers be understood by this term (see Luke 7:8; Acts 10:7; 21:32, 35; 23:23, 31; 27:31, 42; 28:16).[43] In this pericope, Luke identifies the guards as στράτευμα.

In 23:11, Jesus is sent to Herod, who, with a company of his soldiers, mock (ἐμπαίξας) Jesus and dress him in brilliant clothing (περιβαλὼν ἐσθῆτα λαμπρὰν). Matera suggests that Luke abbreviated and edited Mark's account, in order to highlight the fact that even Herod acknowledged Jesus' innocence.[44] Luke draws intentional distinctions between the military forces, so that Creed is correct when he proposes that Luke was "glad to transfer the outrage from

---

[42] Schmidt, "Mark 15:16–32," 15.

[43] Luke uses a variety of words to describe the military: στρατιώτης, στρατευόμενοι, στράτευμα. Στρατιώτης occurs three times in Matthew (8:9; 27:27; 28:12), once in Mark (15:16), and twice in Luke (7:8; 23:36). The term occurs six times in John but only in Chapter 19. In the Gospel, Luke uses the related terms στρατευόμενοι (3:14) and στράτευμα (23:11) once. Ἑκατοντάρχης are found solely in Luke (Luke 7:2, 6; 23:47; Acts 10:1, 22; 21:32; 22:26; 23:17, 23; 27:1, 31, 43), while ἑκατόνταρχος and its various forms are found three times in Matthew (Matt 8:5, 8; 27:54) and once in Acts 22:25.

[44] The inspiration for the Herod incident may be found in Paul's trial before Agrippa and Festus (Acts 25:13–26:32) (F. J. Matera, "Luke 23, 1–25," in *L'Evangile de Luc* [F. Neirynck; Leuven: Peeters, 1989], 545). Also see Krzysztof Bielinski, *Jesus vor Herodes in Lukas 23,6–12: eine narrativ-sozialgeschichtliche Untersuchung* (Stuttgart: Katholisches Bibelwerk, 2003).

the soldiery of Rome to the soldiery of the local tetrarch."[45] Because neither Herodian soldiers[46] nor Roman soldiers are described as physically abusing Jesus, either by striking or by spitting on him, Luke's redaction serves to limit Mark's more negative characterization of soldiers. Nonetheless, the Herodian soldiers do behave according to the stereotype of the brute, mocking Jesus and treating him with contempt. As brutes, they stand in league with the *commilitones* of the beaten soldier in Apuleius' *Metamorphoses*, who hunt down the gardener, searching door to door until they locate him (9.43). Juvenal reports similar behavior among the soldiers of Rome (16.20), who think nothing of abusing the citizenry and standing above the law.

2.2.2 Roman Soldiers Obediently Following Orders

This propensity to minimize the Roman military's responsibility in the death of Jesus continues when Luke fails to designate who actually leads Jesus to his crucifixion: καὶ ὡς ἀπήγαγον αὐτόν, ἐπιλαβόμενοι Σίμωνά τινα Κυρηναῖον (23:26). "A most interesting problem in the closing verses of the passion account is the identity of the mysterious 'they:' *they* led him away; *they* seized one Simon of Cyrene; and when *they* came to the place called 'The Skull,' there *they* crucified him; *they* cast lots to divide his garments."[47] One can assume that "they" are Roman soldiers because Mark is explicit (Οἱ δὲ στρατιῶται ἀπήγαγον αὐτόν, 15:16), but Luke does not identify them. The incident in which Roman soldiers mock Jesus merits only a brief mention and is moved to the foot of the cross,[48] where they do not initiate the taunting but join the rulers (ἄρχοντες, 23:35) in mocking (ἐνέπαιξαν, the same verb found in 23:11) Jesus by offering him a cup of sour wine (ὄξος, 23:36).[49]

Luke has gone to great lengths to minimize explicit references to Roman soldiers in the abuse, mocking, and death of Jesus. But his auditors would presumably know who actually did the crucifixion – the harshest form of Roman

---

[45] J. M. Creed, *The Gospel According to St. Luke* (London: Macmillan, 1930), 280.

[46] Fitzmyer suggests the soldiers were actually bodyguards (*The Gospel According to Luke X–XXIV*, 1482).

[47] Paul W. Walaskay, "The Trial and Death of Jesus in the Gospel of Luke," *JBL* 94 (1975): 92.

[48] However, Walaskay proposes that these soldiers could be Herodian. "That they were Roman is far from certain. More likely, Luke is suggesting that the soldiers were from the Jewish guard" ("The Trial and Death of Jesus in the Gospel of Luke," 92).

[49] Brown sees the mockery of the soldiers as a Lucan simplification of his Marcan source, in order to enhance the narrative's flow. "In my judgment the mockery by the soldiers, peculiar to Luke, is totally a formulation by that evangelist from Marcan raw material, exhibiting his customary flair for rearranged organization, simplification through avoidance of repetition, and preference for smoother narrative flow" (*The Death of the Messiah: from Gethsemane to the Grave* [New York: Doubleday, 1994], 998–99).

execution and humiliation. Like the Carthaginian soldiers defeating the mercenaries (Polyb. 1.86), these soldiers are under orders to crucify rebels, and the text indicates that they obeyed those orders.

2.2.3 The Centurion at the Cross Depicted as Εὐσεβής

The centurion's declaration in Mark 15:39 is often read as an acknowledgment of Jesus' divinity: ἀληθῶς οὗτος ὁ ἄνθρωπος υἱὸς θεοῦ ἦν. But in Luke, the centurion's acknowledgement is understood as glorifying God (ἐδόξαζεν τὸν θεὸν). "Whereas in the other synoptics the centurion was a christologist, in Luke he is an apologist."[50] When the centurion in Luke sees what has occurred,[51] he announces that Jesus is δίκαιος. Thus the centurion at the cross confirms what Pilate (23:4, 14, 22) and Herod (23:15) had declared earlier: οὐθὲν εὗρον ἐν τῷ ἀνθρώπῳ τούτῳ αἴτιον ὧν κατηγορεῖτε κατ᾽ αὐτοῦ (23:14).[52] Roman officials who encounter the apostles will come to similar conclusions (Acts 16:35; 18:15; 23:29 and 25:18–19). Three times Paul will be declared innocent (Acts 23:9; 25:25; 26:31). Scholars disagree as to whether δίκαιος and its cognates should be translated as "innocent"[53] or "righteous."[54] The word and its derivatives occur 14 times within the Gospel (Luke 1:6, 17, 75; 2:25; 5:32; 10:29; 12:57; 14:14; 15:7; 18:9; 20:20; 23:41, 47, 50) and always have the connotation of "righteous." Matera proposes that interpreting the centurion's declaration as

---

[50] Charles H. Talbert, *Reading Acts: A Literary and Theological Commentary on the Acts of the Apostles* (New York: Crossroads, 1997), 225.

[51] While τὸ γενόμενον may refer to the darkness, it may also be meant in regards to Jesus' response to the penitent thief (Fitzmyer, *The Gospel According to Luke X–XXIV*, 1519), Jesus' noble death (Marshall, *Commentary on Luke*, 876), or Jesus' last utterance.

[52] Luke adds to Mark's τί γὰρ ἐποίησεν κακόν (15:14), using the term αἴτος – a basis for legal action – to more strongly infer a juridical scene. But Walaskay concludes that Jesus did not undergo a Roman trial, and thus Pilate's declaration is not a legal finding. Rather, the author reworks the scene as "a lesson for Luke's church to learn that these events, i.e., even the most sophisticated of human institutions, Roman law and justice, must on occasion succumb to the chaos of unlawful men in order to set in motion the plan of God" ("The Trial and Death of Jesus in the Gospel of Luke," 93).

[53] Kilpatrick notes that the theme of innocence occurs both in Luke 23 and in Acts (A Theme of the Lucan Passion Story and Luke xxiii. 47," *JTS* 43 [1942]: 34–36). For the translation of "innocence," see W. J. Harrington, *The Gospel According to St. Luke* (London: Chapman, 1968), 268; F. W. Danker, *Jesus and the New Age According to St. Luke: A Commentary on the Third Gospel* (St. Louis: Clayton, 1972), 242; Marshall, *Commentary on Luke*, 876; and Fitzmyer, *The Gospel According to Luke X–XXIV*, 1520.

[54] Eduard Schweizer, *The Good News According to Luke* (trans. David E. Green; Atlanta: John Knox Press, 1984), 32–363; Robert J. Karris, "Luke 23:47 and the Lucan View of Jesus' Death," *JBL* 105 (1986): 66; and Joel Green, *The Gospel of Luke* (Grand Rapids, MI: Eerdmans, 1997), 826–27.

referencing the righteous sufferer fits within the wider Luke-Acts narrative.[55] Karris notes "further evidence for the view taken here that Jesus dies as a suffering righteous one can be seen in Luke's use of Psalms 22 and 69 and Wis 2:18 in Luke 23:34b–38."[56] But these interpretations overlook the overt political aspect of the trial and crucifixion. The author may have meant for both meanings to be understood. Like Zechariah and Elizabeth, Jesus is righteous, despite the charge διαστρέφοντα τὸ ἔθνος ἡμῶν (23:2). Within the political state, Jesus is innocent, despite the charge κωλύοντα φόρους Καίσαρι διδόναι καὶ λέγοντα ἑαυτὸν χριστὸν βασιλέα εἶναι (23:2).

Of the centurion at the cross, Luke states directly only his rank. His actions (ἐδόξαζεν τὸν θεόν) and his speech (λέγων, ὄντως ὁ ἄνθρωπος οὗτος δίκαιος ἦν) characterize him indirectly. Because Luke does not expressly state why the centurion is at the cross, the audience would surmise that this centurion – as was typical of vexillations – had charge of the crucifixion party. Mark seems to imply this role for the centurion when he includes: ὁ κεντυρίων ὁ παρεστηκὼς ἐξ ἐναντίας αὐτοῦ ὅτι οὕτως ἐξέπνευσεν (15:39). Again, Luke has deleted material that would more explicitly implicate the centurion with the crucifixion. Luke's centurion merely witnesses the event (ἰδὼν δὲ ὁ ἑκατοντάρχης τὸ γενόμενον). Nonetheless, the audience would recognize the centurion's role as chief officer of the execution party.

We shall now examine certain motifs in the account in order to assess Luke's use of stereotypes in his development of the centurion at the cross. This centurion is presented to the authorial audience as obedient and reverent, and therefore a credible witness when he announces, ὄντως ὁ ἄνθρωπος οὗτος δίκαιος ἦν (23:47)

2.2.3.1 An Obedient Officer Glorifying the God of the Jews

The authorial audience is not surprised that the centurion fulfills his duties, as would be expected of an obedient soldier. The literary stereotypes may show a centurion as abusive of civilians, but if he neglects his military duties, he is liable for dire punishment. Petronius's amorous soldier preferred suicide rather than the punishment that awaited him for his dereliction of duty. The centurion who lost his sword in his encounter with Apuleius's gardener hides from his superior officers, lest his loss be discovered.

On first appearance, the centurion at the cross is presented as a typical character. The authorial audience anticipates that he and his fellow soldiers would

---

[55] "While *dikaios* does contain the notion of political innocence, Luke intends that the reader interpret this innocence against the wider background of OT righteousness as manifested in the ordeals of the righteous sufferer" (Frank J. Matera, "The Death of Jesus according to Luke: A Question of Sources," *CBQ* 47 [1985]: 471).

[56] Karris, "Luke 23:47 and the Lucan View of Jesus' Death," 67.

glory in the cruelty of crucifixions (*B.J.* 5.451), seeing them as fitting entertainment (Philo, *Flacc.* 10.84–85). They would not expect the centurion to glorify the gods, let alone the God of the Jews. But this centurion does not respond as anticipated. Instead, his actions mirror those characters in the Gospel of Luke who have been healed or have seen mighty deeds. For example, in Luke 2:20, the shepherds return from witnessing the birth of Jesus, δοξάζοντες καὶ αἰνοῦντες τὸν θεὸν ἐπὶ πᾶσιν οἷς ἤκουσαν καὶ εἶδον καθὼς ἐλαλήθη πρὸς αὐτούς. Not only the healed paralytic but the observing crowds give praise to God (Luke 5:25–26). When Jesus restores the dead man to his widowed mother, again the crowd reacts by glorifying God and recognizing Jesus as a great prophet (ἐδόξαζον τὸν θεὸν λέγοντες ὅτι προφήτης μέγας ἠγέρθη ἐν ἡμῖν, Luke 7:16). Likewise, the bent-over woman praises God when she is made straight (Luke 13:13). In Luke 17:15–16, a pericope unique to the author, a non-Jew glorifies God (δοξάζων τὸν θεόν) for the first time in Luke's Gospel. The healed Samaritan leper returns to thank Jesus and praise God. And finally, the blind beggar in Jericho receives his sight, follows Jesus, and glorifies God, inspiring the crowd to do likewise (δοξάζων τὸν θεόν, Luke 18:43).

When the Roman centurion at the foot of the cross glorifies God, he becomes the first Gentile in the Gospel to do so. The subsequent centurion so inspired[57] will take the next step and be baptized (Acts 10:46–47). This movement of praise outward – first from the Jews, then from a Samaritan, and then from a Roman – replicates the direction of the proclamation announced in Acts 1:8. A Roman centurion supervising a crucifixion exclaiming such piety at such an impious moment would, indeed, cut against the grain of the audience's expectation of how a soldier would typically behave.

2.2.3.2 The Centurion at the Cross Speaks

The authorial audience would expect that, as the chief officer on the scene, the centurion at the cross would speak with authority, reminiscent of the centurion in Luke 7. Earlier in the narrative, Luke emphasized that centurions give orders and receive orders (Luke 7:8). Seldom to do they make their own pronouncements, though the centurion in Acts 22:26 does chide his superior officer when the officer is about to beat Paul, a Roman citizen. In fact, making any public address could label the soldier as a instigator and mutineer, as discussed in Chapter 3. So the audience does not anticipate a declaration from this centurion at the cross, let alone the words of his utterance: ὄντως ὁ ἄνθρωπος οὗτος δίκαιος ἦν.

Unlike the centurion in Mark, this centurion does not declare Jesus as a son of god. Such a remark would have been tantamount to treason, since soldiers

---

[57] Though in the case of Cornelius and his household, the verb is not δοξάζω, but a synonym μεγαλύνω.

swore allegiance to Caesar[58] who was heralded as the son of god.[59] Instead, this centurion calls Jesus δίκαιος. Luke may be intentionally alluding to Wis 2:18 (εἰ γάρ ἐστιν ὁ δίκαιος υἱὸς θεοῦ ἀντιλήμψεται αὐτοῦ καὶ ῥύσεται αὐτὸν ἐκ χειρὸς ἀνθεστηκότων) in 23:34b–38.[60] If so, then οὗτος δίκαιος could be understood as ὁ δίκαιος υἱὸς θεοῦ. Such a verbal ellipsis allows the centurion to remain in character as one who confesses only Caesar as a god, but foreshadows for the authorial audience the idea that not all centurions may be so restrained.

The centurion at the cross may be characterized as a dutiful soldier who confirms what Pilate had earlier declared (*i.e.*, οὐδὲν αἴτιον θανάτου, 23:22). But, more likely, Luke means for the authorial auditor's expectations to be overturned. The centurion's behavior is not a stereotypical behavior of a soldier on assignment in the province. He is neither violent nor mocking,[61] nor does he rescue Jesus. This last centurion encountered in Luke brings to a close the portrait of soldiers in the Gospel. In Luke 3:14, they bear witness to the possibility of conversion, in contradiction to their previous behavior as brutes. In Luke 7, Jesus recognizes the centurion as possessing πίστις. The soldiers of Herod mock Jesus before his crucifixion (Luke 23:11), and Roman soldiers join in the mocking at his crucifixion (Luke 23:26). In Luke 23:47, a centurion responds as would a disciple, by praising God and acknowledging Jesus' righteousness and/or innocence.

3. The Characterization of Soldiers and Officers in the Acts of the Apostles

Most often, the military characters in Acts are depicted stereotypically like their literary compatriots in the works of Chariton, Achilles Tatius, and Petronius, and occasionally even in the comedies of Plautus and Terence. The soldiers guarding Peter in prison (Acts 12) and the soldiers guarding Paul en route to Rome (Acts 27) are little characterized beyond their identification. Luke relies

---

[58] The exact wording of the oath is not recorded, but Epictetus describes it as an oath to assure the safety of the emperor (1.14.15). Tacitus mentions the swearing in of soldiers (*Hist.* 1.12; 2.74; 4.31) by which he may mean both the oath of allegiance and the oath of enlistment. This *sacramentum* was renewed annually. See Daniel G. Van Slyke, "*Sacramentum* in Ancient Non-Christian Authors," Antiphon 9.2 (2005): 167–206; and Campbell, *The Emperor and the Roman Army*, 19–32.

[59] Augustus and his successors were called υἱὸς θεοῦ or *divi filius* in numerous inscriptions (IGR 1.901; 4.309, 315; ILS 107, 113; PRyl 601; POslo 26). Also see T. H. Kim, "The Anarthrous υἱὸς θεοῦ in Mark 15,39 and the Roman Imperial Cult," *Bib* 79 (1998): 221–41.

[60] Karris, "Luke 23:47 and the Lucan View of Jesus' Death."

[61] Luke gives no indication that the soldiers who engage in mocking in 23:36 include the centurion.

on his readers' familiarity with the stereotype to flesh out the characters more fully. The tribune Claudius Lysias (Acts 21–23:32), the centurion Julius (Acts 27), and the lone soldier with Paul in Rome (Acts 28:16) behave both stereotypically and counter to expectations. When we pay attention to their presence and function over the two works, we can see that Luke creates a more complex portrait of these military personae, despite their often brief appearance on the narrative stage. Unlike soldiers in the Greco-Roman histories, the soldiers and officers in Acts of the Apostles are never portrayed in battle. In fact, as did the soldiers in the Gospel, these soldiers function more frequently as a provincial police force. Thus, the narrative setting in Acts of the Apostles is most often "the province."

3.1 The Soldiers of Herod Agrippa: Acts 12:4–11, 18–19

With the sudden demise of the ruler and the exultation of the lowly, Acts 12 reads like a narrative fulfillment of the Magnificat (Luke 1:52),[62] clearly evidencing the Lucan editorial hand. Likewise, Peter's release in Acts 12 (also Acts 5) is an allusion to Luke 4:18//LXX Isaiah 61:1 (κηρύξαι αἰχμαλώτοις ἄφεσιν). Acts 12 begins with the tirade of Herod Agrippa I against the leaders of the Jerusalem community. James, the brother of John, dies by the sword (v. 2), and Peter is imprisoned because the king saw that such action ἀρεστόν ἐστιν τοῖς Ἰουδαίοις (v. 3). The proximity of the Passover prevents a quick dispatch of Peter. Instead, he waits in prison (φυλακή, v. 5), where four squads of four soldiers (τέσσαρσιν τετραδίοις στρατιωτῶν, v. 4) guard him. This is an excessive number for one man, unless one reads the numbering of the squads as a reference to those who kept various watches during the night.[63] The church prays fervently to God on Peter's behalf. At night, Peter is bound by two chains and sleeps between two soldiers[64] while sentries guard the door (v. 6). The detailed description of the tight security serves to heighten the miraculous events to follow. The angel of the Lord appears to Peter as a light shines in the cell. Peter is told ἀνάστα ἐν τάχει (v. 7). The chains fall from his hands. Despite the conversation with the angel and Peter taking time to dress, the guards do not awaken. Peter passes by the first and second guards,[65] the iron gate opens, and he escapes. In the morning, the soldiers are stupefied by Peter's absence (v. 18).

---

[62] David Parry, "Release of the Captives: Reflections on Acts 12," in *Luke's Literary Achievements* (ed. C. M. Tuckett; JSNTS; Sheffield: Sheffield Academic Press, 1995), 157.

[63] Vegetius explains that the night watch was divided into four segments to prevent one guard from falling asleep (*De re militari,* 3.8). Also Barrett, *Acts,* 581.

[64] Josephus recounts that prisoners were chained to soldiers (*A.J.* 18.196).

[65] Haenchen presumes the two guards are the remainder of the four-person squad. Peter had been chained between two, and these two are patrolling the prison (*The Acts of the Apostles: A Commentary* [trans. Bernard Noble and Gerald Shinn; Philadelphia: Westminster, 1971], 384).

When Herod discovers the escape, he examines the guards and commands that they be led away (ἀνακρίνας τοὺς φύλακας ἐκέλευσεν ἀπαχθῆναι, v. 19). In Herodotus (2.114), Plato (*Gorg.* 486a), and Aristophanes (*Ach.* 57), ἀπάγω connotes being led off to prison. Because these soldiers are in dereliction of duty, they will likely be executed. A variant reading (D* sy bo) replaces ἀπαχθῆναι with ἀποκτανθῆναι, making explicit that the guards will be killed.

Although Luke more frequently prefers στρατιῶται for Roman soldiers, he uses the term in verses 4 and 6 probably to refer to soldiers of Herod Agrippa, because Agrippa, and not the prefect, interrogates them for their dereliction of duty. Additionally, Rome preferred that soldiers remain on active duty, and not serve as prison guards (Pliny, *Ep.* 10.19–20). However, Haenchen seems to think these soldiers were Roman, for he cites Roman military procedure on the rotation of guards to explain the four squads of four soldiers.[66] Bruce implies that the guards were Agrippa's private force when he notes that Roman law requires the guard to suffer the fate of the escaped prisoner (*Code of Justinian* 9.4.4) "which, however, was not binding upon Agrippa in the internal administration of his kingdom."[67] As we have seen, Luke attends to differences among the ranks and branches, so he likely meant for the reader to understand these soldiers as being under the jurisdiction of Agrippa.

The authorial audience receives little information from which to form an image of these soldiers. The confusion among the soldiers over Peter's escape (Acts 12:18) despite the heavy guard suggests a comic scene. Reminiscent of the makeshift army marshalled by the braggart Thraso (*Eunuchus*, 784), these soldiers are merely "elements" – figures that lack development as characters and instead serve as props in the story.[68] Their narrative significance is to portray the lengths to which Herod Agrippa would go to secure Peter. They are a manifestation of Herod Agrippa's power, which, as the story reveals, is no match to that of ὁ κύριος (12:23).

3.2 The Roman Soldiers and Officers Quartered in Jerusalem: Acts 21–23

Unlike the military personnel in Acts 12, the soldiers, centurions, and tribune who appear in Acts 21–23 are Roman auxiliary soldiers, who are clearly under the command of the Roman prefect. As such, they are much like the military under the jurisdiction of Pilate in Luke 23:26–38. In addition to their stereotypical role as political muscle for the powers that be, the military men involved with Paul serve as his rescuers. Paul's repeated interactions with the tribune and soldiers stationed near the Temple allow Luke to carefully craft a cumula-

---

[66] Ibid., 382.

[67] F. F. Bruce, *Commentary on the Book of the Acts of the Apostles* (NICNT; Grand Rapids, MI: Eerdmans, 1954), 253 n. 17.

[68] Seymour Chatman, *Story and Discourse,* 96–145.

tive military portrait. In each scene, the authorial audience is given more information with which to build not only the characterization of soldiers and tribune but of Paul as well.

3.2.1 Setting the Scene

In three related but distinct pericopes, Acts 21:27–40; 22:22–29 and 23:16–33, Luke portrays the Roman auxiliary stationed in Jerusalem as promoters – albeit unwitting ones – of the preaching of Paul. Rescuing Paul from the angry mob of Jews, the tribune then allows Paul to address the crowds in the Temple and then later the Sanhedrin. Hearing of a plot to ambush Paul, the tribune amasses an exceedingly large force and, in the middle of the night, whisks Paul to the safety of Caesarea, the provincial headquarters, where he is later invited to address Felix, Festus, Agrippa II, Bernice, and the leading men of the city (25:23). While Paul is "imprisoned" in Herod's praetorium (23:35), a centurion attends to him, and he is allowed to have his supporters minister to his needs (24:23).

3.2.1.1 The Tribune's First Rescue of Paul: Acts 21:27–40

The Jews from Asia (21:27) incite the crowd in the Temple, who attack Paul and drag him out of the precinct. The report of the uproar reaches the tribune[69] of the cohort (ὁ χιλίαρχος τῆς σπείρης, 21:31), who then mobilizes a stout force. The character of the tribune develops during his numerous encounters with Paul.[70] Luke makes mention of two centurions (23:23), suggesting that nearly two hundred soldiers would have been in the vicinity. The use of κατατρέχω (v. 32) hints at the geography of the setting. Though the Temple was on the highest point of the city, the Roman Antonia Fortress overlooked the Temple precinct.[71] A cohort was permanently stationed there in order to quell any disturbances that might arise in the Temple (*B.J.* 5.244). According to Josephus stairs led down from the Antonia tower into the Temple itself. When the soldiers bring Paul up the steps toward the fortress, the crowd is so violent that the rescuing soldiers have to carry him (v. 35). The tribune immediately arrests Paul and has him doubly chained, reminiscent of Peter in Acts 12. However, unlike Peter, Paul will not need a heavenly emissary to free him.

---

[69] LSJ equates the word χιλίαρχος, a leader of a thousand men, with the Latin *tribunus* (1992). The presence of both foot soldiers and cavalry (Acts 23:23) suggests a *cohors equitata milliaria*, which was normally commanded by a tribune (Holder, *Studies in the Auxilia*, 77–80).

[70] "We shall see in the next section how indispensable for the progress of the Lucan narrative is the direction of the whole affair by the tribune himself" (Haenchen, *Acts of the Apostles*, 618)

[71] According to Josephus, the Antonia had a commanding view of the happenings within the Temple precinct (*B.J.* 5.245).

Paul pauses before the fortress to inquire if he may speak to the tribune. Haenchen sees in Paul's request "elaborate politeness."[72] Indeed, Luke is setting up a relationship of deference between Paul and the Roman officer, which will be subtly reversed in the next chapter. The tribune is surprised that Paul speaks Greek (Ἑλληνιστὶ γινώσκεις, v. 37). The authorial audience is meant to recognize – before the tribune discloses how he came by his citizenship and his name – that this tribune is local or, at least, well-versed in the language of the eastern provinces.[73] The tribune obviously thought that Paul was an Egyptian who had been inciting revolt and gathering supporters in the desert (v. 38).[74] According to Josephus, Egyptians had a reputation for promoting sedition (*Ap.* 2.69). In addition, they were frivolous and wholly without sense (*Ap.* 1.225). Tacitus portrayed Egyptian soldiers as cowardly one moment and unrestrained in their passion for war the next (4.14.9). Paul gives a decidedly direct defense to the double-charge of being an Egyptian and being a seditionist. He identifies himself most definitely as a Jew, hailing from Tarsus in the region of Cilicia, οὐκ ἀσήμου πόλεως πολίτης (v. 39). Luke's use of litotes[75] is meant to strengthen his characterization of Paul as an educated man. Paul is no Egyptian, but his zealous acknowledgement of his Cilician roots may stand him in no good stead with a Roman officer. The coast of Cilicia was a notorious haunt of pirates until Pompey subdued them (Dio 36.37).[76] After declaring his provincial citizenship, Paul makes a request of the Tribune that he have permission to speak (v. 30b). Permission granted, Paul now speaks in Hebrew before the angry Jewish crowd. Luke makes much of Paul's language abilities. Paul is able to converse with the Gentiles in Greek and with the Jews in Hebrew. Taking on the role of an orator,[77] Paul gestures to the crowd for their attention and silence, and then begins his defense (v. 40).

---

[72] Haenchen, *Acts of the Apostles*, 619.

[73] The language of the Roman military and particularly its officers was Latin (Watson, *The Roman Soldier*, 38). The assaulted gardener in Apuleius's *Golden Ass* suffered mightily from the language barrier between provincials and Roman soldiers (*Metam.* 9.39).

[74] Gamaliel makes a similar comparison in Acts 5:33–39, where he mentions Theudas and Judas the Galilean with reference to Peter's preaching. Josephus describes two different groups: the *sicarii* (*B.J.* 2.255-257) and those led by the Egyptian false prophet (*B.J.* 2.261-263).

[75] H. J. Cadbury, "Litotes in Acts," in *Festschrift in Honor of F. Wilbur Gingrich* (ed. Eugene Howard Barth and Ronald Edwin Cocroft; Leiden: Brill, 1972), 58–69.

[76] Also see A. N. Sherwin-White, "Rome, Pamphylia and Cilicia, 133–70 B.C.E," *JRS* 66 (1976): 5; and Philip de Souza, *Piracy in the Greco-Roman World* (Cambridge: Cambridge University Press, 1999), 97–148. For a discussion on Roman jurisdiction of Cilicia, see Elias J. Bickerman, "Syria and Cilicia," *American Journal of Philology* 68 (1947): 353–62.

[77] Barrett, *Acts*, 2.1027.

3.2.1.2 The Tribune's Second Rescue of Paul: Acts 22:22–29

The Jews of Jerusalem are at first attentive to Paul's speech, but as Paul announces that the Lord has commanded him to depart from Jerusalem and go to the Gentiles (v. 21), they again riot, calling for his death, waving their garments, and kicking up dust in the air. To quell the eruption of violence, the tribune orders Paul's swift removal. Once inside, he plans to interrogate Paul with whips (μάστιξιν ἀνετάζεσθαι αὐτὸν, v. 24) in order to learn the reason for the crowd's reaction. After his first rescue from the crowd, Paul defended himself against the charge of being an Egyptian seditionist by declaring his provincial citizenship (21:39). Now, to prevent a scourging, Paul asserts his rights as a Roman citizen.[78] Only slaves or non-Roman citizens could have information beaten out of them (Livy, 10.9.4). It is not surprising that the centurion overseeing the examination reports (ἀπήγγειλεν) to the tribune: ὁ γὰρ ἄνθρωπος οὗτος Ῥωμαῖός ἐστιν (v. 26). But his question, τί μέλλεις ποιεῖν, would strike Luke's authorial audience as odd if not outright mutinous, since lower officers did not question the orders of their superior. Equally as strange, the tribune does not rebuke the centurion for his frank remark. Later, the tribune will listen to Paul with similar restraint, even deference.

After questioning Paul to verify his status, the tribune responds by announcing how he had come by his own citizenship, ἐγὼ πολλοῦ κεφαλαίου τὴν πολιτείαν ταύτην ἐκτησάμην (v. 28). Roman citizenship in the East provided the possessor with honor. Additionally, it allowed him to pursue a military career and gain access to the Roman legal system.[79] Acts 22:25–29 may serve as an example of both. The tribune has followed the path of a military career,[80] available to him as a citizen, and Paul invokes his citizenship as a cloak of protection.

---

[78] On Paul's citizenship, see Barrett, *Acts*, 2.1050; and Sherwin-White, *Roman Society and Roman Law in the New Testament*, 144–55. Tajra argues that Paul presents a diploma verifying his status (H. W. Tajra, *The Trial of Paul: A Juridical Exegesis of the Second Half of Acts* [WUNT 2.35; Tübingen: Mohr, 1989], 85). Because Luke enjoys adding details for embellishment (see his description of the lighting in the upper room in Acts 20:8), he would likely have mentioned a diploma should he have envisioned such proof was necessary. Luke paints a generally positive picture of the Empire, so he needed to have his hero, Paul, possess the highly prized Roman citizenship – whether this was historically accurate or not.

[79] See Sherwin-White, *Roman Society and Roman Law in the New Testament*, 180–81.

[80] Officers and soldiers in the Roman legions had to be Roman citizens before their enlistment. Soldiers in the auxiliary need not be citizens but would receive a diploma upon their retirement (Webster, *The Roman Imperial Army*, 102–45). "The individual inhabitant of a great Greek city who happened to possess the Roman franchise could make effective use of it, if he was a proletarian, only by entering the Roman army, or if he was a magnate, by securing admission to the Equestrian order and thence into the public service as an officer. Such promotion required great wealth and considerable personal influence in the

Cassius Dio reports that the franchise of Roman citizenship was indeed up for sale during the reign of Claudius. In fact, it was being sold by the emperor's wife (60.5), though as the tribune notes, it was pricey, μεγάλων τὸ πρῶτον χρημάτων πραθεῖσα (60.5).[81] Despite the ease with which a person could obtain citizenship, Claudius held certain expectations for the comportment of these new citizens. In addition to knowing Latin, the new citizens were expected to adopt Claudius's name and to mention him in their will, though many failed to do this (60.7). One wonders if this expectation was widely known, for the author will reveal in Acts 23 that the tribune's name is Claudius.

Paul's citizenship is untainted; he was born into the privilege (ἐγὼ δὲ καὶ γεγέννημαι, v. 28). The tribune becomes afraid when he confirms Paul's status and recognizes that he has chained a citizen (v. 29). Though the author describes the tribune as ἐφοβήθη, this term is meant to show the tribune's new respect for Paul rather than a fear of retaliation. Previously, Paul has shown deference to the tribune (21:37). Now, the tribune recognizes Paul's status[82] but, curiously, does not unbind him until the next day (v. 30). The fullness of this reversal of authority will be seen in Acts 23:16–22, where Paul makes demands of both the centurion and the tribune.

3.2.1.3 The Tribune Claudius Lysias' Final Rescue of Paul: Acts 23:16–33

Though Paul may have originally been brought into the fortress in chains, he has obviously acquired some clout. His nephew is able to gain access to him so as to warn Paul about the planned ambush (v. 16). The use of ἀπαγγέλειν[83] (vv. 16–17) further suggests that the nephew is acting as a good soldier under authority, sent on a mission and behaving not unlike the centurion of Capernaum (Luke 7:8). Paul's new status is further exemplified when he summons one of the centurions, who actually responds to the call. Using an imperative, Paul commands the centurion to bring his nephew to the commander. In v. 18, the centurion follows Paul's orders, though he acknowledges that Paul is ὁ δέσμιος. The tribune, sensing the importance of the nephew's report, takes the young man by the hand and leads him aside (ἐπιλαβόμενος δὲ τῆς χειρὸς αὐτοῦ ὁ χιλίαρχος καὶ ἀναχωρήσας κατ' ἰδίαν, v. 19). "Never was a tribune so amiable,"

---

right quarters at Rome" (Sherwin-White, *Roman Society and Roman Law in the New Testament*, 177).

[81] Also see Cassius Dio 17.5–7.

[82] Sherwin-White adds, "In the interchange between Lysias and Paul the tribune regards Paul as his social equal" (Sherwin-White, *Roman Society and Roman Law in the New Testament*, 156).

[83] Also see Acts 22:26, where the centurion reports to the tribune that Paul is a Roman citizen.

remarks Loisy.[84] The use of the prohibitive subjunctive emphatically intro-duced by the second personal pronoun (σὺ οὖν μὴ πεισθῇς αὐτοῖς, v. 21) further establishes that Paul and his nephew-emissary are the ones in authority. This unusual role-reversal is foreshadowed for the authorial audience in Acts 22:26 when the centurion dares to question his superior.

The tribune who was willing to use torture on Paul to uncover the truth about the roots of the disturbance (22:24) immediately accepts the report of the young man without further proof or investigation. The tribune, in turn, summons two centurions and directs them to take both of their centuries (στρατιώτας διαχοσίους), seventy cavalry (ἱππεῖς ἑβδομήκοντα), and a sizable squadron of archers (δεξιολάβους διαχοσίους) and to prepare to leave for the headquarters of the prefect at Caesarea (v. 23). Luke uses such excessive numbers to indicate that the level of danger requires a great show of strength. But the authorial au-dience would recognize that, even for a citizen, Paul appears to be receiving extraordinary treatment. The inclusion of cavalry along with infantry suggest a *cohors equitatae*. Luke is familiar enough with the auxiliary system to include specialty soldiers who may have been on a vexillation from their own cohort, perhaps even the *Cohors II Italica Civium Romanorum*, a unit of archers known to be stationed in Syria in the first century. Paul has a mount, so that he may ride, again demonstrating Paul's significance.

The tribune then composes a letter to be carried to the prefect, Felix (v. 25).[85] The letter of Claudius Lysias to Felix injects a bit of realism into the narrative, since it follows the form and content of official military correspondence about an accused Roman citizen.[86] The letter thus serves a narrative purpose of mov-ing the conflict between the Jews of Jerusalem and Paul to the larger arena of Roman judicial affairs. The letter gives an "official" perspective on the events, one which decidedly favors Paul's side, and repudiates the Jews. Additionally, it demonstrates that the tribune is an educated man with good judgment. Verses 25–30 provide the authorial audience with one new piece of information: the name of the tribune. Luke systematically develops the character of the tribune, and only at the moment when he and Paul will separate does Luke introduce his name: Claudius Lysias. His nomen, the reader can assume, he received when he purchased his citizenship (22:28). His Greek cognomen, Lysias, could indicate that he came from the eastern part of the empire. Several inscriptions

---

[84] Alfred Loisy, *Les Actes des Apôtres* (Paris: E. Nourry, 1920), 840.

[85] On the identity of Felix, see *A.J.* 20.137, Suet. *Claud.* 28, Tac. *Hist.* 5:9 and *Ann.* 12.54. Also H. Conzelmann, *Acts of the Apostles*, 194–95.

[86] An *elogium* is a letter that lists a summary of facts when a charge is referred to a higher authority (Suet. *Cal.* 27; Dig. 48.3.11; 49.16.3). Likely Acts 23:26–30 means to echo such an official letter.

identify tribunes who came from the east and received their citizenship from Claudius.[87]

3.2.2 The Characterization of the Tribune Claudius Lysias and His Centurions

More than any other military character in the Gospel and Acts, the tribune and the centurions in Acts 21–23 are developed via their dialogue.[88] Previously, Luke has relied on direct characterization or the more subtle use of actions to depict character. But in these scenes, the conversations among Paul, the Tribune Claudius Lysias, the centurion and the nephew depict a relationship between Paul and the Roman military that is at least cordial if not surprisingly deferential.

The central military character is the tribune Claudius Lysias, whom Luke first describes directly ὁ χιλίαρχος τῆς σπείρης (21:31), and then indirectly through his actions and dialogue with Paul. Luke means for the tribune to exemplify the positive aspects of Roman administration in pre-70 C.E. Judea. He has quelled riots, attempted to investigate the disturbance, sought the assistance of local leaders, and protected the Roman citizen in his midst. He has even showed respect to Paul, perhaps recognizing his superior status as a Roman citizen by birth. By the end of Claudius Lysias's appearance on the Lucan stage, he is taking commands from Paul via his nephew and the centurion. He concludes by writing an official letter to Felix to outline his investigation, and to declare that Paul has done nothing deserving death or imprisonment. The representative of the Roman military authority in Jerusalem recognizes Paul's innocence and protects him. Luke employs stereotypes to portray the tribune and his centurions. Though the officers are typical in some of their behaviors, their deference to Paul suggests that Luke meant that the prisoner be seen as the true one in authority.

3.2.2.1 The Tribune Claudius Lysias Depicted as a Rescuer and Ἀνὴρ Ἀγαθός

The tribune is an auxiliary officer overseeing the cohort of soldiers, cavalry, and archers quartered in Jerusalem. As such, he is much like Polyidus in Xenophon's *Ephesiaca* – the commander of the Egyptian contingent sent to stop the raids of bandits. Charmides, in Achilles Tatius's *Leucippe and Clitophon*, is also depicted as commanding military forces in Egypt. Both of these literary commanders rescue women from the hands of bandits, while steadfastly hold-

---

[87] AE 24, 78, PME C 124; IGR IV 1060. Also see Saddington, "Roman Military and Administrative Personnel in the New Testament," 2416.

[88] Luke uses dialogue to develop the character of the centurion of Capernaum, but the centurion himself is never present to speak. His emissaries speak on his behalf.

ing to their military obligations. The character type of the "rescuer" fits Claudius Lysias who, like his fellow officers, upholds his military obligations and sees to the rescue of Paul – repeatedly! He is the provincial representative of Roman law and order on the side of justice.

The immediate response to a potential riot, the strategic investigation of the disturbance, and the marshalling of troops suggest that Luke meant this tribune to be a reflection of the notable generals of history. Livy records his brief encomium to Scipio as the thoughts of the Numidian Masinissa who has conjured up an image of the ideal man, having already heard of his many achievements (28.35.5). Like Scipio, Claudius Lysias is quick to act and decisive. But his willingness to allow Paul to address the Jews, his toleration of the centurion's question, and his listening to Paul's nephew are characteristic of another type of ἀνὴρ ἀγαθός – that of the good citizen who is temperate in his dealings. As such Claudius Lysias resembles Plautus's Periphanes and Xenophon of Ephesus's retired soldier, Araxus, though they both reside in the narrative setting of the home front.

3.2.2.2 The Tribune Claudius Lysias as Outranked

In some ways, the tribune Claudius Lysias behaves quite unlike other literary leaders. When the centurion questions his command to flog Paul, Claudius Lysias takes the comment seriously and refrains from his original course of action. We do not find in the ranks of military stereotypes an officer who would take direction from a prisoner as the tribune does! Luke seems to have promoted Paul, so that he now outranks the tribune.

In Luke 7, Jesus encounters (via his emissaries) a centurion who recognizes Jesus' authority and defers to him. In Acts of the Apostles, the tribune Claudius Lysias, the highest ranking Roman official in Jerusalem, likewise recognizes Paul's authority. He speeds Paul on his way to Rome, and literally, sends the apostle to the Gentiles (ἔπεμψα πρὸς σὲ, 23:30). From an outpost in Capernaum to the city of Jerusalem, Roman military officers in Luke-Acts are characterized as coming to know both the innocence of Jesus and his apostles and their ultimate authority.

3.2.2.3 The Centurions Depicted as Comic Foils

Luke does little to develop the centurions and soldiers under Lysias' command in comparison to their officer. Their narrative function is to execute the tribune's orders, with a couple of notable exceptions. In Acts 22:26, the centurion, who was about to beat Paul before learning of his citizenship, goes to his commanding officer and demands τί μέλλεις ποιεῖν. Surely such insubordination would not be long tolerated in the ranks. Luke may mean to emphasize the egregious nature of interrogating a Roman citizen by scourging and without a trial, but he has injected into an otherwise stereotypical portrait of an obedient centurion a touch of the comical. The authorial audience does not expect this sudden change nor the lack of punishment from the tribune. Apuleius's centurion may be abusive and a brute, but only towards civilians. When he is on assignment to another town, upon arrival, he goes immediately to report to his commanding officer, also depicted as a tribune. Such acquiescence to authority is expected; an abrupt challenge to a command is not. Because the challenge is unexpected, this centurion's outburst makes him a comic foil, like the wily slaves in the Roman comedies who are able to slander and insult their masters without reproach.

In another example, Paul orders one of centurions guarding him to take his nephew to the tribune (Acts 23:17). Immediately and without argument, the centurion reports to the tribune, relaying the message from the prisoner-cum-commander. When Paul arrives – on horseback no less – at the provincial headquarters guarded by a regiment of foot soldiers, cavalry and archers, the authorial audience is meant to envision with amazement the arrival of the general.

3.3 Julius the Centurion, His Soldiers, and the Praetorian Guard: Acts 27–28

Like Claudius Lysias before them, Festus, Agrippa, and Bernice recognize Paul's innocence (Acts 25:18–19; 26:31). Though Felix holds Paul in custody, he readily summons him to speak. Perhaps Felix is interested in Paul's preaching or, as the text says explicitly, he is hoping for a bribe (24:26). Felix keeps Paul in custody but allows Paul's own to attend to him (καὶ μηδένα κωλύειν τῶν ἰδίων αὐτοῦ ὑπηρετεῖν αὐτῷ, 24:23). If Barrett is correct[89] and Paul is under protective custody,[90] then just as the Roman military saw to Paul's safety in Jerusalem, its soldiers continue to do so in Caesarea. Not surprisingly, a centurion of the σπεῖρα Σεβαστή becomes Paul's escort to Rome in Acts 27.

One could imagine a biography of the centurion Julius, in which Julius, as responsible for the whole voyage, final authority on matters of route, protector of all his charges, stood at the centre; and it would be impossible to find fault with such a biography.[91]

But Acts 27 and 28, as Barrett acknowledges, are actually part of a biography of Paul. Nonetheless, the character of the centurion receives enough authorial

---

[89] Barrett, *Acts*, 2.1112.

[90] See B. Rapske, *The Book of Acts and Paul in Roman Custody* (The Book of Acts in its First Century Setting; Grand Rapids: Eerdmans, 1994). For a narrative-critical perspective that recognizes the significance of setting, see Matthew L. Skinner, *Locating Paul: Places of Custody as Narrative Setting in Acts* (SBL Academia Biblica 13; Atlanta: Society of Biblical Literature, 2003).

[91] Barrett, *Acts*, 2.1179.

attention that one can draw comparisons between this centurion and others encountered in Greco-Roman literature. His companions fare less well, because their characterization is more limited.

3.3.1 Setting the Scene

Acts 27 opens the longest we-section found in the Acts of the Apostles.[92] The unidentified plural narrator joins Paul and the other prisoners under the guard of a centurion of the Augustan Cohort named Julius, as they embark on their voyage to Rome, sailing north along the coast of Syria (v. 2).[93] Julius and the other soldiers appear in Acts 27:3, 6, 11, 31, 42–44 and 28:16. Luke wishes to portray Paul as under protective custody. Verse 3 explains that when the ship reaches Sidon, Julius treats Paul well (φιλανθρώπως τε ὁ Ἰούλιος τῷ Παύλῳ χρησάμενος). Julius's kindness is made manifest when he allows his prisoner, Paul, to go to his friends so that his needs can be met (ἐπέτρεψεν πρὸς τοὺς φίλους πορευθέντι ἐπιμελείας τυχεῖν, v. 3).

In Acts 27, Luke depicts the centurion Julius as responsible for securing transport for Paul and the other prisoners. In Acts 27:6, he locates an Alexandrian ship bound for Italy and ἐνεβίβασεν ἡμᾶς εἰς αὐτό. Despite Paul's warnings, the centurion heeds the advice of the captain and ship owner (v. 11), and the ship is perilously tossed about in a storm. As the ship is about to run aground, the centurion and the soldiers, who are presumably under Julius's command, listen to Paul, who tells them that the sailors must stay on the boat or ὑμεῖς σωθῆναι οὐ δύνασθε (v. 31). The soldiers now follow Paul's orders and cut the ropes to the dingy on which the sailors were to escape (v. 32). Paul encourages those on board to eat some food. Luke's narration resembles the

---

[92] It remains unsettled whether the author of Acts is attempting to legitimize his report with actual first-person sources (Jürgen Roloff, *Die Apostelgeschichte* [NTD; Göttingen: Vandenhoeck & Ruprecht, 1981], 9–10, 238–40, 294–95, 358–59), or is composing from whole cloth (Ernst Haenchen, "Acta 27," in *Zeit und Geschichte: Dankesgabe an Rudolf Bultmann zum 80. Geburtstag* [ed. E. Dinkler; Tübingen: Mohr, 1964], 235–54), or is aiming for veracity in the manner of ancient historiographies (E. Plümacher, "Wirklichkeitserfahrung und Geschichtsschreibung bei Lukas: Erwägungen zu den Wir-Stücken der Apostelgeschichte," *ZNW* 68 [1977]: 2–22) and sea voyages (Vernon Robbins, "By Land and By Sea: The We-Passages and Ancient Sea Voyages," in *Perspectives on Luke-Acts* [ed. C. H. Talbert; Danville, VA: Association of Baptist Professors of Religion, 1978], 215–42). Praeder proposes that "an inclusive account of traditional, source critical, redaction critical, and comparative literary solutions" provides the best scenario for understanding the presence and function of the "we-sections" in Acts (Susan Marie Praeder, "The Problem of First Person Narration in Acts," *NovT* 29 [1987]: 194).

[93] For details on Paul's voyage to Rome, see J. Smith, *The Voyage and Shipwreck of St. Paul* (4th; London; Eugene, OR: Longmans, Green; Wipf & Stock, 1880); E. J. Goodspeed, "Paul's Voyage to Italy," *BW* 34 (1909): 337–45; and Susan Marie Praeder, "Acts 27:1–28:16: Sea Voyages in Ancient Literature and the Theology of Luke–Acts," *CBQ* 46 (1984): 683–706.

Last Supper in Luke 22:19, for Paul in the presence of all (ἐνώπιον πάντων, v. 35), gives thanks to God and breaks the bread. Since Luke notes that all were encouraged and ate (v. 36) and states the number of all the passengers (v. 37), we may presume that Julius and the soldiers were among those who participated in this eucharistic celebration. As the ship nears land, the soldiers intend to kill the prisoners to prevent their escape (v. 42),[94] but the centurion βουλόμενος διασῶσαι τὸν Παῦλον (v. 43) prevents them. Either Paul has found favor with Julius, hence his φιλανθρωπία, or Paul is an important prisoner who must be delivered to Rome unharmed. Those in the ship who are able to swim are to jump overboard first, while the rest are to use planks from the ship to float ashore (v. 44).

After his final arrival in Rome, Paul is placed under "light military custody."[95] The last soldier to appear in Acts is in 28:16, where he is said to serve as a guard for Paul (σὺν τῷ φυλάσσοντι αὐτὸν στρατιώτῃ).[96] Likely, Luke wishes to imply that this soldier was a member of the Praetorian Guard in Rome.[97] Though he is neither named nor described, he does seem to function more as a bodyguard than as a prison guard, for Acts concludes with the statement that Paul remained in Rome for two years at his own expense,[98] κηρύσσων τὴν βασιλείαν τοῦ θεοῦ καὶ διδάσκων τὰ περὶ τοῦ κυρίου Ἰησοῦ Χριστοῦ (28:31). Luke

---

[94] The Code of Justinian (9.4.4) states that the soldiers responsible for the prisoners could be executed if the prisoners escaped. From a period more contemporaneous with Acts, the soldier in Petronius's "Widow of Ephesus" (111–112) seems to fear a similar fate. The Herodian soldiers in Acts 12:19 are dealt with severely when Peter escaped from prison.

[95] Rapske, *The Book of Acts and Paul in Roman Custody*, 182.

[96] The Western text adds ὁ ἑκατόνταρχος παρέδωκεν τοὺς δεσμίους τῷ στρατοπεδάρχῳ τῷ Παύλῳ ἐπετράπη. As Broughton had noted, in the Latin, the term στρατοπέδαρχος could refer to the head of the *castra peregrina*, a camp for legionary officers on furlough in Rome (Broughton, "The Roman Army," 444). Rapske reviews the four identifications for στρατοπέδαρχος, concluding it is just as likely to refer to the head of the Praetorian (Rapske, *The Book of Acts and Paul in Roman Custody*, 175–77).

[97] Saddington, "Roman Military and Administrative Personnel in the New Testament," 2418. In Phil 1:13, Paul mentions the Praetorian Guard who come to know that Paul's imprisonment is for Christ. The Praetorian Guard were the elite soldiers who served as the emperor's bodyguard and military force within the city of Rome. For a discussion of the Praetorian Guard and their functions in Rome, see Sandra Bingham, *The Praetorian Guard: A History of Rome's Elite Special Forces* (London: Tauris, 2013), and Sandra Ottley, "The Role played by the Praetorian Guard in the Events of AD 69, as described by Tacitus in his Historiae" (Ph.D. diss, University of Western Australia, 2009); Watson, *The Roman Soldier*, 16–17; and Keppie, *The Making of the Roman Army*, 187–88.

[98] Henry J. Cadbury, "Lexical Notes on Luke–Acts: III. Luke's Interest in Lodging," *JBL* 45 (1926): 305–22; and Rapske, *The Book of Acts and Paul in Roman Custody*, 177–79.

has Paul mention a chain in verse 20, though this may be metaphorical,[99] because he has not yet stood trial and therefore, according to the *Lex Julia*, should not be bound. Many speculate about why Luke does not narrate Paul's trial in Rome.[100] Luke has carefully established that the Roman Empire, through its envoys and the military, has repeatedly shown deference to Jesus and his apostles and has recognized – if not explicitly, then certainly implicitly – that Jesus is a mighty and worthy κύριος. Thus, Luke could not end his story with the acknowledgement that Rome has the upper hand. Even if Paul is guarded by the attending soldier (28:16), he is still able to preach μετὰ πάσης παρρησίας ἀκωλύτως (28:31), suggesting that far from hindering the spread of the gospel, the presence of a Roman soldier may have actually emboldened Paul.

3.3.2 The Characterization of the Centurion and Soldiers in Chapters 27–28

Luke directly describes the centurion in Acts 27. He has a personal name and a cohort designation, and his behavior toward Paul is described as φιλανθρώπως. Adding to the list of named military characters (Cornelius in Acts 10 and Claudius Lysias in Acts 21–23), the author introduces another centurion, who has a fine Roman moniker – Julius. Speidel proposes on the sole basis of the centurion's name that he was a Roman citizen, and was "of a position and of a status that enabled him to deal with Roman officialdom in the capital."[101] Saddington concurs: "There is no reason to doubt that Julius was himself a Roman citizen."[102] Like Cornelius and Claudius Lysias, Julius has the distinction of not only being named by the author but also as being presented as having Roman citizenship. Broughton is much less certain. In fact, he finds Luke's choice of Julius odd. "It is perhaps surprising that a centurion of a Syrian auxiliary Cohors Augusta should have been given charge of an important prisoner on the road to Rome, for we should expect at least a legionary centurion or else one of the *frumentarii* to perform this duty."[103] Although the *frumentarii* performed a

---

[99] Foakes-Jackson and Lake, *The Beginnings of Christianity,* 346.

[100] Scholars have posited historical, theological and narrative reasons for the ending of Acts. As Barrett noted, "Luke is allowing the legal proceedings against Paul to drop out of the narrative (*Acts*, 2.1232). Failing to narrate Paul's death resulted from the author's theological concerns, according to Trompf ("On Why Luke Declined to Recount the Death of Paul," in *Luke–Acts. New Perspectives from the Society of Biblical Literature Seminar* [ed. Charles H. Talbert; New York: Crossroads Publishing], 225–39). Luke is intentionally evoking "narrative suspension," according to Marguerat, "which allows the author of Acts consciously to use silence and ambivalence in editing the end of his monumental work ("The Enigma of the Silent Closing of Acts [28:16–31]," 304).

[101] Michael P. Speidel, "The Roman Army in Judaea under the Procurators," 240. Neither Speidel nor Saddington question the historicity of the account.

[102] Saddington, "Roman Military and Administrative Personnel in the New Testament," 2417.

[103] Broughton, "The Roman Army," 444.

variety of services, including the transportation of prisoners, they were not organized until the time of Domitian,[104] and thus could not have been involved with Paul's transport.

The identity of the auxiliary cohort to which Julius belonged has long been debated. Schürer identifies the *cohortes Sebastenorum* as the entire garrison at Caesarea. The σπεῖρα Σεβαστή was simply distinguished from among the four other cohorts by its honorary title bestowed by the emperor.[105] However, Schürer's hypothesis is undermined when one accepts that other units, such as the *cohors Italica*, were stationed at Caesarea alongside the *cohortes Sebastenorum*. Speidel critiques Schürer's proposal, remarking that "Schürer is undeniably wrong...when he says that Acts report the Augustan cohort as having been stationed in Caesarea."[106] Schürer is reading Josephus's account of the troops of Herod Antipas into the Acts account, an easily made mistake given the similarity of their names, since Josephus refers to these troops as Σεβαστηνοί (*B.J.* 2.52, 58, 63, 74, 236; *A.J.* 20.122). Inscriptions testify to the early-first-century existence of a *cohors Augusta* and locate the cohort in the Syrian province.[107] Luke could have either unit in mind, though Broughton argues that σπεῖρα Σεβαστή translates into the Latin as *cohors Augusta* and not *cohors Sebastenorum*.[108] The actual title of the unit is less important than its designation as an auxiliary cohort named for Augustus. Luke is again drawing a close connection between Rome and its military personnel serving in the provinces.

3.3.2.1 The Centurion Julius as a Φιλάνθρωπος

Startlingly, a Roman Auxiliary Centurion is described as acting φιλανθρώπως, a virtue one would not associate with the stereotypes of the military rank and file. Rather, it is virtue expected of good generals, like Cyrus, who is described as exceeding in φιλάνθρωπος (Xen, *Cyr.* 1.21.).

The virtue of obedience (so necessary in the soldiers under his command) does not arise in a ruler, but *philanthropia* is all important. This virtue does not count as one of the ordinary soldierly virtues, since soldiers are more concerned with killing the enemy than with making and preserving friendships, but every officer must have it; and the moral virtues of Cyrus are entirely summed up in his *philanthropia*.[109]

---

[104] William G. Sinnigen, "The Roman Secret Service," *CJ* 57 (1961): 65–72 and J. C. Mann, "The Organization of the Frumentarii," *ZPE* 74: 149–50.

[105] Schürer, *The History of the Jewish People in the Age of Jesus Christ*, 363–64.

[106] Speidel, "The Roman Army in Judaea under the Procurators," 238.

[107] B. Haussoullier and H. Ingholt, *Inscriptions grècques de Syrie, Syria* (1924), 316–41; and Speidel, "The Roman Army in Judaea under the Procurators," 238.

[108] Broughton, "The Roman Army," 443.

[109] Lionel Pearson, "Popular Ethics in the World of Thucydides," *CP* 52 (1957): 230.

Luke means for the authorial audience to recognize in Julius an extraordinary character, who, though only an officer of an auxiliary cohort, nonetheless, evidences an exemplary virtue. Luke intends this paradox, as is evident in light of the use of φιλανθρωπία in Acts 28:2, where he writes οἵ τε βάρβαροι παρεῖχον οὐ τὴν τυχοῦσαν φιλανθρωπίαν ἡμῖν. Demosthenes distinguishes the βάρβαροι from the Greeks chiefly because the barbarian does not possess φιλανθρωπία (*Mid.* 49). In fifth-century tragedy and comedy and later in New Comedy, the audience expects φιλανθρωπία to be displayed.[110] In *De vita Mosis I, II,* Philo recasts Moses as a model of φιλανθρωπία, drawing on the philosophy of Hellenistic kingship.[111] In Plutarch's *Lives,*

> it is the virtue par excellence of the civilized, educated man; and it manifests itself in any manner that is proper for such a man, be it affability, courtesy, liberality, kindness, clemency, etc. The *philanthrōpos* is gracious and considerate toward all with whom he associates, he is generous toward the needy, he is also merciful and clement toward his enemies.[112]

Luke describes Julius by a virtue not expected in a centurion whose narrative setting is the province. Soldiers in literature may behave kindly toward their tent mates, as did the comrades in Apuleius's *Metamorphoses*. As in *Leucippe and Clitophon*, a general may be moved with pity by the plight of another (3.14.3). With his demonstration of φιλανθρωπία toward a prisoner, Julius is unlike other stereotypical presentations of soldiers. But like the centurion of Capernaum who sought the aid of Jesus for a dying slave, Julius's actions towards an inferior unsettle the authorial audience's expectations.

3.3.2.2 The Centurion Julius to the Rescue

Julius further exemplifies his kindness toward Paul when he protects him from the other soldiers who intend to kill the prisoners rather than have them escape during the shipwreck. The use of διασῴζω here rather than σῴζω suggests to Barrett that "there may be a desire to distinguish rescue from shipwreck from being saved in a Christian, religious sense."[113] If this were true, how does one read ὑμεῖς σωθῆναι οὐ δύνασθε in 27:31? Does Paul mean that Christian salvation awaits the soldiers and centurion? Though Luke is referring to personal safety in v. 31 and intends that the centurion see Paul safely "through" (διά) the current danger (v. 43), the author could have the theological understanding in mind as well.

---

[110] Robert D. Lamberton, "Philanthropia and the Evolution of Dramatic Taste," *Phoenix* 37 (1983): 95–103.

[111] Milo Van Veldhuizen, "Moses: a Model of Hellenistic Philanthropia," *Reformed Review* 38 (1985): 215–24.

[112] Hubert Martin, "The Concept of *Philanthropia* in Plutarch's Lives," *American Journal of Philology* 82 (1961): 174.

[113] Barrett, *Acts*, 2.1214.

Luke's portrait of Julius mixes stereotypical expectations and unexpected behaviors. Julius, like Claudius Lysias before him, reflects the stereotyped "rescuer," in the vein of Charmides and Polyidus. Yet, Paul is the one who must "rescue" Julius and the others when he recommends they not let the crew escape. The authorial audience expects the centurion to heed the advice of the captain and owner over the advice of Paul, the prisoner (Acts 27:11), but would be surprised when this same centurion prevents his men from carrying out what would seem to be practical procedures – killing the prisoners lest they escape (27:43). This direct identification of Julius's behavior toward Paul as φιλανθρώπως is Luke's final comment on the centurions in his two-volumes. They have demonstrated ἀξίωμα (Luke 7:4), ἀγάπη (Luke 7:5), πίστις (Luke 7:9); εὐσέβεια καὶ φόβος τὸν θεόν (Acts 10:2), and now φιλανθρωπία (Acts 27:3). Surely, Luke's reader would notice that these centurions behave contrary to expectations.

The other soldiers on board are not developed characters but reminiscent of the centurion in Acts 23:17–18, they do respond to Paul's suggestion that they cut the ropes to the boat on which the sailors are to escape. The last soldier encountered in the Acts of the Apostles is little developed. Though Paul may be chained to the soldier, his presence does not seem to limit Paul's proclamation. More than likely, this unnamed soldier is a member of the Praetorian Guard, but Luke does not say so explicitly. Though Luke does not describe him, this soldier perpetuates the positive presentation of the Roman military, who have protected Paul since his rescue in Jerusalem in Acts 21.

4. Conclusion

The literary soldiers portrayed in Luke-Acts are distinguished according to whom they serve. Those soldiers under the jurisdiction of the Herods are ineffectual and little characterized. In Luke 23:11, they are brutes and in Acts 12, they are extensions of the king's power, which is incapable of restraining Peter. Luke transfers the scourging of Jesus from the Roman auxiliary soldiers of his sources onto those in the employ of Herod Antipas. His interest in portraying the Roman soldiers contrary to his source is further evident when he fails to identify precisely who crucified Jesus. He does have the Roman auxiliary soldiers mock Jesus, but only after the rulers have initiated the taunting. At the crucifixion, Luke's Roman soldiers demonstrate uncharacteristic restraint, and their officer acknowledges the crucified prisoner as δίκαιος. When Peter escapes from multiple chains and guards, the Herodian soldiers are the ones who are perplexed (Acts 12:18) and whom Herod Agrippa punishes for their dereliction of duty. When Roman auxiliary soldiers are in a similar position, they propose to kill their prisoners rather than allow them to escape.

Luke pays particular attention to distinctions in rank, demonstrating that he possesses a thorough knowledge of the stereotypes appropriate to foot soldiers and those befitting officers. Those doing their military service question John who directs them to stop shaking down people, which supports the stereotype of the brutish soldier on assignment in the province. The tribune Claudius Lysias, on the other hand, is the model officer. He is clearly in command, giving orders, summoning troops, and contacting his superior officer. Throughout the two volumes, Luke shows particular interest in centurions. He describes them more thoroughly using direct and indirect means. The centurion of Capernaum and Cornelius of Caesarea will be investigated fully in the next chapter, but the centurions analyzed in this chapter – the centurion at the cross, those under the command of the tribune, and Julius of the Augustan Cohort – all demonstrate that a deft hand has portrayed them both as stereotypical and as contrary to the stereotypes, producing much more complex characters. Luke seems more familiar with centurions and more favorably disposed to those of this rank.

The author of the Gospel of Luke and Acts of the Apostles is well aware not only of differences in military units and ranks but also of the variety of literary stereotypes available to characterize soldiers. Nonetheless, Luke has carefully constructed a cumulative portrait of the Roman military that bears only little correlation to the types found in other ancient literature. His characterization suggests that Roman soldiers may be abusive, mocking, and greedy, but they are also likely to be desirous of repentance, humble, and insightful. Where it suits his narrative purpose, Luke portrays his soldiers in keeping with his authorial audience's expectations. Why would soldiers approach John, who preaches a baptism for the repentance of sin, if soldiers were not sinners? As the strong arm of Rome, obedient soldiers are present at Jesus' crucifixion. To save Paul from near death, the tribune rushes into the Temple to quell a riot, as is expected of a good commander. And the centurion listens to the captain of his ship over a prisoner.

In service to his rhetorical agenda, Luke also characterizes soldiers against the grain of expectation. With the exception of those soldiers who are little more than elements, Luke both employs stereotypes and overturns stereotypes in his characterizations of soldiers and officers. Brutes evidence interest in conversion (Luke 3:14). Roman soldiers obediently lead Jesus to his death, but they do not beat him prior to his crucifixion (Luke 23:33). A centurion witnesses the crucifixion, but at Jesus' death, announces him as δίκαιος and glorifies God. As an ἀνὴρ ἀγαθός, the tribune leads his soldiers to investigate a disturbance and captures Paul, a would-be instigator, whom he rescues repeatedly. This commander will, in the end, obey the directions of his prisoner. The stereotype of rescuer is also found in the centurion Julius, who likewise, will, in the end, be rescued by Paul. Though Julius has Paul in custody, he still acts kindly toward him.

Presenting soldiers against the grain of the authorial audience's expectation is not the final step in the Lucan literary portrayal of the Roman military. As will be evident in the following chapter, Luke must actually transcend the stereotype before a soldier can be recognized as possessing πίστις (Luke 7:9) and then be filled with the Holy Spirit and be baptized (Acts 10:44–48).

Chapter 5

Transcending Stereotypes:
The Centurions of Capernaum and Caesarea

1. Introduction

In Luke's employment and contradiction of stereotypes, he has set two types of soldiers at odds with each other. Roman military characters are presented positively, while Herodian soldiers are typed negatively. The soldiers questioning John the Baptist recognize their situation and desire repentance. Though Luke must acknowledge the hand that Roman soldiers played in the crucifixion, he downplays or eliminates their violent actions. Instead, he transposes the scourging of Jesus to Herodian soldiers. The centurion at the foot of the cross announces Jesus' righteousness and/or innocence and responds to the events of Jesus' death by glorifying God – the proper response of a disciple. In the Acts of the Apostles, soldiers of Herod Agrippa are incapable of securing Peter, despite their numbers, while the Roman tribune Claudius Lysias and the centurion Julius will "save" Paul on several occasions. Finally, the person accompanying Paul in Rome is a lone Roman soldier.

In this chapter I investigate two outstanding Roman centurions whom the Lucan author has deliberately developed with great care. Luke portrays them sometimes stereotypically and sometimes against the grain, but in general they transcend expectations. The centurion of Capernaum demonstrates appropriate humility before Jesus and confidence in Jesus' ability to heal. Luke intentionally depicts this centurion to foreshadow the centurion in Caesarea. When finally meeting Cornelius in Acts 10, the authorial audience is not surprised that this centurion is εὐσεβὴς καὶ φοβούμενος τὸν θεόν, odd as that appellation would seem given the characterization of soldiers throughout much of Greco-Roman literature.

2. The Centurion of Capernaum: Luke 7:1–10

The centurion of Capernaum is the most developed military character in the Gospel of Luke. Along with Jesus, he is also a main character in the pericope, though he never appears on stage.[1] Within the Gospel of Luke, the story of the centurion of Capernaum stands mid-way through Jesus' Galilean ministry,[2] a narrative climax of the Sermon on the Plain.[3] In Luke 6:20–49, Jesus exhorts his disciples in a series of beatitudes and woes (vv. 20–26), and commands them to love their enemies (vv. 27–36), and directs them not to judge each other (vv. 37–42). The test of their fidelity to these words will be evident in their good deeds (6:43–45), and their ability to hear and respond to Jesus will result in a sure foundation (6:46–49). Within this larger setting, Luke 7:1–10 serves as an exemplification of the Sermon on the Plain,[4] demonstrating Jesus' ἐξουσία[5] and the appropriate response of a disciple. Specifically, the centurion of Capernaum becomes an unlikely personification for Jesus' teachings in Luke 6:43–45 and 47–48. A good tree produces what is good, and its fruit confirms its goodness (6:43). Likewise, a good person produces goodness from what is stored in his or her heart (6:45). The centurion's good works for the Jewish community evidence his worth (7:5). Everyone who hears (ἀκούων μου τῶν λόγων, 6:47) Jesus' words and responds to them (ποιῶν αὐτούς, 6:47) builds on a sure foundation (6:48). When the centurion hears about Jesus (ἀκούσας δὲ περὶ τοῦ Ἰησοῦ), he sends (ἀπέστειλεν) a delegation to him (7:3). Though a miraculous healing[6] concludes the story, the focus remains on the centurion's faith, which Jesus lauds: οὐδὲ ἐν τῷ Ἰσραὴλ τοσαύτην πίστιν εὗρον

---

[1] Bovon, *Luke 1*, 258.

[2] Alan Kirk proposes that 4:1–13; 6:20b–40; and 7:1–10 "was conceived of and executed as a literary whole in an editorial operation devoted to textualization of Jesus traditions within the framework of Hellenistic-Jewish parenetic genres." The Q source united these three distinct pericopes by their intent to present Jesus as the fulfillment of the prophets ("Some Compositional Conventions of Hellenistic Wisdom Texts and the Juxtaposition of 4:1–13; 6:20b–49; and 7:1–10 in Q," *JBL* 116 [1997]: 257).

[3] Fitzmyer argues that the differences between the Matthean Sermon on the Mount (5:1–7:27) and Luke's Sermon on the Plain result chiefly from Matthew's extensive use of Q material, which Luke includes later in his travel narrative. Additionally, Luke deletes overtly Jewish-Christian concerns and adds some verses of his own (6:24–26, 27c, 28a, 34–35a, 37bc, 38a, 39a). See *The Gospel According to Luke I–IX* (AB; New York: Doubleday, 1981), 628–29.

[4] Athanasius Polag, *Die Christologie der Logienquelle* (WMANT, 45; Neukirchen-Vluyn: Neukirchener-Verlag, 1977), 158.

[5] Uwe Wegner, *Der Hauptmann von Kafarnaum (Mt 7, 28a, 8, 5–10.13 par Lk 7, 1–10) ein Beitrag zur Q-Forschung* (WUNT 2.14; Tübingen: Mohr Siebeck, 1985), 299–300.

[6] The healing takes place at a distance, but it does not occupy the center of the story in either Luke or Matthew. For Luke, see Fitzmyer, *The Gospel According to Luke I–IX*, 649–50; and R. Bultmann, *History of the Synoptic Tradition* (Oxford: Blackwell, 1968), 38. For Matthew, see Ulrich Luz, *Matthew 8–20* (Hermeneia; Minneapolis: Fortress Press, 2001), 8; and W. D. Davies and Dale C. Allison, *The Gospel According to Saint Matthew* (ICC; Edinburgh: T & T Clark, 1991), 17.

(7:9).[7] The narrative serves to challenge and embarrass Israel into a fuller response to Jesus, such as his teachings demand and the centurion demonstrates.[8] Luke structures the Gospel narrative so that the first example of a good Gentile disciple is found in the unlikely person of a Roman centurion,[9] though the soldiers in Luke 3:14 hint at the possibility.

2.1 Intertextual Antecedents

The outline of the passage derives from Q, but the Septuagint may have also influenced this pericope, as it inspired Luke elsewhere.[10] The centurion of Capernaum resembles Naaman, another well-respected Gentile officer for whom a Jewish girl intercedes (2 Kgs 5:1–3).[11] Naaman never actually meets Elisha (2 Kgs 5:5–10), and the healing takes place at a distance (2 Kgs 5:14).[12] The Lucan Jesus' overt reference to the Naaman tale in 4:27 directs the authorial audience to read this centurion in light of Naaman.[13]

The request of the centurion, which originates with Q, shares similarities with both the story of Jairus's daughter and the story of the Syrophoenician

---

[7] Augustin George notes that the central focus of the story is the faith of the centurion and not the healing of the servant ("Guérison de l'esclave d'un centurion," *Assemblées du Seigneur* 40 [1972]: 76).

[8] Richard A. Horsley, "Questions about Redactional Strata and the Social Relations Reflected in Q," *SBL Seminar Papers* (1989): 187.

[9] Matthew distances his centurion (8:5–13) from the Sermon on the Mount, placing the pericope between the healing of a leper (8:1–4) and the healing of others (8:14–18).

[10] For Luke's use of the Septuagint, see C. F. Evans, "The Central Section of St. Luke's Gospel," in *Studies in the Gospels* (ed. D. Nineham; Oxford: Blackwell, 1955), 37–53; James A. Sanders, "From Isaiah 64 to Luke 4," in *Christianity, Judaism and Other Greco-Roman Cults*, vol. 12.1 (ed. Jacob Neusner; Studies in Judaism in Late Antiquity; Leiden: E. J. Brill, 1975), 75–106; and Fitzmyer, *The Gospel According to Luke I–IX*, 114–18.

[11] Joel Green, *The Gospel of Luke* (Grand Rapids, MI: Eerdmans, 1997), 284.

[12] Another comparison is made to Jethro (Deut. 5:27; Exod. 18:13–27). Derrett cited Exod 18:11–27, where Jethro recognizes the supremacy of the God of Moses and recommends that Moses delegate authority to assist him ("Law in the New Testament: The Syro-Phoenician Woman and the Centurion of Capernaum," *NovT* 15 [1973]: 161, 178). The comparison between Jethro and the centurion of Capernaum seems too strained to have been a literary influence for Luke. Also see R. A. J. Gagnon, "Luke's Motives for Redaction in the Account of the Double Delegation in Luke 7:1–10," *NovT* 36 (1994): 128.

[13] Gagnon disagrees, acknowledging that the two pericopes contain a Gentile military officer who requests a healing, which is accomplished at a distance, but he maintains that "little connects the *details* of the two accounts (despite 4:27)" ("Luke's Motives," 128). Derrett suggests that in reading the Q-version, Luke references 2 Kings 1, where Ahaziah sends three delegations to Elijah who refuses to come because the king had first sought the aid of a foreign god ("Law in the New Testament: The Syro-Phoenician Woman and the Centurion of Capernaum," 181), but this comparison is more tenuous.

woman in Mark. Jairus requests that Jesus heal his daughter (Mark 5:22–23). Luke reworks παρακαλεῖ αὐτὸν πολλὰ (Mark 5:23), inserting παρεκάλει αὐτὸν εἰσελθεῖν εἰς τὸν οἶκον αὐτοῦ (Luke 8:41) and changing the direct speech of Jairus in Mark to an explanation of why Jesus was invited to his house. Again, Luke alters Mark's direct speech in the inserted story of the woman with a flow of blood. By limiting dialogue, Luke focuses the auditor's attention on Jesus' pronouncement: θυγάτηρ, ἡ πίστις σου σέσωκέν σε· πορεύου εἰς εἰρήνην (Luke 8:48). Luke's deletion of Mark's καὶ ἴσθι ὑγιὴς ἀπὸ τῆς μάστιγός σου (Mark 5:34) further suggests that Luke meant to focus on the pronouncement about faith and not the healing, as is also seen in Luke 7:1–10. The raising of Jairus's daughter finds its parallel not in Luke 7 but in Acts 9:36–41 where the dead widow Tabitha, also called Dorcas, is raised to life amidst a din of mourning.[14]

In Mark 7:25–26, the Syrophoenician woman seeks the aid of Jesus, though she does not ask that Jesus come to her daughter. Like Jairus and the Syrophoenician woman, the centurion requests that Jesus heal a sick family member. The woman's daughter is healed at a distance (Mark 7:30), as is the centurion's servant (Luke 7:10). The stories share themes of reciprocity, charity, and humility, and parts of the Syrophoenician story may actually appear elsewhere in Luke (11:13; 16:21).[15] But Luke does not include the story of the Syrophoenician mother, preferring to have the centurion be the Gentile whose faith is lauded.

2.2 Luke's Redaction of Q

Echoes of the Septuagint and similar themes in Mark may have affected Luke's redaction, but he begins by building on the skeleton of Q. By rearranging the word order found in Q, changing vocabulary, and inserting new material or deleting Q material, the author develops the portrayal of the centurion and builds the suspense leading to Jesus' pronouncement. John 4:46–54 indicates that this gospel writer also knows a version of the story but redacts it into a healing about a royal official's son rather than a saying of Jesus inspired by a centurion.[16] John shares with the Lucan version (a) that the petitioner has heard of Jesus (ἀκούσας, John 4:47a and Luke 7:3), and (b) the intensity of the illness (ἀποθνῄσκειν, John 4:47 and ἤμελλεν τελευτᾶν, Luke 7:2). But whereas Q and Luke name the petitioner as a centurion, John's fig-

---

[14] Barrett, *Acts,* 1.478.

[15] Derrett, "Law in the New Testament," 184.

[16] "Both traditions, Q and John, thus reflect the same memory, but were transmitted independently thereafter with the result that the direction of the versions now diverge from one another" (Bovon, *Luke 1,* 250). Hans-Josef Klauck has noted that John "has reworked it at least equally as thoroughly as Luke did" (personal correspondence, July 13, 2007).

ure is a royal official (βασιλικός, John 4:46b), and the sick person in John is most often referred to as a son (υἱός, John 4:46b, 47b, 50, 53).

In the reconstruction of Q, where Luke and Matthew diverge in their stories of the centurion of Capernaum, the commentators have chosen the Matthean version,[17] which is essentially a dialogue between Jesus and the centurion. No other actors enter the scene. Immediately evident in a comparison between reconstructed Q 7:1 –10 and the pericope in Luke is the author's placement of ἑκατοντάρχης [18] (7:2). Though the subject of the sentence is δοῦλος, Luke has brought forward the genitive ἑκατοντάρχου (7:2), so that the reader encounters the centurion first. The Q reconstruction opens with a circumstantial participle, followed by the finite verb and then the nominative, ἑκατόνταρχος. A similar alternation is made in Luke 7:6. Where Q reads οὐκ εἰμὶ ἱκανὸς, Luke has switched to οὐ γὰρ ἱκανός εἰμι, stressing the adjective. In verse 9, Q has Jesus speak to those following him: εἶπεν τ(οις) ἀκολουθοῦ(σιν). Luke reverses the order: τῷ ἀκολουθοῦντι αὐτῷ ὄχλῳ εἶπεν. Those Jesus speaks to are introduced first, and Luke specifies that they are in the crowd. Placement can also de-emphasize a word. The Q version notes whose roof is in question: μου ὑπὸ τὴν στέγην. Luke relocates the pronoun to follow the object of the preposition, thus ὑπὸ τὴν στέγην μου (7:6). This pattern of Lucan revision of Q continually adds emphasis to the centurion, his lack of worth, and those following in the crowd.

Luke has also built upon the framework of Q by changing some of the vocabulary, inserting words, or even deleting them. Of particular note is παῖς,[19] found in Matthew 8:6, 8, 13. Luke retains the second reference to δοῦλος (Luke 7:7) but alters the first and third references (Luke 7:2, 10).[20] Luke's

---

[17] The editors of the *Critical Edition of Q* reconstruct Q 7:1–10 giving precedence to the Gospel of Matthew (*The Critical Edition of Q*, 104–17). Fitzmyer concurs that Matthew retains the form originally found in Q (*The Gospel According to Luke I–IX*, 648–49).

[18] Ἑκατοντάρχης and its declined forms are found in the New Testament solely in Luke (Luke 7:2, 6; 23:47; Acts 10:1, 22; 21:32; 22:26; 23:17, 23; 27:1, 31, 43), while ἑκατόνταρχος and its various forms are found three times in Matthew (Matt 8:5, 8; 27:54) and once in Acts 22:25. Like Luke, Josephus uses both terms, sometimes in the same book (ἑκατόνταρχος, *B.J.* 3.124 and ἑκατοντάρχης, *B.J.* 3.333), with no discernible difference between the two.

[19] In addition to the connotation of "child," παῖς often refers to a young man or woman taken as a slave as part of the spoils of battle. In *Anabasis*, the soldiers are forced to divest themselves of all excess baggage, including a handsome boy or woman upon whom a soldier has set his heart (Xen. *Anab.* 4.1.14). The taking of young women and handsome young men by Roman soldiers is recorded by Plautus (*Mil. glor.* 1102–14), Cicero (*Phil* 3.31), Livy (26.13.15) and Tacitus (*Hist.* 3.33) among others.

[20] As Derrett comments, "we are intended to be in doubt" whether the sick one is a slave or a son ("Law in the New Testament," 174). Though John may be preserving the more original version with his reference to son (Hans-Josef Klauck, personal correspond-

exchange of δοῦλος for παῖς [21] is not unlike John's use of υἱός, παῖς, and παιδίον as synonymous terms for the same sick person, though Luke does not present him as a son.[22] The centurion, through his intermediaries, is not asking Jesus to heal his servant (θεραπεύσω αὐτόν, Matt 8:7, Q 7:3) but to save him (διασώσῃ τὸν δοῦλον αὐτοῦ, Luke 7:3). Through his second embassy, the centurion asks Jesus not to trouble himself (μὴ σκύλλου, 7:6), a respectful imperative not found in Q.

Although Luke mostly preserves Q 7:8, he emphasizes the ἐξουσία under which the centurion serves by adding τασσόμενος. Luke uses διατάσσω in Acts 24:23, where it also has a military connotation. The verb τάσσω in the active means "to draw up in order of battle," or "to marshal" (Hdt. 1.191; Thuc. 4.9; Xenophon, *Cyr.* 1.6).[23] Additionally, it has the connotation of "to appoint," or "to order" (Xenophon, *Anab.* 3.1.25; *Cyr.* 7.3.1). In the middle voice, the word can mean "to fall in," "form in order of battle" (Thuc. 1.48; 4.11), and the passive means "to be posted or stationed" (Hdt. 1.84; 7.212; Lysias 14.11). If Luke simply means that the centurion is "under authority," he need not have added the word τασσόμενος. However, with the participle, the centurion, through his ambassadors, is stating that he has been stationed under orders. Whether we are to understand that literally (stationed at Capernaum) or figuratively (commissioned) is less clear. As part of his appointment, he has soldiers at his command, and his authority extends to his household (τῷ δούλῳ μου, v. 8). Additionally, he has authority to send ambassadors (φίλοι) to intercede on his behalf. Verse 9 includes four additions that specify the actions of the verbs. Luke emphasizes that Jesus' amazement is focused on the centurion

---

ence, July 13, 2007), Luke surely means "slave." The length to which the centurion goes for the sake of a slave becomes part of the Lucan characterization, as discussed later. We would expect the centurion to respond to his sick child.

[21] Jennings and Liew argue that the παῖς about whom the centurion is so concerned is actually a sexual slave ("Mistaken Identities but Model Faith: Rereading the Centurion, the Chap, and the Christ in Matthew 8:5–13," *JBL* 123 [2004]: 467–94). That slaves were used to satisfy the master's or mistress's sexual desires is well documented, but Luke is concerned with constructing a portrait of a would-be disciple, so he does not intend sexual overtones. See M. I. Finley, *Ancient Slavery and Modern Ideology* (New York: Viking, 1980) on slaves as sexual property in the Roman context; and Jennifer A. Glancy, "Obstacles to Slaves' Participation in the Corinthian Church," *JBL* 117 (1998): 481–501; Carolyn Osiek, "Female Slaves, Porneia, and the Limits of Obedience," in *Early Christian Families in Context: An Interdisciplinary Dialogue* (ed. David L. Balch and Carolyn Osiek; Grand Rapids: Eerdmans, 2003), 255–74, and J. Albert Harrill, *Slaves in the New Testament: Literary, Social, and Moral Dimensions* (Minneapolis: Fortress Press, 2006) for slavery in early Christian communities.

[22] Ralph P. Martin, "The Healing of the 'Centurion's' Servant/Son," in *Unity and Diversity in New Testament Theology* (ed. Robert A. Guelich; Grand Rapids: Eerdmans, 1978), 21, n. 10.

[23] See LSJ, 1759 and BDAG, 991.

(ἐθαύμασεν αὐτὸν) and results from his having heard specific things (ἀκούσας δὲ ταῦτα). Jesus then pointedly turns (στραφεὶς) to address the crowd (τῷ ἀκολουθοῦντι αὐτῷ ὄχλῳ). Luke also deletes the words καὶ λέγει αὐτῷ and θεραπεύσω αὐτόν, preferring an indirect statement that Jesus went with the first embassy (Luke 7:6).

Both Luke and Matthew couch the Q material within a narrative setting. Matthew is brief, simply stating that as Jesus entered Capernaum, he was approached by a centurion. Matthew reserves his additions for an explanation of what awaits Israel because of its little faith (Matt 8:11–12). Luke, on the other hand, sets a scene in which the centurion actually never appears. A sick slave is at the point of death and is also ἔντιμος to the centurion. The audience does not learn how the Matthean centurion came to know of Jesus, but Luke acknowledges that it is in response to what the centurion has heard concerning Jesus. At the close of the pericope, Jesus responds to what he, in turn, has heard concerning the centurion.

The most lengthy addition into the Q material is found in verses 3–6b. The insertion is often called the double delegation for the two embassies sent by the centurion, and its origin is greatly debated.[24] I propose that, in light of the role the centurion plays as foreshadowing Cornelius in Acts 10,[25] the insertion

---

[24] Schnackenburg argues for the originality of the first delegation in the Q material but suggests that the second delegation is a Lucan creation (*Matthäusevangelium 1,1–16,20* [Würzburg: Echter, 1985], 79–80), a conclusion supported by Bovon (*Luke 1*, 259). Dauer attributes most of vv. 3–6b to Q but sees Luke's editorial hand in v. 7a. (*Johannes und Lukas: Untersuchungen zu den johanneisch-lukanischen Parallelperikopen Joh 4,46–54/Lk 7,1–10 — Joh 12,1–8/Lk 7,36–50; 10, 38–42 — Joh 20, 19–29/Lk 24, 36–49* [Würzburg: Echter, 1984], 146–47). Jeremias goes further in an attempt to distinguish between a Lucan source in the double-delegation and a Lucan redaction. (*Die Sprache des Lukasevangeliums: Redaktion und Tradition im Nicht-Markusstoff des dritten Evangeliums* [Göttingen: Vandenhoeck & Ruprecht, 1980], 151–56). Wegner concludes from a lengthy statistical analysis that the double delegation is originally found in the Lucan source and was not a Lucan redaction, because it has affinities with special Lucan material (*Der Hauptmann*). Gagnon argues that Wegner's summation is incorrect for three reasons: it overemphasizes source over redaction; it presumes that terms found in uniquely Lucan pericopes must have originated in the Lucan source and not been Lucan redactions; and it was overly confident about the conclusiveness of evidence from statistical analysis ("Statistical Analysis and the Case of the Double Delegation in Luke 7:3–7a," *CBQ* 55 [1993]: 711–12). Fitzmyer (*The Gospel According to Luke I–IX*, 649) credits Luke with the composition. Gagnon attributes the insertion to Lucan redaction ("The Case of the Double Delegation" and Gagnon, "Luke's Motives").

[25] "A comparison with Acts 10:1–11:18 suggests that Luke reworked the passage. There, as well, the subject of the story is a pagan but pious centurion, who has been particularly kind to the Jewish population; similarly a legation is sent to him, and something takes place shortly before the bearer of the divine message crosses the threshold" (Bovon, *Luke 1*, 259). The double delegation is therefore purposeful, as Wilson notes, "Luke has added these details both to bring into focus the personality of the centurion

of vv. 3–6a is a Lucan creation. The double delegation allows Luke to develop the centurion more fully while, at the same time, creating a greater resonance with Cornelius in Acts 10, and demonstrates that the Jewish embassy needed to be superseded by a second one. The following demonstrates the relationship between Luke 7:1–10 and Acts 10.[26]

Luke 7	Acts 10
Centurion introduced	Centurion introduced
v. 2 Ἑκατοντάρχου δέ τινος	v. 1 ἑκατοντάρχης ἐκ σπείρης τῆς καλουμένης Ἰταλικῆς ...
Acknowledgment of his virtue	Acknowledgement of his virtue
v. 4 ἄξιός ἐστιν	v. 2a εὐσεβὴς καὶ φοβούμενος τὸν θεὸν σὺν παντὶ τῷ οἴκῳ αὐτοῦ
Examples of virtue "for the people"	Example of virtue "for the people"
v. 5 ἀγαπᾷ γὰρ τὸ ἔθνος ἡμῶν καὶ τὴν συναγωγὴν αὐτὸς ᾠκοδόμησεν ἡμῖν	v. 2b ποιῶν ἐλεημοσύνας πολλὰς τῷ λαῷ καὶ δεόμενος τοῦ θεοῦ διὰ παντός ...
Sends delegations	Sends delegation
v. 3 ἀπέστειλεν πρὸς αὐτὸν πρεσβυτέρους τῶν Ἰουδαίων	v. 7 φωνήσας δύο τῶν οἰκετῶν καὶ στρατιώτην εὐσεβῆ τῶν προσκαρτερούντων
v. 6 ἔπεμψεν φίλους	αὐτῷ...
	v. 8 ἀπέστειλεν αὐτοὺς εἰς τὴν Ἰόππην
Centurion demonstrates humility	Centurion demonstrates humility
v. 6 οὐ γὰρ ἱκανός εἰμι	v. 25 συναντήσας αὐτῷ ὁ Κορνήλιος πεσὼν
v. 7 οὐδὲ ἐμαυτὸν ἠξίωσα	ἐπὶ τοὺς πόδας προσεκύνησεν
Jesus praises Centurion's faith	Holy Spirit falls upon Centurion
v. 9 οὐδὲ ἐν τῷ Ἰσραὴλ τοσαύτην πίστιν εὗρον	v. 44 ἐπέπεσεν τὸ πνεῦμα τὸ ἅγιον ἐπὶ πάντας τοὺς ἀκούοντας τὸν λόγον

In each pericope, Luke introduces the centurion (Luke 7:2//Acts 10:1) and names his virtues (Luke 7:4//Acts 10:2a), and then gives examples of them (Luke 7:5//Acts 10:2b). Both centurions send delegations (Luke 7:3, 6//Acts 10:7–8). Each centurion demonstrates humility (Luke 7:6–7//Acts 10:25) and receives praise or validation (Luke 7:9//Acts 10:44).

---

and his faith, and to enhance the parallel with the narrative of Cornelius, the first Gentile Christian (Acts 10–11)" (Stephen G. Wilson, *The Gentiles and the Gentile Mission in Luke-Acts* [Cambridge: Cambridge University Press, 1973], 31). Also see Fitzmyer, *The Gospel According to Luke I–IX*, 650.

[26] Gagnon finds similar parallels: "Like the suppliant in Luke 7:1–10, Cornelius is (1) a centurion who (2) is admired by the Jews (here for his piety, almsgiving to the Jewish people, and constant prayer, 10:2, 4, 22, 31, 34b–35); (3) sends (albeit single) delegation (here "two of his slaves and a devout soldier," 10:7) to (a) speak of his excellent standing among the Jews (10:22) and (b) bring the Jewish healer (here Peter) to his house; and (4) gives evidence of his humility (here by prostrating himself before the feet of Peter, 10:25)" (Gagnon, "Luke's Motives," 129).

The two embassies act in the *persona* of the centurion, having been commissioned as his ambassadors. The motifs of acknowledgment of unworthiness and confidence in Jesus' authority support the theme of a Gentile's faith exceeding that of Israel's, which is found in both Matthew and Luke and presumably originates with Q. The changes in word order and vocabulary, and insertions into and deletions of the Q material, allow Luke to enhance the portrait of the centurion of Capernaum without altering the narrative at the generic level. Luke 7:1–10 remains a pronouncement story,[27] though the character gets more than the typical cardboard treatment. Luke moves his military figures beyond cookie-cutter stereotypes and into more fully-rounded characterizations.

2.3 Analysis of the Characterization of the Centurion of Capernaum

Luke introduces the first centurion of his two-volumes expecting the authorial audience to bring its own knowledge of the Roman petty officer to the process of characterization. According to the literary stereotype, the authorial audience could anticipate encountering a brute. But the subsequent delegations challenge that assumption. The Jewish πρεσβύτεροι describe this soldier as worthy of Jesus' attention, and his friends relay his humility.

2.3.1 Expecting the Centurion to be Depicted as a Bully

After examining how Luke has intentionally reworked his source, we are able to assess the possible effect of those decisions on the authorial audience. As noted above, Luke redacts Q, relocating the word ἑκατοντάρχης to the beginning of verse 2. This verse contains the first mention of a centurion in the two volumes[28] and sets the standard by which future readers will interpret Lucan centurions. Luke's characterizations rely on the authorial audience's particular expectations of the way a centurion should behave, which are either confirmed or transcended by the figure. To understand the cultural horizon[29] against which Luke's auditors constructed their expectations, one must con-

---

[27] Vincent Taylor (*The Formation of the Gospel Traditions* [London: Macmillan, 1935], 75) and A. Richardson (*The Miracle Stories in the Gospels* [London: SCM, 1941], 78, n. 1) call the pericope a paradigm story, but the story does not exemplify a teaching or saying of Jesus so much as create a context for his pronouncement. The characterization of the centurion is key in recognizing the magnitude of Jesus' statement.

[28] Other centurions appear in Luke 7:6, and 23:47; Acts 10:1, 22; 22:25, 26; 24:23; 27:1, 6, 11, 31, 43.

[29] Klauck clarifies the distinction between questions of history and literary historical concerns within a text. "We work with historical material, yes, but mainly with material already reflected in literary or non-literary sources. And our aim is only to construct a horizon to which Luke's story may be linked. We are asking for the cultural script or the lexicon he is sharing with his addressees" (personal correspondence, July 13, 2007).

sider the military practices that generally would be known by a first-century audience.

The centurion in Luke 7 may be meant to reflect a centurion in the employ of Herod Antipas (*A.J.* 19.357), because Roman legionary soldiers would not have been stationed in the region under a Jewish king.[30] Luke's actual audience may not have noted the difference, since little distinguished a legionary centurion from an auxiliary centurion if both were Roman citizens. Josephus narrates the heroic acts of both, making no distinction between the two (*B.J.* 2.63, 236; *A.J.* 14.69–70; 19.307).[31] Luke will go to great lengths to identify Cornelius in Acts 10 as a Roman. For the sake of foreshadowing, he means to suggest that the centurion here is Roman as well – whether or not this suggestion would be historically accurate.[32] The only unequivocally "Roman" centurion in the Gospel is found in Luke 23:47, where the centurion carries out the dictates of the Roman prefect, Pilate.

Giving no explanation as to what a centurion is, or why one would be in Capernaum, Luke anticipates that his authorial audience is familiar enough with the term "centurion," so as to bring its own knowledge and experience to bear on the character.[33] Luke makes a similar assumption when he uses the word λεγιών in 8:30 with no description. The introduction of the unnamed centurion of Capernaum encourages the authorial auditors to use their own

---

[30] Saddington, "Roman Military and Administrative Personnel in the New Testament," 2413; and Bovon, *Luke 1*, 259.

[31] Josephus's characterizations of Roman centurions and soldiers provide the most relevant models for comparison with those in Luke-Acts because 1) his depictions include auxiliary soldiers as the Lucan narratives do, and 2) are set in Palestine in roughly the same time period.

[32] Schweizer suggests that the significance lies not in the petitioner being a Roman soldier but in fact that he is a Gentile and as such serves to shame Israel (v. 9) (*The Good News According to Luke*, 131).

[33] Fitzmyer writes, "The identification of (the centurion) is of little concern to Luke, for whom he may be rather a foreshadowing of the Roman centurion Cornelius in Acts 10:1" (*The Gospel According to Luke I–IX*, 651). The latter part of his statement is likely, but I disagree that Luke is unconcerned with the centurion's identification. Elsewhere, Luke is precise in designating the various branches of the Roman military and titles of its officers, and throughout his two volumes, he carefully crafts the portrait of the Roman military man of his time. Luke purposely gives his readers little information about this centurion. When the author perceives that a term or situation requires more information in order to be understood, he does include it. For example, the census is described within its political context, so that Joseph's response – despite the pregnancy of his wife – is more clear (Luke 2:1–3). Luke's urban community might have wondered why the shepherds were out at night. Luke adds that they were tending their sheep (Luke 2:8). The Jewish customs that brought Jesus' family to Jerusalem are noted (Luke 2:22–24, 42). In Acts, the Ethiopian's status and his employer are identified (Acts 8:27). And in case his community did not know the name "Tabitha," Luke adds that she is also called "Dorcas" (Acts 9:36).

imagination to flesh out this character. Their very expectations of how a centurion should behave create the paradox that culminates with: οὐδὲ ἐν τῷ Ἰσραὴλ τοσαύτην πίστιν εὗρον (Luke 7:9).

To a late first-century audience, the centurion was *the* face of the Roman military that most provincials would have occasion to see. The centurion stood at the nexus of military success or failure. He received orders from his superiors and ensured that his soldiers completed them. If he failed to keep discipline, adequately prepare his men, or follow through on his orders, he jeopardized Rome's interests and his own life. As noted earlier, centurions and their soldiers performed three essential tasks at the provincial level: mediation between the governor and the provincials, tax protection and/or gathering, and police work. As his title indicates, the centurion supervised one of the six centuries in a cohort. Polybius numbers a century at about 80 men, though most centuries were seldom at full strength. Centurions held significant power both over their men and over any civilians whom they encountered. Their salary evidenced their elevated status. A centurion's stipend was more than three times that of a foot soldier[34] and was supplemented by the bribes extracted from the soldiers under his command who hoped for lighter duty (*Ann.* 1.17).

The Republican centurion was chosen not for his bravery or fearlessness but for his leadership ability under fire. A willingness to stand his ground and die in battle marked the soldier as well-suited for the centurionate (Plb. 6.24.9). Tales of outstanding centurions most often occur in the accounts about the Roman Army of the Republic: "By Caesar's day many centurions had crossed the line from those who restrained to those who needed to be restrained, from the exemplars of *disciplina* to the exemplars of *virtus*,"[35] so that by the end of the first century, provincials would anticipate the worst if they encountered a centurion, and literary portraits often mirror that expectation.[36]

Most centurions were in their thirties by the time they received their staff, the symbol of the centurionate, and most served an average of twenty years. A centurion had a one-in-three chance of promotion to the coveted *primipilate* – if he lived long enough – which was strong incentive to remain in the military service past his initial enlistment period.[37] In fact, Augustus' intent was that

---

[34] Henry C. Boren, "Studies Relating to the Stipendium Militum," *Historia* 32 (1983): 429.

[35] Lendon, *Soldiers and Ghosts*, 218.

[36] See "Chapter 3 Literary Stereotypes of Greco-Roman Soldiers."

[37] Within the legion, the *primus pilus* was the senior centurion, commander of the first century of the first cohort. Retirement as a *primus pilus* assured a substantial grant, enough to elevate a citizen to equestrian status. "The *primipilares* in fact formed a new military aristocracy, the obvious and virtually only route into the equestrian order for the

his soldiers should strive for advancement.[38] Within the Roman auxiliary as well, centurions were also the primary promoters of discipline and supervision among the ranks. When a vexillation was dispatched for provincial service, the centurion would be the senior military official in charge, as evident in the crucifixion scene (Luke 23:47) and Paul's travels to Rome (Acts 27:1–28:10).

The histories are replete with accounts of brutal centurions who extracted blood and bribes from their rank and file soldiers, failed to keep discipline, or instigated mutinies. Tacitus recounts the unhappy end of a centurion named Lucilius whom his troops called "Get Another" (*Ann.* 1.23) because of his tendency to break whipping sticks over the soldiers' backs and call for additional ones. His men eventually revolted, and killed him. During the same Pannonian mutiny, the Fifteenth legion protected the centurion Sirpicus when the Eighth wanted to kill him (*Ann.* 1.23). Aufidienus Rufus, who was promoted from private to centurion and then to camp prefect, was assaulted by his men for attempting to bring back the old harsh military discipline (*Ann.* 1.20). Although centurions were occasionally the victims of the soldiers' anger (*Ann.* 1.32), more often they were bullies themselves.

Satires and comedies also portray the centurion as unjust and unconcerned with the rights of civilians. Juvenal writes that no citizen would dare attack a soldier, and if the citizen himself were abused by a soldier, the citizen better remain silent. The beatings by a soldier left one without teeth, with the likely loss of an eye, and with black-and-blue swelling of one's face (*Sat.* 16.11). But if one sought redress, the judge would be a centurion and the whole cohort would become one's enemies. (*Sat.* 16.20).

As "Chapter 3 Literary Stereotypes of Greco-Roman Soldiers" demonstrated, less frequent are the portrayals of obedient and courageous centurions. Julius Caesar describes the heroic Marcus Petronius, centurion of the Eighth Legion, who sacrificed his own life so that his men could escape in the battle in Gergovia (*Bell. gall.* 7.47–51). Dionysius of Halicarnassus recounts that when Verginius commanded the centurions to disregard the generals' orders, they held fast, not because the generals were right, but because the centurions had made an oath to them. The centurions knew that if they failed to uphold that oath, the generals had the power to execute them (*Ant. rom.* 11.43.2).

---

soldiers of Rome" (Dobson, "The Significance of the Centurion and 'Primipilaris' in the Roman Army and Administration," 432).

[38] Augustus "wanted the army to be a ladder to higher position for everyone from the auxiliary who coveted the citizenship, the legionary who wanted preferment (often to the Guard), the Praetorian who wished to become of the *primi pili* of the legions or something more, as well as the *nobiles* who wanted to reach high command such as *legatus pro praetore*" (Boren, "Studies Relating to the Stipendium Militum," 450).

Against this cultural and historical horizon, the authorial audience would view characters identified as centurions. If Luke hopes to create realistic characters, he needs to respond to the expectations and anticipations of his audience. Luke's placement of the term ἑκατοντάρχης at the beginning of his tale, with no immediate additional information, suggests that he means to evoke the stereotype of a brutish, violent soldier. By so doing, he sets up the auditor to be surprised by the centurion's next steps. This interplay between fulfilling expectations and exceeding them creates the complexity in Luke's carefully fashioned characterization of the centurion of Capernaum, to which we now turn.

2.3.2 Expecting the Centurion to be Depicted as Greedy

The centurion of Capernaum is a slave owner. One of his slaves is ill and about to die. An ancient reader would not be surprised that this centurion possesses a slave as part of his entourage, since slaves were often the spoils of war. The literary archetype is found in the triangle of Agamemnon, Achilles, and their human spoils (*Il.* 1), and Roman comedy is replete with tales of greedy soldiers selling off or purchasing their slaves of battle. After hearing that the centurion of Capernaum possesses a slave, the authorial audience is likely to think immediately of the stereotypes of either the brutish slave owner or the greedy and vulgar soldier. The narrator notes that this nearly-dead slave is ἔντιμος to the centurion. Only in light of the full characterization of this centurion is one able to rightly translate ἔντιμος. Abbott argues that the epithet is misplaced. He proposes that it was meant to distinguish the centurion not the slave. The word ἔντιμος "means (when applied to persons) men of rank, standing, or high repute, who are 'held in honour' for external or internal qualifications. It could not in hardly any context be applied to a young slave."[39] Indeed, various examples verify that the adjective usually describes a person who is perceived as possessing honor (Plato, *Tim.* 21e; *Resp.* 564d; and Xenophon, *Cyr.* 3.1.8). If Luke meant "precious," he might as well have used τίμιος, or if he meant "dear," ἀγαπητός.[40] Given the length to which the centurion goes to secure the aid of a Jew, the subsequent use of ἄξιος (verse 4) and ἀξιόω (verse 7), and Jesus' commendation of the centurion's πίστις, the centurion is not portrayed as greedily concerned with the recovery of his property, as are Plautus's soldiers. Only after realizing that this centurion does not fulfill the stereotype of a brutish, greedy soldier does the authorial audience see, surprisingly, that the sick servant is a respected member of the centurion's household who may also be a prized piece of property. Read in its

---

[39] E. A. Abbott, "A Misplaced Epithet in the Gospel," *Classical Review* 31 (1917): 153.

[40] Abbott, "A Misplaced Epithet in the Gospel," 155.

Lucan location, ἔντιμος qualifies the servant, as it qualifies the dinner guest in 14:8 (μήποτε ἐντιμότερός σου ᾖ κεκλημένος ὑπ' αὐτου). He may have been a servant, but he was nonetheless held in honor by his master, the centurion. Other literary examples of such relationships between masters and slaves suggest that the characterization of an attentive master is not necessarily unusual. But a military character exhibiting such concern is contrary to the common stereotype of the bully, unless the root of his concern is purely financial.

2.3.3 The Centurion and His Embassies

Beginning with verse 3, Luke introduces two different delegations sent on behalf of the centurion, which have the effect of enhancing the characterization of the centurion. Additionally, the delegations function *in persona*, making the centurion present through his ambassadors even though he, himself, never meets Jesus.[41] The impetus to send the first embassy is a report that the centurion receives concerning a Jew who may be capable of saving his slave. Though Luke states that Jesus' words are made within the hearing or "ear" of the people (7:1), this is not where the centurion himself came by his information. Verse 1 implies that those listening to Jesus were Jews, because Luke uses λαός to refer to the people of Israel – the Jews (in Luke 7 alone, see vv. 16, 29).

The Gentile centurion is not said to have heard τὰ ῥήματα of Jesus but περὶ τοῦ Ἰησοῦ. Since Roman military officers kept the peace in the provinces, Luke's authorial audience could expect that this literary centurion would have heard of an itinerant Jewish healer collecting adherents. Claudius Lysias responds similarly when he arrests Paul after the report of a disturbance in the Temple (Acts 21:31–32). Josephus records the procurator's response to this same rebel threat. Felix assembles a large force of cavalry and foot soldiers and attacks the Egyptian and his followers, slaying four hundred and taking two hundred prisoners (*A.J.* 20.172). The actions of the centurion of Capernaum are unusual because rather than send a detachment of soldiers, as Lysias and Felix would do, this centurion first sends a Jewish embassy.[42]

---

[41] "When the centurion sends people to Jesus, he is replicating the process by which the emperor transmits his will throughout the region. Just as the emperor remains out of sight at a distance, so the centurion remains out of sight" (Vernon Robbins, "Luke-Acts: A Mixed Population Seeks a Home in the Roman Empire," in *Images of Empire* [ed. Loveday Alexander; JSOT 122; Sheffield: Sheffield Academic Press, 1991], 208).

[42] Jewish embassies are frequently recorded. Philo writes about his experience as an ambassador to Rome in *Legatio ad Gaium*, and Josephus was sent to Rome to accompany priests charged by Felix on a frivolous matter (*Vita* 13). Occasionally, Jews acted on behalf of Rome. Josephus recounts that when he returned from an embassy to Rome, he found widespread dissension in his home country. Unbidden by Rome, he charges the troublemakers to rethink their planned course of action and to recognize the power that they are about to challenge (*Vita* 17–20). He admittedly fears his remonstrations will

Embassies were governed by official rules and expectations.[43] An ambassador's responsibilities included: giving a report of his meeting and any advice that he offered, carefully observing his instructions during his mission, making good use of the opportunities afforded him, and finally, accomplishing his task with integrity (Demosthenes, *Fals. leg.* 4).[44] Envoys could be bribed (Sallust 40.1),[45] but they did not have the authority to negotiate without consultation with the official who had commissioned them (Appian, *Hist. rom.* 9.3). Theoretically, no ambassador could deviate from his instructions because he had been told what to say and what to do (Demosthenes, *Fals. leg.* 6). The frequency of such delegations necessitated the establishment of imperial protocols. By the first century B.C.E. Rome had created a formula[46] that designated the relative importance and reception that ambassadors should receive.[47] Luke intends such an embassy to be in the mind of his authorial audience, as is evident in light of the vocabulary: ἀπέστειλεν and πρεσβυτέρους (v. 3).

---

label him a collaborator (21). At another time, distinguished Jews of Caesarea went to Felix to implore him to restrain his soldiers during a bloody confrontation. Felix listened to them and called off the army (*A.J.* 20.178).

[43] The use of embassies to appeal to a political power, in order to begin a war (Demosthenes, *Fals. leg.* 19.10) or to negotiate peace (Xenophon, *Hell.* 2.2.35, 3.4.8; Andocides, *De pace* [FGrHist 328 f 149a]), was ubiquitous in ancient Greece and Rome. See Eckart Olshausen, *Prosopographie der hellenistischen Königsgesandten. I. Von Triparadeisos bis Pydna* (Studia hellenistica; Louvain: Studia Hellenistica, 1974); and Canali de Rossi, *Le ambascerie dal mondo greco a Roma in età repubblicana* (Studi pubblicato dall' Istituto Italiano per la Storia Antica; Rome: Instituto Italiano per la storia antica, 1997). For the use of embassies in the New Testament, see Margaret M. Mitchell, "New Testament Envoys in the Context of Greco-Roman Diplomatic and Epistolary Conventions: The Example of Timothy and Titus," *JBL* 111 (1992): 661–82. For the relationship between political embassies and Christian apologetic, see W. R. Schoedel, "Apologetic Literature and Ambassadorial Activities," *HTR* 82 (1989): 55–78.

[44] On the repercussions for failing to follow instructions of the assembly, see Frances Skoczylas Pownall, "'Presbeis Autokratores': Andocides' 'De Pace'," *Phoenix* 49 (1995): 140–49.

[45] Herbert C. Nutting, "The Conviction of Lentulus," *CJ* 3 (1908): 189.

[46] "The *formula sociorum*, then, was expanded to the amorphous *formula amicorum et sociorum* when persons and states came to be listed whose privileges were no longer uniform. The list, as a consequence, ceased to be a convenient reference tool but was perhaps more effective as an instrument of propaganda" (Denvy A. Bowman, "The Formula Sociorum in the Second and First Century B.C," *CJ* 85 [1990]: 336).

[47] For the inscriptional evidence, see Robert Sherk, *Roman Documents from the Greek East. Senatus Consulta and Epistulae to the Age of Augustus* (Baltimore: Johns Hopkins Press, 1969), Inscription 22, 126. For *formula amicorum et sociorum* in literature, see Livy 43.6.5–10; 44.16.5–7; Plut. *Sull.* 23; Appian, *Hist. rom.* 9.4; 12.9.61; and Dio 36.53.5; 37.14.2; 38.34.3; 43.27.3; 53.25.1. Livy noted that ambassadors to Rome should receive lodging and entertainment (42.26.5).

Jews sending an embassy to Roman officials seems a more likely occurrence than, as Luke has portrayed, a Roman officer sending a Jewish delegation to a Jew. Either the authorial audience is meant to see the centurion as anticipating that Jesus would not respond to a Gentile's request (Mark 7:27), or the sending of a Jewish delegation is meant to suggest that the centurion respects the Jews. That latter is confirmed in verse 5. The unlikely mutual respect is contrary to the negative rhetoric of Greco-Roman authors. How could a Gentile seek out a Jew? Tacitus is quite vitriolic in his assessment of the Jews. They are profane toward Roman piety, engage in base and abominable customs, and have little interest in their country or their family (Tacitus, *Hist.* 5.4–5). Juvenal's portrait of Jews is no better (14.96–106). The first embassy already upsets the authorial audience's assumptions.

The second delegation is more in keeping with literary expectations. Accounts report that officers sent soldiers and lower ranked officers as messengers. For example, in Plautus's *Pseudolus*, the soldier Harpax is sent with the general's seal in order to purchase a young woman. Polybius reports that the mutineers, Spendius and Mathos, devised a plan to incite their mercenary troops against the clement General Hamilcar by sending themselves an envoy allegedly from their confederates (Plb. 1.79.8–11). The military messenger appears authentic. Later, when genuine envoys arrive from Hamilcar, the real messengers are turned away and threatened should they try to return (Plb. 1.81.1–4). Appian noted that Marius sent his officers, Aulus Manlius and Cornelius Sulla, to negotiate with Bocchus during the Numidian campaign (*Hist. rom.* 8.4–9).

Soldiers in the narrative setting of the home front often send servants as their representatives. Pyrgopolynices entrusts his slave Palaestrio to negotiate on his behalf in *Miles Gloriosus*, and, as will be seen in the Acts of the Apostles, Cornelius sends his trusted soldier and servants. To send a soldier or a slave as a delegation is within the authority of an officer, as the centurion says expressly in Luke 7:8. His second delegation of φίλοι is a clear example (v. 6). But Luke has this centurion send (ἀπέστειλεν) an assembly of Jewish elders on his behalf to ask Jesus to come and save his slave.

2.3.3.1 The Jewish Πρεσβύτεροι Present the Centurion as Ἄξιος

The first delegation asks Jesus to come and save (διασῴζω) the servant. The act of saving that Jesus extends to the centurion's slave is to be repaid by later centurions in the Acts of the Apostles. Luke will use the word διασῴζω again when the tribune Claudius Lysias orders two centurions and their cohorts to conduct Paul safely to Caesarea (Acts 23:24). A centurion will see to Paul's safety yet again in Acts 27:43.

In Luke 7, the centurion sends the Jews of Capernaum as ambassadors to Jesus to request that he come and save the ailing slave. But these representatives of the centurion do not follow orders.[48] The Jews add their own message, beyond their original commission. They praise the centurion, acknowledging that he is ἄξιος (v. 4). The Jewish ambassadors then present the evidence of his virtue: ἀγαπᾷ γὰρ τὸ ἔθνος ἡμῶν καὶ τὴν συναγωγὴν αὐτὸς ᾠκοδόμησεν ἡμῖν (v. 5). They do not state exactly how the centurion loves the Jews of Capernaum. The use of the conjunction καὶ indicates that the construction of the synagogue[49] is a second proof that the centurion is ἄξιος. Presuming the synagogue was paid for by this centurion, Abbott proposes that the story is about a veteran, because only a retired centurion would have had the money for such a project.[50] More likely Luke is trying to demonstrate the euergetism and φιλανθρωπία of the centurion – something he will state explicitly about the centurion Julius in Acts 27.

2.3.3.2 The Φίλοι Represent the Centurion's Humility

When he learns that Jesus is near his house, the centurion sends a second delegation. The audience may surmise that perhaps spies were keeping the centurion informed.[51] Luke uses the term "spies" (ἐγκαθέτους, Luke 20:20), which suggests that the author and his audience are familiar with the role and func-

---

[48] This may be an example of Luke's questionable depiction of the Jews. For a concise survey of scholarly opinion, see Joseph Tyson, *Luke, Judaism, and the Scholars: Critical Approaches to Luke-Acts* (Columbia, SC: University of South Carolina Press, 1999); and Jon A. Weatherly, *Jewish Responsibility for the Death of Jesus in Luke-Acts* (JSNTSup; Sheffield: Sheffield Academic Press, 1994).

[49] The benefaction of Gentiles toward Jews is evidenced in various building inscriptions. The Aphrodisias inscription, though from the 3rd century, demonstrates that Gentiles were eager to demonstrate their euergetism (Joyce Reynolds and Robert Tannenbaum, *Jews and God-fearers at Aphrodisias: Greek Inscriptions with Commentary* [Cambridge: The Cambridge Philological Society, 1987]). Liftshitz discusses numerous synagogal inscriptions that include names that could belong to Gentiles (B. Lifshitz, *Donateurs et Fondateurs dans les Synagogues Juives* [Cahiers de la Revue Biblique; Paris: J. Gabalda, 1967]). Also see Louis H. Feldman, "Jewish 'Sympathizers' in Classical Literature and Inscriptions," *TAPA* 81 (1950): 200–208.

[50] Abbott, "A Misplaced Epithet in the Gospel," 154. Though most of his stipend would not be paid to him until his retirement, a centurion did receive an allowance and occasionally collected other "funds" from various sources. Therefore, if this referenced a historical event, he need not be retired in order to pay for such a project, particularly because he may have used his own soldiers as the labor for the construction. Inscriptions attest to the use of soldiers in the construction of public buildings as do prescripts preventing the overuse of soldiers for this very task (H. M. D. Parker, *The Roman Legions* [Oxford: Oxford University Press, 1971], 224–25). Haslam proposes that the centurion had an unusual task in building the synagogue ("The Centurion at Capernaum: Luke 7:1–10," *Expository Times* 96 [1985]: 109–10).

[51] Ancient historians report the use of spies in battle to learn the strength of the enemy (Plb. 14.3.7; 15.5.4; *B.J.* 2.487). Josephus records that Herod used spies domestically to ascertain what was being said and done out of his presence (*B.J.* 1.492).

tion of a spy. This time, the centurion sends friends[52] (v. 6) whom one would presume are more closely affiliated with the centurion. Luke frequently refers to the friendship *topos*[53] and is not hesitant to use words for friendship directly (Luke 7:6, 34; 11:5, 6, 8; 12:4; 14:10, 12; 15:6, 9, 29; 16:9; 21:16; 23:12; Acts 10:24; 19:31; 27:3). The centurion of Capernaum and Cornelius, the centurion of Caesarea, are described as having friends, and Julius, the centurion accompanying Paul, exhibits φιλανθρωπία. Since one type of friendship occurred between social equals,[54] the authorial audience may presume the second embassy is made up of those who are at least equal in status to that of the centurion. If Luke had intended that they be military officers as well, likely he would have been explicit. The second possibility is that φίλοι refer to clients who owe obeisance to their patron and are neither social equals nor "friends" in a relational sense.[55] Such "guest friendship" or ξενία held the same necessity for reciprocity but crossed social boundaries.[56] The Lucan auditor could presume these friends were either Gentiles of some renown in the area, or they may have simply been civilians with whom the centurion had some relationship, if guest friendship is meant. Luke characterizes the centurion as having friends – whether social peers or clients – and, therefore, participating in the cultural and social practices of his day. Additionally, the mention of φίλοι

---

[52] For a discussion of ancient friendship, see Horst Hutter, *Politics as Friendship: The Origins of Classical Notions of Politics in the Theory and Practice of Friendship* (Waterloo: Wilfrid Laurier University Press, 1978); J. T. Fitzgerald, ed., *Greco-Roman Perspectives on Friendship* (SBL Resources for Biblical Study; Atlanta: Scholars Press, 1997); D. Konstan, *Friendship in the Classical World* (Cambridge: Cambridge University Press, 1997); and Paul J. Burton, "Amicitia in Plautus: A Study in Roman Friendship Processes," *American Journal of Philology* 125 (2004): 209–43. Mitchell specifically addresses aspects of friendship in Acts (Alan C. Mitchell, "The Social Function of Friendship in Acts 2:44–47 and 4:32–37," *JBL* 111 [1992]: 255–72).

[53] Klauck discusses the ethic of friendship in antiquity and its theological significance in the New Testament, particularly in Paul, Luke, and John. See Hans-Josef Klauck, "Kirche als Freundesgemeinschaft? Auf Spurensuche im Neuen Testament," *MTZ* 42 (1991): 1–14. John stresses that friends lay down their lives for one another, but Luke seems more concerned with the extent of reciprocity and hospitality (P. Marshall, *Enmity in Corinth: Social Conventions in Paul's Relations with the Corinthians* [WUNT 2, Vol 23; Tübingen: J. C. B. Mohr [Paul Siebeck], 1987], 130–31).

[54] Alan C. Mitchell, "The Social Function of Friendship in Acts 2:44–47 and 4:32–37."

[55] The authorial audience could assume that the centurion is a patron of these φίλοι. See Richard P. Saller, "Patronage and Friendship in Early Imperial Rome," in *Patronage in Ancient Society* (ed. Andrew Wallace-Hadrill; London: Routledge, 1989), 49–62.

[56] According to Herman, guest friendship was "a bond of solidarity manifesting itself in an exchange of goods and services between individuals originating from separate social units" (Gabriel Herman, *Ritualized Friendship and the Greek City* [Cambridge: Cambridge University Press, 1987], 10).

could suggest that this centurion, unlike some other literary centurions, does not treat all provincials with disdain.

The second delegation announces κύριε, μὴ σκύλλου, οὐ γὰρ ἱκανός εἰμι ἵνα ὑπὸ τὴν στέγην μου εἰσέλθῃς (v. 6). Μὴ σκύλλου is a Lucan insertion into the Q material. The delegates may be φίλοι on equal footing with the centurion, but they assume the role of ambassadors when they speak in the first person. The centurion could be begging off having to extend hospitality to a Jew who may refuse him.[57] More likely, his character, as Luke has developed him, is only meant to hint at the possibilities of faithfulness to be found among the military. Verse 7 follows Q more closely: διὸ οὐδὲ ἐμαυτὸν ἠξίωσα πρὸς σὲ ἐλθεῖν· ἀλλὰ εἰπὲ λόγῳ, καὶ ἰαθήτω ὁ παῖς μου.

Luke uses the customary practice of embassies to develop an encomiastic portrait of the centurion. The Jews praise the centurion for his worthiness, and then support their judgment with examples. The centurion loves the Jewish ἔθνος and has built their local synagogue. Luke has set up an interesting negative comparison that further characterizes the centurion. The Jews claim that the centurion is worthy, ἄξιος. The second delegation speaks on behalf of the centurion, disclaiming the praise of the first embassy but following a similar pattern. The friends of the centurion announce, in the voice of the centurion, that Jesus should not trouble himself because the centurion, despite the earlier delegation's pronouncement, is not worthy, at least not enough to offer hospitality to Jesus. The centurion's denial of his worthiness – via his second delegation – evidences another virtue, ταπεινοφροσύνης. Peter reacts similarly after the miraculous catch of fish,[58] though he acknowledges not his lack of worth but his sinfulness.

2.3.4 The Centurion Depicted as an Ἀνὴρ Ἀγαθός

Luke's centurion continues to speak directly through his delegation of φίλοι. Luke begins with καὶ γὰρ ἐγὼ indicating that the centurion recognizes that Jesus and he have something in common (v. 8). They are both ὑπὸ ἐξουσίαν. Luke uses the term ἐξουσία to mean authority (Luke 5:24; 9:1; 20:2; Acts 9:14; 26:10, 12), power (Luke 4:32; 10:19; 12:5; 19:17; 20:20; Acts 1:7; 5:4; 8:19; 26:18), those who exercise authority (Luke 12:11), and the area in

---

[57] Derrett makes this point (Derrett, "Law in the New Testament," 179–80) as does Moxnes more fully (Halvor Moxnes, "Patron-Client Relations and the New Community in Luke-Acts," in *The Social World of Luke-Acts* [ed. Jerome Neyrey; Peabody, MA: Hendrickson, 1991], 241–68).

[58] As Kilgallen notes, the centurion's "refusal to put himself in Jesus' presence is noteworthy; no one in the Chapters 4, 5 and 6 reacts to Jesus in this way. (Though Peter's initial response was to ask Jesus to depart from him, he very quickly follows Jesus.)" (John J. Kilgallen, "'I have not found such faith in Israel' [Luke 7,9]," *Melita Theologica* 49 [1998]: 24).

which one can exercise authority (Luke 23:7). Within his two volumes, ἐξουσία can originate from a positive force (Acts 1:7) or a negative one (Luke 22:53; Acts 26:18). Luke uses it to refer to the personal (Acts 5:4) and public (Luke 12:11; Luke 20:20; Acts 26:12) realms. This authority and power can be delegated (Luke 7:8; 10:19; 19:17; Acts 8:19; 9:14). In other instances, where his sources, Mark or Q, have not included ἐξουσία, Luke adds it (Luke 10:19; 12:5; 19:17; 20:20).

In the case of Luke 7:8, Luke found ἐξουσία within his source but added τασσόμενος. While the centurion's denial of worth strikes one as an uncommon behavior among the literary portraits of soldiers, his acknowledgment of his place in the chain of command is not unusual. Soldiers are expected to be obedient to their superiors, and if they hold a rank, they are to demand obedience from those below them. The ideal soldier possesses three virtues: zeal, respect, and obedience to his commanders (Thuc. 5.9.9; Dionysius of Halicarnassus, *Ant. rom.* 9.9.2). As Thucydides enumerates and Vegetius advises, the soldier must be held to constant obedience. Swift and harsh punishment should befall the soldier who fails even in minor tasks (Suet. *Div. Aug.* 24).

Luke 7:8 describes the stereotypical behavior of an obedient soldier, but with a twist. This centurion admits to his place in the chain of command and places Jesus above him. Apuleius's gardener may have assumed equality with the centurion when he pummeled him, but literary sources do not characterize soldiers as acknowledging such equality with provincials, particularly with an itinerant Jewish healer. Luke creates a σύγκρισις that measures both the centurion and Jesus against the stereotype of the obedient soldier. The Lucan addition of τασσόμενος emphasizes that both the centurion and Jesus are under authority and situates them within that chain of command.[59] The authorial audience knows that the centurion is ultimately obedient to Caesar, and that Jesus is obedient to God (Luke 4:8, 43; 5:24; 20:8). Both command those under them. The centurion commands his two delegations, and the presumption that Jesus can heal the centurion's servant from a distance suggests that the centurion recognizes that Jesus also has authority to delegate (Luke 9:1; 22:25). The centurion's confidence is well placed. When the second delegation returns, they find that the servant is well (v. 10). The authorial audience is meant to understand that ready obedience is not simply the blind responsibility of a soldier but the accurate response to God and to his delegate, Jesus. Like the stereotypical obedient soldier, the follower of Jesus must respond to

---

[59] Bovon makes this point as well. "The centurion does not begin with his authority, but stresses his subordination to others .... In military organizations (and this is the point of comparison), the power of the commanding officer is completely delegated to the subordinate" (*Luke 1*, 262). Lucan Christology embodies this sense of being sent. Jesus is the messenger of God, who in turns sends his Spirit, but the ultimate authority rests with God (Act 1:7).

Jesus' command immediately and without excuses. Turning to those following him in the crowd, Jesus praises the centurion, οὐδὲ ἐν τῷ Ἰσραὴλ τοσαύτην πίστιν εὗρον (Luke 7:9).

Fitzmyer sees the centurion's comment on authority as evidence of his modesty,[60] but perhaps Luke means to evoke the image of obedience. Luke is situating the centurion on par with Jesus as one who is commanded and one who commands. Thus the stereotype of the obedient soldier is paradoxically placed on Jesus. Both the soldierly fealty to the superior and the authority to delegate to inferiors point to the divine "chain of command" in which Jesus is situated.

3. Cornelius the Centurion: Acts 10

The praiseworthy centurion of Luke 7 is meant to foreshadow the Centurion Cornelius of Acts 10 upon whom the Holy Spirit will fall signaling divine approbation of the Gentile mission. Luke paints this centurion of Caesarea in similarly encomiastic colors, employing stereotypes as well as transcending them. Part of assessing Luke's characterization of the centurion of Caesarea, requires evaluating the location of the Cornelius incident within the larger narrative, and understanding how the setting of the story in Caesarea may direct the authorial audience in building the character of Cornelius.

In the ever-widening geography initiated by Jesus (Acts 1:8), the Gospel has already been preached to the Jews (Acts 2:14 ff), to the Samaritans (Acts 8:5–8), and to an Ethiopian official whose pilgrimage to Jerusalem and study of the Scriptures suggest a would-be proselyte.[61] Perched on the edge of inter-

---

[60] Fitzmyer, *The Gospel According to Luke I–IX*, 653.

[61] The debate over the significance of Philip's encounter with the Ethiopian eunuch hinges on whether the eunuch is seen as a Gentile or not. Haenchen proposes that the original narrative of the Ethiopian is a competing tale of the first Gentile convert, circulated among the Hellenists. "In other words, the story of the eunuch is the Hellenistic parallel to Luke's account of the first Gentile-conversion by Peter: its parallel – and rival" (*Acts of the Apostles,* 315). In its original form, Dibelius counters that the Cornelius legend stands parallel – not in competition – to that of the story of the Ethiopian official, "in which the implications of the Christian preacher's companionship with the Gentile as he journeyed and also of the latter's baptism, are not fully appreciated" (*Studies in the Acts of the Apostles* [trans. Mary Ling; London: SCM Press, 1956], 121). A more recent narrative approach by Spencer places the Ethiopian eunuch on par with Cornelius. Spencer sees the character of the Ethiopian as a representation of the ends of the earth, and thus he is meant to be seen as a Gentile convert. "The balance of evidence suggests that Luke presents this episode as a pioneering missionary breakthrough to the Gentiles" (F. Scott Spencer, *The Portrait of Philip in Acts* [JSNTSS; Sheffield: Sheffield Academic Press, 1992], 185). Fitzmyer is more definitive when he says, "The Cornelius episode is not just another conversion story, like that of the Ethiopian eunuch (8:26–40), for Cor-

national expansion, under the direction of the Holy Spirit and witnessed by Peter, the Cornelius story opens the gate through which the Gentiles could pass into the Christian way (Acts 10:47–48).

3.1 The Cornelius Event within the Acts of the Apostles

The story of Cornelius occupies all of Acts 10. Then Luke retells it in 11:4–18 and refers to it again in 15:7–9 – the redundancy marking its importance to the author.[62] Not even Paul's conversion receives as many verses as that of the Gentile centurion Cornelius.[63] The story's significance is further emphasized by the prominent role played by Peter, who has functioned as the leader of the community since the outset (Acts 1:15; 2:14; 2:37, etc.). Dibelius emphasizes this point:

Luke does not regard Cornelius as the main character, and Cornelius' adoption of the Christian faith is not the essential content of the story; it is Peter whom we find in the centre of the narrative from Acts 10.1 to 11.18, Peter, his newly acquired knowledge and his defense of it.[64]

However, Dibelius overlooks Luke's extensive development of the character of Cornelius, which begins with his foreshadowing in the centurion of Capernaum in the Gospel. As Peter and those with him experienced Pentecost, so now does the Gentile Cornelius and his household. Peter may, indeed, be the more significant character, but Luke, nonetheless, develops Cornelius as one worthy of receiving the Holy Spirit. The events in Caesarea are interpreted both as a replication of Pentecost (2:1–42), the defining moment of Christianity's institutional history, and as a fulfillment of the dominical prophecy that had opened Luke's account of that history (11:16; cf. 1:5).[65]

The story of Cornelius and his conversion is not only a pivotal scene in the Acts of the Apostles, but it also functions as the realization of the Gospel's

---

nelius and his household symbolize Gentiles, to whom testimony about the Christ even now spreads, not just under the aegis of the leader of the Twelve, but at the direction of heaven itself "(*The Acts of the Apostles*, 447–48). The presence of the Holy Spirit that confirms Cornelius signifies *the* Gentile convert. In Acts 8:36, the eunuch himself initiates the baptism, and the only appearance of the Spirit is when it whisks Philip away.

[62] Witherup proposes that the Lucan repetition functions rhetorically to further the plot, build suspense, and develop the themes of conversion, hospitality, and table-fellowship ("Cornelius Over and Over and Over Again: 'Functional Redundancy' in the Acts of the Apostles," *JSNT* 49 [1993]: 64–65). Also see Barrett, *Acts*, 1.491; and Dibelius, *Studies*, 108.

[63] Best determined that more than 140 lines of the U.B.S. text are devoted to Cornelius, while the three accounts of Paul's conversion receive less than 130 lines (Ernest Best, "Revelation to Evangelize the Gentiles," *JTS* 35 [April 1984]: 11).

[64] Dibelius, *Studies*, 118.

[65] Walter T. Wilson, "Urban Legends: Acts 10:1–11:18 and the Strategies of Greco-Roman Foundation Narratives," *JBL* 120 (2001): 91.

impetus toward universality (Luke 2:32; 3:23; 4:25–27; 24:47). The revelation of a light to the Gentiles is made explicit in the coming of the Holy Spirit upon the Gentile centurion and his household. The prototype, as we have seen, is the centurion of Capernaum, who provides Luke with a "pragmatic justification of the Gentile mission alongside the more 'theological' justifications."[66] Jesus already has announced that the centurion of Capernaum displays greater faith than that which he had seen evidenced in Israel. Though Jesus praises him, the centurion of Capernaum is only a hint of what is to come. The full actualization of the Gentiles' inclusion in the church must await the coming of the Spirit.

In addition to replicating the Pentecost event for the Gentiles, Acts 10:1–11:18 is also the last significant narrative in which Peter has a commanding role.[67] In Acts 11:22, the Jerusalem Church sends Barnabas to Antioch to investigate the Greeks who have come to believe in the Lord (Acts 11:20–21). After Barnabas witnesses ἡ χάρις τοῦ θεοῦ (Acts 11:23) at work among the faithful Greeks in Antioch, he goes to Tarsus to retrieve Paul. In the proclamation of the gospel to the Gentiles, henceforth, Paul will emerge as the central figure. The baptism of Cornelius and his household not only mirrors the Pentecost event for the Gentiles, thereby connecting Acts 2 with Acts 10, but it also serves as the legitimizing event by which Paul begins his mission to the Gentiles, thus linking Acts 10 with the second half of the narrative.[68] Luke has situated the story of Cornelius as the literary mid-point of the Acts narrative.

The setting of Caesarea in Acts 10 centers Luke's narrative geography as well. Acts 1:8 provides the map – ἔν τε Ἰερουσαλὴμ καὶ [ἐν] πάσῃ τῇ Ἰουδαίᾳ καὶ Σαμαρείᾳ καὶ ἕως ἐσχάτου τῆς γῆς. Already the gospel has been preached in Jerusalem and Judea (Acts 2:14ff), and Samaria (8:4). In the first century, Caesarea marked the end of Herodian control; it was a Roman city under the jurisdiction of a Roman prefect. Luke sets Caesarea as the home of Philip the Evangelist (Acts 8:40; 21:8) and other disciples (Acts 21:16). Caesarea is the Mediterranean port city from which Paul departs to Tarsus (Acts 9:30) and returns (Acts 18:22), and the provincial headquarters to where Paul is sent and imprisoned for two years (Acts 23:23, 33). Luke intentionally places the Gentile conversion in the only Roman city on Palestinian soil, signifying, in Luke's theological geography, the beginning of ἐσχάτου τῆς γῆς.

---

[66] Stephen G. Wilson, *The Gentiles and the Gentile Mission*, 177–176.

[67] Acts 12:3–19 recounts Peter's imprisonment and miraculous escape, but he is in a subordinate role, being (literally) led by the angel. The account demonstrates the power of God, not the evangelical work of Peter. With its comical tone, the character of Peter there seems hardly consistent with the portrayal of the great preacher and evangelist from Acts 10:1–11:18. See the previous chapter for a more thorough analysis of Acts 12:3–19.

[68] Conzelmann, *Acts of the Apostles*, xlii.

3.2 Analysis of the Characterization of Cornelius, the Centurion of Caesarea

Because Luke situates Peter as the main character, one could expect that he would portray Cornelius with some brevity. Such is not the case, as will be seen below. In fact, Luke parallels the experiences of Cornelius and Peter.[69] Both receive visions, which confound them (10:3–7). Both report those visions (10:28–33; 11:5–14). Both travel to "foreign" places at the behest of the divine (10:5–8; 20–23) – Cornelius sends envoys from Caesarea, the Roman provincial seat in Judea, to the Jewish town of Joppa, and Peter leaves the security of Joppa for the city of Caesarea. After experiencing transformation, both Peter and Cornelius praise God (10:46; 11:18). Like Peter before him, Cornelius and his household are baptized and receive the Holy Spirit (2:4; 10:47–48). Peter and Cornelius both speak in tongues (2:4; 10:46) and hear and respond to God's word (4:4; 10:44). And both are saved (2:21, 47; 4:12; 11:14).[70] The story of Cornelius is not simply a tale about one exemplary centurion. Luke depicts his household as fearing God (verse 2), and those whom Cornelius has gathered will also receive the Holy Spirit (verse 44).[71] Though Acts 10 introduces Cornelius as a centurion of the Italian cohort, he could be either on active duty or retired. Luke does not explicitly state – as with the Centurion of Capernaum – that he has been stationed at Caesarea (τασσόμενος, Luke 7:8). As in the comedies of Plautus and on inscriptions, retired military men often continued to use their titles or identify themselves with their former military unit. The use of τῷ οἴκῳ αὐτοῦ (vv. 2; 22) and τῷ οἴκῳ μου (v. 30) to describe the quarters of Cornelius and the phrases τοὺς συγγενεῖς αὐτοῦ καὶ τοὺς ἀναγκαίους φίλους (v. 24) to name those whom Cornelius summoned suggest a retired centurion,[72] who has sufficient wealth and status to have a home, extended family, and close friends. The authorial audience would recognize that this centurion is likely a veteran. If, indeed, Cornelius is meant to

---

[69] Wilson outlines this symmetry. "Luke casts the centurion in familiar terms, suggesting that his chief qualities and practices parallel those of devout Jews like Peter" (Walter T. Wilson, "Urban Legends," 90).

[70] Ibid., 91.

[71] As Witherup notes, "The story even from its inception is not just about Cornelius and his conversion but also that of his household" ("Cornelius Over and Over," 56).

[72] Haenchen is silent on the question of Cornelius's military status – whether he is meant to be on active duty or retired, though he does mention the presence of Cornelius's family (*The Acts of the Apostles,* 349, 353, 357). But Broughton ("The Roman Army," 443) and Barrett (*Acts,* 1. 449) recognize that the presence of family and friends could suggest a retired centurion residing in Caesarea. "It is likely that Cornelius was retired – at which time he would have become a Roman citizen – and was living at the center of Roman power for the area: Caesarea" (Howard Clark Kee, *To Every Nation Under Heaven: The Acts of the Apostles* [Harrisburg, PA: Trinity Press International, 1997], 130). However, centurions, even those attached to auxiliary cohorts, were most often already Roman citizens.

be retired, then the historical question of whether the Italian cohort was ever in Caesarea is moot. A centurion was free to settle down wherever he chose after his retirement.

Cornelius would make Menander proud. If he is a retired veteran, he has invested wholly in his new life as a citizen. He engages in benefaction, establishes a home, and develops relationships with φίλοι.[73] Additionally, as the *paterfamilias*, he sets a good example by practicing piety within his household (εὐσεβὴς καὶ φοβούμενος τὸν θεὸν σὺν παντὶ τῷ οἴκῳ αὐτοῦ, 10:2). Cornelius does not display the awkwardness of Polemon (*Perikeiromene*), who struggles to let go of his military brutishness now that he has returned home, but, like Polemon, he takes action to promote domestic harmony. The *miles gloriosus* is much more frequently the presentation of the returned soldier. The character of Cornelius stands as the antithesis of the braggart warrior. He is a literary centurion who may suggest that a military background need not disqualify one from religious zeal, civic benefaction, and ability to promote domestic harmony.

Luke develops the character of Cornelius directly via the narrator's comments and indirectly through his actions and the speech of others. Luke names him, gives his location and occupation, and identifies his cohort. Luke then describes Cornelius as devout, a God-fearer, along with his household, a man who gives alms to the people and prays continually to God. Few other descriptions of Lucan characters are so detailed in their introduction, signaling the significance the author places on the character of Cornelius.[74]

3.2.1 The Centurion Cornelius Depicted as a Roman Ἀνὴρ Ἀγαθός

Luke does not name any of the soldiers and centurions in the Gospel; however, the process of characterization, in itself, creates "nomination," or the sense that the audience can identify a character, regardless of whether the character has a proper name.[75] The centurion of Capernaum is clearly identifiable, though Luke felt no need to give him a personal name. In the Gospel, Luke does not appear to give names to anonymous characters found in his Marcan or Q sources. Likewise, he identifies unique Lucan characters in the Gospel solely by their status, malady, or occupation. The widow of Nain (7:12–17), the crippled woman cured on the Sabbath (13:10–17), the man with dropsy (14:1–6), and the ten lepers (17:12–18) are unnamed like the centurion of Ca-

---

[73] With regard to benefaction and the presence of friends, Cornelius is similar to the centurion in Luke 7; however, that centurion is less ambiguously on active duty and no οἶκος is mentioned.

[74] Parsons recognizes Luke's detailed characterization of Cornelius, comparing it to that of Tabitha. His analysis of Cornelius and Peter addresses the aspect of conversion from a literary perspective. See *Luke: Storyteller, Interpreter, Evangelist,* 149–90.

[75] James Garvey, "Characterization in Narrative," 68.

pernaum. This minimalist tendency is reversed in the Acts of the Apostles, where Luke introduces Barnabas (4:36), Ananias and Sapphira (5:1–6), Stephen (6:8), Philip (8:4ff), Simon the magician (8:9), Ananias (9:10), Tabitha also called Dorcas (9:36), Rhoda (12:13), Bar-Jesus (13:6), Sergius Paulus (13:7), Timothy (16:1), Jason (17:5–9), Aquila and Priscilla (18:2–4), Titius Justus (18:7), Crispus (18:7), Gallio (18:12), Sosthenes (18:17), Apollos (18:24), Demetrius (19:24), Eutychus (20:9), Mnason (21:16), Trophimus (21:29), Claudius Lysias (23:26), Julius (27:1), and Publius (28:7). Doubtless Luke needed to include the names of apostles and significant persons known to his community, but the number of lesser characters, such as Rhoda,[76] who receive little or no characterization save a name suggests that the naming is to add a sense of realism. Therefore, in Acts 10, it is not the act of naming that is necessarily significant,[77] but, rather, the content of the specific name.

Luke or his sources call this centurion "Cornelius," a common name made popular when Publius Cornelius Sulla liberated 10,000 slaves in 82 B.C.E and named them after himself (Appian, *Bell. civ.* 1.100).[78] Cornelius, the Roman centurion of the Italian Cohort, is unambiguously a Gentile and a Roman. Likewise, the other named officers in the Acts of the Apostles bear classically Roman names. Claudius Lysias's name suggests that he is a freedman emancipated by Claudius or a provincial given Roman citizenship.[79] The centurion who accompanies Paul has a double nomination: Julius is of the Augustan cohort. The only gospel writer to name Roman emperors, Luke intends that the reader of Acts recognize the centurions clearly as delegates of Rome and reflections of its imperial leadership. And yet, Cornelius of the Italian cohort, Claudius Lysias, and Julius of the Augustan cohort all demonstrate deference to apostles Peter and Paul.

The centurion Cornelius is a member of the cohort called Italica. By mentioning a cohort, Luke may have wanted again to inject a bit of realism into his narrative, since a cohort by that name was stationed in Syria in the mid-first century. Inscriptional evidence attests to at least two cohorts called Italica – the *cohors I Italica civium Romanorum voluntariorum* (*CIL* XIV 171) and the *cohors II Italica civium Romanorum* (*CIL* III 13483a, *CIL* XVI 106), also known as *cohors II Italica* (*CIL* VI 3528) or *cohors militaria Italica voluntariorum quae est in Syria* (CIL XI 6117). A tomb inscription for Proculus, a member of the *Cohors II Italica,* was found in Carnuntum on the Danube. His

---

[76] Harrill recognizes Rhoda as a stock character, which Luke uses for comic relief ("The Dramatic Function of the Running Slave Rhoda [Acts 12.13–16]: A Piece of Greco-Roman Comedy," *NTS* 46 [2000]: 150–57).

[77] The unimportance of the actual name of the character is confirmed when Peter re-tells the experience but neglects to name the centurion (Acts 11:13).

[78] Bruce, *Commentary on the Book of the Acts of the Apostles*, 214, n. 1.

[79] See section 3 in "Chapter 4: Stereotypical or Against the Grain? The Portrayals of Military Characters in Luke-Acts" on Claudius Lysias and his citizenship.

first name was Roman, but his father's name, Rabilus, was a common Nabatean name. The inscription, which was set up by his brother, Apuleius, who
may have also been in the cohort, identifies the soldier as a native of Philadelphia, one of the cities of the Decapolis.[80] According to the inscription, the II
Italian Cohort formed part of a detachment of archers from the Syrian army.
This cohort may have been sent to the Danube in 69 C.E. by Vespasian, who
hoped to secure his bid for emperor, while he was fighting the Jewish War
(*Hist.* 2.83). Proculus died after seven years of service, which indicates that
the Italian Cohort existed at least as early as 62 C.E. It probably originated in
Italy and may have begun with the enrollment of freedmen, though, as is evident with Proculus, recruitment then occurred locally among Roman citizens
in the province in which the cohort was stationed.[81]

Indeed, Luke's description of the presence of the Italian cohort (Acts 10:1)
and the Sebastian cohort (Acts 27:1) in the province of Syria seems to be cor-
roborated by first-century inscriptions[82] and texts (*B.J.* 2. 52, 58, 63, 74, 236;
A.J. 19.365, 20 122, 176), though the dating of the narrative events is earlier
than the actual evidence of the cohorts. I would argue that the author is less
concerned with dictating a historically viable account of the presence of a
specific cohort in the provincial city at Caesarea. Rather, he is emphasizing
the Romanness of this centurion, who resides in a Roman city built to honor
the Roman emperor and had been enlisted (if he is now retired) in an Italian
military unit.

But Luke adds a twist to the characterization of this soldier of Rome.
Though Cornelius makes no announcement of his being under authority or
commanding others under his own authority, as did the centurion of Capernaum, the character's actions clearly demonstrate these relationships of authority. When Cornelius responds immediately to the angel's command without
asking further questions or arguing, unlike Peter (10:14–16), we meet the face
of military obedience expected of a centurion – but obedience to an unlikely
commander. Cornelius' prompt response suggests that he recognizes the angel
to be in authority over him, as his use of κύριος, indeed, confirms. Cornelius
then summons two of his servants and a fellow soldier who, like himself, is
εὐσεβής, and sends (ἀπέστειλεν, v. 8) them to Joppa. This embassy is reminiscent of the second delegation that the centurion of Capernaum sends, which

---

[80] Proculus | Rabili f. Col. | Philadel., mil. | optio coh. II | Italic. c. R. 7 Fa[us]tini, ex
vexil. sa| git. exer. Syriaci, | stip. VII, vixit an. |XXVI, | Apuleius frater | f. c. (*Inscrip-
tiones Latinae Selectae* no. 9168). Also see Schürer, *The History of the Jewish People in
the Age of Jesus Christ*, 365, no. 54; and Benjamin W. Bacon, "Some 'Western' Variants
in the Texts of Acts," *HTR* 21 (1928): 141, n. 7.

[81] Broughton, "The Roman Army," 442.

[82] Maurice Dunand, *Le Musée de Soueida: Inscriptions et Monuments Figurés* (Paris:
Librairie orientaliste Paul Geuthner, 1934), no. 168; and Speidel, "The Roman Army in
Judaea under the Procurators," 238.

also consisted of those close to the centurion. Luke sets up a similar scene when Peter arrives at Cornelius' home. Cornelius announces, νῦν οὖν πάντες ἡμεῖς ἐνώπιον τοῦ θεοῦ πάρεσμεν ἀκοῦσαι πάντα τὰ προστεταγμένα σοι ὑπὸ τοῦ κυρίου (v. 33). The use of προστάσσω, and its military connotations (Hdt. 5.105; Xenophon, *Cyr.* 8.6.3), suggests that Cornelius understands Peter to be under the authority of ὁ κύριος; Peter is, therefore, an officer sent at the behest of his commander. After the descent of the Holy Spirit, Peter, now acting in authority over Cornelius, commands in the name of Jesus Christ that Cornelius and his household be baptized (προσέταξεν δὲ αὐτοὺς ἐν τῷ ὀνόματι Ἰησοῦ Χριστοῦ βαπτισθῆναι, v. 48).

Like the centurion in Luke 7, Cornelius typifies standard military behavior when he responds with ready obedience and commands with authority. He is able to recognize when one of greater authority is present. By emphasizing his name and cohort, Luke makes explicit that not just any soldier, but an Imperial representative, responds as an ἀνὴρ ἀγαθός.

3.2.2   The Centurion Cornelius Depicted as Εὐσεβής

Inscriptions and altars found on the Roman frontiers attest that real soldiers implored the help of various deities while stationed on the frontier. The Roman soldier on duty in a foreign and hostile environment recognized the importance of placating the gods – whomever they might be – in order to assure his safety. Archaeological finds demonstrate the piety of the military on the march.[83] But aside from the narrative setting of the battlefield, few military characters are portrayed as pious. The centurion Cornelius is unusual in that he is directly declared εὐσεβής and φοβούμενος τὸν θεόν by the narrator, and his actions further demonstrate that he is prayerful and generous in acts of piety.

In the whole narrative of Acts, only Cornelius the centurion and a soldier under his command (10:7) are called εὐσεβής. The author of Luke-Acts more frequently uses the adjective εὐλαβής[84] (Luke 2:25; Acts 2:5; 8:2; 22:12) to

---

[83] See Speidel and Dimitrova-Milceva, "The Cult of the Genii in the Roman Army and the New Military Deity," 1542–55; Birley, "The Religion of the Roman Army," 1506–41; and Helgeland, "Roman Army Religion," 1470–1505. For more recent publications on the religious aspects of the Roman military, see M. Barbara Reeves, "The Feriale Duranum, Roman Military Religion, and Dura-Europos: A Reassessment" (Ph.D. diss., Buffalo, NY: State University of New York, 2005); and Lukas deBlois, et al., *The Impact of the Roman Army (200 BC – AD 478): Economic, Social, Political, Religious and Cultural Aspects: Proceedings of the Sixth Workshop of the International Network Impact of Empire* (Leiden: Brill, 2007).

[84] According to BDAG, the term references religious attitudes of devotion in the LXX (Lev 15:31, Prov 28:14, Micah 7:2, 2 Macc 6:11); Josephus uses the word in reference to "concern" or "anxiety" (*A.J.* 2.217; 6:179). LSJ notes that εὐλαβής projects an air of

express the piety of a character, and only uses the term for Jews, where the word describes their responses to Torah. Simeon is devoutly awaiting the comfort of Israel (Luke 2:25). After the descent of the Holy Spirit, Peter addresses ἄνδρες εὐλαβεῖς ἀπὸ παντὸς ἔθνους τῶν ὑπὸ τὸν οὐρανόν (Acts 2:5), who have presumably gathered in Jerusalem for Pentecost. Devout Jews perform the proper burial rituals after Stephen's death (Acts 8:2). Paul describes Ananias as a follower of the law: ἀνὴρ εὐλαβὴς κατὰ τὸν νόμον (Acts 22:12). A more generic adjective describes Cornelius' religious fervor. The word εὐσεβής most often conveys reverence toward the gods.[85] Platonic writing regards εὐσέβεια as the greatest human virtue (Ps. Plato *Epin.* 989B). Cornelius's virtuous piety and his connection with the Jews lead to his vision, for the angel announces that Cornelius' prayers and alms-giving have ascended as a memorial to God (Acts 10:4).

Cornelius and his fellow soldier are among a select group: *pietas* or εὐσέβεια is far from the stereotypical description of soldiers. Wilson proposes that Luke emphasized Cornelius's piety in order "to show that the Gentiles were not such a bad crowd after all."[86] Or more specifically, in consideration of Luke's overall depiction of soldiers thus far, one could say that not simply Gentiles, but Gentile soldiers, were not such a bad crowd despite the negative stereotypes. Given the rarity of the portrait of pious soldiers and Luke's infrequent use of the term εὐσεβής, one must consider the next descriptor before determining how the reader is to fully understand Cornelius's piety.

The author of Acts uses the adjective εὐσεβής to establish Cornelius's attitude toward God, but because the term may mean reverence for any god, the author of Acts specifies φοβούμενος τὸν θεόν. Luke emphasizes that Cornelius has chosen the one true God out of the plethora available to a soldier in the first century.

Seldom is a centurion or soldier in ancient literature described as φοβούμενος τὸν θεόν, though they may be afraid of their commanders (Xen. *Anab.* 2.6.10) or of the enemy (Thuc. 2.87.4). In the writings of Josephus, the φόβος word group often describes the reactions of those at war, but φοβέομαι is seldom used in relation to God.[87] Philo understood φοβέομαι as fear of God, but a fear shaped by θάρσος (*Her.* 28). In the New Testament, φοβέομαι can mean to become frightened but also to have a respect and reverence. Luke-Acts frequently uses the term to mean "to fear God" (Luke 1:50; 18:2; 23:40; Acts 10:2, 22, 35; 13:16, 26). In Acts 10:2 and 22, Luke calls Cornelius a φοβούμενος. Peter announces in 10:35 that anyone who is a φοβούμενος is ac-

---

caution which, when directed towards the gods, is interpreted as reverence or piety (Plutarch *Num.* 22; Diodorus Siculus, 13.12).

[85] *Die Inschriften von Priene* 117.63; Plato *Smp.* 193d; Isocrates 12.124.

[86] Wilson, *The Gentiles and the Gentile Mission*, 176.

[87] Only in *A.J.* 1.114 is fear of God meant.

ceptable to God. In Acts 13:16 and 26, Paul addresses the men of Israel and the φοβούμενοι in the synagogue at Antioch of Pisidia. According to Hans-Josef Klauck, the presence of God-fearers in the Acts of the Apostles is fore-shadowed in the Gospel: καὶ τὸ ἔλεος αὐτοῦ εἰς γενεὰς καὶ γενεὰς τοῖς φοβουμένοις αὐτόν (Luke 1:50).[88] The word, φοβούμενος, appears in the first part of Acts (10:2; 35; 13:16, 26) and is seemingly replaced by σεβόμενος in the later part (13:43, 50; 16:14; 17:4, 17; 18:7, 13; 19:27), the alteration prob-ably reflecting Luke's sources.[89] However, Wilcox argues that the change of terms signifies the move from Torah-observant piety in the early part of Acts to a broader Gentile understanding.[90] Perhaps, as Lake has suggested, "the reason why these words were used was because they were appropriate to a vague class, not because they were the recognized title limited to a specific group with a definite place in organized Judaism."[91] Cohen concurs that φοβούμενος τὸν θεόν, or "venerators of god," indicates an action of reverence that is not solely constitutive of membership.[92]

Rather than indicating membership in Judaism, perhaps Luke uses "god-fearer" in Acts 10 to describe more fully the parameters of Cornelius's piety. Cornelius was not simply a God-fearer, but devout and a God-fearer, εὐσεβὴς καὶ φοβούμενος τὸν θεὸν (Acts 10:2), who evidences his piety by giving alms and praying to God continually. Both the centurion of Capernaum (though he is not named a God-fearer) and Cornelius of Caesarea are described as providing financial benefaction to the Jews of their respective towns. Unlike the Pharisee justifying himself in prayer by touting his paying of tithes (Luke 18:12), Cornelius's generosity is well received by the divine. The angel an-

---

[88] Hans-Josef Klauck, "Gottesfürchtige im Magnificat?" *NTS* 43 (1997): 134–39.

[89] Kirsopp Lake, "Proselytes and God-fearers," in *The Beginnings of Christianity. The Acts of the Apostles* (ed. F. J. Foakes Jackson and Kirsopp Lake; London; Grand Rapids: MacMillan; Baker Book House, 1933; reprint 1979), 86.

[90] Max Wilcox, "The 'God-fearers' in Acts: A Reconsideration," *JSNT* 13 (1981): 118.

[91] Lake, "Proselytes and God-fearers," 88. The hypothesis that φοβούμενοι or σεβόμενοι τὸν θεόν refer to a distinct group within first-century Judaism, from which the first Gentile Christian converts were culled, has generated an enduring debate, flaring on occasion with new epigraphic discoveries. Inscriptions found in various excavated syna-gogues use the apparently synonymous word θεοσεβής (Josephus uses the term θεοσεβής to describe Poppaea, the wife of Nero, who intercedes on behalf the Jews, *Ant.* 20.195) rather than φοβούμενος or σεβόμενος τὸν θεόν. Kraabel identifies ten occurrences of θεοσεβής from more than 100 inscriptions. Unfortunately, with the exception of the build-ing at Delos, the synagogues under study were built between the second and fourth centu-ry (A. T. Kraabel, "The Disappearance of the 'God-fearers'," *Numen* 28 [1981]: 116).

[92] "If we need to designate all these gentiles with one term, the modern term 'sympa-thizers' seems best precisely because it is so vague and does not imply the existence of a homogeneous category" Shaye J. D. Cohen, "Crossing the Boundary and Becoming a Jew," *HTR* 82 (1989): 31.

nounces: Αἱ προσευχαί σου καὶ αἱ ἐλεημοσύναι σου ἀνέβησαν εἰς μνημόσυνον ἔμπροσθεν τοῦ θεοῦ (10:4). Cornelius repeats to Peter the angel's remark: εἰσηκούσθη σου ἡ προσευχὴ καὶ αἱ ἐλεημοσύναι σου ἐμνήσθησαν ἐνώπιον τοῦ θεου (10:31). Cornelius' generosity is unusual, since more often soldiers are presented in the historiographies, comedies, and novels as greedy. Polybius describes one centurion whose love of money (21.38.3) became his undoing when he tried to ransom his captive. Livy recounts the story of the soldiers of Scipio who were dissatisfied that their pay had been delayed and planned a mutiny in response (28.25.6). Plautus's braggarts are often equally as rapacious when it comes to money and property. Cleomachus of *Bacchides* is worried that he isn't receiving the appropriate amount of money for the woman he is trying to sell, and Therapontigonus in *Curculio* fears he is being swindled in his efforts to purchase a woman. Both are depicted as self-absorbed and overly concerned about being cheated. Only the unnamed soldier in *Epidicus* is willing to spare no expense to retrieve his love. In Apuleius's *Metamorphoses*, the centurion sells the donkey that he has stolen for eleven denarii (10.2). In Cornelius, the authorial audience meets a centurion who contradicts the stereotype of the soldier as extortionist. But his portrayal is in keeping with a developing sense of generosity evident among the military characters of Luke's narrative.

In addition to his alms-giving, Cornelius's fervent prayer is stated by the narrator (Acts 10:2), acknowledged by the angel (Acts 10:4), and repeated by Cornelius himself in verse 31. The audience may be surprised to learn that Cornelius is a God-fearer, but as such his prayer would be expected. In fact, Luke places great emphasis on prayer in the two volumes.[93] Like Cornelius, Zechariah is told by an angel that his prayer is heard (Luke 1:13). Anna is noted for her fasting and prayer (Luke 2:37). The need to pray constantly without tiring is affirmed by Jesus (Luke 18:1). Prayer is particularly necessary during times of tribulation (Luke 21:36). Jesus commands the disciples in the garden to pray that they may not be tested (Luke 22:40, 46). Luke portrays Jesus frequently at prayer (Luke 3:21; 5:16; 6:12; 9:18, 28; 11:1; 22:32). In the Acts of the Apostles, the disciples follow Jesus' example of prayer (Acts 1:4, 24; 2:42; 4:24; 6:14; 8:15; 9:11; 13:3; 14:23; 16:13). Peter and John are on their way to the Temple to pray when they encounter the beggar (Acts 3:1). Peter is praying on a rooftop in Joppa when Cornelius' delegation arrives (Acts 10:9; 11:5). Paul and Silas pray during their imprisonment (Acts 16:25). Paul prays in the Temple (Acts 22:17) and prays before laying his hands on the father of Publius (28:8). "The theological implication is that by prayer God guides the course of redemption history, through its three stages (as Luke

---

[93] Plummer, *The Gospel According to Saint Luke*, xlv.

presents them) of Israel, the period of Jesus and the period of the church."[94] With the repetitive recognition of Cornelius's prayer, Luke signals that the Gentiles are equally guided by God.

Cornelius' commitment to prayer does not distinguish him from other literary soldiers, who are often portrayed in the historiographies as attending to religious obligations, particularly before battle. Polybius recounts that Hannibal praised his men and prayed to the gods (ἐπαινέσας αὐτοὺς καὶ θεοῖς ὑπὲρ ἁπάντων εὐξάμενος, 3.44.13). When taking an oath with the ambassadors sent by King Philip, Hannibal and his soldiers invoked the gods of the army (θεοὶ τῶν συστρατευομένων, 7.9.2). Soldiers prepared for battle only after good omens were declared by the augurs (Livy 10.40). But unlike other soldiers, Cornelius is not petitioning the gods of Rome or the local gods; he is engaged in private and continual prayer to the God of the Jews. The irony is not to be missed. The piety demonstrated by the Horatii and Marcus Curtius is toward their *patria*. The audience would presume if the Centurion Cornelius were pious, as a member of the Roman military, that piety would be directed toward Caesar or at least toward Rome. But, against expectations, Cornelius prays to the God of Israel.

Cornelius is identified as a God-fearer again in v. 22, which forms an inclusion with vv. 1–2, but here the reputation of Cornelius is stated by his embassy rather than by the direct voice of the narrator. In this echo and reaffirmation of the content in verses 1–2, the audience learns one new piece of information about the character of Cornelius. Cornelius the centurion is not simply a pious God-fearer. His piety is specified. He is a righteous God-fearer whose reputation is confirmed by the entire Jewish nation. The Jewish delegation announces that the centurion of Capernaum ἀγαπᾷ γὰρ τὸ ἔθνος ἡμῶν (Luke 7:2), and perhaps their willingness to intercede to Jesus is meant to demonstrate his reputation among the Jews. The whole ἔθνος of the Jews speaking well of Cornelius would seem astonishing for Luke's audience on at least two accounts: that the entire Jewish nation would know of this one centurion and that a centurion would have such a remarkable reputation among a group of provincials.

Luke calls no other Gentile δίκαιος, and literary portraits of righteous soldiers are few. Cornelius is most readily compared to Judas Maccabeus, who is described in 2 Maccabees as noble (γενναῖος, 12:42) and virtuous and brave (ἀνδραγαθία, 14:18). Luke's reader is meant to recognize that this centurion, against all expectations of how literary soldiers behave, actually exemplifies the biblical idea of right relationship with God,[95] a Lucan motif as set forth in Luke 1:6. The pervasive theme of righteousness or justice is found throughout

---

[94] Stephen S. Smalley, "Spirit, Kingdom and Prayer in Luke-Acts," *NovT* 15 (1973): 60.

[95] Fitzmyer, *The Acts of the Apostles*, 322–23.

Luke-Acts. Zachariah and Elizabeth are both δίκαιοι, having followed all the commandments of the Lord. Simeon is introduced as ὁ ἄνθρωπος οὗτος δίκαιος καὶ εὐλαβὴς (Luke 2:25). Likewise, Joseph of Arimathea is ἀνὴρ ἀγαθὸς καὶ δίκαιος (Luke 23:50). The centurion at the cross announces of Jesus, ὁ ἄνθρωπος οὗτος δίκαιος ἦν (Luke 23:47),[96] and in Acts, ὁ δίκαιος refers to Jesus (3:14; 22:14). The second time a soldier declares someone δίκαιος is found in Acts 10, where the soldiers announce that they were sent to Peter by Κορνήλιος ἑκατοντάρχης, ἀνὴρ δίκαιος καὶ φοβούμενος τὸν θεόν (Acts 10:22). Luke portrays the first Gentile convert as possessing the same quality as those of his outstanding Jewish characters: Zechariah, Elizabeth, Simeon, and Joseph of Arimathea. But more significantly, the Roman centurion Cornelius is δίκαιος as is Jesus

3.2.3 The Centurion Cornelius Hosts Peter the Apostle

Anticipating Peter's arrival, Cornelius has prepared to welcome his guests by gathering his family and friends. At Peter's entrance, Cornelius falls at his feet and worships him (v. 25), an action that can also connote "prostrating oneself before a superior."[97] Peter demonstrated similar obeisance before Jesus after seeing the enormous catch of fish (Luke 5:8). The actions of the Centurion Cornelius show that he recognizes that the apostle Peter, who is summoned at the command of an angel of God, must be one of greater authority.

First, the centurion at Capernaum admitted that both he and Jesus stand under authority. Then the centurion at the cross declared Jesus' innocence and/or righteousness, and now a centurion, the representative of Rome, acknowledges the greater authority of his guest, an emissary of ὁ κύριος. Thus Rome bows before Jesus, οὗτός ἐστιν πάντων κύριος (v. 36).[98] Peter commands Cornelius: Ἀνάστηθι· καὶ ἐγὼ αὐτὸς ἄνθρωπός εἰμι (v. 26). Paul will echo this sentiment when the misguided Gentiles of Lystra presume he and Barnabas are Hermes and Zeus (Acts 14:15).

---

[96] The term may also refer to Jesus' innocence. See section 2 of "Chapter 4 Stereotypical Soldiers in Luke-Acts."

[97] Barrett, Acts, 513. Kezbere describes the encounter as a "false apotheosis" (Ilze Kezbere, Umstrittener Monotheismus: Wahre und falsche Apotheose im lukanischen Doppelwerk [NTOA/SUNT 60; Göttingen: Vandenhoeck & Ruprecht, 2006], 4.4).

[98] Rowe recognizes the significance of the demonstrative, οὗτος, in making a counter-claim against the imperial cult. "This one" – Jesus is Lord of all ("Luke-Acts and the Imperial Cult: A Way through the Conundrum?" JSNT 27 [2005]: 291). Against Rowe, Howell has investigated Acts 10:36 in light of imperial propaganda and proposes that Luke's characterization of Cornelius is meant to be ironic. I agree that the author is using rhetorical irony, but, contrary to Howell's finding, I demonstrate that the overall portrait of Cornelius is positive. See Justin R. Howell, "The Imperial Authority and Benefaction of Centurions and Acts 10:34–43: A Response to C. Kavin Rowe," JSNT 31 (2008): 25–51.

As a good host, Cornelius invites his guest to speak to those gathered (v. 33). Effectively, Cornelius hands over command of his household to Peter. Whereas the centurion of Capernaum prevents Jesus from coming to him, saying through his second embassy οὐ γὰρ ἱκανός εἰμι ἵνα ὑπὸ τὴν στέγην μου εἰσέλθῃς (Luke 7:6), Cornelius receives Peter with eagerness and gracious hospitality, ἐξαυτῆς οὖν ἔπεμψα πρὸς σέ, σύ τε καλῶς ἐποίησας παραγενόμενος (v. 33). Luke means for his authorial audience to see a progression. This centurion of Caesarea is worthy enough to receive Peter. Luke has systematically developed the character of Cornelius, so that by the time the apostle and centurion meet, the auditor recognizes that Cornelius is above reproach. And for his part, after his vision, Peter is free to enter the home of a Gentile. Peter explains that Jews had been forbidden to associate (κολλᾶσθαι) or even to visit (προσέρχεσθαι) with a Gentile (v. 28). But such distinctions are no longer valid, for God has shown him that no one is unclean (v. 28).

Peter acknowledges that anyone who fears God and does the work of righteousness is acceptable to God: ὁ φοβούμενος αὐτὸν καὶ ἐργαζόμενος δικαιοσύνην δεκτὸς αὐτῷ ἐστιν (v. 35).[99] The narrator includes in his introduction that Cornelius is a pious God-fearer who gives alms, and his embassy to Peter notes that he is a righteous God-fearer as well. With Peter's words, the reader now knows that this centurion is undoubtedly acceptable to God because he meets the requirements. But the coming of the Holy Spirit confirms Cornelius' acceptability in conjunction with Peter's preaching that Jesus Christ is πάντων κύριος (v. 36).

In verse 22, the embassy states to Peter that Cornelius wants to hear his words (ἀκοῦσαι ῥήματα παρὰ σοῦ). In verse 33, Cornelius gathers his family and friends ἀκοῦσαι πάντα τὰ προστεταγμένα σοι ὑπὸ τοῦ κυρίου. When Peter retells the story to those gathered in Jerusalem, he quotes Cornelius, who was told by the angel to retrieve Peter ὃς λαλήσει ῥήματα πρὸς σὲ ἐν οἷς σωθήσῃ σὺ καὶ πᾶς ὁ οἶκός σου (11:14). The Holy Spirit falls on Cornelius and his household during the attentive hearing of the words (v. 44). Luke's use of the adverb ἔτι, in addition to the present circumstantial participle of λαλέω, stresses that the action of speaking continues as the Spirit falls. As Peter speaks, the Holy Spirit comes. Luke thus emphasizes the connection between proclamation and confirmation. Cornelius's piety, righteousness, and fear of God exist prior to the encounter with Peter. Yet only in hearing the proclamation of Jesus Christ does the Holy Spirit affirm Peter's insight that anyone who fears God and does righteousness is acceptable. As the narrative continues, the authorial audience encounters other notable soldiers in the company of an apostle, but none are portrayed as hearing the word of God. No other soldiers, save Cornelius and those in his household, are baptized.

---

[99] See John Kilgallen, "Clean, Acceptable, Saved – Acts 10," *Expository Times* 109 (1998): 301–2.

Luke does not narrate the actual baptism. Rather, the pericope concludes with the household of Cornelius inviting Peter to remain with them for some days (v. 48). Peter will defend his actions before the circumcision party in Jerusalem (11:4–17), but the pious gentile Cornelius is not named again nor will his character be further developed or described.[100]

4. Conclusion

Luke fashions portraits of soldiers in his double work by engaging various stereotypes, contradicting them, and – as seen in the centurion of Capernaum and Cornelius of Caesarea – transcending those stereotypes. By means of description, example, and comparison, Luke constructs a progressive portrait of Roman centurions that culminates in Cornelius's reception of the Holy Spirit and his baptism. Such honorific portrayals of literary soldiers are infrequent. The historians may paint an encomiastic picture of significant generals (one need only think of Thucydides' characterization of Brasidas, Xenophon on Clearchus, and Livy's Scipio), but the comedies, satires, and novels seldom characterize a soldier fully enough to suggest anything more than a stock character. Therefore, Luke's portrayals of the centurion of Capernaum and Cornelius, the centurion of Caesarea, stand out among the panoply of literary soldiers for their detailed characterization.

4.1 The Centurion of Capernaum as an Example of Πίστις

Luke is well aware of the various stereotypes of soldiers and plays off of them throughout his portrayal of the centurion at Capernaum. He owns slaves, acts as a patron, is set under authority and also holds authority. But Luke also depicts him in a paradoxical fashion. Although he owns slaves, he is concerned enough about the welfare of a sick slave to entreat a Jewish healer to come to his home. His benefactions are not toward Rome's gods but toward the God of the Jews. He sends delegations as ambassadors on his behalf, but one of those embassies is composed of the very people subject to him, whom one would surmise were less loyal. Indeed, this Jewish delegation oversteps its ambassadorial duty, which necessitates a second delegation.

Through his φίλοι, the centurion disclaims any accolades made by the Jewish elders. He is not worthy, despite their comments, to receive Jesus. Such humility is not stereotypical military behavior. In fact, Luke's simple intro-

---

[100] "Peter grows in his stature as a witness and minister of the Word while Cornelius himself fades into the background, his household becoming symbolic of the Gentile world" (Witherup, "Cornelius Over and Over," 60).

duction of the centurion without comment sets up the auditor to be wholly surprised by the atypical behavior that the character then exhibits.

Finally, Luke characterizes this centurion in encomiastic terms. He has friends, engages in public service, possesses wealth, and exhibits compassion. His virtues include worthiness, piety toward the others' god, φιλανθρωπία, humility, and obedience. His actions demonstrate his nobility when he sends for help from a Jew for the sake of a lowly slave, when he sends an additional delegation to humbly deny the first group's boasting on his behalf, and when he prevents Jesus from coming to his home, acknowledging that the healer's power is derivative and can be made manifest even at a distance.

4.2 Cornelius the Centurion as Filled with the Holy Spirit

Through direct attestation by the narrator, and indirectly through the comments by other characters and his own actions, the centurion Cornelius is depicted for the authorial auditor. He hails from a city that needs no introduction by Luke. He engages in acts of benefaction, which evidences some wealth. He has a household, family, and friends. He appropriately commands his attending soldiers and servants. But these elements of his environment do not distinguish him as much as do his virtues.

Cornelius is most immediately identified as εὐσεβὴς καὶ φοβούμενος τὸν θεόν. If Cornelius were still on active duty, such religious obedience to a foreign god of a subject people would be tantamount to treason, which the authorial audience would recognize. Luke not only describes Cornelius as faithful but gives evidence of Cornelius's faith. He participates in Jewish cultic acts by praying continually and giving alms. He has a reputation among the Jews, and his own envoys recognize his righteousness. Luke's authorial audience would presume that such public actions for an active military man would no doubt come to the notice of his superiors. If he is meant to be on active duty, Cornelius is taking great risks to demonstrate his piety.

Cornelius's portrayal is in line with the stereotypical obedient soldier, who recognizes greater authority when he encounters it and submits readily. His actions are equally those of a noble man who risks personal danger to pursue a greater goal. Like other military notables such as Brasidas, Clearchus, and Scipio, Cornelius resembles the stereotype of the ἀνὴρ ἀγαθός, even though his narrative location is not the battlefield. Additionally, Cornelius's behaviors replicate those of a good citizen, who promotes domestic harmony, demonstrates piety, and acts as a patron to both friends and guests alike. His portrayal is also paradoxical, for his giving of alms shows him to be the opposite of the greedy soldier who expects to exploit the provincials or reap the spoils of battle. Finally, the portrayal of Cornelius transcends the stereotypes of literary soldiers. Cornelius and his household are confirmed by the Holy Spirit and baptized into the new cohort of πάντων κύριος.

Luke's portrayals of the centurion of Capernaum and Cornelius of Caesarea stand apart from most characterizations of soldiers in Greco-Roman literature. They play against the authorial audience's expectations of the way literary soldiers stereotypically behave, sometimes following the stereotype, sometimes contradicting it, and sometimes transcending it. The question now becomes, What purpose is served by painting these centurions in such laudatory and unexpected ways?

Chapter 6

The Roman Soldier as a Parabolic Exemplum

1. Introduction

Ancient theorists recognize a relationship between the principles of rhetoric and those of literature. The goal of rhetoric is persuasion, which requires that the orator evoke from the audience a response based on the character of the speaker (ἦθος), the emotions of the audience (πάθος), or the logic of the argument (λόγος, *Rhet.* 1.2.3). Though Aristotle criticizes those teachers of rhetoric who deal solely in πάθος (*Rhet.* 1.2.5), he, nonetheless, reckons that stirring the emotions of the hearers affects their response. Aristotle "seems to imagine the playwright himself, like an orator, standing before the audience himself, and playing on their emotions (being 'persuasive' or 'realistic') through his own capacity for emotional self-involvement."[1] The writer is concerned no less than the orator with the impact of πάθος on his or her audience's reception of the text.[2]

Because audience-oriented approaches consider the affective response of the reader, they share with ancient rhetorical theory an interest in what Aristotle termed πάθος.

This rhetorical concern with the impact of subjective predisposition on interpretation, *the pathos principle*, is parallel to the basic assumption of reader-response criticism: the premise that the act of understanding the meaning of textual features is affected by the predisposition of the reading mind.[3]

The modern recognition of the relationship between πάθος and an audience-centered interpretative model replicates something of which ancient writers were already aware: the audience responds to characters with whom they can identify (*Rhet.* 2.13.16). The narratives of Luke demonstrate that the author understood rhetorical theory and was able to integrate aspects of it into his work.[4]

---

[1] Gill, "The Ēthos/Pathos Distinction," 152.

[2] Ibid., 158.

[3] Nan Johnson, "Reader-Response and the Pathos Principle," *Rhetoric Review* 6 (1988): 152–53.

[4] Several scholars have explored various aspects of Luke's use of rhetoric. See George Kennedy, "The Speeches in Acts," in *New Testament Interpretation through Rhetorical Criticism* (Chapel Hill, NC: University of North Carolina Press, 1984), 114–40; Jerome Neyrey, "The Forensic Defense Speech and Paul's Trial Speeches in Acts 22–26: Form and Function," in *Luke–Acts: New Perspectives from the Society of Biblical Literature*

"In order to appreciate Luke's abilities to tell the story of Jesus in an elegant, learned, and clear manner, we must place him squarely in the rhetorical tradition, a tradition he apparently was intimately familiar with, and to which his audience would have responded."[5] In attempting to persuade his actual audience to a greater sense of certainty (Luke 1:4), Luke engages and upsets the expectations of his authorial one. Roman soldiers who do not behave as anticipated provoke Luke's authorial audience to reconsider its assumptions and come to new conclusions. If Luke has successfully created an authorial audience closely aligned with his actual one, then the latter will come to the same recognition.

Luke employs, contradicts, and transforms the stereotypes of literary soldiers familiar to his authorial audience as part of his cumulative characterization of the Roman military. The developing portrait invites the authorial audience to recognize that even a soldier possesses the possibilities of conversion and commitment. Thus, the characterization of the Roman military functions as a parabolic exemplum of true discipleship.

1.1 Greco-Roman Literary Stereotypes of Soldiers

As is the case with all literary characters, soldiers in Greco-Roman literature are drawn to conform to the expectations of the audience, which brings its experience of the genre and its horizon of cultural knowledge into the character-building process. The audience recognizes that the location of real soldiers often affects how they would behave. An action that would gain positive recognition on the battlefield would bring disgrace on the home front. When these different expectations are translated into prose, the narrative settings – "the battlefield," "on assignment in the provinces," or "the home front" – become the lens through which the authorial audience views the literary soldier's behavior. Repetitive, similar, or contrasting behaviors lead to generalizations and impli-

---

Seminar (ed. Charles H. Talbert; New York: Crossroads, 1984), 210–24; Bruce Winter, "The Importance of the Captatio Benevolentiae in the Speeches of Tertullus and Paul in Acts 24:1–21," *JTS* 42 (1991): 505–31; Robert Morgenthaler, *Lukas und Quintilian. Rhetorik als Erzählkunst* (Zürich: Gotthelf, 1993); Philip E. Satterthwaite, "Acts Against the Background of Classical Rhetoric," in *The Book of Acts in Its Ancient Literary Setting. Vol. 1* (eds Bruce W. Winter and Andrew D. Clarke; Grand Rapids: Eerdmans, 1993), 337–79; Todd Penner, "Narrative as Persuasion: Epideictic Rhetoric and Scribal Amplification in the Stephen Episode in Acts," *SBLSP* 35 (1996): 352–67; Philip Shuler, "The Rhetorical Character of Luke 1–2," in *Literary Studies in Luke-Acts* (ed. Thomas Phillips and Richard Thomspon; Macon, GA: Mercer University Press, 1998), 173–89; Todd Penner and Caroline Vander Stichele, eds., *Contextualizing Acts: Lukan Narrative and Greco-Roman Discourse* (SBLSS 20; Atlanta: SBL, 2003); Mikeal C. Parsons, *Luke: Storyteller, Interpreter, Evangelist*, 15–50; and Patrick E. Spencer, *Rhetorical Texture and Narrative.*

[5] Parsons, *Luke: Storyteller, Interpreter, Evangelist*, 17.

cations, which result in the designation of various commonplaces or stereotypes. In addition to affecting the plot, ancient characters are also meant to demonstrate qualities that the audience would identify with and evaluate. Of those military characters developed enough to be classified, nine general stereotypes emerge. In the narrative setting of the battlefield, positive stereotypes include "The Brave Soldier," and "The Holy Warrior," while negative stereotypes are "The Coward," "The Greedy Soldier," and "The Mutineer." Soldiers and officers depicted on active duty in the narrative setting of the province are generally either rescuers or bullies. Veterans and soldiers on the home front can be depicted as "The Good Citizen," or "The Braggart." This analysis acknowledges that a stereotype forms the basis of the characterization, upon which an author could build a more complex character.

As would be expected, more types are found on the battlefield, where the locus of action involves soldiers. Here, a soldier could be vicious in several ways, but a virtuous soldier is above all brave and occasionally reverent. In works that do not center on military conflicts, soldiers as characters are fewer and seldom influence the plot dramatically. Though the braggart warrior of Plautus is certainly a vivid character, he is a foil to the protagonist, as are most of the soldiers in Roman comedy. Likewise, the heroes of novels encounter military figures, but these figures do not play significant roles.

Luke's depiction of soldiers are not limited to the stereotypes generally found in the specific narrative settings of the battlefield, the province, and the home front. The obedient and reverent soldier is found in the province, along with the rescuing and kind soldier. The brute is appropriately found patrolling the Judean countryside, but the good citizen is also encountered. Additionally, Luke combines several, sometimes contradictory, stereotypes in a single portrait. Soldiers who are brutes exhibit repentance. The obedient soldier seeks out the aid of a Jew and reveres the Jewish God.

The narrative settings for soldiers in both the Gospel of Luke and Acts of the Apostles is "on assignment in the provinces." Like their actual counterparts, the Lucan soldiers appear to be serving as a police force in Judea under the command of the prefect or auxiliary tribune. The crucifixion is an episode in a provincial setting in which the authorial audience would hold certain expectations for the soldiers' conduct, but those expectations would not be satisfied. Luke says very little about the soldiers' role in the death of Jesus. Like their literary comrades, Lucan soldiers play only minor roles in the two volumes. Jesus praises the centurion of Capernaum, but the centurion is represented in absentia by his embassies. Cornelius's baptism is significant because he is a Gentile, not because he is a soldier. Though Cornelius and Claudius Lysias are involved in lengthy episodes, Peter and Paul, respectively, remain the chief protagonists.

1.2 Luke's Use of Stereotypes

In his economy of characterization, the author of Luke-Acts often engages a stereotype to introduce a new narrative persona. The authorial audience is meant to recognize what Zechariah does and his religious and ethnic identity by the use of ἱερεύς (Luke 1:5). Widows are frequent in the two volumes (Luke 2:37; 4:26; 7:12; 18:3; 20:47; 21:2; Acts 6:1; 9:39). Likewise, tax collectors appear (Luke 3:12; 5:27; 7:29; 7:34; 15:1; 18:10; 19:2) with no description beyond the title τελώνης. Luke expects his authorial audience to be familiar with those who practice magic (μαγεύω, Acts 8:9; μάγοι, Acts 13:6) and engage in the magical arts (τὰ περίεργα, Acts 19:19). But unlike Matthew (2:1), Luke anticipates that his authorial audience would hold a negative view of such practices. The author depicts Simon, despite his baptism, as attempting to purchase the power of God (Acts 8:19). Bar-Jesus is portrayed as opposing Barnabas and Saul (Acts 13:6), and those who would be believers burn their magical books (Acts 19:19).

The Lucan stereotypical characters function on the level of the narrative to forward the plot. The characters are also meant to encourage an experience of πάθος within the authorial audience, which is expected to be sympathetic to widows, distrusting of tax collectors, and suspicious of magicians. But occasionally, Luke turns the stereotype on its head. The unjust judge is afraid that the persistent widow will sucker punch him (ἵνα μὴ εἰς τέλος ἐρχομένη ὑπωπιάζῃ με, Luke 18:5). The repentant tax collector shows greater remorse than the Pharisee (18:9–14). The chief tax collector, Zacchaeus, offers to repay generously anyone whom he has defrauded (Luke 19:8). Of the criminals crucified beside Jesus, one behaves stereotypically (Εἷς δὲ τῶν κρεμασθέντων κακούργων ἐβλασφήμει αὐτόν, Luke 23:39), and the other is repentant (ἀποκριθεὶς δὲ ὁ ἕτερος ἐπιτιμῶν αὐτῷ ἔφη· οὐδὲ φοβῇ σὺ τὸν θεόν, ὅτι ἐν τῷ αὐτῷ κρίματι εἶ, Luke 23:40). The barbarians on Malta demonstrate φιλανθρωπία (Acts 28:2).

Luke contradicts the authorial audience's judgment of a stereotype when a figure behaves against expectations. The widow (stereotypically "helpless and vulnerable") is capable of instilling fear by her persistence. The Samaritan is the one who aids the injured man in the parable (Luke 10:30–37), and a Samaritan leper, not the Jewish ones, return to thank Jesus (Luke 17:16). But how does the author anticipate that the authorial audience will react when the character exemplifies part of the stereotype, contradicts another, and in the end, transforms the stereotype? Such a reversal, as Ricoeur notes, is paradoxical. It "disorients only to reorient."[6] When the authorial audience recognizes the characters, they are drawn in.

---

[6] Paul Ricoeur, "Biblical Hermeneutics," *Semeia* 4 (1975): 126.

They buy into a kind of world with which they believe themselves to be familiar. But when the second shoe drops, the parabolic world to which they have already committed themselves inverts. The drop of the second shoe requires a revision of the first, and the parable presents readers with an alternative vision that also challenges them to a revision of their own lives.[7]

This "divergence from the familiar," as Iser termed it,[8] has the potential to provoke the authorial audience into a new way of seeing the characters, which can lead to a new interpretation of the episode. In his portrait of soldiers, Luke clearly recognizes the role of stereotypes in characterization. As demonstrated in the previous chapters, Luke uses and contradicts these stereotypes. He also creates a rupture instead of a continuity, so that the authorial audience must reconsider their original assumptions.

2. The Cumulative Characterization of Soldiers in Luke-Acts

The centurion of Capernaum and Cornelius of Caesarea are outstanding examples of Luke's successful manipulation of stereotypes. But these exemplary centurions are not meant to be evaluated singularly. The use of *inclusio*, comparison, foreshadowing, and repetition demonstrate that the authorial audience is expected to create a cumulative portrait of the Roman military as a whole.

In a character *inclusio*, the first soldiers in the Gospel witness the baptizing ministry of John, and the last one testifies to Jesus' death. The centurion in Caesarea is acknowledged as δίκαιος. Another centurion makes this same statement about Jesus. Peter and Cornelius both have visions to which they respond. Paul's citizenship is compared to that of the tribune Claudius Lysias. The story of the centurion in Luke 7 foreshadows that of Cornelius in Acts 10. The repetitive rescues of Paul by the tribune culminate in Paul's safe arrival in Caesarea. The φιλανθρωπία of the Centurion Julius towards Paul is not surprising, given the ἀγάπη τοῦ ἔθνου of the centurion of Capernaum, and the almsgiving of the Centurion Cornelius. The full implication of this use of literary devices to build a corporate portrait of the Roman military is only recognized in hindsight, however. When the authorial audience first encounters Lucan soldiers, it expects them to behave according to the stereotypes.

In Luke 3:14, John admonishes the soldiers to stop extorting and making false accusations. John's words do not surprise the authorial audience. Indeed, the most frequently occurring negative stereotype of soldiers in the narrative setting of "on assignment in the provinces" is that of the brute. In light of the stereotype, the auditors may interpret the soldier's question, τί ποιήσωμεν, as mocking. Only with the introduction of the centurion of Capernaum does the

---

[7] Brawley, *Text to Text Pours Forth Speech*, 28.
[8] Iser, *The Implied Reader*, 34.

authorial audience have an interpretive clue. The unnamed centurion has demonstrated an interest in the Jews and now is concerned about his slave. His comment about obedience, via the second embassy, supports the positive stereotype of the good soldier. In light of this centurion's actions, the authorial audience is meant to reinterpret the question of the soldiers coming to John. Luke's editorial work on the crucifixion narrative diminishes the overt role of the soldiers. The centurion at the cross acknowledges that Jesus is δίκαιος, a remarkable statement from one who oversaw the execution of an innocent man. Even more surprisingly, this Gentile centurion praises the God of Israel.

When the first soldier is encountered in the Acts of the Apostles, the authorial audience is prepared to interpret his character in light of those found in the Gospel. Nonetheless, Luke is explicit is his description of Cornelius. He is a devout God-fearer. He is also the only soldier to whom the word of God is proclaimed. During Peter's speech, the Holy Spirit falls upon Cornelius and his household – holy approbation that the Gentiles are to be included in the Way. No other soldier will receive the Holy Spirit or be baptized, nor will Luke use any further negative stereotypes in his characterization of soldiers. The tribune Claudius Lysias is portrayed as efficient and attentive. The centurion who interrupts the tribune's near beating of Paul is a comic foil meant to heighten the drama. He does not function as a mutineer. The centurion Julius treats Paul with respect and even listens to his suggestions. Like the tribune, Julius rescues Paul, exemplifying the stereotype of "The Rescuer." The authorial audience might have wondered how to interpret the appearance of the first soldiers in the Gospel, but by the time Luke introduces the last soldier in Acts, the audience has little doubt. Though the author gives no direct description, the authorial audience would see him in light of his fellow soldiers, particular Claudius Lysias and Julius, who had previously guarded Paul. The two volumes thus come to a close with Paul freely preaching, accompanied by a soldier.

3. The Function of the Lucan Portrait of Soldiers

The author of the Gospel of Luke and the Acts of the Apostles intended to pen a planned narrative, as is evident in the Gospel's prologue (Luke 1:3). The plot is made more explicit in the prologue of the second volume: ἀλλὰ λήμψεσθε δύναμιν ἐπελθόντος τοῦ ἁγίου πνεύματος ἐφ᾿ ὑμᾶς καὶ ἔσεσθέ μου μάρτυρες ἔν τε Ἰερουσαλὴμ καὶ [ἐν] πάσῃ τῇ Ἰουδαίᾳ καὶ Σαμαρείᾳ καὶ ἕως ἐσχάτου τῆς γῆς (Acts 1:8). Further, the ordered work focuses on the deeds and teachings of Jesus (volume one) and those of his followers (volume two).

The author expressly states in the prologue of the Gospel that the narrative is meant as an assurance of the reliability of what has been taught (Luke 1:4). According to Tannehill, the unifying purpose of Luke-Acts is the βουλὴ τοῦ θεοῦ referred to in Luke 7:30 and Acts 2:23; 4:28; 5:38–39; 13:36; and 20:27. Specific episodes within the two volumes "represent particular steps in the realization of this purpose or portray human resistance to this purpose."[9] To that end, Luke introduces characters who support the plot and encourage the audience to evaluate their ἦθος. As has been demonstrated with the soldiers in other literary accounts, Luke's development of a character's ἦθος is particularly evident in his use and manipulation of stereotypes. Thus certain characters in the narrative are meant to confirm faith and exemplify the appropriate response of a disciple to the will of God.

Tannehill outlines four aspects of a narrative that provide clues to the divine purpose: previews and reviews, Old Testament quotes, commission statements, and interpretative statements made by reliable characters.[10] The first and last have particular resonance with regard to the characterization of soldiers. The use of foreshadowing and review allows the author to direct the reader's interpretation of the story. A light revealed to the Gentiles prophesied by Simeon in the Temple and announced by Jesus in 4:23–30 is first realized in Luke 7 when the centurion of Capernaum seeks the aid of Jesus. But the prediction is only fully experienced in Acts 10 when the Holy Spirit falls upon the centurion of Caesarea and his household, and all are baptized by Peter. This inclusion of the Gentiles receives ecclesial approbation in Acts 15. Paul reprises Simeon's words in his defense before Agrippa and Bernice in Acts 26:23. Finally, under the protection of a soldier in Rome, Paul concludes γνωστὸν οὖν ἔστω ὑμῖν ὅτι τοῖς ἔθνεσιν ἀπεστάλη τοῦτο τὸ σωτήριον τοῦ θεοῦ· αὐτοὶ καὶ ἀκούσονται (Acts 28:28).

A more explicit way of interpreting the events in the narrative is through the statements of reliable characters. Jesus, Peter, Stephen, and Paul are considered reliable and authoritative voices.[11] But a reliable voice can equally come from a minor character who is an eyewitness.[12] Pilate announces οὐδὲν εὑρίσκω αἴτιον ἐν τῷ ἀνθρώπῳ τούτῳ (Luke 23:4), which he repeats two more times (23:14, 22). Likewise, the centurion at the cross declares Jesus δίκαιος (Luke 23:47). Surely the declaration of innocence from the highest ranking Roman official in Judea and a representative of the Roman military have more narrative weight than the declaration of a disciple, from whom the auditor would expect such a claim. In fact, soldiers are present in several episodes where interpretative statements are made. The appropriate question in response to John's preaching of

---

[9] Robert C. Tannehill, "Israel in Luke–Acts: A Tragic Story," *JBL* 104 (1985): 69.

[10] Ibid., 69–70.

[11] Ibid., 70.

[12] Luke places a significant value on witnesses (Luke 1:2; 24:48; Acts 1:22; 4:33; 10:43; 14:17; 15:8; 20:1, 24; 22:15, 20; 23:11x2; 26:16; and 28:23). He even has God bearing witness by granting the Holy Spirit in Acts 15:8. Here, Peter is referring to Cornelius and the coming of the spirit.

repentance is echoed three times, the final one coming from the soldiers (Luke 3:14). In Luke 7:9, it is not a soldier who speaks, but Jesus who speaks of a soldier, commending his faith. In Acts 10:47, Peter confirms the actions of the Holy Spirit, which fall upon Cornelius and those gathered. The tribune of the Jerusalem cohort pens a letter to Felix, declaring that Paul has done nothing deserving death (Acts 23:26–30).

Through foreshadowing, reviews, and interpretative statements made by reliable characters, episodes involving soldiers promote the unity of the two volumes. The portrait of the Roman military must then be understood as confirming what is known and (given its positive and deliberate construction) witnessing a response to the will of God. In fact, as the narrative progresses, the cumulative characterization of soldiers and centurions shows that, contrary to the authorial audience's expectations, the military representatives not only witness to the will of God but act in accord with it.

3.1 The Narrative Audience and Lucan Soldiers

The portrait of the Roman soldier functions on several different audience levels. At the level of the narrative audience, the characters whom the audience is likely to identify with – John the Baptist, Jesus, Peter, and Paul – all have encounters with Roman soldiers. These soldiers respond positively to the message presented, though they are not initially the intended recipients of the message. The soldiers in Luke 3:14 ask what they are to do; the centurion in Luke 7 acknowledges Jesus' authority; Cornelius (Acts 10) receives the Holy Spirit during Peter's preaching; and Claudius Lysias (Acts 21–23) rescues Paul instead of beating him.

The narrative audience does not interpret the characters in light of stereotypes. No distinction is made by John the Baptist between the soldiers and the others who have gathered. Jesus does not praise the centurion because he defies a stereotype. In actuality, Jesus approves of the soldier's military obedience. Jesus praises him because his πίστις exceeds that of Israel. When Peter defends his actions before the council, no mention is made of Cornelius or his status as a Roman centurion, save that he is a Gentile.

At the level of the narrative audience, Luke constructs a portrait of a would-be disciple – one who is first a sinner but desires repentance (Luke 3:14), recognizes Jesus' authority (Luke 7), proclaims Jesus to be δίκαιος (Luke 23:47), seeks out the preaching of Peter, receives the Holy Spirit and is baptized (Acts 10), protects Paul and delivers him to safety (Acts 21–23, 27), and finally, attends to the Apostle in Rome (Acts 28). This cumulative presentation of a soldier as a near disciple would have a decidedly different impact on Luke's authorial audience for whom the literary stereotype of soldiers was most often negative.

3.2 The Roman Soldier as a Parabolic Exemplum

The cumulative portrait of military characters in Luke-Acts is of a soldier who is ἄξιος (Luke 7:4), evidences ἀγάπη (Luke 7:5), is lauded for his πίστις (Luke 7:9), is called εὐσεβὴς καὶ φοβούμενος τὸν θεὸν σὺν παντὶ τῷ οἴκῳ αὐτοῦ, ποιῶν ἐλεημοσύνας πολλὰς τῷ λαῷ (Acts 10:2) and is regarded for his φιλανθρωπία (Acts 27:3). Luke's characterization of soldiers demonstrates that the author not only knew of the stereotypes and assumed his authorial audience did as well, but could readily turn them to his advantage. In fact, the stereotypes are a springboard from which Luke elicits typical expectations only to upset them later. The image of a centurion in Luke 7:2 conjured up by the authorial audience is wholly transformed by verse 9. Jesus responds to the centurion with amazement – the reaction normally ascribed to the crowd witnessing Jesus' own behavior in a miracle story (Luke 2:23; 4:22, 36; 8:25; 9:46; 11:14; 20:26; 24:12, 41) or the actions of his disciples (Acts 2:7; 3:10–12; 4:13). Luke's audience likely was equally amazed because the centurion of Capernaum does not resemble the literary portraits the audience had come to expect.

Nor does Cornelius ultimately reflect the military stereotypes, though he is first depicted as a stereotypically obedient soldier who submits to authority. Luke not only establishes that this character is a remarkable man, but also indicates that his military affiliation has contributed positively to his character and his quest for salvation. He is obedient, recognizes authority, and is willing to take risks. Yet, he worships the God of the Jews, invites a Jew into his home, and receives the Holy Spirit. Luke's portrait of Cornelius is at once typical, paradoxical, and laudatory.

The soldiers in the Gospel and Acts serve Luke's narrative rhetoric in one of three ways. First, those enlisted under the Herods function as extensions of the kings' power, which proves violent and ineffectual. Those serving Rome, as manifestations of Roman power and authority, demonstrate that the aims and interest of the empire are not threatened by the proclamation of the Way. Third, Luke means his soldiers to represent to his readers the very ones whom Jesus had come to call (Luke 5:32) – those who had been lost (Luke 19:10). The author intends these characters, despite their stereotypes, to be narrative examples of the Lucan motifs for discipleship: appropriate use of possessions, right recognition of authority, and praise of God. But, with the exception of the centurion at the cross, they do not make a profession of faith, and, with the exception of Cornelius, are not baptized. Such expressions of faith require hearing and responding to the word of God (Luke 8:21). At Peter's preaching, the Holy Spirit descends upon Cornelius, but he is the only soldier for whom the word is proclaimed.

Though Roman soldiers seek out John, Jesus, Peter, and Paul, these soldiers are not portrayed directly as disciples, but rather, they serve as parabolic exempla,[13] unexpected examples of the appropriate response to Jesus and his apostles. Aristotle recognizes that a παράδειγμα or exemplum, like ἐνθύμημα, is a means of proof common to all species of rhetoric (*Rhet.* 2.20.1). An exemplum could be either historical or fictional (*Rhet.* 2.20.2). An author could present an exemplum in three basic ways: narration, allusion, or direct naming of a character. The narrative forms are most elaborate and can be found in the form of a διήγημα, χρεία, or σύγκρισις.[14] The author of an allusion expects the reader or auditor to be able to understand and interpret the exemplum without any direct designation from the author. Given the temporal nature of allusions, later audiences may not be able to recognize authorial allusions. The third type of exemplum is the naming of a character, which may have included a description relating the character to the relevant episode. This type requires that the audience be familiar with the character mentioned.

An exemplum can function as convincing evidence or as a moral example to be imitated. In deliberative and judicial rhetoric, orators utilize exempla as evidence to persuade the audience of a decision or judgment. Historical examples can make a point more believable (Cicero, *Part. or.* 40) and add to the credibility of the speaker, while delighting the audience (Cicero, *Or.* 34.120). The moralists in their diatribes often employ exempla "as edifying or deterrent models, so as to influence more efficiently the attitude and opinions of the audience or addressee."[15] Inherent in the exemplum as a model is the expectation that the audience will identify, evaluate, and imitate the example presented.[16] According to Quintilian, examples work by adducing "some past action real or assumed which may serve to persuade the audience of the truth of the point which we are trying to make" (*Inst.* 5.11.6 [Butler, LCL]).

The portrait of Roman soldiers in Luke-Acts serves as a parabolic exemplum, anticipating that the authorial audience will be familiar with the character but will initially come to the wrong conclusions. The authorial audience is repulsed by the soldiers, expecting them to behave according to the negative stereotypes found in other Greco-Roman literature. But, as with parables, the story is not what it first appears to be. Once the authorial audience uses its horizon

---

[13] Demoen defines παράδειγμα or exemplum as "the evoking of a history which has or has not actually occurred, which is similar or related to the matter under discussion, which is implicitly or explicitly brought into connection with this matter as argument (evidence or model) or as ornament, and which takes the form of a narration, a name-mentioning, or an allusion" (Kristoffel Demoen, "A Paradigm for the Analysis of Paradigms: The Rhetorical Exemplum in Ancient and Imperial Greek Theory," *Rhetorica* 15 [1997]: 148).

[14] Ibid., 142.

[15] Ibid., 130.

[16] "As a means of accomplishing that imitation, the audience is expected to enter or continue a program of instruction and formation as outlined by the author," (Benjamin Fiore, "Paul, Exemplification, and Imitation," in *Paul in the Greco-Roman World* [ed. J. Paul Sampley; Harrisburg, PA: Trinity Press International, 2003], 236).

of cultural knowledge to begin to construct a character, the author adds a twist. The brutes may actually be seeking the baptism of John. A centurion guarding the outpost of Capernaum attends to the town's Jews. A Gentile centurion in the Roman city of Caesarea sends for Peter at the direction of an angelic messenger. Though only one soldier is baptized, he is the first unequivocal Gentile to be baptized and, as such, demonstrates that the possibility exists for all soldiers, despite the stereotypes Luke's envisioned audience may have held. As an exemplum of appropriate discipleship, the characterization of the Roman soldier calls the authorial audience to imitation.

The Lucan soldier may represent any person whom Luke's authorial audience might have summarily dismissed as unworthy. As such, the soldier resembles the tax collectors and sinners, who were viewed negatively by Luke's narrative audience (5:30; 7:34), only to be exonerated by Jesus (Luke 5:32; 15:1–2). The cumulative characterization of Roman soldiers may serve as a parabolic exemplum to the authorial audience that imperial representatives can find a place in the community of faith, just as tax collectors and sinners. But the majority of Luke's Roman soldiers do not become disciples. They do, however, foster the mission. Given Luke's larger interest in promoting a positive view of the empire, through his depiction of imperial representatives, and the repeated declaration of Jesus' and Paul's innocence, the author of Luke-Acts likely intends to demonstrate that the imperial support shown to the narrative audience can be anticipated by Luke's actual audience.

Thus the characterization of Roman soldiers and centurions in Luke-Acts functions both as a parabolic exemplum of a good disciple, and as the author's optimistic expectation of imperial benevolence. Not until the Edict of Milan would the latter be realized (Eusebius, *Hist. eccl.* 8.17).

Bibliography

Ancient Sources: Texts, Editions, Translations

Achilles Tatius. *Leucippe and Clitophon*. Translated by S. Gaselee. Loeb Classical Library. Cambridge, MA: Harvard University Press, 1984.

Apuleius. *Metamorphoses*. Translated by J. Arthur Hanson. Loeb Classical Library. Cambridge, MA.: Harvard University Press, 1989.

Aristophanes. *Acharnians, Knights*. Translated by Jeffrey Henderson. Loeb Classical Library. Cambridge, MA: Harvard University Press, 1998.

Aristotle. *Art of Rhetoric*. Translated by J. H. Freese. Loeb Classical Library. Cambridge, MA: Harvard University Press, 2000.

–. *Nicomachean Ethics*. Translated by H. Rackham. Loeb Classical Library. Cambridge, MA: Harvard University Press, 1926.

–. *Poetics*. Translated by Stephen Halliwell. Loeb Classical Library. Cambridge, MA: Harvard University Press, 1995.

–. *Posterior Analytics*. Translated by Hugh Tredennick, and E S. Forster. Cambridge, MA: Harvard University Press, 1960.

–. *Rhetoric and Poetics*. Translated by W. Rhys Roberts and Ingram Bywater. New York: Modern Library, 1954.

Chariton. *Callirhoe*. Translated by G. P. Goold. Loeb Classical Library. Cambridge, MA: Harvard University Press, 1995.

Cicero. *De Invention. De Optino Genere Oratorum. Topica*. Translated by H. M. Hubbell. Loeb Classical Library. Cambridge, MA: Harvard University Press, 1969.

Dio. *Roman History*. Translated by Eanest Cary. Loeb Classical Library. New York: G. P. Putnam's Sons, 1917.

Dionysius of Halicarnassus. *Roman Antiquities*. 7 Vols. Translated by Earnest Cary. Loeb Classical Library. Cambridge, MA: Harvard University Press, 1937–1950.

Frontinus. *The Stratagems and The Aqueducts of Rome*. Translated by Charles E. Bennett. Loeb Classical Library. New York: G. P. Putnam, 1925.

Josephus. *Jewish Antiquities, Books I–IV*. Translated by H. St. John Thackeray. Loeb Classical Library. Cambridge, MA: Harvard University Press, 1967.

–. *Jewish Antiquities. Books V–VIII*. Translated by H. St. John Thackeray and Ralph Marcus. Loeb Classical Library. Cambridge, MA: Harvard University Press, 1988.

–. *Jewish Antiquities, Books IX–XI*. Translated by Ralph Marcus. Loeb Classical Library. Cambridge, MA: Harvard University Press, 1995.

–. *Jewish Antiquities. Books XII–XIV*. Translated by Ralph Marcus. Loeb Classical Library. Cambridge, MA: Harvard University Press, 1986.

–. *Jewish Antiquities. Books XV–XVII*. Translated by Ralph Marcus and Allen Wikgren. Loeb Classical Library. Cambridge, MA: Harvard University Press, 1990.

–. *Jewish Antiquities. Books XVIII–XIX*. Translated by L. H. Feldman. Loeb Classical Library. Cambridge, MA: Harvard University Press, 1965.

–. *Jewish Antiquities, Book XX*. Translated by L. H. Feldman. Loeb Classical Library. Cambridge, MA: Harvard University Press, 1981.

–. *The Jewish War. Books I–II.* Translated by H. St. John Thackeray. Loeb Classical Library. Cambridge, MA: Harvard University Press, 1997.

–. *The Jewish War. Books III–IV.* Translated by H. St. John Thackeray. Loeb Classical Library. Cambridge, MA: Harvard University Press, 1997.

–. *The Jewish War. Books V–VII.* Translated by H. St. John Thackeray. Loeb Classical Library. Cambridge, MA: Harvard University Press, 1997.

–. *The Life, Against Apion.* Translated by H. St. J. Thackeray. Loeb Classical Library. Cambridge, MA: Harvard University Press, 1997.

Julius Caesar. *The Gallic War.* Translated by H. J. Edwards. Loeb Classical Library. Cambridge, MA: Harvard University Press, 1917.

Juvenal, and Persius. *Juvenal and Persius.* Translated by G. G. Ramsay. Loeb Classical Library. Cambridge, MA: Harvard University Press, 1996.

Livy, Titus. *Livy.* Translated by B. O. Foster. Vols. 1–5. Loeb Classical Library. Cambridge, MA: Harvard University Press, 1919–29.

Longus and Xenophon of Ephesus. *Daphnis and Chloe. Anthia and Habrocomes.* Translated by Jeffrey Henderson. Loeb Classical Library. Cambridge, MA: 2009.

Menander. *Menandri quae supersunt.* Translated and edited by Alfredus Koerte. Leipzig: Teubner, 1945.

Petronius. *Petronius and Seneca.* Translated and edited by Michael Heseltine and W. H. D. Rouse. NY: G. P. Putnam's Sons, 1916.

Plutarch. *Moralia.* Vol. 3. Translated by Frank Cole Babbitt. Loeb Classical Library. Cambridge, MA: Harvard University Press, 1931.

Plautus, Titus Maccius. *Plautus.* 5 vols. Translated by Wolfgang de Mello. Loeb Classical Library. Cambridge, MA: Harvard University Press, 2011–2013.

Polybius. *The Histories.* Translated by W. R. Paton. 6 vols. Loeb Classical Library. Cambridge, MA: Harvard University Press, 1979–2000.

Quintilian. *The Institutio Oratoria of Quintilian.* Translated by H. E. Butler. Loeb Classical Library. New York: G. P. Putnam's Sons, 1921.

Tacitus. *The Histories.* Translated and edited by Clifford H. Moore. Loeb Classical Library. Cambridge, MA: Harvard University Press, 1937.

–. *The Histories and The Annals.* Translated and edited by John Jackson. Loeb Classical Library. Cambridge, MA: Harvard University Press, 1931.

Terence. *The Woman of Andros. The Self-Tormentor. The Eunuch.* Vol. 1. Translated by John Barsby. Loeb Classical Library. Cambridge, MA: Harvard University Press, 2001.

Theophrastus. *Characters.* Translated by Jeffrey Rusten and I. C. Cunningham. Loeb Classical Library. Cambridge, MA: Harvard University Press, 1993.

Thucydides. History of the Peloponnesian War. Translated by C. F. Smith. 4 vols. Loeb Classical Library. Cambridge, MA: Harvard University Press, 1996–1999.

Vegetius. *Epitoma Rei Militaris.* Leo Stelten. New York: P. Lang, 1990.

Velleius Paterculus, *The Caesarian and Augustan Narrative (2.41–93).* Translated by A.J. Woodman. New York: Cambridge University Press, 1983.

Xenophon. Translated by Carleton L. Brownson. 7 vols. Loeb Classical Library. Cambridge, MA: Harvard University Press, 1922; revised ed. 1998.

Secondary Sources

Abbott, E. A. "A Misplaced Epithet in the Gospel." *Classical Review* 31 (1917): 153-55.

Abbott, F. F., and A. C. Johnson. *Municipal Administration in the Roman Empire.* Princeton: Princeton University Press, 1926.

Achtemeier, Paul J. "Omne verbum sonat: The New Testament and the Oral Environment of Late Western Antiquity." *JBL* 109 (1990): 3-27.

Aichele, George, ed. *The Postmodern Bible: The Bible and Culture Collective*. New Haven, CT: Yale University Press, 1995.

Alexander, Loveday. "Ancient Book Production and the Circulation of the Gospels." Pp. 71–112 in *The Gospels for All Christians: Rethinking the Gospel Audiences*. Edited by Richard Bauckham. Grand Rapids, MI: Eerdmans Publishing, 1998.

–. "Formal Elements and Genre: Which Greco-Roman Prologues Most Closely Parallel the Lukan Prologues?" Pp. 9–26 in *Jesus and the Heritage of Israel*. Edited by David P. Moessner. Harrisburg, PA: Trinity Press International, 1999.

–. *Acts in its Ancient Literary Context: A Classicist Looks at the Acts of the Apostles*. Library of New Testament Studies 298. New York: T & T Clark, 2005.

–. "The Acts of the Apostles as an Apologetic Text." Pp. 15–44 in *Apologetics in the Roman Empire*. Edited by Mark Edwards, Martin Goodman, and Simon Price. Oxford: Oxford University Press, 1999.

–. "Geography and the Bible (Early Jewish)." P. 978 in *ABD*, vol. 2. Edited by David Noel Freedman. New York: Doubleday, 1992.

–. "'In Journeyings Often': Voyaging in the Acts of the Apostles and in Greek Romance." Pp. 17-49 in *Luke's Literary Achievement: Collected Essays*. Edited by C.M. Tuckett. Sheffield: Sheffield Academic Press, 1995.

–. "Mapping Early Christianity: Acts and the Shape of Early Church History." *Interpretation* 57 (2003): 163–73.

–. *Preface to Luke's Gospel: Literary Convention and Social Context in Luke 1:1–4 and Acts 1:1*. Cambridge; New York: Cambridge University Press, 1993.

–. "What If Luke Had Never Met Theophilus." *BibInt* 8 (2000): 161–70.

Alford, C. Fred. "Greek Tragedy and Civilization: The Cultivation of Pity." *Political Research Quarterly* 46 (1993): 259-80.

Allen, O. W. *The Death of Herod: The Narrative and Theological Function of Retribution in Luke-Acts*. SBLDS 158. Atlanta: Scholars Press, 1997.

Alston, Richard. *Aspects of Roman History: A.D. 17-117*. London: Routledge, 1998.

–. *Soldier and Society in Roman Egypt: A Social History*. London: Routledge, 1995.

Alter, Robert. *The Art of Biblical Narrative*. New York: Basic, 1981.

Ameling, Walter. *Inscriptiones Judaicae Orientis II*. TSAJ 99. Tübingen: Mohr Siebeck, 2004.

Amossy, Ruth. "Introduction to the Study of Doxa." *Poetics Today* 23 (2002): 369–94.

Amossy, Ruth, and Therese Heidingsfeld. "Stereotypes and Representation in Fiction." *Poetics Today* 5 (1984): 689–700.

Anderson, H. "3 Maccabees (First Century B.C.)." Pp. 509–30 in *The Old Testament Pseudepigrapha*. Edited by James H. Charlesworth. ABRL. New York: Doubleday, 1985.

Applebaum, Shimon. *Judaea in Hellenistic and Roman Times*. NY: Brill, 1989.

Appleby, Joyce, Lynn Hunt, and Margaret Jacob. *Telling the Truth About History*. New York: Norton, 1994.

Auerbach, E. *Mimesis*. Princeton: Princeton University Press, 1953.

Aune, D. E. *The New Testament in Its Literary Environment*. Philadelphia: Westminster, 1987.

Bacon, Benjamin W. "Some 'Western' Variants in the Texts of Acts." *HTR* 21 (1928): 113–45.

Bainton, Roland. "The Early Church and War." *HTR* 39 (July 1946): 189–212.

Baird, William. *History of New Testament Research*. Minneapolis, MN: Fortress Press, 2003.

Bakirtzis, Charalambos, and Helmut Koester. *Philippi at the Time of Paul and after His Death*. Harrisburg, PA.: Trinity Press International, 1998.

Balch, David L. "The Genre of Luke-Acts: Individual Biography, Adventure Novel, or Political History?" *SWJT* 33 (1990): 5–19.

Bannon, Cynthia J. *The Brothers of Romulus: Fraternal Pietas in Roman Law, Literature, and Society.* Princeton: Princeton University Press, 1997.

Barrett, C. K. *A Critical and Exegetical Commentary on the Acts of the Apostles.* Edinburgh: T & T Clark, 1994–98.

Bauckham, Richard, ed. *The Book of Acts in Its Palestinian Setting.* Vol. 4 of *The Book of Acts in Its First Century Setting.* Edited by Bruce W. Winter. Grand Rapids, MI: Eerdmans, 1995.

–, ed. *The Gospels for All Christians: Rethinking the Gospel Audiences.* Grand Rapids, MI: Eerdmans Publishing, 1998.

–. "For Whom Were the Gospels Written?" Pp. 9–48 in *The Gospels for All Christians. Rethinking the Gospel Audiences.* Edited by Richard Bauckham. Grand Rapids: Eerdmans Publishing, 1998.

–. "Response to Philip Esler." *Scottish Journal of Theology* 51 (1998): 249–53.

Bauman, Richard A. *Women and Politics in Ancient Rome* (London: Routledge, 1994.

Beard, Mary. *The Roman Triumph.* Cambridge, MA: Belknap Press, 2007.

Belfiore, Elizabeth. "Aristotle's Concept of Praxis in the Poetics." *CJ* 79 (1984): 110–24.

Bell, H. I. "Philanthropia in the Papyri of the Roman Period." Pp. 31–7 in *Hommages à Joseph Bidez et à Franz Cumont.* Collection Latomus 2. Bruxelles: Latomus, 1949.

Best, Ernest. "Revelation to Evangelize the Gentiles." *JTS* 35 (April 1984): 1–30.

Betz, Hans Dieter. *The Sermon on the Mount.* Hermeneia. Minneapolis: Fortress Press, 1995.

Bickerman, Elias J. "Syria and Cilicia." *American Journal of Philology* 68 (1947): 353–62.

Bielinski, Krzysztof. *Jesus vor Herodes in Lukas 23,6–12: eine narrativ-sozialgeschichtliche Untersuchung.* Stuttgart: Katholisches Bibelwerk, 2003.

Bigelmair, Andreas. *Die Beteiligung der Christen am öffentlichen Leben in vorconstantinischer Zeit.* München: J. J. Lentner, 1902.

Bingham, Sandra. *The Praetorian Guard: A History of Rome's Elite Special Forces.* London: Tauris, 2013.

Bird, Michael F. "The Unity of Luke-Acts in Recent Discussion." *JSNT* 29 (2007): 425–48.

Birley, A. *Garrison Life at Vindolanda.* Charleston, SC: Tempus Publishing, 2002.

Birley, E. "The Religion of the Roman Army." *ANRW* II.16.2 (1978): 1506–41.

Blake, Warren E. "Chariton's Romance. The First European Novel." *CJ* 29 (1934): 284–88.

Blume, Horst-Dieter. "Komische Soldaten: Entwicklung und Wandel einer typischen Bühenfigur in der Antike." Pp. 175–95 in *Rezeption des antiken Drama auf der Bühne und in der Literatur.* Edited by Bernhard Zimmermann. Stuttgart: Metzler, 2001.

Bonz, Marianne Palmer. *The Past As Legacy: Luke-Acts and Ancient Epic.* Minneapolis: Fortress Press, 2000.

Boorsch, Jean. "About Some Greek Romances." *Yale French Studies* 38 (1967): 72–88.

Boren, Henry C. "Studies Relating to the Stipendium Militum." *Historia* 32 (1983): 427–60.

Bovon, François. *Luke 1.* Hermeneia. Minneapolis, MN: Fortress Press, 2002.

–. "Studies in Luke-Acts: Retrospect and Prospect." *HTR* 85 (1992): 175–96.

Bowman, Alan K., and Dominic Rathbone. "Cities and Administration in Roman Egypt." *JRS* 82, no. 1992 (1992): 107–27.

–. and J. D. Thomas. "A military strength report from Vindolanda." *JRS* 81 (1991): 62–73.

Bowman, Denvy A. "The Formula Sociorum in the Second and First Century B.C." *CJ* 85 (1990): 330–36.

Brawley, Robert L. "Abrahamic Covenant Traditions and the Characterization of God." Pp. 109-132 in *The Unity of Luke-Acts.* Edited by J. Verheyden. BETL 142. Leuven: Peeters, 1999.

–. *Text to Text Pours Forth Speech: Voices of Scripture in Luke-Acts*. Bloomington, IN: Indiana University Press, 1995.

Breeze, D. J. "The Career Structure below the Centurionate during the Principate." *ANRW* II.1 (1974): 435–51.

Brink, Laurie. "A General's Exhortation to His Troops: Paul's Military Rhetoric in 2 Cor 10:1–11. Part I." *Biblische Zeitschrift* 49 (2005): 191–201.

–. "A General's Exhortation to His Troops: Paul's Military Rhetoric in 2 Cor 10:1–11. Part II." *Biblische Zeitschrift* 50 (2006): 74–89.

–. "Going the Extra Mile: Reading Matt 5:41 Literally and Metaphorically." In *The History of Religions School Today: Essays in Honor of Hans Dieter Betz*. Edited by T. Blanton, R. Matthew Calhoun and C. K. Rothschild. WUNT. Tübingen: Mohr Siebeck, 2014.

Brock, Ann Graham. "The Significance of φιλέω and φίλος in the Tradition of Jesus Sayings and in the Early Christian Communities." *HTR* 90 (1997): 393–409.

Brodie, T. "Not Q but Elijah: The Saving of the Centurion's Servant (Luke 7:1–10) as an Internalization of the Saving of the Widow and her Child (1 Kgs 17:1–16)." *Irish Biblical Studies* 14 (1992): 54–71.

Broughton, T.R.S. "The Roman Army." Pp. 427–44 in *The Beginnings of Christianity: The Acts of the Apostles*. Edited by F. J. Foakes Jackson and Kirsopp Lake. London: MacMillan, 1933; repr., Grand Rapids, MI: Baker Book House, 1979.

Brown, Peter McC. "Soldiers in New Comedy: Insiders and Outsiders." *Leeds International Classical Studies* 3, no. 8 (2004): 1–16.

Brown, Raymond. *The Death of the Messiah: from Gethsemane to the Grave*. New York: Doubleday, 1994.

Bruce, F. F. "The Acts of the Apostles: Historical Record or Theological Reconstruction." *ANRW* II.25.3 (1985): 2569–2603.

–. *Commentary on the Book of the Acts of the Apostles*. NICNT. Grand Rapids, MI: Eerdmans, 1954.

Bryan, Christopher. "Cornelius's Conversion and the Plain Meaning of Scripture." *Sewanee Theological Review* 43 (2000): 251–58.

Büchler, Adolf. *Types of Jewish–Palestinian Piety from 70 B.C.E. to 70 C.E.* London: Oxford University Press, 1922.

Bultmann, R. *History of the Synoptic Tradition*. Oxford: Blackwell, 1968.

Burgess, Theodore. *Epideictic Literature*. Chicago: University of Chicago Press, 1902.

Burnett, Fred W. "Characterization and Reader Construction of Characters in the Gospels." Pp. 3–23 in *Characterization in Biblical Literature*. Edited by Elizabeth Struthers Malbon and Adele Berlin. Semeia 63. Atlanta: Scholars Press, 1993.

Burton, G. P. "Proconsuls, Assizes and the Administration of Justice." *JRS* 65 (1975): 92–106.

Burton, Paul J. "Amicitia in Plautus: A Study in Roman Friendship Processes." *American Journal of Philology* 125 (2004): 209–43.

Cadbury, Henry J. *The Book of Acts in History*. New York: Harper and Bros, 1955.

–. "Lexical Notes on Luke-Acts: III. Luke's Interest in Lodging." *JBL* 45 (1926): 305–22.

–. "Litotes in Acts." Pp. 58–69 in *Festschrift in Honor of F. Wilbur Gingrich*. Edited by Eugene Howard Barth and Ronald Edwin Cocroft. Leiden: Brill, 1972

–. *The Making of Luke-Acts*. London: SPCK, 1927; reprint 1958.

–. "Some Semitic Personal Names in Luke-Acts," Pp. 45–56 in *Amicitiae Corolla: a Volume of Essays Presented to James Rendel Harris, D. Litt. On the Occasion of His Eightieth Birthday*. H. G. Wood. London: University of London Press, 1933.

Cadoux, C. J. *The Early Christian Attitude toward War*. London: Headley Brothers, Ltd., 1919.

Campbell, J. B. *The Emperor and the Roman Army: 31 BC–AD 235*. Oxford: Clarendon, 1984.

–. "The Marriage of Soldiers under the Empire." *JRS* 68 (1978): 153–166.

Cancik, Hubert. "The History of Culture, Religion and Institutions in Ancient Historiography: Philological Observations Concerning Luke's History." *JBL* 116 (1997): 673–95.

Caragounis, Chrys. "ΟΨΩΝΙΟΝ: A Reconsideration of its Meaning." *NovT* 16 (1974): 35–57.

Carawan, Edwin M. "The Tragic History of Marcellus and Livy's Characterization." *CJ* 80 (1984): 131–41.

Chalmers, Walter R. "Plautus and his Audience." Pp. 21–50 in *Roman Drama*. Edited by T. A. Dorey and Donald R. Dudley. London: Routledge & Kegan Paul, 1965.

Chance, J. Bradley. "Divine Prognostications and the Movement of Story: An Intertextual Exploration of Xenophon's Ephesian Tale and the Acts of the Apostles." Pp. 219–34 in *Ancient Fiction and Early Christian Narrative*. Edited by R. F. Hock, J. B. Chance, and J. Perkins. SBL Symposium Series 6. Atlanta: Scholars Press, 1998.

Chancey, Mark A. *The Myth of a Gentile Galilee*. SNTSMS 118. Cambridge: Cambridge University Press, 2002.

Charlesworth, M. P. "The Virtues of a Roman Emperor: Propaganda and the Creation of Belief." *Proceedings of the British Academy* 23 (1937): 105–33.

Chatman, Seymour. *Story and Discourse: Narrative Structure in Fiction and Film*. Ithaca, NY: Cornell University Press, 1978.

Cheesman, G. L. *The Auxilia of the Roman Imperial Army*. Oxford: Clarendon Press, 1914.

Cherry, David. *Frontier and Society in Roman North Africa*. Oxford: Oxford University Press, 1998.

Chew, Kathryn. "Achilles Tatius and Parody." *CJ* 96 (2000): 57–70.

Cohen, Shaye J. D. "Crossing the Boundary and Becoming a Jew." *HTR* 82 (1989): 13–33.

–. "Josephus, Jeremiah, and Polybius." *History and Theory* 21 (1982): 366–81.

Coleman, K. M. "Launching into History: Aquatic Displays in the Early Empire." *TAPA* 70 (1939): 46–50.

Collart, P. *Philippes, ville de Macédoine*. Paris: E. De Boccard, 1937.

Conzelmann, H. *Acts of the Apostles*. Hermeneia. Philadelphia: Fortress Press, 1987.

Cook, Cornelia. "The Sense of Audience in Luke: A Literary Examination." *New Blackfriars* 72 (1991): 19–30.

Creech, R. Robert. "The Most Excellent Narratee: The Significance of Theophilus in Luke-Acts." Pp. 107–26 in *With Steadfast Purpose: Essays on Acts in Honor of Henry Jackson Flanders Jr.* Edited by Naymond H. Keathley. Waco, TX: Baylor University Press, 1990.

Creed, J. M. *The Gospel According to St. Luke*. London: Macmillan, 1930.

Culler, Jonathan. "Literary Competence." Pp. 101–17 in *Reader-Response Criticism. From Formalism to Post-Structuralism*. Edited by Jane P. Tompkins. Baltimore; London: Johns Hopkins University Press, 1980.

–. *Structuralist Poetics: Structuralism, Linguistics and the Study of Literature*. London: Routledge, 1975.

Culpepper, R. Alan. *Anatomy of the Fourth Gospel: A Study in Literary Design*. Philadelphia: Fortress, 1983.

D'Angelo, Mary R. "Εὐσέβεια: Roman Imperial Family Values and the Sexual Politics of 4 Maccabees and the Pastorals." *Biblical Interpretation* 11 (2003): 139–65.

Daitz, Stephen G. "Tacitus' Technique of Character Portrayal." *The American Journal of Philology* 81 (1960): 30–52.

Danker, F. W. *Jesus and the New Age According to St. Luke: A Commentary on the Third Gospel*. St. Louis: Clayton, 1972.

Darr, John A. *On Character Building: The Reader and the Rhetoric of Characterization in Luke-Acts*. Literary Currents in Biblical Interpretation. Louisville, KY: Westminster John Knox, 1992.

–. *Herod the Fox: Audience Criticism and Lukan Characterization.* JSNTSS. Sheffield: Sheffield Academic Press, 1998.

–. "Narrator as Character: Mapping a Reader-Oriented Approach to Narration in Luke-Acts." *Semeia* 63 (1993): 43–60.

Dauer, Anton. *Johannes und Lukas: Untersuchungen zu den johanneisch-lukanischen Parallelperikopen Joh 4,46–54/Lk 7,1–10 – Joh 12,1–8/Lk 7,36–50; 10, 38–42 –Joh 20, 19–29/Lk 24 36–49.* Würzburg: Echter, 1984.

Davies, W. D., and Dale C. Allison. *The Gospel According to Saint Matthew.* ICC. Edinburgh: T & T Clark, 1991.

Davis, R. W. "The Daily Life of the Roman Soldier under the Principate." *ANRW* II.1 (1974): 299–338.

Dawsey, James M. "What's in a name: Characterization in Luke." *BTB* 16 (1986): 143–47.

de Blois, Lukas. "Volk und Soldaten bei Cassius Dio." *ANRW* II.34.3 (1997): 2650–76.

–, Lukas, Elio LoCascio, and Gerda de Kleijn Hekster, eds. *The Impact of the Roman Army (200 BC – AD 478): Economic, Social, Political, Religious and Cultural Aspects: Proceedings of the Sixth Workshop of the International Network Impact of Empire.* Leiden: Brill, 2007.

de Rossi, Canali. *Le ambascerie dal mondo greco a Roma in età repubblicana.* Studi pubblicato dall' Istituto Italiano per la Storia Antica. Rome: Instituto Italiano per la storia antica, 1997.

de Souza, Philip. *Piracy in the Greco-Roman World.* Cambridge: Cambridge University Press, 1999.

Demoen, Kristoffel. "A Paradigm for the Analysis of Paradigms: The Rhetorical Exemplum in Ancient and Imperial Greek Theory." *Rhetorica* 15 (1997): 125–58.

Derrett, J. Duncan M. "Law in the New Testament: The Syro-Phoenician Woman and the Centurion of Capernaum." *NovT* 15 (1973): 161–86.

Detweiler, Robert, ed. "Reader Response Approaches to Biblical and Secular Texts." *Semeia* 31 (1985).

Devijver, H. "The Roman Army in Egypt (with Special Reference to the Militiae Equestres)." *ANRW* II.1 (1974): 452–92.

Dibelius, Martin. *Studies in the Acts of the Apostles.* Translated by Mary Ling. London: SCM Press, 1956.

Dickerson, Patrick L. "The New Character Narrative in Luke-Acts and the Synoptic Problem." *JBL* 116 (1997): 291–312.

Dobson, Brian. "The Significance of the Centurion and 'Primipilaris' in the Roman Army and Administration." *ANRW* II.1 (1974): 392–434.

Donlan, Walter. "The Origin of Καλὸς Κἀγαθός." *American Journal of Philology* 94 (1973): 365–74.

Doran, Robert. "2 Maccabees and 'Tragic History'." *Hebrew Union College Annual* 50 (1979): 107–14.

–. *Temple Propaganda: The Purpose and Character of 2 Maccabees.* Washington, D.C.: Catholic Biblical Association, 1981.

Dorey, T. A. "Aristophanes and Cleon." *Greece & Rome* 3 (1956): 132–139.

–. *Livy.* London: Routledge and K. Paul, 1971.

Dover, Kenneth James. "Aristophanes." Pp. 163-65 in *The Oxford Classical Dictionary.* Edited by Simon Hornblower and Anthony Spawforth. Oxford: Oxford University Press, 1996.

–. *Aristophanic Comedy.* Berkeley: University of California Press, 1972.

Downing, F. Gerald. "Redaction Criticism. Josephus' Antiquities and the Synoptic Gospels. I." *JSNT* 8 (1980): 46–65.

–. "Redaction Criticism. Josephus' Antiquities and the Synoptic Gospels. II." *JSNT* 9 (1980): 29–48.

du Plessis, Isak. "The Lukan Audience Rediscovered? Some Reactions to Bauckham's Theory." *Neotestamentica* 34 (2000): 243–61.

Duckworth, George E. *The Nature of Roman Comedy*. Princeton: Princeton University Press, 1952, repr. Norman, OK; University of Oklahoma Press, 1994.

Dunand, Maurice. *Le Musée de Soueida. Inscriptions et Monuments Figurés*. Paris: Librairie orientaliste Paul Geuthner, 1934.

Durham, Donald Blythe. "Parody in Achilles Tatius." *Classical Philology* 33 (1938): 1–19.

Eck, Werner. "Provincial Administration and Finance." Pp. 266–92 in *The Cambridge Ancient History XI The High Empire A.D. 70–192*. Edited by Alan K. Bowman, Peter Garnsey, and Dominic Rathbone. Cambridge: Cambridge University Press, 2000.

Edwards, M J. "Quoting Aratus : Acts 17,28." *Zeitschrift Für Die Neutestamentliche Wissenschaft Und Die Kunde Der Älteren Kirche* 83 (January 1, 1992): 266–269.

Eggs, Ekkehard. "Doxa in Poetry: A Study in Aristotle's Poetics." *Poetics Today* 23 (2002): 395–426.

Ehrenberg, V. *The People of Aristophanes: A Sociology of Old Attic Comedy*. 3rd revised. New York: Schocken Books, 1962.

Esler, Philip Francis. "Community and Gospel in Early Christianity: A Response to Richard Bauckham's Gospels for All Christians." *Scottish Journal of Theology* 51 (1998): 235–48.

–. *Community and Gospel in Luke-Acts*. Cambridge: Cambridge University Press, 1987.

Evans, Christopher F. "The Central Section of St. Luke's Gospel." Pp. 37–53 in *Studies in the Gospels*. Edited by D. Nineham. Oxford: Blackwell, 1955.

–. *Saint Luke*. Philadelphia: Trinity Press International, 1990.

Evans, H. H. *St. Paul the Author of Acts of the Apostles and of the Third Gospel*. London: Wyman, 1884.

Farmer, William R. *The Synoptic Problem: A Critical Analysis*. 2nd. Dillsboro, NC: Western North Carolina Press, 1976.

Feld, Maury D. *The Structures of Violence: Armed Forces and Social Systems*. Sage Series on Armed Forces and Society 10. Beverly Hills, CA: Sage Publications, 1977.

Feldman, Louis. *Jew and Gentile in the Ancient World*. Princeton: Princeton University Press, 1993.

Fensham, F. C., "Widows, Orphan, and the Poor in Ancient Near Eastern Legal and Wisdom Literature," *Journal of Near Eastern Studies* 21 (1962): 129–139.

Finley, M. I. *Ancient Slavery and Modern Ideology*. New York: Viking, 1980.

Finn, Thomas. "The God-fearers Reconsidered." *CBQ* 47 (1985): 75–84.

Fiore, Benjamin. "Paul, Exemplification, and Imitation." Pp. 228–57 in *Paul in the Greco-Roman World*. Edited by J. Paul Sampley. Harrisburg, PA: Trinity Press International, 2003.

Fish, Stanley. "Interpreting the Variorum." *Critical Inquiry* 2 (1976): 465–85.

–. *Is There a Text in This Class?: The Authority of Interpretive Communities*. Cambridge, MA: Harvard University Press, 1980.

Fitzgerald, J. T., ed. *Greco-Roman Perspectives on Friendship*. SBL Resources for Biblical Study. Atlanta: Scholars Press, 1997.

Fitzmyer, Joseph. *The Acts of the Apostles*. AB. New York: Doubleday, 1998.

–. *The Gospel According to Luke I–IX*. AB. New York: Doubleday, 1981.

–. *The Gospel According to Luke X–XXIV*. AB. New York: Doubleday, 1985.

Flessen, Bonnie J. *An Exemplary Man: Cornelius and Characterization in Acts 10*. Eugene, OR: Wipf & Stock, 2011.

Flickinger, Roy C. "Terence and Menander." *CJ* 26 (1931): 676–94.

Foakes-Jackson, F. J., and K. Lake. *The Beginnings of Christianity. The Acts of the Apostles*. London: Macmillan, 1933; repr., Grand Rapids, MI: Baker Book House, 1979.

Forni, G. "Estrazione etnica e sociale dei soldati delle legioni nei primi tre secoli dell'impero." *ANRW* II.1 (1974): 339–91.

Forrest, W. G. "Acharnians." *Phoenix* 17, no. 1 (Spring 1963): 1–12.

Forster, E. M. *Aspects of the Novel*. New York: Harmondsworth, 1962.

Forsythe, Gary. *Livy and Early Rome: A Study in Historical Method and Judgement*. Stuttgart: Franz Steiner, 1999.

Fowler, Robert M. *Let the Reader Understand: Reader-Response Criticism and the Gospel of Mark*. Minneapolis: Augsburg/Fortress, 1991.

Fox, Matthew. "History and Rhetoric in Dionysius of Halicarnassus." *JRS* 83 (1993): 31–47.

Frein, Brigid Curtin. "Genre and Point of View in Luke's Gospel." *BTB* 38 (2008): 1–14.

Frend, W. H. C. "Church Historians of the Early Twentieth Century: Adolf von Harnack (1851–1930)." *Journal of Ecclesiastical History* 52 (2001): 83–102.

–. "A Third-Century Inscription Relating to Angareia in Phrygia." *JRS* 46 (1956): 46–56.

Freyne, Sean. *Galilee and Gospel*. Boston: Brill, 2002.

Frost, Maurice. "'I also am a Man under Authority'." *Expository Times* 45 (1933–34): 477–78.

Fuhrmann, Christopher J. *Policing the Roman Empire: Soldiers, Administration, and Public Order*. Oxford; New York: Oxford University Press, 2012.

Funk, Robert W., and et al. *The Five Gospels. The Search for the Authentic Words of Jesus*. New York: Macmillan, 1993.

Gabba, Emilio. *Dionysius and The History of Archaic Rome*. Berkeley: University of California Press, 1991.

Gadamer, Hans-Georg. *Truth and Method*. 2nd. rev. ed. Edited by Joel Weinsheimer and Donald G. Marshall. New York: Continuum, 1994.

Gagnon, R. A. J. "Luke's Motives for Redaction in the Account of the Double Delegation in Luke 7:1–10." *NovT* 36 (1994): 122–45.

–. "Statistical Analysis and the Case of the Double Delegation in Luke 7:3–7a." *CBQ* 55 (1993): 709–31.

Garrett, S. R. "Exodus from Bondage: Luke 9:31 and Acts 12:1–24." *CBQ* 52 (1990): 656–80.

Garrison, Roman. *The Significance of Theophilus as Luke's Reader*. Studies in the Bible and Early Christianity 62. Lewiston, NY: Edwin Mellen Press, 2004.

Garvey, James. "Characterization in Narrative." *Poetics* 7 (1978): 63–78.

Gaventa, Beverly R. *Acts*. Abingdon New Testament Commentaries. Nashville, TN: Abingdon Press, 2003.

George, Augustin. "Guérison de l'esclave d'un centurion." *Assemblées du Seigneur* 40 (1972): 66–77.

Gibson, Walker. "Authors, Speakers, Readers, and Mock Readers." *College English* 11 (1950): 265–69.

Gilbert, Allan H. "Aristotle's Four Species of Tragedy (Poetics 18) and Their Importance for Dramatic Criticism." *AJP* 68 (1947): 363–81.

Gilbert, Gary. "The List of Nations in Acts 2: Roman Propaganda and the Lukan Response." *JBL* 121 (2002): 497–529.

Gilchrist, J. M. "The Historicity of Paul's Shipwreck." *JSNT* 61 (1996): 29–51.

Gill, Christopher. "The Ēthos/Pathos Distinction in Rhetorical and Literary Criticism." *CQ* 34 (1984): 149–66.

–. "The Question of Character-Development: Plutarch and Tacitus." *CQ* 33 (1983): 469–87.

Gill, David W. J., and Conrad Gempf, eds. *The Book of Acts in Its Graeco-Roman Setting*. Vol 2 of *Book of Acts in Its First Century Setting*. Edited by Bruce W. Winter. Grand Rapids, MI: Eerdmans, 1993.

Gilliard, Frank D. "More Silent Reading in Antiquity: Non Omne Verbum Sonabat." *JBL* 112 (1993): 689–94.

Glancy, Jennifer A. "Obstacles to Slaves' Participation in the Corinthian Church." *JBL* 117 (1998): 481–501.

Goldberg, S. M. *Understanding Terence*. Princeton: Princeton University Press, 1986.

Goldsworthy, Adrian K. *The Roman Army at War 100 B.C. – A.D. 200*. Oxford: Oxford University Press, 1996.

González, Justo L. *Acts: The Gospel of the Spirit*. Maryknoll, NY: Orbis Books, 2001.

Goodman, Martin. *The Roman World: 44 BC–AD 180*. New York: Routledge, 1997.

Goodspeed, E. J. "Paul's Voyage to Italy." *BW* 34 (1909): 337–45.

–. "Was Theophilus Luke's Publisher." *JBL* 73 (1954): 84–92.

Gordon, Mary L. "The Patria of Tacitus." *JRS* 26 (1936): 145–51.

Goulder, Michael D. *Luke: A New Paradigm*. JSNTSup 20. Sheffield: Sheffield Academic Press, 1989.

–. "Luke's Knowledge of Matthew." Pp. 143–62 in *Minor Agreements: Symposium Göttingen 1991*. Edited by Georg Strecker. Göttingen: Vandenhoeck & Ruprecht, 1993.

Gowler, David B. "Characterization in Luke: A Socio-Narratological Approach." *BTB* 19 (1989): 57–62.

–. "Hospitality and Characterization in Luke 11:37–54: A Socio-Narratological Approach." *Semeia* 64 (1993): 213–52.

–. *Host, Guest, Enemy, and Friend: Portraits of the Pharisees in Luke and Acts*. Emory Studies in Early Christianity. New York: P. Lang, 1991.

–. "Text, Culture, and Ideology in Luke 7:1-10: A Dialogic Reading." Pp. 89–125 in *Fabrics of Discourse: A Festschrift in honor of Professor Vernon K. Robbins*. Edited by David B. Gowler, Gregory Bloomquist and Duane F. Watson. Philadelphia: Trinity Press International, 2003.

Graff, Richard. "Prose verses Poetry in Early Greek Theories of Style," *Rhetorica* 23 (2005): 303–335.

Grant, Robert M. "Early Christian Geography." *VC* 46 (1992): 105–11.

Green, Joel. *The Gospel of Luke*. Grand Rapids, MI: Eerdmans, 1997.

–, Scot McKnight and I. Howard Marshall. *Dictionary of Jesus and the Gospels: A Compendium of Contemporary Biblical Scholarship*. Downers Grove, IL: Intervarsity Press, 1992.

Gregory, Andrew. "The Reception of Luke and Acts and the Unity of Luke-Acts." *JSNT* 29 (2007): 459–72.

–. *The Reception of Luke and Acts in the Period before Irenaeus*. WUNT 2.169. Tübingen: Mohr Siebeck, 2003.

Grenfell, B. P., A. S. Hunt, and eds. *The Oxyrhynchus Papyri*. London: Oxford University Press, 1899.

Grube, G. M. A. *The Greek and Roman Critics*. London: Methuen, 1965.

Grundmann, W. *Das Evangelium nach Lukas*. THKNT 3. Berlin: Evangelische Verlagsanstalt, 1966.

Gulley, Norman. *Aristotle on the Purposes of Literature*. Cardiff: University of Wales Press, 1971.

Hackett, John. "Echoes of Euripides in the Acts of the Apostles," *Irish Theological Quarterly* 23 [1956]: 218–27; 350–66.

Haenchen, Ernst. "Acta 27." Pp. 235–54 in *Zeit und Geschichte: Dankesgabe an Rudolf Bultmann zum 80. Geburtstag*. Edited by E. Dinkler. Tübingen: Mohr, 1964.

–. *The Acts of the Apostles: A Commentary*. Translated by Bernard Noble and Gerald Shinn. Philadelphia: Westminster, 1971.

Hägg, Thomas. "The Naming of the Characters in the Romance of Xenophon of Ephesus." *Eranos* 69 (1971): 25–59.

–. *The Novel in Antiquity*. Berkeley: University of California Press, 1983.

Haley, S. P. "Livy, Passion and Cultural Stereotypes." *Historia* 39 (1990): 375–81.

Hall, John F. "The Roman Province of Judea: A Historical Overview," *BYU Studies Quarterly* 36:3 (1996–1997): 319–336.

Halliwell, Stephen. "Aristophanes' Apprenticeship." *CQ* 30 (1980): 33–45.

–. "Aristotle Poetics." Pp. 1–142 in *Aristotle Poetics, Longinus On the Sublime, Demetrius On Style*. Translated and edited by Stephen Halliwell, W. H. Fyfe, Donald Russell, and Doreen C. Innes. Loeb Classical Library. Cambridge, MA: Harvard University Press, 1995.

–. "Traditional Greek Conceptions of Character." In *Characterization and Individuality in Greek Literature*. Edited by Christopher Pelling. Oxford: Clarendon Press, 1990.

Hamblin, William J. "The Roman Army in the First Century," *BYU Studies Quarterly* 36:3 (1996–1997): 337–349.

Hansen, Mogens Herman. "The Battle Exhortation in Ancient Historiography: Fact or Fiction?" *Historia* 42 (1993): 161–80.

Hanson, John Arthur. "The Glorious Military." Pp. 51–85 in *Roman Drama*. Edited by T. A. Dorey and D. R. Dudley. London: Routledge & Kegan Paul, 1965.

Harmand, J. "Les origines de l'armée impériale: Un témoignage sur la réalité du pseudo-principat et sur l'évolution militaire de l'Occident." *ANRW* II.1 (1974): 263–98.

Harnack, Adolf. *Militia Christi: Die christliche Religion und der Soldatenstand in den ersten drei Jahrhunderten*. Tübingen: Mohr Siebeck, 1905.

–. *Militia Christi: The Christian Religion and the Military in the First Three Centuries*. Translated by David McInnes Gracie. Philadelphia: Fortress Press, 1982.

–. *The Mission and Expansion of Christianity in the First Three Centuries*. Translated by James Moffatt. Theological Translation Library. New York: Putnam, 1904–5.

–. *Die Mission und Ausbreitung des Christentums in den ersten drei jahrhunderten*. Leipzig: J. C Hinrichs, 1902.

–. *New Testament Studies III: The Acts of the Apostles*. Translated by John Richard Wilkinson. New York: G. P. Putnam, 1909.

Harner, Philip. *Relation Analysis of the Fourth Gospel: A Study in Reader-Response Criticism*. Lewiston, NY: Edwin Mellen Biblical Press, 1993.

Harrill, J. Albert. "The Dramatic Function of the Running Slave Rhoda (Acts 12.13–16): A Piece of Greco-Roman Comedy." *NTS* 46 (2000): 150–57.

–. *Slaves in the New Testament: Literary, Social, and Moral Dimensions*. Minneapolis: Fortress Press, 2006.

Harrington, W. J. *The Gospel According to St. Luke*. London: Chapman, 1968.

Harris, O. G. "Prayer in Luke-Acts: A Study in the Theology of Luke." Nashville: Vanderbilt University, 1966.

Harrison, S. J. *Apuleius. A Latin Sophist*. Oxford: Oxford University Press, 2000.

–. "Petronius Arbiter." Pp. 1149–50 in *The Oxford Classical Dictionary*. 3rd. Edited by Simon Hornblower and Anthony Spawforth. Oxford: Oxford University Press, 1996.

Haslam, J. A. G. "The Centurion at Capernaum Luke 7:1–10." *Expository Times* 96 (1985): 109–10.

Haussoullier, B., and H. Ingholt. *Inscriptions grècques de Syrie, Syria*, 1924.

Hawthorne, Tim. "A Discourse Analysis of Paul's Shipwreck: Acts 27:1–44." *JOTT* 6 (1993): 253–73.

Heath, Malcolm. "Aristotelian Comedy." *The Classical Quarterly* 39 (1989): 344–54.

Heil, John Paul. *The Meal Scenes in Luke-Acts: An Audience-Oriented Approach*. SBLMS 52. Atlanta: Society of Biblical Literature, 1999.

Helgeland, John. "Christians and Military Service, A.D. 173–337." University of Chicago, 1973.

–. "Christians and the Roman Army from Marcus Aurelius to Constantine." *ANRW* II.23.1 (1979): 724–834.

–. "Roman Army Religion." Pp. 199–205 in *SBL Seminar Papers*. George MacRae. Missoula: Scholars Press, 1975.

–. "Roman Army Religion." *ANRW* II.16.2 (1978): 1470–1505.

Helgeland, John, Robert J. Daley, and J. Patout Burns. *Christians and the Military: The Early Experience*. Philadelphia: Fortress, 1985.

Hemer, Colin J. *The Book of Acts in the Setting of Hellenistic History*. Edited by Conrad H. Gempf. Winona Lake, IN: Eisenbrauns, 1990.

Herman, Gabriel. *Ritualized Friendship and the Greek City*. Cambridge: Cambridge University Press, 1987.

Hewitt, Joseph W. "Elements of Humor in the Satire of Aristophanes." *CJ* 8 (1913): 293–300.

Hildesheimer, Hirsch, and Samuel Klein. *Gevulot ha-Arets: Studies in the Geography of Eretz-Israel*. Jerusalem: Mosad ha-Rav Kuk, 1965.

Hobbs, T. R. "Soldiers in the Gospels: A Neglected Agent." Pp. 328–48 in *Social-Scientific Models for Interpreting the Bible: Essays by the Context Group in Honor of Bruce J. Malina*. Edited by John J. Pilch. Boston; Leiden: Brill, 2001.

Hochman, Baruch. *Character in Literature*. Ithaca, NY: Cornell University Press, 1985.

Holder, Paul A. *Studies in the Auxilia of the Roman Army from Augustus to Trajan*. Oxford: BAR, 1980.

Hoover, Roy W. "Selected Special Lukan Material in the Passion Narrative (Luke 23:33–43, 47b–49)." *Forum* 1 (1998): 119–27.

Horsley, G. H. R. "Speeches and Dialogue in Acts." *NTS* 32 (1986): 609–14.

Horsley, Richard A. *Galilee. History, Politics, People*. Valley Forge, PA: Trinity Press International, 1995.

–. "Questions about Redactional Strata and the Social Relations Reflected in Q." *SBL Seminar Papers* (1989), 186–203.

Howell, Justin R. "The Imperial Authority and Benefaction of Centurions and Acts 10:34–43: A Response to C. Kavin Rowe." *JSNT* 31 (2008): 25–51.

Howgego, Christopher. "The Supply and Use of Money in the Roman World 200 B.C. to A.D. 300." *JRS* 82 (1992): 1–31.

Hult, Christine A. "Reader Reception Theory." Pp. 255–57 in *Theorizing Composition: A Critical Sourcebook of Theory and Scholarship in Contemporary Composition Studies*. Edited by Mary Lynch Kennedy. Westport, CT: Greenwood Press, 1998.

Hutter, Horst. *Politics as Friendship: The Origins of Classical Notions of Politics in the Theory and Practice of Friendship*. Waterloo: Wilfrid Laurier University Press, 1978.

Isaac, Benjamin. "The Roman Army in Judaea: Police Duties and Taxation." Pp. 458–61 in *Roman Frontier Studies*. Edited by V.A. Maxfield and M. I. Dobson. Exeter: University of Exeter Press, 1991.

–. "Roman Colonies in Judaea: The Foundation of Aelia Capitolina." *Talanta* 12/13 (1980 January): 38–43.

Iser, Wolfgang. *The Implied Reader*. Baltimore: Johns Hopkins University Press, 1974.

–. "The Reading Process: A Phenomenological Approach." *New Literary History* 3, no. 2 (Winter 1972): 279–99.

Iverson, Stanley Allen. "The Military Theme in Juvenal's Satires." Ph.D. diss., Vanderbilt University, 1975.

Jacobson, A. D. *The First Gospel: An Introduction to Q*. Sonoma, CA: Polebridge, 1992.

–. "The History of the Composition of the Synoptic Sayings Source, Q." *SBL Seminar Papers 1987* (1987), 285–94.

Jauss, Hans-Robert. "Literary History as a Challenge to Literary Theory." *New Literary History* 2 (1970): 7–37.

–. *Toward an Aesthetic of Reception*. Translated by Timothy Bahti. Minneapolis: University of Minnesota Press, 1982.

Jennings, Theodore W., and Tat-Siong Benny Liew. "Mistaken Identities but Model Faith: Rereading the Centurion, the Chap, and the Christ in Matthew 8:5–13." *JBL* 123 (2004): 467–94.

Jensen, Jorgen Skafte. "God-Fearers or Sympathizers: A Special Social Group?" *Temenos* 28 (1992): 199–207.

Jeremias, J. *Die Sprache des Lukasevangeliums: Redaktion und Tradition im Nicht-Markusstoff des dritten Evangeliums*. Göttingen: Vandenhoeck & Ruprecht, 1980.

Johnson, Earl S. "Mark 15,39 and the So-Called Confession of the Roman Centurion." *Biblica* 81 (2000): 406–13.

Johnson, Luke Timothy. *The Acts of the Apostles*. Sacra Pagina. Collegeville, MN: Liturgical Press, 1992.

–. *The Literary Function of Possessions in Luke-Acts*. SBL Dissertation Series. Missoula, Mt: Scholars Press, 1977.

–. "On Finding the Lukan Community: A Cautious Cautionary Essay." *SBLSP* 1 (1979): 87–100.

Johnson, Nan. "Reader-Response and the Pathos Principle." *Rhetoric Review* 6 (1988): 152–66.

Judge, E. A. "Jews, Proselytes and God-fearers Club Together." Pp. 73–81 in *New Documents Illustrating Early Christianity*. Edited by S.R. Llewelyn. Sydney: Ancient History Documentary Research Centre, Macquarie University, 2002.

–. "The Regional Kanon for Requistioned Transport." Pp. 36–44 in *New Documents Illustrating Early Christianity*. Edited by G. H. R. Horsley. North Ryde, Australia: Macquarie University, 1976.

Judge, J. P. "Luke 7:1–10: Sources and Redaction." Pp. 473–90 in *L'Evangile de Luc*. Edited by F. Neirynck. Leuven: Peeters, 1989.

Jung, J. H. "Das Eherecht der romischen Soldaten." *ANRW* II.14 (1982): 302–46.

–. "Die Rechtsstellung der römischen Soldaten: Ihre Entwicklung von den Anfängen Roms bis auf Diokletian." *ANRW* II.14 (1982): 882–1013.

Karris, Robert J. "Luke 23:47 and the Lucan View of Jesus' Death." *JBL* 105 (1986): 65–74.

–. Windows and Mirrors: Literary Criticism and Luke's *Sitz im Leben*," *SBL Seminar Papers* (1979): 47–58.

Kasher, Aryeh, "The Isopoliteia Question in Caesarea Maritima." *JQR* 68 (1977): 16–27.

Kee, Howard Clark. *To Every Nation Under Heaven: The Acts of the Apostles*. Harrisburg, PA: Trinity Press International, 1997.

Kelber, Werner. "Redaction Criticism: On the Nature and Exposition of the Gospels." *PRSt* 6 (1979): 4–16.

Kennedy, George A. "The Speeches in Acts." Pp. 114–40 in *New Testament Interpretation through Rhetorical Criticism*. Chapel Hill, NC: University of North Carolina Press, 1984.

–. *Progymnasmata. Greek Textbooks of Prose Composition and Rhetoric*. Writings from the Greco-Roman World. Atlanta: SBL, 2003.

Keener, Craig S. *Acts. An Exegetical Commentary*. Vol. 1. Grand Rapids, MI: Baker Academic, 2012.

Kenyon, F. G., H. I. Bell, and eds. *Greek Papyri in the British Museum III*. London: Oxford University Press, 1907.

Keppie, Lawrence. *Legions and Veterans*. Stuttgart: Franz Steiner, 2000.

–. *The Making of the Roman Army: From Republic to Empire*. Norman, OK: University of Oklahoma, 1998.

Kermode, F. *The Genesis of Secrecy: On the Interpretation of Narrative* Cambridge, MA: Harvard University Press, 1979.

Kezbere, Ilze. *Umstrittener Monotheismus: Wahre und falsche Apotheose im lukanischen Doppelwerk*. NTOA/SUNT 60. Göttingen: Vandenhoeck & Ruprecht, 2006.

Kiley, M. "Roman Legends and Luke-Acts." *Biblical Theology Bulletin* 39 (2009): 135–142.

Kilgallen, John. "Clean, Acceptable, Saved – Acts 10." *Expository Times* 109 (1998): 301–2.

–. "'I have not found such faith in Israel' (Luke 7,9)." *Melita Theologica* 49 (1998): 19–24.

Kilpatrick, G. D. "A Theme of the Lucan Passion Story and Luke xxiii. 47." *JTS* 43 (1942): 34–36.

Kim, Seyoon. *Christ and Caesar: The Gospel and the Roman Empire in the Writings of Paul and Luke*. Grand Rapids, Mich.: William B. Eerdmans, 2008.

Kim, T. H. "The Anarthrous υἱὸς θεοῦ in Mark 15,39 and the Roman Imperial Cult." *Bib* 79 (1998): 221–41.

Kingsbury, Jack Dean. "Reflections on 'the Reader' of Matthew's Gospel," NTS 34 (1988): 442–460.

Kirk, A. "'Love Your Enemies,' the Golden Rule, and Ancient Reciprocity (Luke 6:27–35)," 2003.

–. "Some Compositional Conventions of Hellenistic Wisdom Texts and the Juxtaposition of 4:1–13; 6:20b–49; and 7:1–10 in Q." *JBL* 116 (1997): 235–57.

Klauck, Hans-Josef. "Gottesfürchtige im Magnificat?" *NTS* 43 (1997): 134–39.

–. "Kirche als Freundesgemeinschaft? Auf Spurensuche im Neuen Testament." *MTZ* 42 (1991): 1–14.

–. *Magic and Paganism in Early Christianity: The World of the Acts of the Apostles*. Edinburgh: T & T Clark, 2000.

–. *The Religious Context of Early Christianity*. Edinburgh: T & T Clark, 2000.

Klink III, Edward W. "The Gospel Community Debate: State of the Question." *CBR* 3 (2004): 60–85.

–. *The Sheep of the Fold: The Audience and Origin of the Gospel of John*. Cambridge: Cambridge University Press, 2007.

Kloppenborg, John. *The Formation of Q: Trajectories in Ancient Wisdom Collections*. Philadelphia: Fortress Press, 1987.

Koester, Helmut. *Introduction to the New Testament. Vol 1. History, Culture, and Religion of the Hellenistic Age*. Hermeneia. Philadelphia: Fortress Press, 1982.

–. *Introduction to the New Testament. Vol 2. History and Literature of Early Christianity*. Hermeneia. Philadelphia: Fortress Press, 1982.

Konstan, D. *Friendship in the Classical World*. Cambridge: Cambridge University Press, 1997.

Korfmacher, William Charles. "Three Phases of Classical Type Characterization." *Classical Weekly* 27 (1934): 85–86.

Kraabel, A. T. "The Disappearance of the 'God-fearers'." *Numen* 28 (1981): 113–26.

–. "The God-fearers Meet the Beloved Disciple." Pp. 276–84 in *The Future of Early Christianity: Essays in Honour of Helmut Koester*. Edited by B. A. Pearson, A. T. Kraabel, G.W.E. Nickelsbourg, and N. R. Peterson. Minneapolis: Fortress Press, 1991.

Krodel, Gerhard A. *Acts*. Augsburg Commentary on the New Testament. Minneapolis, MN: Augsburg Press, 1986.

Kurz, William. *Reading Luke-Acts: Dynamics of Biblical Narrative*. Louisville: Westminster John Knox, 1993.

Lake, Kirsopp. "Proselytes and God-fearers." Pp. 74–96 in *The Beginnings of Christianity. The Acts of the Apostles*. Edited by F. J. Foakes Jackson and Kirsopp Lake. London; Grand Rapids: MacMillan; Baker Book House, 1933; reprint 1979.

Lamberton, Robert D. "Philanthropia and the Evolution of Dramatic Taste." *Phoenix* 37 (1983): 95–103.

Lane, Thomas J. *Luke and the Gentile Mission: Gospel Anticipates Acts*. Frankfurt: Peter Lang, 1996.

Laney, James T. "Characterization and Moral Judgments." *JR* 55 (1975): 405–14.

Lehmann, B. "Das Eigenvermögen der römischen Soldaten unter väterlicher Gewalt." *ANRW* II.14 (1982): 183–284.

Lehtipuu, Outi. "Characterization and Persuasion: The Rich Man and the Poor Man in Luke 16:19–31." Pp. 73–105 in *Characterization in the Gospels*. Edited by David Rhoads and Kari Syreeni. JSNTSup 184. Sheffield: Sheffield Academic Press, 1999.

Lendon, J. E. *Soldiers and Ghosts: A History of Battle in Classical Antiquity*. New Haven, CT: Yale University Press, 2005.

Lentricchia, Frank. *After the New Criticism*. Chicago: University of Chicago Press, 1980.

Lettich, Giovanni. *Itinerari Epigrafici Aquileiesi*. Trieste: Editreg SRL, 2003.

Levick, Barbara. *Roman Colonies in Southern Asia Minor*. Oxford: Clarendon, 1967.

–. "Two Pisidian Colonial Families." *JRS* 48, no. 1/2 (1958): 74–78.

Levinska, I. A. *The Book of Acts in its Diaspora Setting*. Book of Acts in its First Century Setting. Grand Rapids: Eerdmans, 1996.

Lewis, Naphtali, Yigael Yadin, and Jonas C. Greenfield, eds. *The Documents from the Bar Kokhba Period in the Cave of Letters. Greek Papyri*. Jerusalem: Israel Exploration Society, 1989.

Lifshitz, B. *Donateurs et Fondateurs dans les Synagogues Juives*. Cahiers de la Revue Biblique. Paris: S. Gabalda, 1967.

Little, Alan McN. G. "Plautus and Popular Drama." *Harvard Studies in Classical Philology* 49 (1938): 205–28.

Llewelyn, S. R., ed. *New Documents Illustrating Early Christianity. Volume 7*. North Ryde, N.S.W. Australia: Macquarie University, 1994.

Loisy, Alfred. *Les Actes des Apôtres*. Paris: E. Nourry, 1920.

Löning, Karl. "Die Korneliustradition." *BZ* 18 (1974): 1–19.

Luce, T. J. *Livy: The Composition of his History*. Princeton: Princeton University Press, 1977.

Luomanen, Petri. "Corpus Mixtum – An Appropriate Description of Matthew's Community?" *JBL* 117, no. 3 (1998): 469–80.

Luz, Ulrich. *Matthew 8–20*. Hermeneia. Minneapolis: Fortress Press, 2001.

Lüdemann, Gerd. *Early Christianity According to the Traditions in Acts*. Minneapolis: Fortress Press, 1987.

MacCary, W. Thomas. "Menander's Soldiers: Their Names, Roles and Masks." *The American Journal of Philology* 93 (1972): 279–98.

MacDonald, D. R. *Does the New Testament Imitate Homer? Four Cases from the Acts of the Apostles*. New Haven, CT: Yale University Press, 2003.

–. "Luke's Emulation of Homer: Acts 12:1–17 and Iliad 24." *Forum* 3 (2000): 197–205.

–. "The Shipwrecks of Odysseus and Paul." *NTS* 45 (1999): 88–107.

MacMullen, Ramsay. "The Epigraphic Habit in the Roman Empire." *AJP* 103 (1982): 233–46.

–. "How Big was the Roman Imperial Army?" *Klio* 62 (1980): 451–60.

–. "The Legion as a Society." *Hist.* 33 (1984): 440–56.

–. "The Roman Emperor's Army Costs." *Latomus* 43 (1984): 571–80.

Maddox, Robert. *The Purpose of Luke-Acts*. Studies of the New Testament and its World. Edinburgh: T&T Clark, 1982.

Mailloux, Steven. *Interpretive Conventions: The Reader in the Study of American Fiction*.
    Ithaca, NY; London: Cornell University Press, 1982.
Major, Wilfred. "Menander in a Macedonian World." *Greek, Roman and Byzantine Studies* 38
    (1997): 41–73.
Malbon, Elizabeth Struthers. "The Jewish Leaders in the Gospel of Mark: A Literary Study of
    Marcan Characterization." *JBL* 108 (1989): 259–81.
Malherbe, Abraham J. "Antisthenes and Odysseus, and Paul at War." *HTR* 76 (1983): 143–73.
–. *Social Aspects of Early Christianity*. Eugene, OR: Wipf & Stock, 2003.
Mann, J. C. "The Development of the Auxiliary and Fleet Diplomas." *Epigraphische Studien* 9
    (1972): 233–41.
–. *Legionary Recruitment and Veteran Settlement During the Principate*. London: Institute of
    Archaeology, 1983.
–. "The Organization of the Frumentarii." *ZPE* 74 (1988): 149–50.
Marguerat, Daniel. "The Enigma of the Silent Closing of Acts (28:16–31)." Pp. 285–304 in
    Jesus and the Heritage of Israel: Luke's Narrative Claim upon Israel's Legacy. Edited by
    David P. Moessner. Harrisburg, PA.: Trinity Press International, 1999.
–. "Saul's Conversion (Acts 9, 22, 26) and the Multiplication of Narrative in Acts." Pp. 127–
    55 in *Luke's Literary Achievement*. Edited by C. M. Tuckett. Sheffield: Sheffield Academic
    Press, 995.
Marples, Morris. "Plautus." *Greece and Rome* 8 (October 1938): 1–7.
Marshall, I. Howard. *The Acts of the Apostles: An Introduction and Commentary*. TNTC. Grand
    Rapids, MI: Eerdmans, 1980.
–. *Commentary on Luke*. NIGTC. Grand Rapids, MI: Eerdmans, 1978.
–. "Former Treatise." Pp. 163–82 in *The Book of Acts in Its Ancient Literary Setting*. Edited
    by Bruce W. Winter and Andrew D. Clarke. Grand Rapids, MI: Eerdmans Publishing, 1993.
Marshall, P. *Enmity in Corinth: Social Conventions in Paul's Relations with the Corinthians*.
    WUNT 2.23. Tübingen: Mohr Siebeck, 1987.
Martin, Hubert. "The Concept of Philanthropia in Plutarch's Lives." *American Journal of
    Philology* 82 (1961): 164–75.
Martin, Ralph P. "The Healing of the 'Centurion's' Servant/Son." Pp. 14–22 in *Unity and
    Diversity in New Testament Theology*. Edited by Robert A. Guelich. Grand Rapids:
    Eerdmans, 1978.
Martin, René. *Pétrone: Le Satyricon*. Paris: Ellipses, 1999.
Mason, Steve. "Flavius Josephus in Flavian Rome." Pp. 559–89 in *Flavian Rome.Culture,
    Image, Text*. Edited by A. J. Boyle and W. J. Dominik. Boston: Brill, 2003.
–. *Josephus and the New Testament*. 2nd. Peabody, MA: Hendrickson, 2003.
Matera, Frank J. "Luke 23, 1–25." Pp. 535–51 in *L'Evangile de Luc*. Edited by F. Neirynck.
    Leuven: Peeters, 1989.
–. "The Death of Jesus according to Luke: A Question of Sources." *CBQ* 47 (1985): 469–85.
–. "Luke 22, 66–71: Jesus before the Presbyterion." *Ephemerides Theologicae Lovanienses* 65
    (1989): 43–59.
Mattill, A. J. "The Jesus–Paul Parallels and the Purpose of Luke-Acts: H. H. Evans
    Reconsidered." *NovT* 17, no. 1 (January 1975): 15–46.
Mattingly, Harold. "The Roman 'Virtues'." *HTR* 30 (1937): 103–17.
McCown, C. C. "The Geography of Luke's Central Section." *JBL* 57 (1938): 51–66.
McDonald, A. H. "The Style of Livy." *JRS* 47 (1957): 155–72.
McDonnell, Myles. "Roman Men and Greek Virtue." Pp. 235–61 in *Andreia. Studies in
    Manliness and Courage in Classical Antiquity*. Edited by Ralph M. Rosen and Ineke Sluiter.
    Boston: Brill, 2003.

McKeon, Richard. "Aristotle's Conception of Language and the Arts of Language." Pp. 176–231 in *Critics and Criticism: Ancient and Modern*. Edited by R. S. Crane. Chicago: University of Chicago Press, 1952.

McKnight, Edgar V. "Reader Perspectives on the New Testament." *Semeia* 48 (1989), 1–206.

–. "Reader-Response Criticism." Pp. 230–52 in *To Each Its Own Meaning: An Introduction to Biblical Criticisms and Their Application*. Edited by Steven L. McKenzie and Stephen R. Haynes. Louisville: Westminster John Knox Press, 1999.

Meeks, Wayne. *The First Urban Christians: The Social World of the Apostle Paul*. New Haven, CT: Yale University Press, 1983.

Merelahti, Petri, and Raimo Hakola. "Reconceiving Narrative Criticism." Pp. 13–48 in *Characterization in the Gospel. Reconceiving Narrative Criticism*. Edited by David Rhoads and Kari Syreeni. JSNT Suppl. Series 184. Sheffield: Sheffield Academic Press, 1999.

Michaels, J. Ramsey. "The Centurion's Confession and the Spear Thrust." *CBQ* 29 (1967): 102–9.

Miles, Gary B., and Garry Trompf. "Luke and Antiphon: The Theology of Acts 27–28 in the Light of Pagan Beliefs about Divine Retribution, Pollution, and Shipwreck." *HTR* 69 (1976): 259–67.

Millar, Fergus. "Empire and City, Augustus to Julian: Obligations, Excuses and Status." *JRS* 73 (1983): 76–96.

–. "The Roman Coloniae of the Near East: A Study of Cultural Relations." In *Roman Eastern Policy and Other Studies in Roman History*. Edited by H. Solin and M. Kajava. Helsinki: Finnish Society of Science and Letters, 1990.

–. *The Roman Near East: 31 BC–AD 337*. Cambridge, MA: Harvard University Press, 1993.

–. "The World of the Golden Ass." *JRS* 71 (1981): 63–75.

Miller, D. L. "Empaizein: Playing the Mock Game (Luke 22:63–64)." *JBL* 90 (1971): 309–13.

Mitchell, Alan C. "'Greet Friends by Name': New Testament Evidence for the Greco-Roman Topos on Friendship." Pp. 225–62 in *Greco-Roman Perspectives on Friendship*. Edited by John T. Fitzgerald. SBL Resources for Biblical Study 34. Atlanta: Scholars Press, 1997.

–. "The Social Function of Friendship in Acts 2:44–47 and 4:32–37." *JBL* 111 (1992): 255–72.

Mitchell, Margaret M. *The Heavenly Trumpet: John Chrysostom and the Art of Pauline Interpretation*. Louisville, KY: Westminster John Knox Press, 2002.

–. "New Testament Envoys in the Context of Greco-Roman Diplomatic and Epistolary Conventions: The Example of Timothy and Titus." *JBL* 111 (1992): 661–82.

–. "Patristic Counter-Evidence to the Claim that 'The Gospels Were Written for All Christians'." *NTS* 51 (2005): 36–79.

–. *Paul and the Rhetoric of Reconciliation: An Exegetical Investigation of the Language and Composition of 1 Corinthians*. Tübingen; Louisville, KY: Mohr Siebeck; Westminster/John Knox Press, 1991.

–. "Review: Homer in the New Testament?" *JR* 83 (2003): 244–60.

–. "Rhetorical and New Literary Criticism." Pp. 615–33 in *The Oxford Handbook of Biblical Studies*. Edited by J. W. Rogerson and Judith M. Lieu. Oxford: Oxford University Press, 2006.

Mitchell, Stephen. "Legio VII and the Garrison of Augustan Galatia." *Classical Quarterly* 26 (1976): 298–308.

–. "Requisitioned Transport in the Roman Empire: A new Inscription from Pisidia." *JRS* 66 (1976): 106–31.

Moessner, David P. *Lord of the Banquet: The Literary and Theological Significance of the Lukan Travel Narrative*. Minneapolis, MN: Fortress Press, 1989; repr., Harrisburg, PA: Trinity Press International, 1998.

–. "'The Christ Must Suffer': New Light on the Jesus–Peter, Stephen, Paul Parallels in Luke-Acts." *NovT* 28, no. 3 (July 1986): 220–56.

Moffatt, James. "War." Pp. 646–73 in *Dictionary of the Apostolic Church*. NY: Charles Scribner's Sons, 1918.

Moles, John. "'Philanthropia' in the Poetics." *Phoenix* 38 (1984): 325–35.

Mommsen, Theodore. *Römische Geschichte V*. Berlin: Weidmann, 1885.

Montefiore, H. W. "Josephus and the New Testament (Continued)." *NovT* 4 (1960): 307–18.

Moore, Stephen D. "Doing Gospel Criticism as/with a 'Reader'." *BTB* 19 (1989): 85–93.

–. *Literary Criticism and the Gospels: The Theoretical Challenge*. New Haven, CT: Yale University Press, 1989.

–. "Narrative Homiletics: Lucan Rhetoric and the Making of the Reader." Dublin: University of Dublin, 1986.

–. "Negative Hermeneutics, Insubstantial Texts: Stanley Fish and the Biblical Interpreter." *JAAR* 54 (1986): 707–19.

Morgenthaler, Robert. *Lukas und Quintilian. Rhetorik als Erzählkunst*. Zürich: Gotthelf, 1993.

Moscato, M.A. "Current Theories Regarding the Audience of Luke-Acts." *Currents in Theology and Mission* 3 (1976): 355–61.

Moxnes, Halvor. *The Economy of the Kingdom. Social Conflict and Economic Relations in Luke's Gospel*. Philadelphia: Fortress Press, 1988.

–. "Patron-Client Relations and the New Community in Luke-Acts." Pp. 241–68 in *The Social World of Luke-Acts*. Edited by Jerome Neyrey. Peabody, MA: Hendrickson, 1991.

–. "The Social Context of Luke's Community." *Int* 48 (1994): 379–89.

Murphy-O'Connor, Jerome. "Lots of God-fearers? THEOSEBEIS in the Aphrodisias Inscription." *RB* 99 (1992): 418–24.

Navone, J. "The Journey Theme in Luke-Acts." *Scr* 20 (1972): 24–30.

Nesselrath, Heinz-Günther. *Die attische mittlere Komödie: ihre Stellung in der antiken Literaturkritik und Literaturgeschichte*. Untersuchungen zur antiken Literatur und Geschichte. Berlin: Walter de Gruyter, 1990.

Neyrey, Jerome H. "Acts 17, Epicureans and Theodicy: A Study in Stereotypes." Pp. 118–34 in *Greeks, Romans and Christians: Essays in Honor of Abraham J. Malherbe*. Edited by David L. Balch, Everett Ferguson, and Wayne A. Meeks. Minneapolis: Fortress Press, 1990.

–. "The Forensic Defense Speech and Paul's Trial Speeches in Acts 22–26: Form and Function." Pp. 210–24 in *Luke-Acts: New Perspectives from the Society of Biblical Literature Seminar*. Edited by Charles H. Talbert. New York: Crossroads, 1984.

Nguyen, vanThanh. *Peter and Cornelius: A Story of Conversion and Mission*. ASM Scholarly Monograph Series 15. Eugene, OR: Pickwick Publications, 2012.

Nissen, Heinrich. *Kritische Untersuchungen über die Quellen der vierten und fünften Dekade des Livius*. Berlin: Weidmann, 1863.

Norden, Eduard. *Agnostos Theos: Untersuchungen zur Formengeschichte religiöser Rede*. Darmstadt: Wissenschaftliche Buchgesellschaft, 1913; reprint 1956.

Nutting, Herbert C. "The Conviction of Lentulus." *CJ* 3 (1908): 186–91.

O'Donoghue, N. D. *Pathos and Significance*. Philosophical Studies, National University of Ireland 19. Dublin: National University of Ireland, 1970.

O'Sullivan, James N. *Xenophon of Ephesus: His Compositional Technique and the Birth of the Novel*. Berlin: Walter de Gruyter, 1995.

Ogilvie, R. M. A. *The Romans and Their Gods in the Age of Augustus*. New York: Norton, 1970.

Olshausen, Eckart. *Prosopographie der hellenistischen Königsgesandten. I. Von Triparadeisos bis Pydna*. Studia hellenistica. Louvain: Studia Hellenistica, 1974.

Ong, Walter J. "The Writer's Audience Is Always a Fiction." *PMLA* 90 (1975): 9–21.

Osiek, Carolyn. "Female Slaves, Porneia, and the Limits of Obedience." Pp. 255–74 in *Early Christian Families in Context: An Interdisciplinary Dialogue*. Edited by David L. Balch and Carolyn Osiek. Grand Rapids: Eerdmans, 2003.

Ottley, Sandra. "The Role played by the Praetorian Guard in the Events of AD 69, as described by Tacitus in his *Historiae*." Ph.D. diss, University of Western Australia, 2009.

Overman, J. Andrew. "The God-fearers: Some Neglected Features." *JSNT* 32 (1988): 17–26.

Papanikolaou, Antonios D. *Chariton-Studien: Untersuchungen zur Sprache und Chronologie der griechischen Romane*. Hypomnemata. Göttingen: Vandenhoeck and Ruprecht, 1973.

Parker, H. M. D. *The Roman Legions*. Oxford: Oxford University Press, 1971.

Parker, Holt N. "Plautus v. Terence: Audience and Popularity Re-Examined." *American Journal of Philology* 117 (1996): 585–617.

Parry, David. "Release of the Captives: Reflections on Acts 12." Pp. 156–64 in *Luke's Literary Achievements*. Edited by C. M. Tuckett. JSNTS. Sheffield: Sheffield Academic Press, 1995.

Parsons, Mikeal C. *Body and Character in Luke and Acts: The Subversion of Physiognomy in Early Christianity*. Grand Rapids, MI: Baker Academic, 2006.

–. "The Character of the Lame Man in Acts 3–4." *JBL* 124 (2005): 295–312.

–. *The Departure of Jesus in Luke-Acts: The Ascension Narratives in Context*. JSNTSup 21. Sheffield: JSOT, 1987.

–. *Luke: Storyteller, Interpreter, Evangelist*. Peabody, MA: Hendrickson, 2007.

Parsons, Mikeal C., and Richard I. Pervo. *Rethinking the Unity of Luke and Acts*. Minneapolis, MN: Fortress Press, 1993.

Patterson, "The Widow, Orphan and the Poor in the Old Testament and Extra-Biblical Literature," *Bibliotheca Sacra* 130 (1973): 223–34.

Pearson, Lionel. "Characterization in Drama and Oratory–Poetics 1450a20." *Classical Quarterly* 18, no. 1 (May 1968): 76–83.

–. "Popular Ethics in the World of Thucydides." *CP* 52 (1957): 228–44.

Penner, Todd. "Madness in the Method? The Acts of the Apostles in Current Study." *CBR* 2 (2004): 223–93.

–. "Narrative as Persuasion: Epideictic Rhetoric and Scribal Amplification in the Stephen Episode in Acts." *SBLSP* 35 (1996): 352–67.

Penner, Todd, and Caroline Vander Stichele, eds. *Contextualizing Acts: Lukan Narrative and Greco-Roman Discourse*. SBLSS 20. Atlanta: SBL, 2003.

Perry, Ben E. *The Ancient Romances*. Berkeley: University of California Press, 1967.

–. "Chariton and His Romance from a Literary-Historical Point of View." *American Journal of Philology* 51 (1930): 93–134.

–. "The Literary Art of Apuleius." *TAPA* 54 (1923): 196–227.

Pervo, Richard I. *Dating Acts: Between the Evangelists and the Apologists*. Santa Rosa, CA: Polebridge Press, 2006.

–. "Direct Speech in Acts and the Question of Genre." *JSNT* 28 (2006): 285–307.

–. *Profit with Delight: The Literary Genre of the Acts of the Apostles*. Philadelphia: Fortress Press, 1987.

Peterson, H. "Livy and Augustus." *TAPA* 91 (1961): 440–52.

Phang, Sara Elise. "The Families of Roman Soldiers (First and Second Centuries A.D.): Culture, Law, and Practice." *Journal of Family History* 27 (October 2002): 352–73.

–. *The Marriage of Roman Soldiers (13 B.C. – A.D. 235): Law and Family in the Imperial Army*. Columbia Studies in the Classical Tradition 24. Leiden; Boston: Brill, 2001.

Phelan, James. "'Self-Help' for Narratee and Narrative Audience: How 'I'–and 'You'?–read 'How.' Lorrie Moore's Short Story 'How' from the Collection 'Self-Help'– Second-Person Narrative." *Style* 28 (1994): 350–65.

Phillips, Thomas E. "The Genre of Acts: Moving Toward Consensus?" *CBR* 4 (2006): 365–96.

Plummer, Alfred. *The Gospel According to Saint Luke*. 5th. ICC. Edinburgh: T & T Clark, 1901.

Plümacher, E. "Wirklichkeitserfahrung und Geschichtsschreibung bei Lukas: Erwägungen zu den Wir-Strücken der Apostelgeschichte." *ZNW* 68 (1977): 2–22.

Polag, Athanasius. *Die Christologie der Logienquelle*. WMANT 45. Neukirchen-Vluyn: Neukirchener-Verlag, 1977.

Polhill, John. *Acts*. The New American Commentary. Nashville, TN: Broadman Press, 1992.

Pollard, Nigel. "The Roman army as 'total institution' in the Near East? Dura-Europos as a case study." Pp. 211–27 in *The Roman Army in the East*. D. L. Kennedy. Ann Arbor, MI: Journal of Roman Archaeology, 1996.

Porter, Stanley E. "Reader-Response Criticism and New Testament Study: A Response to A. C. Thiselton's New Horizons in Hermeneutics." *Journal of Literature and Theology* 8 (1994): 94–102.

–. "Why Hasn't Reader-Response Criticism Caught on in New Testament Studies?" *Journal of Literature and Theology* 4 (1990): 278–92.

Post, L. A. "Aristotle and Menander." *TAPA* 69 (1938): 1–42.

Powell, Mark Allan. "The Religious Leaders in Luke: A Literary-Critical Study." *JBL* 109 (1990): 93–110.

–. *What is Narrative Criticism?* Minneapolis: Fortress Press, 1990.

Pownall, Frances Skoczylas. "'Presbeis Autokratores': Andocides' 'De Pace'." *Phoenix* 49 (1995): 140–49.

Praeder, Susan Marie. "Acts 27:1–28:16: Sea Voyages in Ancient Literature and the Theology of Luke-Acts." *CBQ* 46 (1984): 683–706.

–. "The Problem of First Person Narration in Acts." *NovT* 29 (1987): 193–218.

Price, S. R. F. "Soter." Pp. 1427–28 in *OCD 3rd*. Edited by Simon Hornblower and Anthony Spawforth. Oxford: Oxford University Press, 1996.

Prince, Gerald. "Introduction to the Study of the Narratee." In *Reader-Response Criticism: From Formalism to Post-Structuralism*. Edited by Jane P. Tompkins. Baltimore: Johns Hopkins University Press, 1980.

Pritchett, W. Kendrick. *Essays in Greek History*. Amsterdam: J. C. Gieben, 1994.

Rabinowitz, Peter J. *Before Reading: Narrative Conventions and the Politics of Interpretation*. Columbus: Ohio State University Press, 1998.

–. "Truth or Fiction: A Reexamination of Audiences." *Critical Inquiry* 4 (1977): 121–41.

–. "What Readers Do When They Read/What Authors Do When They Write." Pp. 48–72 in *Authorizing Readers. Resistance and Respect in the Teaching of Literature*. Edited by P. J. Rabinowitz and Michael W. Smith. New York: Teachers College Press, 1998.

–. "Whirl without End: Audience-Oriented Criticism." Pp. 81–100 in *Contemporary Literary Theory*. Edited by G. Douglas Atkins. Amherst: University of Massachusetts Press, 1989.

Rackham, Richard B. *The Acts of the Apostles*. London; Grand Rapids: Metheun, Baker Book House, 1901.

Rajak, Tessa. *Josephus*. 2nd ed. London: Duckworth, 2002.

Ramsay, W. M., and A. Margaret Ramsay. "Roman Garrisons and Soldiers in Asia Minor." *JRS* 18 (1928): 181–90.

Rapske, B. *The Book of Acts and Paul in Roman Custody*. Vol. 3 of *The Book of Acts in its First Century Setting*. Edited by Bruce W. Winter. Grand Rapids: Eerdmans, 1994.

Reardon, B. P. "Aspects of the Greek Novel." *Greece & Rome* 23 (1976): 118–31.

–. "The Greek Novel." *Phoenix* 23 (1969): 291–309.

Reeves, M. Barbara. "The Feriale Duranum, Roman Military Religion, and Dura-Europos: A Reassessment." Ph.D. diss. Buffalo, NY: State University of New York, 2005.

Reinmuth, E. *Pseudo-Philo und Lukas: Studien zum Liber Antiquitatum Biblicarum und seiner Bedeutung für die Interpretation des lukanischen Doppelwerkes.* WUNT 74. Tübingen: Mohr Siebeck, 1994.

Renon, Vega L. "Aristotle's Endoxa and Plausible Argumentation." *Argumentation* 12 (1998): 95–113.

Reynolds, Joyce, and Robert Tannenbaum. *Jews and God-fearers at Aphrodisias: Greek Inscriptions with Commentary.* Cambridge: The Cambridge Philological Society, 1987.

Rhoads, David, Joanna Dewy, and Donald Michie. *Mark as Story: An Introduction to the Narrative of a Gospel.* 2nd. Minneapolis, MN: Fortress Press, 1999.

Richardson, Alan. *The Miracle Stories in the Gospels.* London: SCM, 1941.

Richter, David H. *The Critical Tradition: Classic Texts and Contemporary Trends.* New York: St. Martin's Press, 1989.

Ricoeur, Paul. "Biblical Hermeneutics." *Semeia* 4 (1975): 29–148.

–. *Interpretation Theory: Discourses and the Surplus of Meaning.* Fort Worth: Texas Christian University Press, 1976.

Rife, J. L. "Officials of the Roman Provinces in Xenophon's Ephesiaca." *ZPE* 138 (2002): 93–108.

Rimmon-Kenan, Shlomith. *Narrative Fiction.* London: Routledge, 1983.

Robbins, Vernon. "By Land and By Sea: The We-Passages and Ancient Sea Voyages." Pp. 215–42 in *Perspectives on Luke-Acts.* Edited by C. H. Talbert. Danville, VA: Association of Baptist Professors of Religion, 1978.

–. "Luke-Acts: A Mixed Population Seeks a Home in the Roman Empire." Pp. 201–21 in *Images of Empire.* Edited by Loveday Alexander. JSOT 122. Sheffield: Sheffield Academic Press, 1991.

Robert, L. "Sur un papyrus de Bruxelles." *Revue de Philogie* 3rd series 17 (1943): 111.

Robinson, James M., Paul Hoffman, and John S. Kloppenborg. *The Critical Edition of Q.* Hermeneia. Minneapolis: Fortress Press, 2000.

Roloff, Jürgen. *Die Apostelgeschichte.* NTD. Göttingen: Vandenhoeck & Ruprecht, 1981.

Rose, Peter W. "Thersites and the Plural Voices of Homer." *Arethusa* 21 (1988): 5–25.

Rostowzew, Michail I. "Angariae." *Klio* 6 (1906): 250–51, 253–57.

Roth, Jonathan P. "The Army and the Economy in Judaea and Palestine." Pp. 375–97 in *The Roman Army and the Economy.* Edited by Paul Erdkamp. Amsterdam: J. C. Gieben, 2002.

–. *The Logistics of the Roman Army at War (264 B.C. – A.D. 235).* Columbia Studies in the Class Tradition. 23. Leiden; Boston: Brill, 1998.

Roth, S. John. *The Blind, the Lame, and the Poor: Character Types in Luke-Acts.* JSNTSup 144. Sheffield: Sheffield Academic Press, 1997.

Rothschild, Clare K. *Luke-Acts and the Rhetoric of History.* WUNT 175. Tübingen: Mohr Siebeck, 2004.

Rowe, C. Kavin. "Literary Unity and Reception History: Reading Luke-Acts as Luke and Acts." *JSNT* 29 (2007): 449–57.

–. "Luke-Acts and the Imperial Cult: A Way through the Conundrum?" *JSNT* 27 (2005): 279–300.

Russell, D. A., and N. G. Wilson. *Menander Rhetor.* Oxford: Clarendon Press, 1981.

Ryan, Edward. "The Rejection of Military Service by the Early Christians." *Theological Studies* 12 (March 1952): 1–32.

Saddington, Denis B. "The Administration and the Army in Judaea in the Early Roman Period (From Pompey to Vespasian, 63 BC–AD 79)." Pp. 33–40 in *The Holy Land in History and Thought.* Edited by Moshe Sharon. NY: Brill, 1988.

–. "The Development of the Roman Auxiliary Forces from Augustus to Trajan." *ANRW* II.3 (1975): 176–201.

–. *The Development of the Roman Auxiliary Forces from Caesar to Vespasian (49 B.C.–A.D. 79)*. Harare, Zimbabwe: University of Zimbabwe, 1982.
–. "Roman Military and Administrative Personnel in the New Testament." *ANRW* II.26.3 (1996): 2410–35.
–. "Tacitus and the Roman Army." *ANRW* II.33.5 (1991): 3484–3555.
Saller, Richard P. *Patriarchy, Property and Death in the Roman Family*. Cambridge: Cambridge University Press, 1994.
–. "Patronage and Friendship in Early Imperial Rome." Pp. 49–62 in *Patronage in Ancient Society*. Edited by Andrew Wallace-Hadrill. London: Routledge, 1989.
–. and Brent D. Shaw, "Tombstones and Roman Family Relations in the Principate: Civilians, Soldiers and Slaves," *JRS* 74 (1984): 134.
Sanders, James A. "From Isaiah 64 to Luke 4." Pp. 75–106 in *Christianity, Judaism and Other Greco-Roman Cults*, vol. 12.1. Edited by Jacob Neusner. Studies in Judaism in Late Antiquity. Leiden: E. J. Brill, 1975.
Sanford, Eva Matthews. "Contrasting Views of the Roman Empire." *The American Journal of Philology* 58 (1937): 437–56.
Satterthwaite, Philip E. "Acts against the Background of Classical Rhetoric." Pp. 337–79 in *The Book of Acts in Its Ancient Literary Setting*. Edited by Bruce W. Winter and Andrew D. Clarke. Grand Rapids: Eerdmans, 1993.
Schaaf, Lothar. *Der Miles Gloriosus des Plautus und sein griechisches Original. Ein Beitrag zur Kontaminationsfrage*. Munich: Wilhelm Kink, 1977.
Schmeling, Gareth. *Chariton*. TWAS 295. New York: Twayne Publishers, 1974.
–. *Xenophon of Ephesus*. TWAS. Boston: Twayne Publishers, 1980.
Schmidt, T. E. "Mark 15:16–32: The Crucifixion Narrative and the Roman Triumphal Procession." *NTS* 41 (1995): 1-18.
Schnackenburg, Rudolf. *Matthäusevangelium 1,1–16,20*. Würzburg: Echter, 1985.
Schoedel, W. R. "Apologetic Literature and Ambassadorial Activities." *HTR* 82 (1989): 55–78.
Schoenfeld, Andrew J. "Sons of Israel in Caesar's Service: Jewish Soldiers in the Roman Military." *Shofar: An Interdisciplinary Journal of Jewish Studies* 24 (2006): 115–26.
Schultze, Clemence. "Dionysius of Halicarnassus and His Audience." Pp. 121–41 in *Past Perspectives. Studies in Greek and Roman Historical Writing*. Edited by I. S. Moxon and et al. Cambridge: Cambridge University Press, 1986.
Schürer, Emil. *Geschichte des jüdischen Volkes im Zeitalter Jesu Christi*. Leipzig: C. Hinrichs, 1898–1901.
–. *The History of the Jewish People in the Age of Jesus Christ*. Edited by G. Vermes, F Millar, and M. Black. Edinburgh: T &T Clark, 1973, reprint 1993.
–. *A History of the Jewish People in the Time of Jesus*. Edited by Nahum N. Glatzer. New York: Schocken Books, 1961.
–. *A History of the Jewish People in the Time of Jesus Christ*. 3rd, 4th. John Macpherson, Sophia Taylor, and Peter Christie. Edinburgh: T & T Clark, 1885–96.
Schürmann, Heinz. *Das Lukasevangelium*. HTKNT. Freiburg,: Herder & Herder, 1969.
Schweizer, Eduard. *The Good News According to Luke*. Translated by David E. Green. Atlanta: John Knox Press, 1984.
Segovia, Fernando. *What is John? Readers and Readings of the Fourth Gospel*. Atlanta, GA: Scholars Press, 1996.
Semenchencko, L. V. "The Conception of Piety in the Jewish Antiquities of Flavius Josephus." *Vestnik drevnej istorii* 3 (2003): 36–45.
Shepherd, William H. *The Narrative Function of the Holy Spirit as a Character in Luke-Acts*. SBLDS. Atlanta: Society of Biblical Literature, 1994.

Sherk, R. K. *The Roman Empire: Augustus to Hadrian*. Cambridge: Cambridge University Press, 1988.
–. "Roman Geographical Exploration and Military Maps." *ANRW* II.1 (1974): 534–62.
–. *Roman Documents from the Greek East. Senatus Consulta and Epistulae to the Age of Augustus*. Baltimore: Johns Hopkins Press, 1969.
Sherwin-White, A. N. *The Roman Citizenship*. Oxford: Oxford University Press, 1973.
–. *Roman Society and Roman Law in the New Testament*. Oxford: Clarendon Press, 1963.
–. "Rome, Pamphylia and Cilicia, 133–70 B.C.E." *JRS* 66 (1976): 1–14.
Shiner, W. T. "The Ambiguous Pronouncement of the Centurion and the Shrouding of Meaning in Mark." *JSNT* 78 (2000): 3–22.
Shuler, Philip. "The Rhetorical Character of Luke 1–2." Pp. 173–89 in *Literary Studies in Luke-Acts*. Edited by Thomas Phillips and Richard Thomspon. Macon, GA: Mercer University Press, 1998.
Sibinga, J. Smit. "The Making of Luke 23:26–56." *Revue Biblique* 104 (1997): 378–404.
Siker, Jeffrey S. "'First to the Gentiles': A Literary Analysis of Luke 4:16–30." *JBL* 111 (1992): 73–90.
Silk, M. S. *Aristophanes and the Definition of Comedy*. Oxford: Oxford University Press, 2000.
Simson, P. "The Drama of the City of God: Jerusalem in St. Luke's Gospel." *Scr* 15 (1963): 65–80.
Sinnigen, William G. "The Roman Secret Service." *CJ* 57 (1961): 65–72.
Skinner, Matthew L. *Locating Paul: Places of Custody as Narrative Setting in Acts*. SBL Academia Biblica 13. Atlanta: Society of Biblical Literature, 2003.
Slatoff, Walter J. *With Respect to Readers: Dimensions of Literary Response*. Ithaca, NY: Cornell University Press, 1970.
Slusser, Michale. "Reading Silently in Antiquity." *JBL* 111 (1992): 499.
Smalley, Stephen S. "Spirit, Kingdom and Prayer in Luke-Acts." *NovT* 15 (1973): 59–71.
Smith, Charles Forster. "Character-Drawing in Thucydides." *The American Journal of Philology* 24 (1903): 369–87.
Smith, E. Marion. "The Egypt of the Greek Romances." *CJ* 23 (1928): 531–37.
Smith, J. *The Voyage and Shipwreck of St. Paul*. 4th. London; Eugene, OR: Longmans, Green; Wipf & Stock, 1880.
Smith, Mark D. "Of Jesus and Quirinius." *CBQ* 62 (2000): 278–93.
Southern, Pat. *The Roman Army: A Social and Institutional History*. Oxford: Oxford University Press, 2007
Speidel, M. Alexander. "Roman Army Pay Scales." *JRS* 82 (1992): 87–106.
Speidel, Michael P. "The Captor of Decabalus: A New Inscription of Philippi." *JRS* 60 (1970): 142–53.
–. "Legionaries from Asia Minor." *ANRW* II.7.2 (1980): 730–746.
–. "The Rise of Ethnic Units in the Roman Imperial Army." *ANRW* II.3 (1975): 202–31.
–. "The Roman Army in Arabia." *ANRW* II.8 (1977): 687–730.
–. "The Roman Army in Judaea under the Procurators." Pp. 224–32 in *Roman Army Studies 2*. Edited by Michael P. Speidel. Stuttgart: Franz Steiner, 1992.
–. "A Tile Stamp of Cohors I Thracum Milliaria from Hebron/Palestine." *Zeitschrift für Papyrologie und Epigraphik* 35 (1979): 170–72.
Speidel, Michael P., and A. Dimitrova-Milceva. "The Cult of the Genii in the Roman Army and the New Military Deity." *ANRW* II.16.2 (1978): 1542–55.
Spencer, F. Scott. "Acts and Modern Literary Approaches." Pp. 38–414 in *The Book of Acts in Its Ancient Literary Setting*. Grand Rapids, MI: Eerdmans Publishing, 1993.
–. *The Portrait of Philip in Acts*. JSNTSS. Sheffield: Sheffield Academic Press, 1992.

Spencer, Patrick E. *Rhetorical Texture and Narrative: Trajectories of the Lukan Galilean Ministry Speeches.* Library of New Testament Studies 341. New York: T & T Clark, 2007.

Springer, Mary Doyle. *A Rhetoric of Literary Character: Some Women of Henry James.* Chicago: University of Chicago Press, 1978.

Stainsby, Herbert H. "'Under Authority'." *Expository Times* 30 (1918–19): 328–29.

Standhartinger, Angela. "Eusebeia in den Pastoralbriefen. Ein Beitrag zum Einflus römischen Denkens auf das Enstehende Christentum." *NovT* 48 (2006): 51–82.

Starr, Chester G. *The Roman Imperial Navy 31 B.C.–A.D. 324.* 3nd. Chicago: Ares Publishing, 1993.

Stein, Robert H. "Redaction Criticism (NT)." Pp. 647–50 in *The Anchor Bible Dictionary.* Edited by David Noel Freedman and et al. New York: Doubleday, 1992.

–. "What is Redaktionsgeschichte?" *JBL* 88 (1969): 45–56.

Stenschke, C. W. *Luke's Portrait of Gentiles Prior to their Coming to Faith.* WUNT 2.108. Tübingen: Mohr Siebeck, 1999.

Sterling, Gregory. *Historiography and Self-Definition: Josephos, Luke-Acts, and Apologetic Historiography.* Leiden: Brill, 1992.

–. "Luke-Acts and Apologetic Historiography." *SBL Seminar Papers* 28 (1989): 326–42.

Stow, H. Lloyd. "Aristophanes' Influence upon Public Opinion." *CJ* 38 (1942): 83–92.

Suleiman, Susan, and Inge Crosman, eds. *The Reader in the Text: Essays on Audience and Interpretation.* Princeton: Princeton University Press, 1980.

Summers, Richard. "Roman Justice and Apuleius' Metamorphoses." *TAPA* 101 (1970): 511–31.

Swain, Simon. "Biography and Biographic in the Literature of the Roman Empire." Pp. 1–37 in *Portraits. Biographical Representation in the Greek and Latin Literature of the Roman Empire.* Edited by M. J. Edwards and Simon Swain. Oxford: Clarendon Press, 1997.

Swartley, W. M. "War and Peace in the New Testament." *ANRW* II.26.3 (1996): 2298–2408.

Syme, Ronald. "How Tacitus Came to History." *Greece & Rome* 4 (1957): 160–67.

–. "Livy and Augustus." *Harvard Studies in Classical Philology* 64 (1959): 27–87.

–. *Tacitus.* Oxford: Clarendon Press, 1958.

Tajra, H. W. *The Trial of Paul: A Jurdical Exegesis of the Second Half of Acts.* WUNT 2.35. Tübingen: Mohr Siebeck, 1989.

Talbert, Charles H. *Literary Patterns, Theological Themes, and the Genre of Luke-Acts.* SBLMS. Missoula, MT: Scholars Press, 1974.

–. *Reading Acts: A Literary and Theological Commentary on the Acts of the Apostles.* New York: Crossroads, 1997.

–. *Reading Luke: A Literary and Theological Commentary on the Third Gospel.* New York: Crossroads, 1982.

–. *Reading Luke-Acts in Its Mediterranean Milieu.* NovTSup 107. Leiden: Brill, 2003.

Talbert, Charles H., and John H. Hayes. "A Theology of Sea Storms in Luke-Acts." Pp. 267–283 in *Jesus and the Heritage of Israel.* Edited by David P. Moessner. Harrisburg, PA: Trinity Press International, 1999.

Tannehill, Robert C. "The Disciples in Mark: The Function of a Narrative Role." *JR* 57 (1977): 386–405.

–. "Israel in Luke-Acts: A Tragic Story." *JBL* 104 (1985): 69–85.

–. *Luke.* Abingdon New Testament Commentaries. Nashville, TN: Abingdon Press, 1996.

–. *The Narrative Unity of Luke-Acts: A Literary Interpretation.* 2 vols; Philadelphia; Minneapolis, MN: Fortress Press, 1986–90.

Tatum, James. *Apuleius and The Golden Ass.* Ithaca NY: Cornell University Press, 1979.

Taylor, S. M. "The Roman Empire in the Acts of the Apostles." *ANRW* II.26.3 (1996): 2436–2500.

–. "St. Paul and the Roman Empire: Acts of the Apostles 13–14." *ANRW* II.26.2 (1995): 1189–1231.

Taylor, Vincent. *The Passion Narrative of St. Luke: A Critical and Historical Investigation.* SNTSMS. Cambridge: Cambridge University Press, 1972.

–. *The Formation of the Gospel Traditions.* London: Macmillan, 1935.

de Temmerman, K. "Ancient Rhetoric as a Hermeneutical Tool for the Analysis of Characterization in Narrative Literature." *Rhetorica*, 28 (2010): 23–51.

Thompson, Richard P. "Believers and Religious Leaders in Jerusalem: Contrasting Portraits of Jews in Acts 1–7." Pp. 327–344 in *Literary Studies in Luke-Acts: Essays in Honor of Joseph B. Tyson.* Edited by Richard P. Thompson and Thomas E. Phillips; Macon, GA: Mercer University Press, 1998.

–. *Keeping the Church in Its Place.* New York: T & T Clark, 2006.

Tolbert, Mary Ann. *Sowing the Gospel: Mark's World in Literary-Historical Perspective.* Minneapolis, MN: Fortress Press, 1989.

Tompkins, Jane P. "An Introduction to Reader-Response Criticism." Pp. ix–xxvi in *Reader-Response Criticism. From Formalism to Post-Structuralism.* Edited by Jane P. Tompkins. Baltimore; London: Johns Hopkins University Press, 1980.

–. "The Reader in History: The Changing Shape of Literary Response." Pp. 201–32 in *Reader-Response Criticism. From Formalism to Post-Structuralism.* Edited by Jane P. Tompkins. Baltimore; London: Johns Hopkins University Press, 1980.

–. *Reader-Response Criticism: From Formalism to Post-Structuralism.* Baltimore: Johns Hopkins University Press, 1980.

Tränkle, Hermann. *Livius und Polybios.* Stuttgart: Basel, 1977.

Trompf, G. W. "On Why Luke Declined to Recount the Death of Paul." Pp. 225–39 in *Luke-Acts. New Perspectives from the Society of Biblical Literature Seminar.* Edited by Charles H. Talbert. New York: Crossroads Publishing.

Tyson, Joseph. "The Gentile Mission and the Authority of Scripture in Acts." *NTS* 33 (1987): 619–31.

–. "Jews and Judaism in Luke-Acts: Reading as a Godfearer." *NTS* 41 (1995): 19–38.

–. "The Lukan Version of the Trial of Jesus." *NovT* 3 (1959): 249–58.

–. *Luke, Judaism, and the Scholars: Critical Approaches to Luke-Acts.* Columbia, SC: University of South Carolina Press, 1999.

Ullman, B. L. "History and Tragedy." *TAPA* 73 (1942): 25–53.

Ussher, R. G. "Old Comedy and 'Character': Some Comments." *GR* 24 (1977): 71–79.

Van Der Toorn, Karel. "Torn between Vice and Virtue: Stereotypes of the Widow in Israel and Mesopotamia." Pages 1–14 in *Female Stereotypes in Religious Traditions.* Edited by Ria Kloppenborg and Wouter J. Hanegraaff. Leiden: Brill, 1995.

Van Slyke, Daniel. "*Sacramentum* in Ancient Non-Christian Authors," Antiphon 9 (2005): 167–206.

Van Veldhuizen, Milo. "Moses: a Model of Hellenistic Philanthropia." *Reformed Review* 38 (1985): 215–24.

Verheyden, J. "The Unity of Luke-Acts: What Are We Up To?" Pp. 3–56 in *The Unity of Luke-Acts.* Edited by J. Verheyden. Leuven: Leuven University Press, 1999.

Vögel, Otto. "Lukas und Euripides," *TZ* 9 (1953): 415–438.

Volkmann, Hans. *Res Gestae Divi Augusti. Das Monumentum Ancyranum.* Berlin: Walter de Gruyter, 1964.

Wagenvoort, Hendrik. *Pietas: Selected Studies in Roman Religion.* Leiden: Brill, 1980.

Walaskay, Paul W. "The Trial and Death of Jesus in the Gospel of Luke." *JBL* 94 (1975): 81–93.

Walbank, F. W. *A Historical Commentary on Polybius.* Oxford: Clarendon Press, 1957–79.

–. "Polemic in Polybius." *JRS* 52 (1962): 1–12.

Wall, Robert W. "Peter, 'Son' of Jonah: The Conversion of Cornelius in the Context of the Canon." *JSNT* 29 (1987): 79–90.

Wallace-Hadrill, Andrew. "The Emperor and His Virtues." *Historia* 30 (1981): 298–323.

Walsh, P. G. *Livy: His Historical Methods and Aims.* Cambridge: Cambridge University Press, 1961.

–. *The Roman Novel.* Cambridge, London: Cambridge University Press, Bristol Classical Press, 1970, reprint 1995.

Warnecke, H. *Die tatsächliche Romfahrt des Apostels Paulus.* Stuttgart: Katholisches Bibelwerk, 1987.

Watson, D. F. "People, Crowds." Pp. 605 –609 in *Dictionary of Jesus and the Gospels.* Edited by Joel Green, Scot McKnight and I. Howard Marshall. Downers Grove, IL: IVP, 1992.

Watson, G. R. "Documentation in the Roman Army." *ANRW* II.1 (1974): 493–507.

–. *The Roman Soldier.* Ithaca, NY: Cornell University Press, 1969.

Weatherly, Jon A. *Jewish Responsibility for the Death of Jesus in Luke-Acts.* JSNTsup. Sheffield: Sheffield Academic Press, 1994.

Weaver, John B. *Plots of Epiphany: Prison-Escape in Acts of the Apostles.* BZNW 131. New York: DeGruyter, 2004.

Webber, Randall. *Reader Response Analysis of the Epistle of James.* San Francisco: International Scholars Publications, 1996.

Webster, Graham. *The Roman Imperial Army of the First and Second Centuries A.D.* 3rd ed. Norman, OK: University of Oklahoma, 1998.

Webster, T. B. L. *Studies in Later Greek Comedy.* Manchester: Manchester University Press, 1970.

–. *Studies in Menander.* Manchester: Manchester University Press, 1950.

Weeden, Theodore J. *Mark: Traditions in Conflict.* Philadelphia: Fortress Press, 1971.

Wegner, Uwe. *Der Hauptmann von Kafarnaum (Mt 7, 28a, 8, 5–10.13 par Lk 7, 1–10) ein Beitrag zur Q–Forschung.* WUNT 2.14. Tübingen: Mohr Siebeck, 1985.

Weinreich, Otto. *Gebet und Wunder: zwei Abhandlungen zur Religions- und Literatur- geschichte.* Tübinger Beiträge zur Altertumswissenschaft 5. Stuttgart: Kohlhammer, 1929.

West, Andrew F. "On a Patriotic Passage in the Miles Gloriosus of Plautus." *American Journal of Philology* 8 (1887): 15–33.

West, Louis C. "Imperial Publicity on Coins of the Roman Emperors." *CJ* 45 [1949]: 19–26.

Westlake, H. D. *Individuals in Thucydides.* Cambridge: Cambridge University Press, 1968.

Wilcox, Max. "The 'God-fearers' in Acts: A Reconsideration." *JSNT* 13 (1981): 102–22.

Wilkes, J. J. "The Danube Provinces." Pp. 577–603 in *The Cambridge Ancient History XI The High Empire A.D. 70–192.* Edited by Alan K. Bowman, Peter Garnsey, and Dominic Rathbone. Cambridge: Cambridge University Press, 2000.

Wilson, Marcus. "After the Silence: Tacitus, Suetonius, Juvenal." Pp. 523–42 in *Flavian Rome. Culture, Image, Text.* Edited by A. J. Boyle and W. J. Dominik. Boston: Brill, 2003.

Wilson, Stephen G. *The Gentiles and the Gentile Mission in Luke-Acts.* Cambridge: Cambridge University Press, 1973.

–. "The Jews and the Death of Jesus in Acts." Pp. 1.127–53 in *Anti-Judaism in Early Christianity.* Edited by P. Richardson. Waterloo, Ont.: Wilfrid Laurier University Press, 1986.

Wilson, Walter T. "Urban Legends: Acts 10:1–11:18 and the Strategies of Greco-Roman Foundation Narratives." *JBL* 120 (2001): 77–99.

Winter, B. W., and A. D. Clarke. *The Book of Acts in Its Ancient Literary Setting.* Vol. 1 of *The Book of Acts in Its First Century Setting.* Edited by Bruce W. Winter. Grand Rapids: Eerdmans, 1993.

Winter, Bruce. "The Importance of the Captatio Benevolentiae in the Speeches of Tertullus and Paul in Acts 24:1–21." *JTS* 42 (1991): 505–31.

Witherington, Ben. *Acts of the Apostles*. Grand Rapids, MI: Eerdmans, 1998.

Witherup, Ronald. "Cornelius Over and Over and Over Again: 'Functional Redundancy' in the Acts of the Apostles." *JSNT* 49 (1993): 45–66.

Wolter, Michael. *Das Lukasevangelium*. HNT 5. Tübingen: Mohr Siebeck, 2008.

Yamada, Kota. "A Rhetorical History: The Literary Genre of the Acts of the Apostles." Pp. 230–250 in *Rhetoric, Scripture and Theology*. Edited by Stanley E. Porter and Thomas H. Olbricht. Sheffield: Sheffield Academic Press, 1996.

Youtie, H. C., and O. M. Pearl. *Michigan Papyri VI. Papyri and Ostraca from Karanis*. Ann Arbor: University of Michigan, 1944.

Zahn, Thomas. *Das Evangelium des Lukas: Ausgelegt*. Kommentar zum Neuen Testament 3. Leipzig/Erlangen: Deichert, 1913.

Index of Ancient Sources

Old Testament

New Testament

Ancient Authors

Index of Modern Authors

Index of Subjects

Wissenschaftliche Untersuchungen zum Neuen Testament
Alphabetical Index of the First and Second Series

Bauer, Thomas Johann: Paulus und die kaiser-
zeitliche Epistolographie. 2011. *Vol. 276.*

Bauernfeind, Otto: Kommentar und Studien zur
Apostelgeschichte. 1980. *Vol. 22.*

Baum, Armin Daniel: Pseudepigraphie und
literarische Fälschung im frühen Christentum. 2001. *Vol. II/138.*

Bayer, Hans Friedrich: Jesus' Predictions
of Vindication and Resurrection. 1986.
Vol. II/20.

Becker, Eve-Marie: Das Markus-Evangelium
im Rahmen antiker Historiographie. 2006.
Vol. 194.

Becker, Eve-Marie and *Peter Pilhofer* (Ed.):
Biographie und Persönlichkeit des Paulus.
2005. *Vol. 187.*

– and *Anders Runesson* (Ed.): Mark and
Matthew I. 2011. *Vol. 271.*

– Mark and Matthew II. 2013. *Vol. 304.*

Becker, Michael: Wunder und Wundertäter
im frührabbinischen Judentum. 2002.
Vol. II/144.

Becker, Michael and *Markus Öhler* (Ed.): Apo-
kalyptik als Herausforderung neutestamentlicher Theologie. 2006. *Vol. II/214.*

Bell, Richard H.: Deliver Us from Evil. 2007.
Vol. 216.

– The Irrevocable Call of God. 2005. *Vol. 184.*

– No One Seeks for God. 1998. *Vol. 106.*

– Provoked to Jealousy. 1994. *Vol. II/63.*

Bennema, Cornelis: The Power of Saving
Wisdom. 2002. *Vol. II/148.*

Bergman, Jan: see *Kieffer, René.*

Bergmeier, Roland: Das Gesetz im Römerbrief
und andere Studien zum Neuen Testament.
2000. *Vol. 121.*

Bernett, Monika: Der Kaiserkult in Judäa unter
den Herodiern und Römern. 2007. *Vol. 203.*

Betho, Benjamin: see *Clivaz, Claire.*

Betz, Otto: Jesus, der Messias Israels. 1987.
Vol. 42.

– Jesus, der Herr der Kirche. 1990. *Vol. 52.*

Beyerle, Stefan: see *Assel, Heinrich.*

Beyschlag, Karlmann: Simon Magus und die
christliche Gnosis. 1974. *Vol. 16.*

Bieringer, Reimund: see *Koester, Craig.*

Bird, Michael F. and *Jason Maston* (Ed.): Earliest Christian History. 2012. *Vol. II/320.*

Bittner, Wolfgang J.: Jesu Zeichen im Johannesevangelium. 1987. *Vol. II/26.*

Bjerkelund, Carl J.: Tauta Egeneto. 1987.
Vol. 40.

Blackburn, Barry Lee: Theios Aner and the
Markan Miracle Traditions. 1991. *Vol. II/40.*

Blackwell, Ben C.: Christosis. 2011. *Vol. II/314.*

Blanton IV, Thomas R.: Constructing a New
Covenant. 2007. *Vol. II/233.*

Bock, Darrell L.: Blasphemy and Exaltation in
Judaism and the Final Examination of Jesus.
1998. *Vol. II/106.*

– and *Robert L. Webb* (Ed.): Key Events in the
Life of the Historical Jesus. 2009. *Vol. 247.*

Bockmuehl, Markus: The Remembered Peter.
2010. *Vol. 262.*

– Revelation and Mystery in Ancient Judaism
and Pauline Christianity. 1990. *Vol. II/36.*

– see *Stanton, Graham.*

Bøe, Sverre: Cross-Bearing in Luke. 2010.
Vol. II/278.

– Gog and Magog. 2001. *Vol. II/135.*

Böhlig, Alexander: Gnosis und Synkretismus.
Vol. 1 1989. *Vol. 47* – Vol. 2 1989. *Vol. 48.*

Böhm, Martina: Samarien und die Samaritai bei
Lukas. 1999. *Vol. II/111.*

Börstinghaus, Jens: Sturmfahrt und Schiff-
bruch. 2010. *Vol. II/274.*

Böttrich, Christfried: Weltweisheit – Mensch-
heitsethik – Urkult. 1992. *Vol. II/50.*

– and *Herzer, Jens* (Ed.): Josephus und das
Neue Testament. 2007. *Vol. 209.*

– see *Assel, Heinrich.*

Bolyki, János: Jesu Tischgemeinschaften. 1997.
Vol. II/96.

Bosman, Philip: Conscience in Philo and Paul.
2003. *Vol. II/166.*

Bovon, François: The Emergence of Christianity. 2013. *Vol. 319.*

– New Testament and Christian Apocrypha.
2009. *Vol. 237.*

– Studies in Early Christianity. 2003. *Vol. 161.*

Brändl, Martin: Der Agon bei Paulus. 2006.
Vol. II/222.

Braun, Heike: Geschichte des Gottesvolkes und
christliche Identität. 2010. *Vol. II/279.*

Breytenbach, Cilliers: see *Frey, Jörg.*

Brink, Laurie: Soldiers in Luke-Acts. 2014.
Vol. II/362.

Broadhead, Edwin K.: Jewish Ways of Following Jesus Redrawing the Religious Map of
Antiquity. 2010. *Vol. 266.*

Brocke, Christoph vom: Thessaloniki – Stadt
des Kassander und Gemeinde des Paulus.
2001. *Vol. II/125.*

Brown, Paul J.: Bodily Resurrection and Ethics
in 1 Cor 15. 2014. *Vol. II/360.*

Brunson, Andrew: Psalm 118 in the Gospel of
John. 2003. *Vol. II/158.*

Büchli, Jörg: Der Poimandres – ein paganisier-
tes Evangelium. 1987. *Vol. II/27.*

Bühner, Jan A.: Der Gesandte und sein Weg im
4. Evangelium. 1977. *Vol. II/2.*

Burchard, Christoph: Untersuchungen zu
Joseph und Asenath. 1965. *Vol. 8.*

– Studien zur Theologie, Sprache und Umwelt des Neuen Testaments. Ed. by D. Sänger. 1998. *Vol. 107.*

Burnett, Richard: Karl Barth's Theological Exegesis. 2001. *Vol. II/145.*

Byron, John: Slavery Metaphors in Early Judaism and Pauline Christianity. 2003. *Vol. II/162.*

Byrskog, Samuel: Story as History – History as Story. 2000. *Vol. 123.*

Calaway, Jared C.: The Sabbath and the Sanctuary. 2013. *Vol. II/349.*

Calhoun, Robert M.: Paul's Definitions of the Gospel in Romans 1. 2011. *Vol. II/316.*

Calpino, Teresa: Women, Work and Leadership in Acts. 2014. *Vol. II/361.*

Canavan, Rosemary: Clothing the Body of Christ at Colossae. 2012. *Vol. II/334.*

Cancik, Hubert (Ed.): Markus-Philologie. 1984. *Vol. 33.*

Capes, David B.: Old Testament Yaweh Texts in Paul's Christology. 1992. *Vol. II/47.*

Caragounis, Chrys C.: The Development of Greek and the New Testament. 2004. *Vol. 167.*

– New Testament Language and Exegesis. 2014. *Vol. 323.*

– The Son of Man. 1986. *Vol. 38.*

– see *Fridrichsen, Anton.*

Carleton Paget, James: The Epistle of Barnabas. 1994. *Vol. II/64.*

– Jews, Christians and Jewish Christians in Antiquity. 2010. *Vol. 251.*

Carson, D.A., O'Brien, Peter T. and Mark Seifrid (Ed.): Justification and Variegated Nomism.
Vol. 1: The Complexities of Second Temple Judaism. 2001. *Vol. II/140.*
Vol. 2: The Paradoxes of Paul. 2004. *Vol. II/181.*

Caulley, Thomas Scott and Hermann Lichtenberger (Ed.): Die Septuaginta und das frühe Christentum – The Septuagint and Christian Origins. 2011. *Vol. 277.*

– see *Lichtenberger, Hermann.*

Chae, Young Sam: Jesus as the Eschatological Davidic Shepherd. 2006. *Vol. II/216.*

Chapman, David W.: Ancient Jewish and Christian Perceptions of Crucifixion. 2008. *Vol. II/244.*

Chester, Andrew: Future Hope and Present Reality. Vol. I: Eschatology and Transformation in the Hebrew Bible. 2012. *Vol. 293.*

– Messiah and Exaltation. 2007. *Vol. 207.*

Chibici-Revneanu, Nicole: Die Herrlichkeit des Verherrlichten. 2007. *Vol. II/231.*

Ciampa, Roy E.: The Presence and Function of Scripture in Galatians 1 and 2. 1998. *Vol. II/102.*

Classen, Carl Joachim: Rhetorical Criticsm of the New Testament. 2000. *Vol. 128.*

Claußen, Carsten (Ed.): see *Frey, Jörg.*

Clivaz, Claire, Andreas Dettwiler, Luc Devillers, Enrico Norelli with Benjamin Bertho (Ed.): Infancy Gospels. 2011. *Vol. 281.*

Colpe, Carsten: Griechen – Byzantiner – Semiten – Muslime. 2008. *Vol. 221.*

– Iranier – Aramäer – Hebräer – Hellenen. 2003. *Vol. 154.*

Cook, John G.: Roman Attitudes Towards the Christians. 2010. *Vol. 261.*

Coote, Robert B. (Ed.): see *Weissenrieder, Annette.*

Coppins, Wayne: The Interpretation of Freedom in the Letters of Paul. 2009. *Vol. II/261.*

Crump, David: Jesus the Intercessor. 1992. *Vol. II/49.*

Dahl, Nils Alstrup: Studies in Ephesians. 2000. *Vol. 131.*

Daise, Michael A.: Feasts in John. 2007. *Vol. II/229.*

Deines, Roland: Acts of God in History. Ed. by Christoph Ochs and Peter Watts. 2013. *Vol. 317.*

– Die Gerechtigkeit der Tora im Reich des Messias. 2004. *Vol. 177.*

– Jüdische Steingefäße und pharisäische Frömmigkeit. 1993. *Vol. II/52.*

– Die Pharisäer. 1997. *Vol. 101.*

Deines, Roland, Jens Herzer and Karl-Wilhelm Niebuhr (Ed.): Neues Testament und hellenistisch-jüdische Alltagskultur. III. Internationales Symposium zum Corpus Judaeo-Hellenisticum Novi Testamenti. 21.–24. Mai 2009 in Leipzig. 2011. *Vol. 274.*

– and *Karl-Wilhelm Niebuhr* (Ed.): Philo und das Neue Testament. 2004. *Vol. 172.*

Dennis, John A.: Jesus' Death and the Gathering of True Israel. 2006. *Vol. 217.*

Dettwiler, Andreas and Jean Zumstein (Ed.): Kreuzestheologie im Neuen Testament. 2002. *Vol. 151.*

– see *Clivaz, Claire.*

Devillers, Luc: see *Clivaz, Claire.*

Dickson, John P.: Mission-Commitment in Ancient Judaism and in the Pauline Communities. 2003. *Vol. II/159.*

Dietzfelbinger, Christian: Der Abschied des Kommenden. 1997. *Vol. 95.*

Dimitrov, Ivan Z., James D.G. Dunn, Ulrich Luz and Karl-Wilhelm Niebuhr (Ed.): Das Alte Testament als christliche Bibel in orthodoxer und westlicher Sicht. 2004. *Vol. 174.*

Dobbeler, Axel von: Glaube als Teilhabe. 1987. *Vol. II/22.*

Docherty, Susan E.: The Use of the Old Testament in Hebrews. 2009. *Vol. II/260.*

Dochhorn, Jan: Schriftgelehrte Prophetie. 2010. *Vol. 268.*

Doering, Lutz: Ancient Jewish Letters and the Beginnings of Christian Epistolography. 2012. *Vol. 298.*

Doole, J. Andrew: What was Mark for Matthew? 2013. *Vol. II/344.*

Downs, David J.: The Offering of the Gentiles. 2008. *Vol. II/248.*

Dryden, J. de Waal: Theology and Ethics in 1 Peter. 2006. *Vol. II/209.*

Dübbers, Michael: Christologie und Existenz im Kolosserbrief. 2005. *Vol. II/191.*

Dunn, James D.G.: The New Perspective on Paul. 2005. *Vol. 185.*

Dunn, James D.G. (Ed.): Jews and Christians. 1992. *Vol. 66.*

– Paul and the Mosaic Law. 1996. *Vol. 89.*

– see *Dimitrov, Ivan Z.*

–, *Hans Klein, Ulrich Luz,* and *Vasile Mihoc* (Ed.): Auslegung der Bibel in orthodoxer und westlicher Perspektive. 2000. *Vol. 130.*

Dunson, Ben C.: Individual and Community in Paul's Letter to the Romans. 2012. *Vol. II/332.*

Ebel, Eva: Die Attraktivität früher christlicher Gemeinden. 2004. *Vol. II/178.*

Eberhart, Christian A.: Kultmetaphorik und Christologie. 2013. *Vol. 306.*

Ebertz, Michael N.: Das Charisma des Gekreuzigten. 1987. *Vol. 45.*

Eckstein, Hans-Joachim: Der Begriff Syneidesis bei Paulus. 1983. *Vol. II/10.*

– Verheißung und Gesetz. 1996. *Vol. 86.*

–, *Christoph Landmesser* and *Hermann Lichtenberger* (Ed.): Eschatologie – Eschatology. The Sixth Durham-Tübingen Research Symposium. 2011. *Vol. 272.*

Edwards, J. Christopher: The Ransom Logion in Mark and Matthew. 2012. *Vol. II/327.*

Ego, Beate: Im Himmel wie auf Erden. 1989. *Vol. II/34.*

Ego, Beate, Armin Lange and *Peter Pilhofer* (Ed.): Gemeinde ohne Tempel – Community without Temple. 1999. *Vol. 118.*

– and *Helmut Merkel* (Ed.): Religiöses Lernen in der biblischen, frühjüdischen und frühchristlichen Überlieferung. 2005. *Vol. 180.*

Ehrlich, Carl S., Anders Runesson and *Eileen Schuller* (Ed.): Purity, Holiness, and Identity in Judaism and Christianity. 2013. *Vol. 305.*

Eisele, Wilfried: Welcher Thomas? 2010. *Vol. 259.*

Eisen, Ute E., Christine Gerber and *Angela Standhartinger* (Ed.): Doing Gender – Doing Religion. 2013. *Vol. 302.*

Eisen, Ute E.: see *Paulsen, Henning.*

Elledge, C.D.: Life after Death in Early Judaism. 2006. *Vol. II/208.*

Ellis, E. Earle: Prophecy and Hermeneutic in Early Christianity. 1978. *Vol. 18.*

– The Old Testament in Early Christianity. 1991. *Vol. 54.*

Elmer, Ian J.: Paul, Jerusalem and the Judaisers. 2009. *Vol. II/258.*

Endo, Masanobu: Creation and Christology. 2002. *Vol. 149.*

Ennulat, Andreas: Die 'Minor Agreements'. 1994. *Vol. II/62.*

Ensor, Peter W.: Jesus and His 'Works'. 1996. *Vol. II/85.*

Eskola, Timo: Messiah and the Throne. 2001. *Vol. II/142.*

– Theodicy and Predestination in Pauline Soteriology. 1998. *Vol. II/100.*

Farelly, Nicolas: The Disciples in the Fourth Gospel. 2010. *Vol. II/290.*

Fatehi, Mehrdad: The Spirit's Relation to the Risen Lord in Paul. 2000. *Vol. II/128.*

Feldmeier, Reinhard: Die Krisis des Gottessohnes. 1987. *Vol. II/21.*

– Die Christen als Fremde. 1992. *Vol. 64.*

Feldmeier, Reinhard and *Ulrich Heckel* (Ed.): Die Heiden. 1994. *Vol. 70.*

Felsch, Dorit: Die Feste im Johannesevangelium. 2011. *Vol. II/308.*

Finnern, Sönke: Narratologie und biblische Exegese. 2010. *Vol. II/285.*

Fletcher-Louis, Crispin H.T.: Luke-Acts: Angels, Christology and Soteriology. 1997. *Vol. II/94.*

Förster, Niclas: Jesus und die Steuerfrage. 2012. *Vol. 294.*

– Marcus Magus. 1999. *Vol. 114.*

Forbes, Christopher Brian: Prophecy and Inspired Speech in Early Christianity and its Hellenistic Environment. 1995. *Vol. II/75.*

Fornberg, Tord: see *Fridrichsen, Anton.*

Fossum, Jarl E.: The Name of God and the Angel of the Lord. 1985. *Vol. 36.*

Foster, Paul: Community, Law and Mission in Matthew's Gospel. *Vol. II/177.*

Fotopoulos, John: Food Offered to Idols in Roman Corinth. 2003. *Vol. II/151.*

Frank, Nicole: Der Kolosserbrief im Kontext des paulinischen Erbes. 2009. *Vol. II/271.*

Frenschkowski, Marco: Offenbarung und Epiphanie. Vol. 1 1995. *Vol. II/79* – Vol. 2 1997. *Vol. II/80.*

Frey, Jörg: Eugen Drewermann und die biblische Exegese. 1995. *Vol. II/71.*

– Die Herrlichkeit des Gekreuzigten. Studien zu den Johanneischen Schriften I. 2013. *Vol. 307.*
– Die johanneische Eschatologie. Vol. I. 1997. *Vol. 96.* – Vol. II. 1998. *Vol. 110.* – Vol. III. 2000. *Vol. 117.*
Frey, Jörg (Ed.)*: see Avemarie, Friedrich.*
– *Carsten Claußen* and *Nadine Kessler* (Ed.): Qumran und die Archäologie. 2011. *Vol. 278.*
– and *Cilliers Breytenbach* (Ed.): Aufgabe und Durchführung einer Theologie des Neuen Testaments. 2007. *Vol. 205.*
– *Jens Herzer, Martina Janßen* and *Clare K. Rothschild* (Ed.): Pseudepigraphie und Verfasserfiktion in frühchristlichen Briefen. 2009. *Vol. 246.*
– *James A. Kelhoffer* and *Franz Tóth* (Ed.): Die Johannesapokalypse. 2012. *Vol. 287.*
– *Stefan Krauter* and *Hermann Lichtenberger* (Ed.): Heil und Geschichte. 2009. *Vol. 248.*
– and *Udo Schnelle (Ed.):* Kontexte des Johannesevangeliums. 2004. *Vol. 175.*
– and *Jens Schröter* (Ed.): Deutungen des Todes Jesu im Neuen Testament. 2005. *Vol. 181.*
– Jesus in apokryphen Evangelienüberlieferungen. 2010. *Vol. 254.*
–, *Jan G. van der Watt,* and *Ruben Zimmermann* (Ed.): Imagery in the Gospel of John. 2006. *Vol. 200.*
Freyne, Sean: Galilee and Gospel. 2000. *Vol. 125.*
Fridrichsen, Anton: Exegetical Writings. Ed. by C.C. Caragounis and T. Fornberg. 1994. *Vol. 76.*
Gadenz, Pablo T.: Called from the Jews and from the Gentiles. 2009. *Vol. II/267.*
Gäbel, Georg: Die Kulttheologie des Hebräerbriefes. 2006. *Vol. II/212.*
Gäckle, Volker: Die Starken und die Schwachen in Korinth und in Rom. 2005. *Vol. 200.*
Garlington, Don B.: 'The Obedience of Faith'. 1991. *Vol. II/38.*
– Faith, Obedience, and Perseverance. 1994. *Vol. 79.*
Garnet, Paul: Salvation and Atonement in the Qumran Scrolls. 1977. *Vol. II/3.*
Garský, Zbyněk: Das Wirken Jesu in Galiläa bei Johannes. 2012. *Vol. II/325.*
Gemünden, Petra von (Ed.): see *Weissenrieder, Annette.*
Gerber, Christine (Ed.): see *Eisen, Ute E.*
Gese, Michael: Das Vermächtnis des Apostels. 1997. *Vol. II/99.*
Gheorghita, Radu: The Role of the Septuagint in Hebrews. 2003. *Vol. II/160.*

Gibson, Jack J.: Peter Between Jerusalem and Antioch. 2013. *Vol. II/345.*
Gordley, Matthew E.: The Colossian Hymn in Context. 2007. *Vol. II/228.*
– Teaching through Song in Antiquity. 2011. *Vol. II/302.*
Gräbe, Petrus J.: The Power of God in Paul's Letters. 2000, ²2008. *Vol. II/123.*
Gräßer, Erich: Der Alte Bund im Neuen. 1985. *Vol. 35.*
– Forschungen zur Apostelgeschichte. 2001. *Vol. 137.*
Grappe, Christian (Ed.): Le Repas de Dieu / Das Mahl Gottes. 2004. *Vol. 169.*
Gray, Timothy C.: The Temple in the Gospel of Mark. 2008. *Vol. II/242.*
Green, Joel B.: The Death of Jesus. 1988. *Vol. II/33.*
Gregg, Brian Han: The Historical Jesus and the Final Judgment Sayings in Q. 2005. *Vol. II/207.*
Gregory, Andrew: The Reception of Luke and Acts in the Period before Irenaeus. 2003. *Vol. II/169.*
Grindheim, Sigurd: The Crux of Election. 2005. *Vol. II/202.*
Grünstäudl, Wolfgang: Petrus Alexandrinus. 2013. *Vol. II/353.*
Gundry, Robert H.: The Old is Better. 2005. *Vol. 178.*
Gundry Volf, Judith M.: Paul and Perseverance. 1990. *Vol. II/37.*
Häußer, Detlef: Christusbekenntnis und Jesusüberlieferung bei Paulus. 2006. *Vol. 210.*
Hafemann, Scott J.: Suffering and the Spirit. 1986. *Vol. II/19.*
– Paul, Moses, and the History of Israel. 1995. *Vol. 81.*
Hahn, Ferdinand: Studien zum Neuen Testament.
Vol. I: Grundsatzfragen, Jesusforschung, Evangelien. 2006. *Vol. 191.*
Vol. II: Bekenntnisbildung und Theologie in urchristlicher Zeit. 2006. *Vol. 192.*
Hahn, Johannes (Ed.): Zerstörungen des Jerusalemer Tempels. 2002. *Vol. 147.*
Hamid-Khani, Saeed: Relevation and Concealment of Christ. 2000. *Vol. II/120.*
Hanges, James C.: Paul, Founder of Churches. 2012. *Vol. 292.*
Hannah, Darrel D.: Michael and Christ. 1999. *Vol. II/109.*
Hardin, Justin K.: Galatians and the Imperial Cult? 2007. *Vol. II /237.*
Harrison, James R.: Paul and the Imperial Authorities at Thessolanica and Rome. 2011. *Vol. 273.*

- Paul's Language of Grace in Its Graeco-Roman Context. 2003. *Vol. II/172.*
Hartman, Lars: Approaching New Testament Texts and Contexts. 2013. *Vol. 311.*
- Text-Centered New Testament Studies. Ed. by D. Hellholm. 1997. *Vol. 102.*
Hartog, Paul: Polycarp and the New Testament. 2001. *Vol. II/134.*
Hasselbrook, David S.: Studies in New Testament Lexicography. 2011. *Vol. II/303.*
Hays, Christopher M.: Luke's Wealth Ethics. 2010. *Vol. 275.*
Heckel, Theo K.: Der Innere Mensch. 1993. *Vol. II/53.*
- Vom Evangelium des Markus zum viergestaltigen Evangelium. 1999. *Vol. 120.*
Heckel, Ulrich: Kraft in Schwachheit. 1993. *Vol. II/56.*
- Der Segen im Neuen Testament. 2002. *Vol. 150.*
- see *Feldmeier, Reinhard.*
- see *Hengel, Martin.*
Heemstra, Marius: The Fiscus Judaicus and the Parting of the Ways. 2010. *Vol. II/277.*
Heiligenthal, Roman: Werke als Zeichen. 1983. *Vol. II/9.*
Heininger, Bernhard: Die Inkulturation des Christentums. 2010. *Vol. 255.*
Heliso, Desta: Pistis and the Righteous One. 2007. *Vol. II/235.*
Hellholm, D.: see *Hartman, Lars.*
Hemer, Colin J.: The Book of Acts in the Setting of Hellenistic History. 1989. *Vol. 49.*
Henderson, Timothy P.: The Gospel of Peter and Early Christian Apologetics. 2011. *Vol. II/301.*
Hengel, Martin: Jesus und die Evangelien. Kleine Schriften V. 2007. *Vol. 211.*
- Die johanneische Frage. 1993. *Vol. 67.*
- Judaica et Hellenistica. Kleine Schriften I. 1996. *Vol. 90.*
- Judaica, Hellenistica et Christiana. Kleine Schriften II. 1999. *Vol. 109.*
- Judentum und Hellenismus. 1969, ³1988. *Vol. 10.*
- Paulus und Jakobus. Kleine Schriften III. 2002. *Vol. 141.*
- Studien zur Christologie. Kleine Schriften IV. 2006. *Vol. 201.*
- Studien zum Urchristentum. Kleine Schriften VI. 2008. *Vol. 234.*
- Theologische, historische und biographische Skizzen. Kleine Schriften VII. 2010. *Vol. 253.*
- and *Anna Maria Schwemer:* Paulus zwischen Damaskus und Antiochien. 1998. *Vol. 108.*

- Der messianische Anspruch Jesu und die Anfänge der Christologie. 2001. *Vol. 138.*
- Die vier Evangelien und das eine Evangelium von Jesus Christus. 2008. *Vol. 224.*
- Die Zeloten. ³2011. *Vol. 283.*
Hengel, Martin and *Ulrich Heckel* (Ed.): Paulus und das antike Judentum. 1991. *Vol. 58.*
- and *Hermut Löhr* (Ed.): Schriftauslegung im antiken Judentum und im Urchristentum. 1994. *Vol. 73.*
- and *Anna Maria Schwemer* (Ed.): Königsherrschaft Gottes und himmlischer Kult. 1991. *Vol. 55.*
- Die Septuaginta. 1994. *Vol. 72.*
-, *Siegfried Mittmann* and *Anna Maria Schwemer* (Ed.): La Cité de Dieu / Die Stadt Gottes. 2000. *Vol. 129.*
Hentschel, Anni: Diakonia im Neuen Testament. 2007. *Vol. 226.*
Hernández Jr., Juan: Scribal Habits and Theological Influence in the Apocalypse. 2006. *Vol. II/218.*
Herrenbrück, Fritz: Jesus und die Zöllner. 1990. *Vol. II/41.*
Herzer, Jens: Paulus oder Petrus? 1998. *Vol. 103.*
- see *Böttrich, Christfried.*
- see *Deines, Roland.*
- see *Frey, Jörg.*
- (Ed.): Papyrologie und Exegese. 2012. *Vol. II/341.*
Hill, Charles E.: From the Lost Teaching of Polycarp. 2005. *Vol. 186.*
Hoegen-Rohls, Christina: Der nachösterliche Johannes. 1996. *Vol. II/84.*
Hoffmann, Matthias Reinhard: The Destroyer and the Lamb. 2005. *Vol. II/203.*
Hofius, Otfried: Katapausis. 1970. *Vol. 11.*
- Der Vorhang vor dem Thron Gottes. 1972. *Vol. 14.*
- Der Christushymnus Philipper 2,6–11. 1976, ²1991. *Vol. 17.*
- Paulusstudien. 1989, ²1994. *Vol. 51.*
- Neutestamentliche Studien. 2000. *Vol. 132.*
- Paulusstudien II. 2002. *Vol. 143.*
- Exegetische Studien. 2008. *Vol. 223.*
- and *Hans-Christian Kammler:* Johannesstudien. 1996. *Vol. 88.*
Holloway, Paul A.: Coping with Prejudice. 2009. *Vol. 244.*
- see *Ahearne-Kroll, Stephen P.*
Holmberg, Bengt (Ed.): Exploring Early Christian Identity. 2008. *Vol. 226.*
- and *Mikael Winninge* (Ed.): Identity Formation in the New Testament. 2008. *Vol. 227.*
Holmén, Tom (Ed.): Jesus in Continuum. 2012. *Vol. 289.*

Holtz, Traugott: Geschichte und Theologie des Urchristentums. 1991. *Vol. 57.*

Hommel, Hildebrecht: Sebasmata. Vol. 1 1983. *Vol. 31.* Vol. 2 1984. *Vol. 32.*

Horbury, William: Herodian Judaism and New Testament Study. 2006. *Vol. 193.*

Horn, Friedrich Wilhelm and *Ruben Zimmermann* (Ed.): Jenseits von Indikativ und Imperativ. Vol. 1. 2009. *Vol. 238.*

–, *Ulrich Volp* and *Ruben Zimmermann* (Ed.): Ethische Normen des frühen Christentums. Kontexte und Normen neutestamentlicher Ethik / Context and Norms of New Testament Ethics, Vol. IV. 2013. *Vol. 313.*

Horst, Pieter W. van der: Jews and Christians in Their Graeco-Roman Context. 2006. *Vol. 196.*

Hultgård, Anders and *Stig Norin* (Ed): Le Jour de Dieu / Der Tag Gottes. 2009. *Vol. 245.*

Hume, Douglas A.: The Early Christian Community. 2011. *Vol. II/298.*

Hunt, Steven A., D. Francois Tolmie and *Ruben Zimmermann* (Ed.): Character Studies in the Fourth Gospel. 2013. *Vol. 314.*

Hvalvik, Reidar: The Struggle for Scripture and Covenant. 1996. *Vol. II/82.*

Inselmann, Anke: Die Freude im Lukasevangelium. 2012. *Vol. II/322.*

Jackson, Ryan: New Creation in Paul's Letters. 2010. *Vol. II/272.*

Janßen, Martina: see *Frey, Jörg.*

Jauhiainen, Marko: The Use of Zechariah in Revelation. 2005. *Vol. II/199.*

Jensen, Morten H.: Herod Antipas in Galilee. 2006; ²2010. *Vol. II/215.*

Johns, Loren L.: The Lamb Christology of the Apocalypse of John. 2003. *Vol. II/167.*

Joseph, Simon J.: Jesus, Q, and the Dead Sea Scrolls. 2012. *Vol. II/333.*

Jossa, Giorgio: Jews or Christians? 2006. *Vol. 202.*

Joubert, Stephan: Paul as Benefactor. 2000. *Vol. II/124.*

Judge, E. A.: The First Christians in the Roman World. 2008. *Vol. 229.*

– Jerusalem and Athens. 2010. *Vol. 265.*

Jungbauer, Harry: „Ehre Vater und Mutter". 2002. *Vol. II/146.*

Kähler, Christoph: Jesu Gleichnisse als Poesie und Therapie. 1995. *Vol. 78.*

Kamlah, Ehrhard: Die Form der katalogischen Paränese im Neuen Testament. 1964. *Vol. 7.*

Kammler, Hans-Christian: Christologie und Eschatologie. 2000. *Vol. 126.*

– Kreuz und Weisheit. 2003. *Vol. 159.*

– see *Hofius, Otfried.*

Karakolis, Christos, Karl-Wilhelm Niebuhr and *Sviatoslav Rogalsky* (Ed.): Gospel Images of Jesus Christ in Church Tradition and in Biblical Scholarship. Fifth International East-West Symposium of New Testament Scholars, Minsk, September 2 to 9, 2010. 2012. *Vol. 288.*

– see *Alexeev, Anatoly A.*

Karrer, Martin und *Wolfgang Kraus* (Ed.): Die Septuaginta – Texte, Kontexte, Lebenswelten. 2008. *Vol. 219.*

– see *Kraus, Wolfgang.*

Kazen, Thomas: Scripture, Interpretation, or Authority? 2013. *Vol. 320.*

Kelhoffer, James A.: The Diet of John the Baptist. 2005. *Vol. 176.*

– Miracle and Mission. 2000. *Vol. II/112.*

– Persecution, Persuasion and Power. 2010. *Vol. 270.*

– see *Ahearne-Kroll, Stephen P.*

– see *Frey, Jörg.*

Kelley, Nicole: Knowledge and Religious Authority in the Pseudo-Clementines. 2006. *Vol. II/213.*

Kennedy, Joel: The Recapitulation of Israel. 2008. *Vol. II/257.*

Kensky, Meira Z.: Trying Man, Trying God. 2010. *Vol. II/289.*

Kessler, Nadine (Ed.): see *Frey, Jörg.*

Kieffer, René and *Jan Bergman* (Ed.): La Main de Dieu / Die Hand Gottes. 1997. *Vol. 94.*

Kierspel, Lars: The Jews and the World in the Fourth Gospel. 2006. *Vol. 220.*

Kim, Seyoon: The Origin of Paul's Gospel. 1981, ²1984. *Vol. II/4.*

– Paul and the New Perspective. 2002. *Vol. 140.*

– "The 'Son of Man'" as the Son of God. 1983. *Vol. 30.*

Klauck, Hans-Josef: Religion und Gesellschaft im frühen Christentum. 2003. *Vol. 152.*

Klein, Hans, Vasile Mihoc und *Karl-Wilhelm Niebuhr* (Ed.): Das Gebet im Neuen Testament. Vierte, europäische orthodox-westliche Exegetenkonferenz in Sambata de Sus, 4. – 8. August 2007. 2009. Vol. 249.

– see *Dunn, James D.G.*

Kleinknecht, Karl Th.: Der leidende Gerechtfertigte. 1984, ²1988. *Vol. II/13.*

Klinghardt, Matthias: Gesetz und Volk Gottes. 1988. *Vol. II/32.*

Kloppenborg, John S.: The Tenants in the Vineyard. 2006, student edition 2010. *Vol. 195.*

Koch, Michael: Drachenkampf und Sonnenfrau. 2004. *Vol. II/184.*

Koch, Stefan: Rechtliche Regelung von Konflikten im frühen Christentum. 2004. *Vol. II/174.*

Köhler, Wolf-Dietrich: Rezeption des Matthäus-evangeliums in der Zeit vor Irenäus. 1987. *Vol. II/24.*

Köhn, Andreas: Der Neutestamentler Ernst Lohmeyer. 2004. *Vol. II/180.*

Koester, Craig and *Reimund Bieringer* (Ed.): The Resurrection of Jesus in the Gospel of John. 2008. *Vol. 222.*

Konradt, Matthias: Israel, Kirche und die Völker im Matthäusevangelium. 2007. *Vol. 215.*

– and *Esther Schläpfer* (Ed.): Anthropologie und Ethik im Frühjudentum und im Neuen Testament. 2013. *Vol. 322.*

Kooten, George H. van: Cosmic Christology in Paul and the Pauline School. 2003. *Vol. II/171.*

– Paul's Anthropology in Context. 2008. *Vol. 232.*

Korn, Manfred: Die Geschichte Jesu in ver-änderter Zeit. 1993. *Vol. II/51.*

Koskenniemi, Erkki: Apollonios von Tyana in der neutestamentlichen Exegese. 1994. *Vol. II/61.*

– The Old Testament Miracle-Workers in Early Judaism. 2005. *Vol. II/206.*

Kraus, Thomas J.: Sprache, Stil und historischer Ort des zweiten Petrusbriefes. 2001. *Vol. II/136.*

Kraus, Wolfgang: Das Volk Gottes. 1996. *Vol. 85.*

– see *Karrer, Martin.*

– see *Walter, Nikolaus.*

– and *Martin Karrer* (Hrsg.): Die Septua-ginta – Texte, Theologien, Einflüsse. 2010. *Bd. 252.*

– and *Karl-Wilhelm Niebuhr* (Ed.): Frühjuden-tum und Neues Testament im Horizont Bib-lischer Theologie. 2003. *Vol. 162.*

Krauter, Stefan: Studien zu Röm 13,1-7. 2009. *Vol. 243.*

– see *Frey, Jörg.*

Kreplin, Matthias: Das Selbstverständnis Jesu. 2001. *Vol. II/141.*

Kreuzer, Siegfried, Martin Meiser and *Marcus Sigismund* (Ed.): Die Septuaginta – Entste-hung, Sprache, Geschichte. 2012. *Vol. 286.*

Kuhn, Karl G.: Achtzehngebet und Vaterunser und der Reim. 1950. *Vol. 1.*

Kvalbein, Hans: see *Ådna, Jostein.*

Kwon, Yon-Gyong: Eschatology in Galatians. 2004. *Vol. II/183.*

Laansma, Jon: I Will Give You Rest. 1997. *Vol. II/98.*

Labahn, Michael: Offenbarung in Zeichen und Wort. 2000. *Vol. II/117.*

– (Ed.): see *Roth, Dieter T.*

Lambers-Petry, Doris: see *Tomson, Peter J.*

Lampe, Peter: Die stadtrömischen Christen in den ersten beiden Jahrhunderten. 1987, ²1989. *Vol. II/18.*

Landmesser, Christof: Wahrheit als Grundbe-griff neutestamentlicher Wissenschaft. 1999. *Vol. 113.*

– Jüngerberufung und Zuwendung zu Gott. 2000. *Vol. 133.*

– see *Eckstein, Hans-Joachim.*

Lange, Armin: see *Ego, Beate.*

Lau, Andrew: Manifest in Flesh. 1996. *Vol. II/86.*

Lawrence, Louise: An Ethnography of the Gospel of Matthew. 2003. *Vol. II/165.*

Lee, Aquila H.I.: From Messiah to Preexistent Son. 2005. *Vol. II/192.*

Lee, DooHee: Luke-Acts and 'Tragic History'. 2013. *Vol. II/346.*

Lee, Pilchan: The New Jerusalem in the Book of Relevation. 2000. *Vol. II/129.*

Lee, Sang M.: The Cosmic Drama of Salvation. 2010. *Vol. II/276.*

Lee, Simon S.: Jesus' Transfiguration and the Believers' Transformation. 2009. *Vol. II/265.*

Lichtenberger, Hermann: Das Ich Adams und das Ich der Menschheit. 2004. *Vol. 164.*

– see *Avemarie, Friedrich.*

– see *Caulley, Thomas Scott.*

– see *Eckstein, Hans-Joachim.*

– see *Frey, Jörg.*

Lierman, John: The New Testament Moses. 2004. *Vol. II/173.*

– (Ed.): Challenging Perspectives on the Gospel of John. 2006. *Vol. II/219.*

Lieu, Samuel N.C.: Manichaeism in the Later Roman Empire and Medieval China. ²1992. *Vol. 63.*

Lindemann, Andreas: Die Evangelien und die Apostelgeschichte. 2009. *Vol. 241.*

– Glauben, Handeln, Verstehen. Studien zur Auslegung des Neuen Testaments. 2011. *Vol. II/282.*

Lincicum, David: Paul and the Early Jewish Encounter with Deuteronomy. 2010. *Vol. II/284.*

– see *Stanton, Graham.*

Lindgård, Fredrik: Paul's Line of Thought in 2 Corinthians 4:16–5:10. 2004. *Vol. II/189.*

Liu, Yulin: Temple Purity in 1-2 Corinthians. 2013. *Vol. II/343.*

Livesey, Nina E.: Circumcision as a Malleable Symbol. 2010. *Vol. II/295.*

Loader, William R.G.: Jesus' Attitude Towards the Law. 1997. *Vol. II/97.*

Löhr, Gebhard: Verherrlichung Gottes durch Philosophie. 1997. *Vol. 97.*

Löhr, Hermut: Studien zum frühchristlichen und frühjüdischen Gebet. 2003. *Vol. 160.*

– see *Hengel, Martin.*
Löhr, Winrich Alfried: Basilides und seine Schule. 1995. *Vol. 83.*
Lorenzen, Stefanie: Das paulinische Eikon-Konzept. 2008. *Vol. II/250.*
Luomanen, Petri: Entering the Kingdom of Heaven. 1998. *Vol. II/101.*
Luz, Ulrich: see *Alexeev, Anatoly A.*
– see *Dunn, James D.G.*
Lykke, Anne und *Friedrich T. Schipper* (Ed.): Kult und Macht. 2011. *Vol. II/319.*
Lyu, Eun-Geol: Sünde und Rechtfertigung bei Paulus. 2012. *Vol. II/318.*
Mackay, Ian D.: John's Relationship with Mark. 2004. *Vol. II/182.*
Mackie, Scott D.: Eschatology and Exhortation in the Epistle to the Hebrews. 2006. *Vol. II/223.*
Magda, Ksenija: Paul's Territoriality and Mission Strategy. 2009. *Vol. II/266.*
Maier, Gerhard: Mensch und freier Wille. 1971. *Vol. 12.*
– Die Johannesoffenbarung und die Kirche. 1981. *Vol. 25.*
Marguerat, Daniel: Paul in Acts and Paul in His Letters. 2013. *Vol. 310.*
Markley, John R.: Peter – Apocalyptic Seer. 2013. *Vol. II/348.*
Markschies, Christoph: Valentinus Gnosticus? 1992. *Vol. 65.*
Marshall, Jonathan: Jesus, Patrons, and Benefactors. 2009. *Vol. II/259.*
Marshall, Peter: Enmity in Corinth: Social Conventions in Paul's Relations with the Corinthians. 1987. *Vol. II/23.*
Martin, Dale B.: see *Zangenberg, Jürgen.*
Maston, Jason: Divine and Human Agency in Second Temple Judaism and Paul. 2010. *Vol. II/297.*
– see *Bird, Michael F.*
Mayer, Annemarie: Sprache der Einheit im Epheserbrief und in der Ökumene. 2002. *Vol. II/150.*
Mayordomo, Moisés: Argumentiert Paulus logisch? 2005. *Vol. 188.*
McDonough, Sean M.: YHWH at Patmos: Rev. 1:4 in its Hellenistic and Early Jewish Setting. 1999. *Vol. II/107.*
McDowell, Markus: Prayers of Jewish Women. 2006. *Vol. II/211.*
McGlynn, Moyna: Divine Judgement and Divine Benevolence in the Book of Wisdom. 2001. *Vol. II/139.*
McNamara, Martin: Targum and New Testament. 2011. *Vol. 279.*
Meade, David G.: Pseudonymity and Canon. 1986. *Vol. 39.*

Meadors, Edward P.: Jesus the Messianic Herald of Salvation. 1995. *Vol. II/72.*
Meiser, Martin: see *Kreuzer, Siegfried.*
Meißner, Stefan: Die Heimholung des Ketzers. 1996. *Vol. II/87.*
Mell, Ulrich: Die „anderen" Winzer. 1994. *Vol. 77.*
– see *Sänger, Dieter.*
Mengel, Berthold: Studien zum Philipperbrief. 1982. *Vol. II/8.*
Merkel, Helmut: Die Widersprüche zwischen den Evangelien. 1971. *Vol. 13.*
– see *Ego, Beate.*
Merklein, Helmut: Studien zu Jesus und Paulus. Vol. 1 1987. *Vol. 43.* – Vol. 2 1998. *Vol. 105.*
Merkt, Andreas: see *Nicklas, Tobias*
Metzdorf, Christina: Die Tempelaktion Jesu. 2003. *Vol. II/168.*
Metzler, Karin: Der griechische Begriff des Verzeihens. 1991. *Vol. II/44.*
Metzner, Rainer: Die Rezeption des Matthäusevangeliums im 1. Petrusbrief. 1995. *Vol. II/74.*
– Das Verständnis der Sünde im Johannesevangelium. 2000. *Vol. 122.*
Michalak, Aleksander: Angels as Warriors in Late Second Temple Jewish Literature. 2012. *Vol. II/330.*
Mihoc, Vasile: see *Dunn, James D.G.*
– see *Klein, Hans.*
Mineshige, Kiyoshi: Besitzverzicht und Almosen bei Lukas. 2003. *Vol. II/163.*
Mittmann, Siegfried: see *Hengel, Martin.*
Mittmann-Richert, Ulrike: Magnifikat und Benediktus. 1996. *Vol. II/90.*
– Der Sühnetod des Gottesknechts. 2008. *Vol. 220.*
Miura, Yuzuru: David in Luke-Acts. 2007. *Vol. II/232.*
Moll, Sebastian: The Arch-Heretic Marcion. 2010. *Vol. 250.*
Morales, Rodrigo J.: The Spirit and the Restorat. 2010. *Vol. 282.*
Mournet, Terence C.: Oral Tradition and Literary Dependency. 2005. *Vol. II/195.*
Mußner, Franz: Jesus von Nazareth im Umfeld Israels und der Urkirche. Ed. by M. Theobald. 1998. *Vol. 111.*
Mutschler, Bernhard: Das Corpus Johanneum bei Irenäus von Lyon. 2005. *Vol. 189.*
– Glaube in den Pastoralbriefen. 2010. *Vol. 256.*
Myers, Susan E.: Spirit Epicleses in the Acts of Thomas. 2010. *Vol. 281.*
Myers, Susan E. (Ed.): Portraits of Jesus. 2012. *Vol. II/321.*
Nguyen, V. Henry T.: Christian Identity in Corinth. 2008. *Vol. II/243.*

Nicklas, Tobias, Andreas Merkt und *Joseph Verheyden* (Ed.): Gelitten – Gestorben – Auferstanden. 2010. *Vol. II/273.*
– and *Janet E. Spittler* (Ed.): Credible, Incredible. 2013. *Vol. 321.*
– see *Verheyden, Joseph.*
Nicolet-Anderson, Valérie: Constructing the Self. 2012. *Vol. II/324.*
Niebuhr, Karl-Wilhelm: Gesetz and Paränese. 1987. *Vol. II/28.*
– Heidenapostel aus Israel. 1992. *Vol. 62.*
– see *Deines, Roland.*
– see *Dimitrov, Ivan Z.*
– see *Karakolis, Christos.*
– see *Klein, Hans.*
– see *Kraus, Wolfgang.*
Nielsen, Anders E.: "Until it is Fullfilled". 2000. *Vol. II/126.*
Nielsen, Jesper Tang: Die kognitive Dimension des Kreuzes. 2009. *Vol. II/263.*
Nissen, Andreas: Gott und der Nächste im antiken Judentum. 1974. *Vol. 15.*
Noack, Christian: Gottesbewußtsein. 2000. *Vol. II/116.*
Noormann, Rolf: Irenäus als Paulusinterpret. 1994. *Vol. II/66.*
Norelli, Enrico: see *Clivaz, Claire.*
Norin, Stig: see *Hultgård, Anders.*
Novakovic, Lidija: Messiah, the Healer of the Sick. 2003. *Vol. II/170.*
Obermann, Andreas: Die christologische Erfüllung der Schrift im Johannesevangelium. 1996. *Vol. II/83.*
Ochs, Christoph: Matthaeus Adversus Christianos. 2013. *Vol. II/350.*
– see *Deines, Roland.*
Öhler, Markus: Barnabas. 2003. *Vol. 156.*
– see *Becker, Michael.*
– (Ed.): Aposteldekret und antikes Vereinswesen. 2011. *Vol. 280.*
Oestreich, Bernhard: Performanzkritik der Paulusbriefe. 2012. *Vol. 296.*
Okure, Teresa: The Johannine Approach to Mission. 1988. *Vol. II/31.*
Oliver, Isaac W.: Torah Praxis after 70 CE. 2013. *Vol. II/355.*
Onuki, Takashi: Heil und Erlösung. 2004. *Vol. 165.*
Oppong-Kumi, Peter Y.: Matthean Sets of Parables. 2013. *Vol. II/340.*
Oropeza, B. J.: Paul and Apostasy. 2000. *Vol. II/115.*
Orr, Peter: Christ Absent and Present. 2013. *Vol. II/354.*
Ostmeyer, Karl-Heinrich: Kommunikation mit Gott und Christus. 2006. *Vol. 197.*
– Taufe und Typos. 2000. *Vol. II/118.*

Ounsworth, Richard: Joshua Typology in the New Testament. 2012. *Vol. II/328.*
Pale Hera, Marianus: Christology and Discipleship in John 17. 2013. *Vol. II/342.*
Pao, David W.: Acts and the Isaianic New Exodus. 2000. *Vol. II/130.*
Pardee, Nancy: The Genre and Development of the Didache. 2012. *Vol. II/339.*
Park, Eung Chun: The Mission Discourse in Matthew's Interpretation. 1995. *Vol. II/81.*
Park, Joseph S.: Conceptions of Afterlife in Jewish Insriptions. 2000. *Vol. II/121.*
Parsenios, George L.: Rhetoric and Drama in the Johannine Lawsuit Motif. 2010. *Vol. 258.*
Pate, C. Marvin: The Reverse of the Curse. 2000. *Vol. II/114.*
Paulsen, Henning: Studien zur Literatur und Geschichte des frühen Christentums. Ed. by Ute E. Eisen. 1997. *Vol. 99.*
Pearce, Sarah J.K.: The Land of the Body. 2007. *Vol. 208.*
Peres, Imre: Griechische Grabinschriften und neutestamentliche Eschatologie. 2003. *Vol. 157.*
Perry, Peter S.: The Rhetoric of Digressions. 2009. *Vol. II/268.*
Pierce, Chad T.: Spirits and the Proclamation of Christ. 2011. *Vol. II/305.*
Philip, Finny: The Origins of Pauline Pneumatology. 2005. *Vol. II/194.*
Philonenko, Marc (Ed.): Le Trône de Dieu. 1993. *Vol. 69.*
Pilhofer, Peter: Presbyteron Kreitton. 1990. *Vol. II/39.*
– Philippi. Vol. 1 1995. *Vol. 87.* – Vol. 2 ²2009. *Vol. 119.*
– Die frühen Christen und ihre Welt. 2002. *Vol. 145.*
– see *Becker, Eve-Marie.*
– see *Ego, Beate.*
Pitre, Brant: Jesus, the Tribulation, and the End of the Exile. 2005. *Vol. II/204.*
Plümacher, Eckhard: Geschichte und Geschichten. 2004. *Vol. 170.*
Pöhlmann, Wolfgang: Der Verlorene Sohn und das Haus. 1993. *Vol. 68.*
Poirier, John C.: The Tongues of Angels. 2010. *Vol. II/287.*
Pokorný, Petr and *Josef B. Souček:* Bibelauslegung als Theologie. 1997. *Vol. 100.*
– and *Jan Roskovec* (Ed.): Philosophical Hermeneutics and Biblical Exegesis. 2002. *Vol. 153.*
Popkes, Enno Edzard: Das Menschenbild des Thomasevangeliums. 2007. *Vol. 206.*
– Die Theologie der Liebe Gottes in den johanneischen Schriften. 2005. *Vol. II/197.*

– and *Gregor Wurst* (Ed.): Judasevangelium und Codex Tchacos. 2012. *Vol. 297.*

Porter, Stanley E.: The Paul of Acts. 1999. *Vol. 115.*

Prieur, Alexander: Die Verkündigung der Gottesherrschaft. 1996. *Vol. II/89.*

Probst, Hermann: Paulus und der Brief. 1991. *Vol. II/45.*

Puig i Tàrrech, Armand: Jesus: An Uncommon Journey. 2010. *Vol. II/288.*

Rabens, Volker: The Holy Spirit and Ethics in Paul. ²2013. *Vol. II/283.*

Räisänen, Heikki: Paul and the Law. 1983, ²1987. *Vol. 29.*

Rehfeld, Emmanuel L.: Relationale Ontologie bei Paulus. 2012. *Vol. II/326.*

Rehkopf, Friedrich: Die lukanische Sonderquelle. 1959. *Vol. 5.*

Rein, Matthias: Die Heilung des Blindgeborenen (Joh 9). 1995. *Vol. II/73.*

Reinmuth, Eckart: Pseudo-Philo und Lukas. 1994. *Vol. 74.*

Reiser, Marius: Bibelkritik und Auslegung der Heiligen Schrift. 2007. *Vol. 217.*

– Syntax und Stil des Markusevangeliums. 1984. *Vol. II/11.*

Reynolds, Benjamin E.: The Apocalyptic Son of Man in the Gospel of John. 2008. *Vol. II/249.*

Rhodes, James N.: The Epistle of Barnabas and the Deuteronomic Tradition. 2004. *Vol. II/188.*

Richards, E. Randolph: The Secretary in the Letters of Paul. 1991. *Vol. II/42.*

Richardson, Christopher A.: Pioneer and Perfecter of Faith. 2012. *Vol. II/338.*

Riesner, Rainer: Jesus als Lehrer. 1981, ³1988. *Vol. II/7.*

– Die Frühzeit des Apostels Paulus. 1994. *Vol. 71.*

Rissi, Mathias: Die Theologie des Hebräerbriefs. 1987. *Vol. 41.*

Röcker, Fritz W.: Belial und Katechon. 2009. *Vol. II/262.*

Röhser, Günter: Metaphorik und Personifikation der Sünde. 1987. *Vol. II/25.*

Rogalsky, Sviatoslav: see *Karakolis, Christos.*

Rose, Christian: Theologie als Erzählung im Markusevangelium. 2007. *Vol. II/236.*

– Die Wolke der Zeugen. 1994. *Vol. II/60.*

Roskovec, Jan: see *Pokorný, Petr.*

Roth, Dieter T., Zimmermann, Ruben and *Labahn, Michael* (Ed.): Metaphor, Narrative, and Parables in Q. 2014. *Vol. 315.*

Rothschild, Clare K.: Baptist Traditions and Q. 2005. *Vol. 190.*

– Hebrews as Pseudepigraphon. 2009. *Vol. 235.*

– Luke Acts and the Rhetoric of History. 2004. *Vol. II/175.*

– see *Frey, Jörg.*

– and *Jens Schröter* (Ed.): The Rise and Expansion of Christianity in the First Three Centuries of the Common Era. 2013. *Vol. 301.*

– and *Trevor W. Thompson* (Ed.): Christian Body, Christian Self. 2011. *Vol. 284.*

Rudolph, David J.: A Jew to the Jews. 2011. *Vol. II/304.*

Rüegger, Hans-Ulrich: Verstehen, was Markus erzählt. 2002. *Vol. II/155.*

Rüger, Hans Peter: Die Weisheitsschrift aus der Kairoer Geniza. 1991. *Vol. 53.*

Ruf, Martin G.: Die heiligen Propheten, eure Apostel und ich. 2011. *Vol. II/300.*

Runesson, Anders: see *Becker, Eve-Marie.*

– see *Ehrlich, Carl S.*

Sänger, Dieter: Antikes Judentum und die Mysterien. 1980. *Vol. II/5.*

– Die Verkündigung des Gekreuzigten und Israel. 1994. *Vol. 75.*

– see *Burchard, Christoph.*

– and *Ulrich Mell* (Ed.): Paulus und Johannes. 2006. *Vol. 198.*

Salier, Willis Hedley: The Rhetorical Impact of the Semeia in the Gospel of John. 2004. *Vol. II/186.*

Salzmann, Jörg Christian: Lehren und Ermahnen. 1994. *Vol. II/59.*

Samuelsson, Gunnar: Crucifixion in Antiquity. ²2013. *Vol. II/310.*

Sandelin, Karl-Gustav: Attraction and Danger of Alien Religion. 2012. *Vol. 290.*

Sandnes, Karl Olav: Paul – One of the Prophets? 1991. *Vol. II/43.*

Sato, Migaku: Q und Prophetie. 1988. *Vol. II/29.*

Schäfer, Ruth: Paulus bis zum Apostelkonzil. 2004. *Vol. II/179.*

Schaper, Joachim: Eschatology in the Greek Psalter. 1995. *Vol. II/76.*

Schimanowski, Gottfried: Die himmlische Liturgie in der Apokalypse des Johannes. 2002. *Vol. II/154.*

– Weisheit und Messias. 1985. *Vol. II/17.*

Schipper, Friedrich T.: see *Lykke, Anne.*

Schläpfer, Esther: see *Konradt, Matthias.*

Schlichting, Günter: Ein jüdisches Leben Jesu. 1982. *Vol. 24.*

Schließer, Benjamin: Abraham's Faith in Romans 4. 2007. *Vol. II/224.*

Schnabel, Eckhard J.: Law and Wisdom from Ben Sira to Paul. 1985. *Vol. II/16.*

Schnelle, Udo: see *Frey, Jörg.*

Schröter, Jens: Von Jesus zum Neuen Testament. 2007. *Vol. 204.*

– see *Frey, Jörg.*

– see *Rothschild, Clare K.*
Schuller, Eileen: see *Ehrlich, Carl S.*
Schultheiß, Tanja: Das Petrusbild im Johannes-evangelium. 2012. *Vol. II/329.*
Schutter, William L.: Hermeneutic and Composition in I Peter. 1989. *Vol. II/30.*
Schwartz, Daniel R.: Reading the First Century. 2013. *Vol. 300.*
– Studies in the Jewish Background of Christianity. 1992. *Vol. 60.*
Schwemer, Anna Maria: see *Hengel, Martin*
Scott, Ian W.: Implicit Epistemology in the Letters of Paul. 2005. *Vol. II/205.*
Scott, James M.: Adoption as Sons of God. 1992. *Vol. II/48.*
– Paul and the Nations. 1995. *Vol. 84.*
Shi, Wenhua: Paul's Message of the Cross as Body Language. 2008. *Vol. II/254.*
Shum, Shiu-Lun: Paul's Use of Isaiah in Romans. 2002. *Vol. II/156.*
Siegert, Folker: Drei hellenistisch-jüdische Predigten. Teil I 1980. *Vol. 20* – Teil II 1992. *Vol. 61.*
– Nag-Hammadi-Register. 1982. *Vol. 26.*
– Argumentation bei Paulus. 1985. *Vol. 34.*
– Philon von Alexandrien. 1988. *Vol. 46.*
Siggelkow-Berner, Birke: Die jüdischen Feste im Bellum Judaicum des Flavius Josephus. 2011. *Vol. II/306.*
Sigismund, Marcus: see *Kreuzer, Siegfried.*
Simon, Marcel: Le christianisme antique et son contexte religieux I/II. 1981. *Vol. 23.*
Smit, Peter-Ben: Fellowship and Food in the Kingdom. 2008. *Vol. II/234.*
Smith, Claire S.: Pauline Communities as 'Scholastic Communities'.2012. *Vol. II/335.*
Smith, Julien: Christ the Ideal King. 2011. *Vol. II/313.*
Snodgrass, Klyne: The Parable of the Wicked Tenants. 1983. *Vol. 27.*
Snyder, Glenn E.: Acts of Paul. 2013. *Vol. II/352.*
Söding, Thomas: Das Wort vom Kreuz. 1997. *Vol. 93.*
– see *Thüsing, Wilhelm.*
Sommer, Urs: Die Passionsgeschichte des Markusevangeliums. 1993. *Vol. II/58.*
Sorensen, Eric: Possession and Exorcism in the New Testament and Early Christianity. 2002. *Vol. II/157.*
Souček, Josef B.: see *Pokorný, Petr.*
Southall, David J.: Rediscovering Righteousness in Romans. 2008. *Vol. 240.*
Spangenberg, Volker: Herrlichkeit des Neuen Bundes. 1993. *Vol. II/55.*
Spanje, T.E. van: Inconsistency in Paul? 1999. *Vol. II/110.*

Speyer, Wolfgang: Frühes Christentum im antiken Strahlungsfeld. Vol. I: 1989. *Vol. 50.*
– Vol. II: 1999. *Vol. 116.*
– Vol. III: 2007. *Vol. 213.*
Spittler, Janet E.: Animals in the Apocryphal Acts of the Apostles. 2008. *Vol. II/247.*
– see *Nicklas, Tobias.*
Sprinkle, Preston: Law and Life. 2008. *Vol. II/241.*
Stadelmann, Helge: Ben Sira als Schriftgelehrter. 1980. *Vol. II/6.*
Standhartinger, Angela (Ed.): see *Avemarie, Friedrich.*
– see *Eisen, Ute E.*
Stanton, Graham: Studies in Matthew and Early Christianity. Ed. by Markus Bockmuehl and David Lincicum. 2013. *Vol. 309.*
Stein, Hans Joachim: Frühchristliche Mahlfeiern. 2008. *Vol. II/255.*
Stenschke, Christoph W.: Luke's Portrait of Gentiles Prior to Their Coming to Faith. *Vol. II/108.*
Stephens, Mark B.: Annihilation or Renewal? 2011. *Vol. II/307.*
Sterck-Degueldre, Jean-Pierre: Eine Frau namens Lydia. 2004. *Vol. II/176.*
Stettler, Christian: Der Kolosserhymnus. 2000. *Vol. II/131.*
– Das letzte Gericht. 2011. *Vol. II/299.*
Stettler, Hanna: Die Christologie der Pastoralbriefe. 1998. *Vol. II/105.*
Stökl Ben Ezra, Daniel: The Impact of Yom Kippur on Early Christianity. 2003. *Vol. 163.*
Strobel, August: Die Stunde der Wahrheit. 1980. *Vol. 21.*
Stroumsa, Guy G.: Barbarian Philosophy. 1999. *Vol. 112.*
Stuckenbruck, Loren T.: Angel Veneration and Christology. 1995. *Vol. II/70.*
–, *Stephen C. Barton* and *Benjamin G. Wold* (Ed.): Memory in the Bible and Antiquity. 2007. *Vol. 212.*
Stuhlmacher, Peter (Ed.): Das Evangelium und die Evangelien. 1983. *Vol. 28.*
– Biblische Theologie und Evangelium. 2002. *Vol. 146.*
Sung, Chong-Hyon: Vergebung der Sünden. 1993. *Vol. II/57.*
Svendsen, Stefan N.: Allegory Transformed. 2009. *Vol. II/269.*
Tajra, Harry W.: The Trial of St. Paul. 1989. *Vol. II/35.*
– The Martyrdom of St.Paul. 1994. *Vol. II/67.*
Tellbe, Mikael: Christ-Believers in Ephesus. 2009. *Vol. 242.*
Thate, Michael J.: Remembrance of Things Past? 2013. *Vol. II/351.*

Theißen, Gerd: Studien zur Soziologie des Urchristentums. 1979, ³1989. *Vol. 19.*
Theobald, Michael: Studien zum Corpus Iohanneum. 2010. *Vol. 267.*
– Studien zum Römerbrief. 2001. *Vol. 136.*
– see *Mußner, Franz.*
Thompson, Trevor W.: see *Rothschild, Clare K.*
Thornton, Claus-Jürgen: Der Zeuge des Zeugen. 1991. *Vol. 56.*
Thüsing, Wilhelm: Studien zur neutestamentlichen Theologie. Ed. by Thomas Söding. 1995. *Vol. 82.*
Thurén, Lauri: Derhethorizing Paul. 2000. *Vol. 124.*
Thyen, Hartwig: Studien zum Corpus Iohanneum. 2007. *Vol. 214.*
Tibbs, Clint: Religious Experience of the Pneuma. 2007. *Vol. II/230.*
Tilling, Chris: Paul's Divine Christology. 2012. *Vol. II/323.*
Toit, David S. du: Theios Anthropos. 1997. *Vol. II/91.*
Tolmie, D. Francois: Persuading the Galatians. 2005. *Vol. II/190.*
– see *Hunt, Steven A.*
Tomson, Peter J. and *Doris Lambers-Petry* (Ed.): The Image of the Judaeo-Christians in Ancient Jewish and Christian Literature. 2003. *Vol. 158.*
Toney, Carl N.: Paul's Inclusive Ethic. 2008. *Vol. II/252.*
– siehe *Frey, Jörg.*
Tóth, Franz: see *Frey, Jörg.*
Trebilco, Paul: The Early Christians in Ephesus from Paul to Ignatius. 2004. *Vol. 166.*
Treloar, Geoffrey R.: Lightfoot the Historian. 1998. *Vol. II/103.*
Troftgruben, Troy M.: A Conclusion Unhindered. 2010. *Vol. II/280.*
Tso, Marcus K.M.: Ethics in the Qumran Community. 2010. *Vol. II/292.*
Tsuji, Manabu: Glaube zwischen Vollkommenheit und Verweltlichung. 1997. *Vol. II/93.*
Tuval, Michael: From Jerusalem Priest to Roman Jew. 2013. *Vol. II/357.*
Twelftree, Graham H.: Jesus the Exorcist. 1993. *Vol. II/54.*
Ulrichs, Karl Friedrich: Christusglaube. 2007. *Vol. II/227.*
Urban, Christina: Das Menschenbild nach dem Johannesevangelium. 2001. *Vol. II/137.*
Vahrenhorst, Martin: Kultische Sprache in den Paulusbriefen. 2008. *Vol. 230.*
Vegge, Ivar: 2 Corinthians – a Letter about Reconciliation. 2008. *Vol. II/239.*
Verheyden, Joseph, Korinna Zamfir and *Tobias Nicklas* (Ed.): Prophets and Prophecy in Jewish and Early Christian Literature. 2010. *Vol. II/286.*
– see *Nicklas, Tobias*
Visotzky, Burton L.: Fathers of the World. 1995. *Vol. 80.*
Vollenweider, Samuel: Horizonte neutestamentlicher Christologie. 2002. *Vol. 144.*
Volp, Ulrich: see *Horn, Friedrich Wilhelm.*
Vos, Johan S.: Die Kunst der Argumentation bei Paulus. 2002. *Vol. 149.*
Vuong, Lily C.: Gender and Purity in the Protevangelium of James. 2013. *Vol. II/358.*
Waaler, Erik: The *Shema* and The First Commandment in First Corinthians. 2008. *Vol. II/253.*
Wagener, Ulrike: Die Ordnung des „Hauses Gottes". 1994. *Vol. II/65.*
Wagner, J. Ross: see *Wilk, Florian.*
Wahlen, Clinton: Jesus and the Impurity of Spirits in the Synoptic Gospels. 2004. *Vol. II/185.*
Walker, Donald D.: Paul's Offer of Leniency (2 Cor 10:1). 2002. *Vol. II/152.*
Walser, Georg A.: Old Testament Quotations in Hebrews. 2013. *Vol. II/356.*
Walter, Nikolaus: Praeparatio Evangelica. Ed. by Wolfgang Kraus und Florian Wilk. 1997. *Vol. 98.*
Wander, Bernd: Gottesfürchtige und Sympathisanten. 1998. *Vol. 104.*
Wardle, Timothy: The Jerusalem Temple and Early Christian Identity. 2010. *Vol. II/291.*
Wasserman, Emma: The Death of the Soul in Romans 7. 2008. *Vol. 256.*
Waters, Guy: The End of Deuteronomy in the Epistles of Paul. 2006. *Vol. 221.*
Watt, Jan G. van der (Ed.): Eschatology of the New Testament and Some Related Documents. 2011. *Vol. II/315.*
– and *Ruben Zimmermann* (Ed.): Rethinking the Ethics of John. 2012. *Vol. 291.*
– see *Frey, Jörg.*
– see *Zimmermann, Ruben.*
Watts, Peter: see *Deines, Roland.*
Watts, Rikki: Isaiah's New Exodus and Mark. 1997. *Vol. II/88.*
Webb, Robert L.: see *Bock, Darrell L.*
Wedderburn, Alexander J.M.: Baptism and Resurrection. 1987. *Vol. 44.*
– The Death of Jesus. 2013. *Vol. 299.*
– Jesus and the Historians. 2010. *Vol. 269.*
Wegner, Uwe: Der Hauptmann von Kafarnaum. 1985. *Vol. II/14.*
Weiß, Hans-Friedrich: Frühes Christentum und Gnosis. 2008. *Vol. 225.*
Weissenrieder, Annette: Images of Illness in the Gospel of Luke. 2003. *Vol. II/164.*

–, and *David L. Balch* (Ed.): Contested Spaces. 2012. *Vol. 285.*

–, and *Robert B. Coote* (Ed.): The Interface of Orality and Writing. 2010. *Vol. 260.*

–, *Friederike Wendt* and *Petra von Gemünden* (Ed.): Picturing the New Testament. 2005. *Vol. II/193.*

Welck, Christian: Erzählte ‚Zeichen'. 1994. *Vol. II/69.*

Wendt, Friederike (Ed.): see *Weissenrieder, Annette.*

Weyer-Menkhoff, Karl: Die Ethik des Johannesevangeliums im sprachlichen Feld des Handelns. 2014. *Vol. II/359.*

Wiarda, Timothy: Peter in the Gospels. 2000. *Vol. II/127.*

Wifstrand, Albert: Epochs and Styles. 2005. *Vol. 179.*

Wilk, Florian and *J. Ross Wagner* (Ed.): Between Gospel and Election. 2010. *Vol. 257.*

– see *Walter, Nikolaus.*

Williams, Catrin H.: I am He. 2000. *Vol. II/113.*

Williams, Margaret H.: Jews in a Graeco-Roman Environment. 2013. *Vol. 312.*

Wilson, Todd A.: The Curse of the Law and the Crisis in Galatia. 2007. *Vol. II/225.*

Wilson, Walter T.: Love without Pretense. 1991. *Vol. II/46.*

Winn, Adam: The Purpose of Mark's Gospel. 2008. *Vol. II/245.*

Winninge, Mikael: see *Holmberg, Bengt.*

Wischmeyer, Oda: Von Ben Sira zu Paulus. 2004. *Vol. 173.*

Wisdom, Jeffrey: Blessing for the Nations and the Curse of the Law. 2001. *Vol. II/133.*

Witmer, Stephen E.: Divine Instruction in Early Christianity. 2008. *Vol. II/246.*

Witulski, Thomas: Apk 11 und der Bar Kokhba-Aufstand. 2012. *Vol. II/337.*

Wold, Benjamin G.: Women, Men, and Angels. 2005. *Vol. II/2001.*

Wolter, Michael: Theologie und Ethos im frühen Christentum. 2009. *Vol. 236.*

– see *Stuckenbruck, Loren T.*

Worthington, Jonathan: Creation in Paul and Philo. 2011. *Vol. II/317.*

Wright, Archie T.: The Origin of Evil Spirits. 2005, ²2013. *Vol. II/198.*

Wucherpfennig, Ansgar: Heracleon Philologus. 2002. *Vol. 142.*

Wurst, Gregor: see *Popkes, Enno Edzard.*

Wypadlo, Adrian: Die Verklärung Jesu nach dem Markusevangelium. 2013. *Vol. 308.*

Yates, John W.: The Spirit and Creation in Paul. 2008. *Vol. II/251.*

Yeung, Maureen: Faith in Jesus and Paul. 2002. *Vol. II/147.*

Young, Stephen E.: Jesus Tradition in the Apostolic Fathers. 2011. *Vol. II/311.*

Zamfir, Corinna: see *Verheyden, Joseph*

Zangenberg, Jürgen, Harold W. Attridge and *Dale B. Martin* (Ed.): Religion, Ethnicity and Identity in Ancient Galilee. 2007. *Vol. 210.*

Zelyck, Lorne R.: John among the Other Gospels 2013. *Vol. II/347.*

Zimmermann, Alfred E.: Die urchristlichen Lehrer. 1984, ²1988. *Vol. II/12.*

Zimmermann, Johannes: Messianische Texte aus Qumran. 1998. *Vol. II/104.*

Zimmermann, Ruben: Christologie der Bilder im Johannesevangelium. 2004. *Vol. 171.*

– Geschlechtermetaphorik und Gottesverhältnis. 2001. *Vol. II/122.*

– (Ed.): Hermeneutik der Gleichnisse Jesu. 2008. *Vol. 231.*

– and *Jan G. van der Watt* (Ed.): Moral Language in the New Testament. Vol. II. 2010. *Vol. II/296.*

– see *Frey, Jörg.*

– see *Horn, Friedrich Wilhelm.*

– see *Hunt, Steven A.*

– see *Roth, Dieter T.*

– see *Watt, Jan G. van der.*

Zugmann, Michael: „Hellenisten" in der Apostelgeschichte. 2009. *Vol. II/264.*

Zumstein, Jean: see *Dettwiler, Andreas*

Zwiep, Arie W.: Christ, the Spirit and the Community of God. 2010. *Vol. II/293.*

– Judas and the Choice of Matthias. 2004. *Vol. II/187.*

For a complete catalogue of this series please write to the publisher
Mohr Siebeck • P.O. Box 2030 • D–72010 Tübingen/Germany
Up-to-date information on the internet at www.mohr.de

2015.11.09   118.00 (105.00)